INSIDER DEALING AND MONEY LAUNDERING IN THE EU: LAW AND REGULATION

Insider Dealing and Money Laundering in the EU: Law and Regulation

R.C.H. ALEXANDER
University of London, UK

LONDON AND NEW YORK

First published 2007 by Ashgate Publishing

Published 2016 by Routledge
2 Park Square, Milton Park, Abingdon, Oxon OX14 4RN
711 Third Avenue, New York, NY 10017, USA

Routledge is an imprint of the Taylor & Francis Group, an informa business

Copyright © R.C.H. Alexander 2007

R.C.H. Alexander has asserted his moral right under the Copyright, Designs and Patents Act, 1988, to be identified as the author of this work.

All rights reserved. No part of this book may be reprinted or reproduced or utilised in any form or by any electronic, mechanical, or other means, now known or hereafter invented, including photocopying and recording, or in any information storage or retrieval system, without permission in writing from the publishers.

Notice:
Product or corporate names may be trademarks or registered trademarks, and are used only for identification and explanation without intent to infringe.

British Library Cataloguing in Publication Data
Alexander, R. C. H.
　Insider dealing and money laundering in the EU : law and regulation
　1. Insider trading in securities - Law and legislation - European Union countries 2. Money laundering - law and legislation - European Union countries
　I. Title
　345.4'0268

Library of Congress Cataloging-in-Publication Data
Alexander, R. C. H.
　Insider dealing and money laundering in the EU : law and regulation / by R.C.H. Alexander
　　　p. cm.
　Includes bibliographical references and index.
　ISBN-13: 978-0-7546-4926-7 1. Money laundering--European Union countries. I. Title.

KJE2188.A954 2006
345.24'0268--dc22

2006025015

ISBN 13: 978 0 7546 4926 7 (hbk)

Contents

Table of Cases		*vii*
Table of Legislation		*ix*
Preface		*xv*
Chapter 1	**Why Regulate Insider Dealing and Money Laundering?**	**1**
	Insider Dealing	2
	Money Laundering	21
	International Pressure	28
Chapter 2	**Who is an Insider?**	**37**
	The Directive	38
	Austria	47
	Belgium	51
	Denmark	54
	Finland	55
	France	56
	Germany	61
	Greece	66
	Ireland (Republic)	67
	Italy	69
	Luxembourg	71
	Netherlands	71
	Portugal	72
	Spain	75
	Sweden	76
	United Kingdom	77
	Conclusion	80
Chapter 3	**Inside Information**	**83**
	The Directive	83
	Austria	85
	Belgium	87
	Denmark	92
	Finland	94
	France	95
	Germany	99
	Greece	102

		Ireland	102
		Italy	103
		Luxembourg	104
		Netherlands	106
		Portugal	107
		Spain	108
		Sweden	109
		United Kingdom	110
Chapter 4		**Criminal Offences of Insider Dealing**	**113**
		Introduction	113
		Dealing	114
		Exemptions Relating to Dealing Offence	116
		Penalties for Dealing	121
		Encouraging to Deal	135
		Allowing to Deal	138
		Unauthorised Disclosure	139
Chapter 5		**Money Laundering: The EU Directive and the UK Statutory Response**	**143**
		Introduction	143
		The EU Position	145
		United Kingdom	156
Chapter 6		**Impact on the Financial Services Industry**	**181**
		Insider Dealing	181
		Money Laundering	188
		Conclusion	199
Chapter 7		**Civil and Administrative Offences**	**201**
		Substantive Insider Dealing Offences	201
		Failure to Report Significant Developments	222
Chapter 8		**Conclusion: A Model for Enforcement**	**229**
		Insider Dealing	229
		Money Laundering	237
		Current Trends	244
		The Future	250

Bibliography   *255*
Index   *259*

Table of Cases

Belgium

Office of Public Prosecutor of Ghent v Bekaert and Storme, trial
Ghent Criminal Court, 27 September 1995; appeal reported in
Le Soir, 5 May 1997. 52-3, 54-5, 89, 91

England and Wales

*Amalgamated Metal Trading Ltd. v City of London Police Financial
Investigation Unit and others* [2003] 1 WLR 2711 195-6
Boardman v Phipps [1966] 3 All ER 721 16-18, 161, 220
Bray v Ford [1896] AC 44 14-15
C v S and others [1999] 2 All ER 345 193-4, 197
Fibrosa Spolka Akcyjna v Fairbairn Lawson Combe Barbour Ltd.
[1943] AC 32) 186, n.16
Foley v Hill (1848) 2 HL Cas. 28 195
Governor and Company of the Bank of Scotland v A [2001] 1 WLR 751 195
H.R. Bolton (Engineering) Co. v Graham [1957] 1 QB 159 50, n.32
ex p. James (1803) 8 Ves. 337 15
Keech v Sandford (1726) Sel. Cas. Ch. 61 14
Lennards Carrying Co. v Asiatic Petroleum Co. [1915] AC 705 50, n.32
Mahon and another v Rahn and others (No. 2) [2000] 4 All ER 41 144, n.6, 198
Oxford v Moss (1979) 68 Crim. App. Rep. 183, [1979] Crim. LR 119
20, n.88, 116, 160, 161-2
R v Andrews Weatherfoil Ltd. 56 Cr. App. R 31 50, n.33
R v Bentley (1998) The Times, July 31 251, n.49
Regal (Hastings) Ltd. v Gulliver [1942] 1 All ER 378 15-16, 17
Hosni Tayeb v HSBC Bank plc and Al Foursan International
Company [2004] EWHC 1529 (Comm.) 197
Taylor v Serious Fraud Office [1999] 2 AC 177, 219 [1998] 4 All
ER 801, 818 144, n.6, 198
United Dominions Trust Ltd. v Kirkwood [1966] 2 QB 431 195, n.40

European Court of Human Rights

Saunders v United Kingdom 23 EHRR 313, 17 December 1996 217

France

Delalande / Synthélabo   61, n.60, 125, 218, 219, 234
La Ruche Méridionale, Cour de Cassation, Chambre Criminel, 26 June 1995   96, n.19,
Pechiney, Cour de Cassation, Chambre Criminel, 26 October 1995   59, 98, 116, n.9, 125, 230

Germany

Weru, Amtsgericht Frankfurt am Main, January 1997. Reported, Frankfurter Allgemeine Zeitung, 27 February 1997   126

Greece

Capital Markets Commission v Trifon   205

Netherlands

HCS, Hoge Raad 27 June 1995, Netherlands Jurisprudence (NJ) 1995, 662   71
Weweler, Rb. Amsterdam, 3 January 1997   71, n.86

New Zealand

A-G for Hong Kong v Reid [1994] 1 AC 324; [1994] 1 All ER 1 (Privy Council)   16, n.65, 20, n.88, 162, n.65, 220

Singapore

Royal Brunei Airlines Sdn Bhd v Tan [1995] 2 AC 378 (Privy Council)   195, n.38

United States

Diamond v Oreamuno (1969) 24 NY 2d 494   161
SEC v Texas Gulf Sulfur Co. (1968) 401 F 2d 833   10, 19
SEC v Wang and Lee (1991) 944 F.2d 80   1, n.4, 30
U.S. v Vincent F. Chiarella (1980) 445 U.S. 222   19
U.S. v Newman (1981) 664 F 2d 12   19-20, 25, n.108, 26-7, 147
U.S. v O'Hagan (1997) 117 S. Ct. 2199   20

Table of Legislation

Austria

Criminal Code (*Strafgesetzbuch*, StGB)	123
Securities Supervisory Act (*Wertpapieraufsichtsgesetz*, WAG) 1996, BGBl. 1996/753	47-8
Stock Exchange Act (*Börsegesetz*, BörseG) 1993, BGBl. 1993/529	85-7, 123, 223

Belgium

Law of 22 December 1995	51-2, 53, 87-92, 124, 223-4
Penal Code	122, n.32
Royal Act No. 64 of 10 November 1967	89
Royal Decree of 18 September 1990	223-4

Denmark

Securities, etc. Consolidated Act, Consolidated Act No. 168 of 14 March 2001	54, 92-4, 124-5, 224

European Union

EC Treaty	22
Consolidated Banking Directive, Directive of the European Parliament and Council 2000/12/EC	152, 164, n.70
Capital Adequacy Directive, Council Directive 93/6/EEC	106, n.41
Insider Dealing Directive, Council Directive 89/592/EEC	xv, xvii, 31, 38-46, 83-5, 181-8, 222
Investment Services Directive, Council Directive 93/22/EEC	31-2, 106, n.41, 164, n.70, 219
Market Abuse Directive, Directive of the European Parliament and Council 2003/6/EC, implemented by Directive of the European Parliament and Council 2004/72/EC	ix, 63, 78, 137, 204, 233, 245
Markets in Financial Instruments Directive, Directive of the European Parliament and Council 2004/39/EC	31, n.28, 164, n.70
Money Laundering Directive, Council Directive 91/308/EEC	xvii, xviii, 23, n.102, 28, n.111, 31, 46, 143, 145-56, 188, 192

Second Banking Directive, Council Directive 89/646/EEC xvii, 152
Second Money Laundering Directive, Directive of the European
Parliament and Council 2001/97/EC 145, 146-8, 149, 151-2, 164, 243
Third Money Laundering Directive, Directive of the European
Parliament and Council 2005/60/EC xvii, 145, 148, 149, 153-4, 239, 241, 243

Finland

Securities Market Act (*Arvopaperimarkkinalaki*), Act
No. 1989/495 of 26 May 1995 55-6, 94-5, 125, 224

France

Law of 23 December 1970 1
Monetary and Financial Code (*Code Monétaire et Financier*) 21, n.90, 56-60, 95-8, 125, 138, 139, 224
Ordinance 67-833 of 28 September 1967 56-7, 96, 58
Penal Code (*Code Pénal*) 21, n.90, 57, 58, 98, 116, 126, 241

Germany

Criminal Code (*Strafgesetzbuch*, StGB) 66, 126, 146
Criminal Procedure Code (*Strafprozessordnung*, StPO) 126
Regulatory Offences Act (*Ordnungswidrigkeitengesetz*, OWiG) 66
Securities Trade Act (*Wertpapierhandelsgesetz*, WpHG) of 9
September 1998, as amended by Article 9 of the Act of 15 December 2003 61-2, 99-100, 126
Securities Trade Act (*Wertpapierhandelsgesetz*, WpHG) of 9 September
1998, as amended by Article 3 of the Act of 15 December 2004 62-6, 98-101, 205, 224-5
Stock Code (*Aktiengesetz*) 63

Greece

Law 1806/1988 126
Presidential Decree 53/1992 66, 102, 136, 205-6, 225

Ireland (Republic)

Companies Act 1990 67-9, 102-3, 127, 206-7
Companies Act 1990 (Insider Dealing Regulations) 1992, SI 131/1992 103
Constitution 67, n.77
Criminal Law (Jurisdiction) Act 1976 67, n.77
Euro Changeover (Amounts) Act 2001 122

Italy

Law No. 157 of 17 May 1991	70, 103, 127-8
Legislative Decree No. 58 of 24 February 1998 (as amended by Legislative Decree No. 61 of 11 April 2002)	69-71, 103-4, 127-9, 207-8

Luxembourg

Law of 3 May 1991	71, 104-6, 129, 137
Ministerial Regulation of 25 October 1996	226
Penal Code	105, n.39, 129

Netherlands

Economic Offences Act	129-30
Securities Trade Supervision Act (*Wet toezicht effectenverkeer*) 1995	71-2, 106-7, 129, 226-7

Portugal

Securities Code (*Código dos Valores Mobiliários*) of 13 November 1999, last amended by Decree-Law 66/2004 of 24 March 2004	72-5, 107, 130

South Africa

Criminal Procedure Act 1977	57, n.49
Firearms Control Act 2000	57, n.50
Insider Trading Act 1998	40, 57, 124, n.37, 220, 233

Spain

Penal Code (*Código Penal*)	66, n.73, 75, 76, 115, 131, 149
Securities Market Law (*Ley del Mercado de Valores*)	75-6, 108, 115, 208-11, 227

Sweden

Criminal Code	132
Financial Instruments Trade Act (*Lagen om Handel med Finansiella Instrument*)	110
Insider Act (*Insiderlagen*)	76-7, 108-10, 132, 137

United Kingdom

Anti-Terrorism, Crime and Security Act 2001	145, n.7, 157, 173, 237, 240
Companies Act 1980	1, 10, n.37, 78, n.100
Companies Act 1985	52, n.37, 91, n.12
Computer Misuse Act 1990	44, n.23
Criminal Justice Act 1988	157, 159-60
Criminal Justice Act 1993	77-8, 110-1, 132, 157, 170, 171, n.87, 202, 212, 238
Drug Trafficking (Offences) Act 1986	156
Drug Trafficking Act 1994	159-60, 165, 170, 171, n.87, 238, 239, n.21
Financial Services Act 1986	12, 211-2, 249
Financial Services and Markets Act 2000	13, 77, 78-80, 145, n.7, 186-7, 212-22, 228
Financial Services and Markets Act (Regulated Activities) Order 2001, SI 2001/544	111
Human Rights Act 1998	216, 252-3
Limited Liability Partnership Act 2000	183, n.5
Magistrates' Courts (Unit Fines) Rules 1992, SI 1992/1856	123
Money Laundering Regulations 1993, SI 1993/1933	143, n.3, 152, 156, 188
Money Laundering Regulations 2001, SI 2001/3641	156
Money Laundering Regulations 2003	143, n.3, 145, n.8, 157, 165, n.71, 249
Official Secrets Act 1989	41, n.13,
Proceeds of Crime Act 2002	133, 134-5, 143, 145, n.8, 156, 157-73, 178, 189-90, 235-6, 237, 239-40, 249
Terrorism Act 2000	143, 157, 173, 175-9, 237-8, 249

United States

Bank Secrecy Act 1970	22, 243
Securities Exchange Act 1934	19, 29, n.113, 116
USA PATRIOT Act (Uniting and Strengthening America by Providing Appropriate Tools Required to Intercept and Obstruct Terrorism) 2001	22, 30

Regulatory Instruments

Finland

Rahoitustarkastus (Financial Supervision), Guidance Notes	55, 94

France

Commission des Opérations de Bourse, COB (Stock
Exchange Operations Commission) Regulation 90-08   56, 60-1, 95, 96, 98,
204-5

Greece

Capital Markets Commission Decision No. 86 of 15 October 1996   225

Ireland

"Yellow Book" (Stock Exchange Regulations)   225-6

Italy

Commissione Nazionale per la Società e la Borsa, CONSOB
(National Company and Stock Exchange Commission) Regulation
No. 5553 of 14 November 1991   69-70
CONSOB Resolution 14 November 1991   207-8
CONSOB Regulation 11971 of 14 May 1999   226

Organisation for Economic Cooperation and Development

Financial Action Task Force Forty Recommendations (2003)   23, n.102, 28,
n.111, 33, 148, 241

Spain

Governing Body of Madrid Stock Exchange, Guidance Note, 1990   227

United Kingdom

Financial Services Authority, Regulatory Handbook
- Code of Market Conduct (MAR)   79-80, 120, 187, 214, 217
- Enforcement Manual (ENF)   218, n.48, 219, 234
- Threshold Conditions (COND)   221

Law Society of England and Wales, "Guide to Professional
Conduct"   140, n.95,
Law Society of England and Wales, Practice Notes, Council
Statements (1974) 71 Law Society Gazette 395   10-11, 186, n.19

Preface

Insider dealing has, as a legal issue at least, come increasingly to the fore in the last 20 years or so. Although it was criminalised in the United States as early as 1934 and the remarks of both lawyers and economists there have featured in books and articles alike at fairly frequent intervals since, other jurisdictions have only taken action somewhat more recently. This is certainly true of Europe, in which even the first jurisdiction, France, did not pass legislation prohibiting insider dealing until 1970. Eight years after that, Professor Barry Rider, writing on the subject in *The Conveyancer*, commented in his opening sentences that the use by a fiduciary of confidential information was an issue rather less considered in the UK than in the United States.[1] His call, at the article's close, for legislation outlawing insider dealing in the UK would not be heeded for a further 2 years.

This has now changed. The introduction by the European Community of the Insider Dealing Directive ("the Directive"[2]) in 1989[3] led, by legal necessity, to implementing legislation, prohibiting insider dealing, across, initially, 12 Member States[4] with a further three and then an additional ten following over time. Earlier discussions as to whether insider dealing really is a bad thing and the arguments of some that it may be positively beneficial have largely ceased as a consensus has arisen that it is bad and must therefore be stopped. Insider dealing legislation has spread beyond North America and Europe to the other major financial centres and on to the developing jurisdictions, such as South Africa and mainland China. In place of the old debates have arisen new ones: are the measures that have now been introduced to prevent, or at least control, insider dealing actually effective and what can be done to improve them?

The introduction of the EC Directive meant that a large number of jurisdictions introduced anti insider-dealing legislation over really quite a short period of time. At the same time, the latitude given to the Member States, as with all Directives, enables considerable variation in the implementing methods adopted. The opportunity was therefore created for a comparative study, examining the different measures taken and considering the advantages and drawbacks of each.

---

1 Rider, B.A.K. (1978) "The Fiduciary and the Frying Pan" 42 *The Conveyancer* 114.

2 Throughout this book, unless otherwise stated, "the Directive" refers to the Insider Dealing Directive, i.e. Directive 89/592/EEC. The exception to this rule is in Chapter 5, where it refers to the First Money Laundering Directive, 91/108, as amended, by Directive 2001/97/EC.

3 Council Directive 89/592/EEC.

4 Even the two Member States with existing anti-insider dealing measures, namely France and the UK, amended their legislation in order to comply fully with the Directive.

It is, however, noticeable that this opportunity was not taken. A study compiled for the European Commission was published in 1998, but this simply set out which measures were taken in each of the (then) 15 Member States in order to establish the extent to which each complied with the Directive. It therefore contained little or no comment or analysis. Rather, the literature, whether books or journal articles, has tended to take one of two approaches. Many deal with one jurisdiction alone: the United States, the UK, Australia, Japan, etc. The comparative works, which are in any case fewer in number, tend to focus on the major financial centres: the United States,[5] the United Kingdom, Japan, Germany. A notable exception to this rule is Rider and Ffrench's *The Regulation of Insider Trading*,[6] which counts as one of very few global studies: it covers over 40 jurisdictions on every continent except South America. With the exception of the UK and France, however, even this does not deal with Europe in detail: the other European countries are considered in a total of 34 pages. Further, it was published in 1979, several years before the introduction of the EC Directive and indeed of any kind of legislative anti insider-dealing provisions in a number of jurisdictions.[7]

This book therefore sets out, first and foremost, to be a comparative study of the provisions relating to insider dealing under the Directive and in each of the 15 jurisdictions that were Member States of the European Union prior to 1 May 2004.[8] Unlike the European Commission study, it does not merely set out the provisions, but goes on to provide comment and analysis. The measures are compared to the EC Directive, but also, where appropriate, to the measures taken by other Member States and even, on occasion, by jurisdictions outside Europe.

Although, inevitably, the Insider Dealing Directive is considered in some detail, the book does not seek to be a treatise on European Community law. Such issues as the achievement of the European single market (an important factor in the introduction of the Directive) are therefore not considered, nor, except in the most general terms, is the discretion of Member States in implementing European Directives. Nor is the legislation of the twelve Member States which have acceded to the European Union in May 2004 covered.[9]

The "old" Member States continue to encompass most of the main financial centres of Europe and, in any case, there remain in force a number of transition provisions

---

5   It is difficult to over-state the influence of the United States globally in every aspect of financial services regulation. In view of this, and also of the fact that the United States was for some considerable time the only major jurisdiction to possess anti insider-dealing legislation, most works on insider dealing have tended to refer to it.

6   Rider, B.A.K. and Ffrench, H.L. (1979) *The Regulation of Insider Trading*, Macmillan Press.

7   Rider and Ffrench comment that, for example, Spain and Austria had no such provisions at the time.

8   Austria, Belgium, Denmark, Finland, France, Germany, Greece, Ireland, Italy, Luxembourg, the Netherlands, Portugal, Spain, Sweden, and the United Kingdom.

9   Cyprus, Czech Republic, Estonia, Hungary, Latvia, Lithuania, Malta, Poland, Slovakia and Slovenia, (2004); Bulgaria and Romania (2007).

in relation to the new states. Consideration of the insider dealing provisions of "the ten" may therefore be left to a later book.

The EU Market Abuse Directive is similarly not addressed. Its implementation by the Member States is still ongoing; indeed, the initial Directive – Directive 2003/6/EC – was merely a framework Directive, requiring implementation at Community level in the form of Directive 2004/72/EC. This was only passed at the end of April 2004 and the history of previous Directives, including the Insider Dealing Directive, would suggest that implementation will not be fully complete for some years yet to come. This being the case, although the Insider Dealing Directive has been formally repealed, it is it, not the Market Abuse Directive, which continues to be the basis of the national legislation across the Member States.[10] Further, in those Member States, such as Germany, where the Market Abuse Directive has already been implemented, the influence of its predecessor remains strong.[11] Indeed, the term "market abuse" is first found not in the context of the Directive now in place, but of the UK civil / administrative provisions introduced to supplement the criminal measures which themselves were enacted to implement the Insider Dealing Directive.[12]

The same is true of the EU Third Money Laundering Directive. Although this came into force on 15 December 2005, Member States have until 15 December 2007 to implement it. The legislation of the Member States continues, therefore, for the time being to be based on the First Money Laundering Directive,[13] as amended,[14] just as has been stated above of the Insider Dealing Directive.

A final point to be made in relation to what material is and is not covered in this work concerns the provisions in the United States. Much of the initiatives against financial crime, including insider dealing, have their origins in the United States and, as both the world superpower and the world's leading financial centre, the United States is a country that continues to have a significant influence on developments around the world. That influence is discussed in Chapter 1, where the reasons for

---

10 English translations of the insider dealing legislation of a number of the Member States are available on the national regulators' websites. See, for example, the Italian CONSOB, www.consob.it, the Portuguese Comissão do Mercado dos Valores Mobiliarios: www.cmvm.pt, the Swedish Finansinspektionen, www.fi.se, the Danish Finanstilsynet, www.ftnet.dk and the Finnish Rahoitustarkastus, www.rata.bof.fi. Other regulators' websites contain the legislation, but only in the local language, for example the German BaFin, www.bafin.de and the Spanish Comisión Nacional del Mercado de Valores, www.cnmv.es. In other cases, it may be found on websites devoted to publishing national legislation in general (on all subjects): examples are the French www.legifrance.gouv.fr, the Irish Statute Book, www.irishstatutebook.ie, and more recent Acts of the Oireachtas on the Oireachtas website, www.oireachtas.ie and indeed the UK Acts of Parliament, www.opsi.gov.uk/acts.htm.

11 The German provision, for example, relating to actual dealing (as opposed to the offences of encouragement to deal or unauthorised disclosure) is unchanged.

12 For the way in which the two run in parallel in the UK, see the discussion of the civil/administrative provisions in Chapter 7: pp. 211-22.

13 Council Directive 91/308/EEC.

14 By the Second Money Laundering Directive, 2001/97/EC.

regulating both insider dealing and money laundering are discussed. The work as a whole, however, explicitly has as its focus the European Union. Although, therefore, other jurisdictions are referred to in passing, it is the measures of the EU and of its Member States, in particular the 15 prior to the 2004 enlargement, which are discussed in detail. Discussion of the US measures may be left to the considerable literature that has already been devoted to it.

The principal subject of the book is the control of insider dealing. It is, however, impossible now to consider any form of crime, certainly economic crime, in isolation. Economic crime, including insider dealing, gives rise to profits; indeed, this is its purpose and motivation. Handling such profits constitutes money laundering, an offence often considered to be even more serious than insider dealing.[15] The anti money-laundering measures need, therefore, also to be considered in a study of this nature. The wide definition of criminal proceeds to cover not just financial profits but any property originating from a criminal offence only emphasises this. To deal in detail, however, with both the insider dealing and money laundering legislation of 15 jurisdictions would be unduly cumbersome for one study; it is to be noted that multinational studies of either subject regularly fill entire books. It would also detract from the book's main focus on insider dealing. Money laundering is therefore dealt with rather more briefly: Chapter 5 considers the First Money Laundering Directive (as amended)[16] and, as an example, the UK primary legislation.

The book begins with a general consideration of the rationale for regulating financial services in general and controlling insider dealing and money laundering in particular. It then goes on, in Chapters 2, 3 and 4, to examine, in respect of each of the 15 Member States, the definition of an insider and of inside information and the various criminal offences relating to insider dealing. Chapter 5 then deals with the anti money-laundering regime. It is recognised that the measures, in relation to both insider dealing and money laundering, have a considerable impact on the financial sector and this is considered in Chapter 6. The criminal law has, however, been judged to be of limited effect in controlling insider dealing and there is therefore an increasing trend to deal with it by means of civil/administrative measures, considered in Chapter 7. Finally, Chapter 8 makes some suggestions as to possible models for insider dealing and money laundering legislation and concludes by considering what the likely trends will be in this area in the coming years.

A brief note should be made regarding the titles of legislation, regulators and courts. This book covers 15 Member States and therefore 11 different official languages. In general, the preference has been to refer to the legislation, at least

---

15 For example, in the UK, insider dealing carries a maximum prison sentence of 7 years, precisely half that for money laundering. Similarly, EC legislation requires that money laundering be punished by criminal sanctions; no such stipulation is made in respect of insider dealing.

16 Council Directive 91/308/EEC, as amended by Directive of the European Parliament and Council 2001/97/EC. Mention is also made in Chapter 5 of the Third Money Laundering Directive: although this is now in force, the Member States have until December 2007 to implement it.

in the first reference, by its title both in its original language and in translation, for example, "Securities Trade Act (*Wertpapierhandelsgesetz*)". In certain cases, however, this has not been practical as the sources in English refer to the legislation only by an English translation; this is true, for example, of the Danish legislation. In such cases, the translation stands alone. A further exception has been made in relation to what may be described as generic titles, e.g. "Penal Code" or "Law No. 2001-1062 of 15 November 2001", since no useful purpose would be served by citing their titles in the original languages. With regulators, the practice has been to use the name in the original language (again, with translation) for the first reference; thereafter, if there is a commonly used abbreviation, such as the French COB, it is used, otherwise, for ease of reference, the translation is used.

As regards courts, the general practice has been to translate their names, save where no real translation exists. For example, the French Cour de Cassation has no real English-language equivalent and hence its French title has been used. Its chambers are, however, translated for ease of reference (e.g. Cour de Cassation, Criminal Division).

In the tradition of legal literature, the language in this study is non-gender specific.

Chapter 1

Why Regulate Insider Dealing and Money Laundering?

The question of why one should regulate financial markets at all is not as strange as it may seem. Outright fraud has always attracted disapproval with the ensuing penalties imposed on those caught perpetrating it. Certain other forms of conduct, however, such as insider dealing, which would now generally be considered as market abuse, were long viewed, at least in certain quarters, as normal and legitimate business practices, particularly in Europe. (Money laundering, with which this book also deals, is a separate issue and the arguments for its control are therefore discussed separately towards the end of this chapter.) Even after insider dealing had been criminalised in a number of European jurisdictions, the perception, notably in the United States, was that it was still not viewed particularly seriously there. In 1989, when insider dealing had been a criminal offence for nearly a decade in the UK[1] and nearly two in France,[2] the *Asian Wall Street Journal* carried an article by an American journalist, entitled "Insider Trading, Illegal in US, is Customary in Europe".[3] A year later, Judge Owen of the Southern District Court of New York commented that in Hong Kong, at that time still under British administration, a conviction for insider dealing was tantamount to a commendation from the Queen.[4] Even today, commentators have been known to say, albeit rarely in print, that no one in the commercial world would wish to be considered an "outsider".

A major factor has been the mentality, not amongst the public at large but amongst the financial services community. Insider dealing, some have argued, is a victimless crime and thus there is nothing intrinsically wrong with it. Robbery, murder, rape – all these offences have clear, identifiable victims. The same can be said of fraud, whether it is perpetrated by the con man who persuades someone to entrust to him their savings or the embezzler who at some later date appropriates funds originally accepted for legitimate investment. The public outcry at the misappropriation of pension funds in the Maxwell affair was as great as at any act of physical violence.

---

1 Part V, Companies Act 1980.
2 Law of 23 December 1970, amending Ordinance of 28 September 1967.
3 Forman, C. (1989) *Asian Wall Street Journal*, 9 February 1989.
4 See *SEC v Wang and Lee* 944 F.2d 80 (2nd Circuit, 1991).

Insider Dealing

A core question, however, is, who are the victims of insider dealing? Traditionally, it has been argued that it is the market that suffers,[5] but some have considered this to be too vague. To this, in turn, it has been pointed out that the law condemns a number of offences against the community at large: treason has no specific individual victims[6] but rather the nation as a whole. In other jurisdictions, a variety of attitudes emerge. In a number of Central and Eastern European states, insider dealing was, until recently,[7] seen simply as one version of corruption. The approach that insider dealing is simply a perk of holding certain positions is widespread, both in developing countries and more established financial centres. In the UK, it was said that "well into [the 20th] century, such insider trading in shares was perceived by many as a perk of the job in a system often regarded as fair game and always in season".[8] James Fishman similarly remarked, "Particularly in the context of takeovers, within a relatively closed environment, [insider] dealing was considered a customary way of doing business in the City, a sort of fringe benefit."[9]

Attitudes in Germany have been said to be even more blatant:

> So called 'fireside chats', during which German journalists, financial analysts and others heard inside information prior to its public announcement, were a common phenomena. One foreign banker based in Frankfurt noted that it became a real 'joke' to watch prices move first and then data being issued.[10]

A similar anecdote is told of a conference delegate in Hong Kong, who asked with incredulity, "But what kind of idiot would invest on the stock market if he did not have inside information?" Perhaps when Craig Forman wrote his article, he should have looked a little closer at hand.

---

5   For example, by Herzel, L. and Harris, D. "Do we need insider trading laws?" [1989] Co. Law 34: see pp. 9-10..

6   Except in its more arcane form of adultery with the wife of the King or the heir to the throne, which in any case would not appear now to be prosecuted! Even assassinating the monarch, or conspiring to do so, is viewed not as harm against them personally (although it clearly involves that!) but against the state of which they are the head.

7   The accession of eight of these states to the European Union on 1 May 2004 (together with Cyprus and Malta) has meant that they have now been compelled to introduce specific anti-insider-dealing legislation in order to comply with EU law.

8   Ashe, T.M. and Counsell, L. (1993) *Insider Trading*, 2nd Edition, Tolley Publishing Company Ltd., cited in Small, R.G. (2001) *Path dependence and the law: A law and economics analysis of the development of the insider trading laws of the United States, United Kingdom and Japan*, PhD thesis, University of London.

9   "A comparison of enforcement of securities law violations in the UK and US" (1993) 14 Co. Law 163, 169.

10   Pfeil, U.C. (1996), "Finanzplatz Deutschland: Germany Enacts Insider Trading Legislation" 11 Am. U.J. International Law and Policy, 137, cited in R.G. Small, *supra*.

Economic Arguments for Permitting Insider Dealing

Indeed some have gone further, perhaps no one more so than Professor Henry Manne. He has argued, in not only in an article appropriately titled "In Defense of Insider Trading"[11] but also in an entire book, *Insider Trading and the Stock Market*,[12] that not only is there nothing wrong with insider dealing, it is positively beneficial in a number of respects. It should be noted that all Manne's arguments are put forward from an economic, rather than legal, perspective, perhaps one too often overlooked.[13]

Manne begins by arguing that insider dealing encourages persons to engage in the securities markets. In particular, he focuses on corporate managers. Few do anything out of pure altruism, he says: they require the incentive of a reward. Those involved in trading in securities, therefore, require the perk of a nice profit ahead of the game now and again in order to make what they do worthwhile. While, he argues, the old-style entrepreneur who founded his own business was rewarded by receiving directly the profits ensuing from his skill, the modern entrepreneur who is a corporate officer, and hence an employee, does not. There are a number of responses to this. The first and most obvious is that the rewards of insider dealing do not make it desirable to society. One could equally well say that the smuggling of tobacco and of controlled drugs is a good thing because it encourages people to be international truck drivers.[14]

Secondly, securities traders, corporate executives and the professionals with whom they work are already rewarded with some of the highest salaries in the economy. In addition, many of them receive a handsome annual bonus that may equal or even exceed the salary itself. One could suggest that it is this, rather than the opportunities to engage in insider dealing (which inevitably will be unpredictable) that leads people to go into this sector of work. Professor Barry Rider and Leigh Ffrench, although they roundly refute Professor Manne's theories, suggest that, in times of recession, the salaries received by corporate executives no longer prove

---

11 44 Harvard Business Review, No. 6, 113.

12 (1966) Collier-Macmillan.

13 William L. Cary, former chairman of the US Securities and Exchange Commission has remarked, "there has been too much dominance of lawyers and legal thinking in the work of the Securities and Exchange Commission ... The Commission can never afford to be without economic as well as legal counsel." (Foreword to Robbins, S.G. (1966) *The Securities Markets: Operations and Issues*, vii, viii, cited in Wu, H.K. (1968) "An Economist Looks At Section 16 Of The Securities Exchange Act Of 1934" 68 *Columbia Law Review* 260.) The ethical/moral perspective is also, for the most part, rejected as being hypocritical, although some of the arguments Manne puts forward in favour of insider dealing are, in fact, moral ones: see pp. 5-6.

14 In fact, Professor Petrus Van Duyne has argued that the high levels of taxation on tobacco products in the UK are harmful because they give rise to smuggling by organised crime groups: (2003) "Organizing cigarette smuggling and policy making, ending up in smoke" 39 *Crime, Law and Social Change* 285–317.

a sufficient incentive.[15] But this must be questioned: even in a downturn in the economy, corporate salaries remain distinctly attractive in comparison to those of other positions. Manne explicitly says that salaries and bonuses are not, in fact, adequate recompense for corporate entrepreneurs but only for those merely exercising management functions, and he cites J.A. Schumpeter in support of this view.[16] This, he says, is because they are not directly linked to the profits that the officer has achieved: they cannot be because they are by definition fixed in advance. Even though bonuses are linked to the profits of the company, they are linked to the overall profits, of which each officer receives a share: the individual officer does not receive a bonus directly linked to the profits that he brought in. This may be true in principle. On the other hand, a corporate officer who delivers, who through his own efforts and initiative brings in profits to his company, is far more likely to retain his job and thus his large salary. This will perhaps never be more true than in the times of recession to which Rider and Ffrench refer: in the rounds of lay-offs and redundancies, it will be the least productive who go first and those who most visibly bring in profits whom the company will take most pains to keep in order to ensure that some profits continue to come in and the company survives.

Thirdly, as Manne himself acknowledges, insider dealing comprises a very small percentage of the total number of securities transactions. If it is an incentive, therefore, it cannot be a great one.

Before moving on to Manne's second argument, two more points need to be made in relation to his first. Since, as is seen below, the basic theory of Manne and others that insider dealing is beneficial has now largely been dismissed, these points may be of academic interest only, but they are still worth making. Manne focuses on corporate executives, who he feels are rightly rewarded through insider dealing for their entrepreneurism. He overlooks the fact, however, that such executives are only one category of insider dealer. The executive's lawyer and accountant are also insiders. So are, in many cases, some of his junior employees.[17] The first persons in a pharmaceutical company, for example, to learn that the tests of a new drug or vaccine have been successful will not be the CEO, but the rather more junior employees in the Research and Development department. More common still are the cases of junior insiders buying stock in the target of a takeover bid: executives will generally be barred, not just by legislation but by their own companies, from buying such stock.[18] These players are not entrepreneurs: although their fortunes are linked to those of their client or employer, as the case may be, they do not take the same risks for it. Yet Manne would offer them the same reward.

---

15 Rider, B.A.K. and Ffrench, H.L. (1979) *The Regulation of Insider Trading*, Macmillan, p. 4.

16 Schumpeter, J.A. (1942) *Capitalism, Socialism and Democracy*.

17 For a full consideration of the range of persons who may qualify as insiders, see Chapter 2.

18 Herzel, L. and Harris, D., "Do we need insider trading laws?" [1989] Co. Law 34.

To this, it could be argued that researchers should similarly be provided with an incentive, since many companies rely on them to develop their products. Further, in some cases, such as the pharmaceutical industry, the results of the researchers' labours may benefit not only their company but society at large: this would, at least in principle, be true of new drugs.[19] Such researchers already, however, receive a substantial incentive: the continued success of their employer. This is not an idealistic argument; it is a highly pragmatic one. It is through developing new products, often in a highly competitive industry, that companies remain profitable and hence in business. The labours of the researcher are therefore rewarded directly by the security of his job. Less starkly, the successful researcher (or other more junior employee) may well be rewarded with greater prospects in the job market, either through internal promotion or a move to another employer in the industry. The bar to insider dealing does not deprive them of an incentive to work well any more than it does the entrepreneur.

It is also to be noted that Manne's argument focuses on executives who make a profit from insider dealing. Attention should also be paid to the other side: those who obtain information indicating that securities are about to fall in price, rather than rise. A lack of prohibition on insider dealing would mean that executives could, if their company suffered a major setback, minimise their personal loss by selling out ahead of the rest of the market, i.e. dump much of their losses on other investors. To an extent, corporate structures, particularly those of limited liability, enable entrepreneurs to do this in any event: when a company becomes insolvent, the losses generally fall on its creditors, not its directors. Just as the principles of company law allow this, since, if they did not, few would take the risk of setting up a new business in the first place, so, one could perhaps argue, should the law regarding dealing by entrepreneurs. James Fishman has, albeit disapprovingly, said that this has been an argument supporting insider dealing: "Insider trading was tolerated because it helped maintain an 'orderly market', that is, one in which professionals did not lose money."[20] In response, however, one should point out the disquiet already prevalent amongst the public regarding those who set up a business, watch it fail and then walk away leaving others to "carry the can". The public are hardly likely to be mollified by such persons not only being able to walk away from the company's debts but also recoup their personal investment before the final day of reckoning.[21]

Manne's second argument is linked to the first: he suggests that the opportunity to engage in insider dealing is a just reward for corporate entrepreneurism. That executives are entitled to certain perks in addition to their salary is not in dispute: a

---

19 Provided that society at large is permitted to benefit from the research: the practical realities of drugs research are considered in direct terms by Dersowltz, R.S. (2002), *Federal Bodysnatchers and the New Guinea Virus: Tales of Parasites, People and Politics*, W.W. Norton & Co., especially (although not exclusively) in Chapter 7.

20 Fishman, J.J. (1993), "A comparison of enforcement of securities law violations in the UK and US" 14 Co. Law 163, 170.

21 Indeed, public opinion has in general played a large part in securing the regulation of financial markets: see pp. 11-13.

luxury car or the opportunity to attend conferences in very pleasant locations[22] are examples. The profits derived from insider dealing, he suggests, are simply another legitimate perk of the job. To this, however, may be raised in rebuttal the same argument as that above: the rewards for corporate entrepreneurs are already quite adequate.

Thirdly, Manne suggests that insider dealing benefits the market as a whole. His thesis here is that insider dealers by their activities ensure that the rise or fall in price of the security concerned is more gentle than it would otherwise be. Insiders' buying will be noticed by other investors, who will therefore see that there is something attractive about the securities and themselves start to buy. This will gradually increase the price until the information, up to now confidential, is announced. The result will be that the announcement will cause the price to rise, but not as sharply because the increase has already begun. Conversely, if no insider dealing takes place, there will be a sudden, substantial change in the price as soon as the news is announced. This will cause unnecessary volatility, which is harmful to the market.

In addition, Manne argues, the more gradual rise set off by the insider dealers counters the argument of unfairness that some critics of insider dealing raise. Yes, investors who are not "in the know" will lose out in comparison to the insiders, but not by as much as they would otherwise do. Indeed, many of them will have been drawn in to buy in the days preceding the announcement simply because of the upward trend in the price. The insiders will profit most, a fitting reward for securing the contract. But far fewer "outside" investors will lose by the full difference between the price before the insider dealing started and the price after the announcement. One could add that the process will also avoid investors winning by sheer luck: if there were no insider dealing, an investor who has no knowledge whatsoever of the contract but who has generally been impressed by the company's performance, could buy shares and make an instant windfall when the price shot up a few days later. If this is fairer than the insiders being allowed to make a profit, it arguably has the fairness of the lottery![23] Furthermore, under a system that prohibits insider dealing, that investor, through absolutely no fault of his own, would then be likely to face an investigation by the financial regulators or, worse still, the police for insider dealing. Is that fair?

In response, Rider and Ffrench point out, again, that insider dealing represents a very small proportion of the total dealing in a given security. This is not surprising: insiders rarely have the available spare capital to buy large numbers of shares. Even someone on a "fat cat" salary of the type highlighted in the press is likely only to be able at a moment's notice to buy securities worth, say, £20,000: a decidedly small amount compared to the amounts that institutions routinely buy and sell. To quote Rider and Ffrench, who here summarise Manne's own argument, "the scope of the

---

22 This last is of course less common in the harsher economic environment of the 21st century, but it was the norm in the 1960s and 1970s when Manne proposed his theories.

23 Manne in fact compares the securities markets, with open approval, to gambling: see p. 11.

problem posed by insider trading on privileged information in relation to the market for shares in the particular corporation will be negligible".[24] Insiders may be able to raise more funds over time but they rarely have a great deal of time. The flurry of trading activity to which Manne refers is therefore likely in practice to raise barely a blip on the radar screen of the market.

The point about the unfortunate "outsider" dealer who happens to buy the securities just before the announcement is made, only to find himself under investigation is my own, not Manne's. In response, however, it must be pointed out that insider dealing charges are notoriously difficult to prove.[25] This is particularly true in the criminal justice arena, but even under the civil/administrative systems, some connection will need to be shown between the dealer and the information if an allegation and subsequent penalty for insider dealing is likely to stick.

It is not only Manne, however, who argues that insider dealing benefits the markets as a whole. The argument, albeit on different grounds, is put forward by Professor Hsiu-kwang Wu in "An Economist Looks at Section 16 of the Securities Exchange Act of 1934".[26] Wu does not advocate insider dealing in as strong terms as Manne. He does, however, seek to examine the economic issues. He states, "federal securities law ... places serious obstacles in the way of exploitation of inside information and thereby makes insiders more reluctant to trade their shares."[27] Thus far, few would take issue with him; indeed, many would consider this a testament to the success of the legislation.[28] But he continues, "The economic implications of this reluctance should be taken into account, or at least recognised in legal discussions."

Wu's argument centres around the "classical" economic model. He starts off by stating that insiders, unless restrained, will deal speculatively in the relative securities, i.e. buy and re-sell (or sell and re-buy) within a short period in order to gain an immediate profit, rather than investing, i.e. buying the relevant securities with the intention of retaining them for a significant period of time. He then goes on to say that, according to classical economic theory, speculators create liquidity in the market both by providing a broad and active market and by reducing differences in the price of securities over a short period of time. In addition, they provide stability: since they know what price is normal for a given security, they will buy it when its price is above this level and will sell when it is below it. This will in turn lead others to do so, thus correcting the price.

Speculators will, however, only thrive in the markets if they have "better-than-average foresight", enabling them to judge which securities are likely to move in which direction (and by how much). If they are not able to judge this correctly, Wu

---

24 Rider, B.A K and Ffrench, H.L. (1979) *The Regulation of Insider Trading*, Macmillan, p. 2.

25 For the reasons for this, see p. 202.

26 (1968) 68 *Columbia Law Review* 260.

27 *Ibid.*, p. 262.

28 Although some have questioned the effectiveness of the existing insider dealing legislation in a number of jurisdictions, including the UK, they do acknowledge the approach of the United States as being among the most effective.

argues, they will sustain losses more often than they make profits and thus be driven out of the market altogether. It follows that those with the best foresight of all as to which direction securities are likely to move in will be those in possession of inside information. It is no longer a matter of an educated guess, it is actual knowledge. Indeed, Wu says, it is the "informed" who have better foresight and thrive and the "uninformed" who do not and leave the market.

There are, however, some drawbacks to this theory, some of which Wu himself acknowledges. The first is that it is doubtful whether speculators do in fact enhance the stability of the markets. Certainly their injecting of money into the markets and ensuring that securities are traded frequently is likely to result in a broad and active market and certainly they provide additional liquidity. But whether they iron out price differences is, however, another matter: on occasion, speculators cause sudden and very significant price changes. Indeed, Keynes' view was that speculators are harmful to the market *per se*.[29]

Secondly, as Wu states, the theory pre-supposes that there is a "normal" price for a given security that can accurately be foreseen. This is by no means necessarily the case. The price of securities can be affected by many factors on a day-to-day basis, of which the "big news" to which the inside information relates may only be one. So, an insider will be able confidently to predict that the price of the company's shares will rise, but he will not so easily be able to predict to what level, certainly not with the accuracy that the example set out suggests. There may be a bubble triggered by the insiders' dealing which pushes the price higher than expected; alternatively, other factors, relating either to the company specifically or to the market in general, may cause the rise to be dampened. But, Wu suggests, insiders are likely to hold out for the profit which their information leads them to expect; consequently, they will sell after the price has reaches its peak or buy after it has reached its trough. This will contrast with other types of speculators who will often sell before the peak is reached, not wishing to hold on too long and risk an unexpected downturn.[30] Such

---

29 Two examples will suffice. By speculating heavily against sterling in September 1992, George Soros triggered a series of events that caused a sharp devaluation of the currency and indeed its unceremonious removal from the European Exchange Rate Mechanism. Similarly, on 27 December 1995, two banks speculated heavily on the Madrid Stock Exchange, resulting in an overall fall in value of securities across the Exchange of 2%. Although it could be argued that in both these cases, the speculators' aim was not the usual one of making a short-term profit but to prove, in the one case, that investors are more powerful than governments and, in the other, simply to cause destabilisation, they do appear to give weight to Keynes' view that, far from having a beneficial effect, speculators tend in fact to cause harm to the markets.

30 This point can be overstated: some traders will commit funds to backing their prediction in order to make a greater profit. A now famous example of where this went wrong is the activities of Nick Leeson in 1994-5: although the offence for which he was convicted related to his hiding of his losses, rather than his sustaining them in the first place, it is salutary to recall that those losses were sustained as a result of his holding on and continuing to invest, believing that the market would turn. Inevitably, some investors do take this high-

"on-the-edge" trading, he says, leaves insider dealers vulnerable to the effects of "sentiment": a downturn in the price can easily cause them to change their view of the likely rise and sell out suddenly. The result of this, far from stabilising the market, can be the very reverse. Keynes' view, that all speculators have a destabilising effect, would therefore appear to apply as much to insiders as to anyone else.

Although Wu acknowledges the arguments against his economic theory, he ultimately says that they merely show that there are exceptions to the otherwise valid rule. This is unfortunate: such negative effects as destabilisation of the market should not be so dismissed. Further, the admission that insider dealing is not, in fact, always beneficial to the markets seriously undermines the case that it should be permitted.

Others, however, have put forward economic arguments against insider dealing. Dr Giorgios Zekos states that the very flurry of activity caused by the insiders' dealing being observed can destabilise the price of the security concerned.[31] If the information, when published, is likely to cause the share-price to rise from £3.60 to £4.10, the increased demand caused by the insiders' dealing may raise it from £3.60 to £3.75 or perhaps even £3.80. But then the speculators notice the price rise and start buying in order to "get in on the action". This fuels further price rises such that, by the time of the announcement, the share price is £4.40. Since the release of information will only set the share price at £4.10, this increased price is unsustainable: a bubble has been created. This will of course not happen in every case of insider dealing, but in an environment as fast moving as a modern securities market, bubbles can never be ruled out. When it bursts and the share price returns to £4.10, the insiders who bought at £3.60 have made a nice profit while the losers are not only those who were not "in the know" at the beginning, but also those who bought towards the end of the flurry, which the insiders triggered, and hence bought too high. The same will apply where the inside information is bad news, not good: the flurry of selling will drive the share price down further than the information actually warrants and those who sell in panic just before the announcement will lose by having sold at a price lower than they need have done.

Herzel and Harris, in the paper referred to above, also argue that insider dealing is harmful to the market, but on different grounds. They state that it impedes, or even prevents, information being disseminated to the markets:

Misuse by an agent of valuable information acquired in the course of his agency damages the principal. More importantly, it also damages society because the execution of policy

---

risk approach, resulting in their profits and losses being greater than they would otherwise be, while others take a more cautious approach, based on the adage, "A bull makes money and a bear makes money, but a pig makes nothing."

31 Zekos, G.I., *Insider Dealing/Trading – An Economic Overview of an Established Offence*, ch. 3: Economic View of Insider Trading. Published on Internet at http://diavlos.com/zekos. That said, Zekos acknowledges Keynes' view that all speculative trading has a destabilising fact: Keynes, J.M. (1936) *The General Theory of Employment, Interest and Money*.

and the accumulation of socially useful information becomes more difficult and expensive or even impossible.[32]

Grounds for the Prohibition of Insider Dealing

These arguments address the particular thesis that insider dealing is beneficial. There are, however, a number of others advanced, in the UK[33] and elsewhere, as to why it should be prohibited. The most direct is that it is seen as unfair. It is considered unjust that those who are privy to information that is quite simply unavailable to other investors should be able to profit from it. In one of the key decisions on insider dealing, *SEC v Texas Gulf Sulfur Co.*,[34] the court stated:

> inequities based upon unequal access to knowledge should not be shrugged off as inevitable in our way of life or, in view of the congressional concern in the area, remain uncorrected.[35]

Arthur Levitt, Chairman of the US Securities and Exchange Commission, similarly stated, in a speech in 1998:

> Our system of law demands that the economy be organized to achieve more than just ruthless, relentless, efficiency. Honest commerce must also be guided by a spirit of fairness.[36]

The Law Society took a similar view, disapproving of insider dealing in 1974, when, unlike in the United States, it was not yet an offence anywhere in the UK:[37]

---

32 Herzel, L. and Harris, D., "Do we need insider trading laws?" [1989] Co. Law 34, 35.

33 The United Kingdom in fact consists of not one but three principal jurisdictions: England and Wales, Scotland and Northern Ireland. In the context of the "UK", the law as set out in this book is that of England and Wales, where most of the financial centres are located, unless stated otherwise. That said, the law in the areas considered in this book is frequently similar in Scotland and Northern Ireland to that in England and Wales. The Isle of Man, Jersey and Guernsey, although part of the United Kingdom for certain purposes, all have a considerably greater degree of autonomy than do Scotland or Northern Ireland, including their own financial services laws and regulations. Although all three jurisdictions are significant financial centres, no comment is therefore made in this book in respect of them.

34 (1968) 401 F 2d 833.

35 See pp. 851–52.

36 Arthur Levitt, "A Question of Integrity: Promoting Investor Confidence by Fighting Insider Trading", SEC Conference, 27 February 1998, cited in Small, R.G. (2001) *Path dependence and the law: A law and economics analysis of the development of the insider trading laws of the United States, United Kingdom and Japan*, PhD thesis, University of London.

37 The first UK prohibition of insider dealing, contained in the Companies Act 1980, only applied to England and Wales and to Scotland. The offence was only extended to Northern Ireland in 1993 with the Criminal Justice Act 1993.

it would be improper conduct for a solicitor to use for his own personal advantage *or for the advantage of any client of his*, or of his firm, *or for the advantage of any trust of which he or his partners are trustees*, or to communicate to any other person any confidential information obtained by him or his firm in the course of his professional practice.[38]

Some may argue that life is unfair: not everyone has the same opportunities and we might as well just accept the fact. But this has not proved the general view.

A second rationale for controlling market abuse is the maintenance of investor confidence. To quote Professor Barry Rider, "Integral to the efficient operation of any market is the maintenance of confidence in the integrity of its functions".[39] If a market is therefore seen to be a tool of the unscrupulous, it will be unattractive to investors. Investor confidence must then be restored by means of clear regulatory action.

Such regulation has not always served, even in recent years, to safeguard the securities markets' reputation in the eyes of the public. The view that those who deal on the securities markets were by definition a bunch of crooks has persisted in some quarters to the present day. Manne, in setting out his arguments in favour of insider dealing, or at least the permitting of it, openly states: "It cannot and should not be denied that the stock market provides the greatest competition to Las Vegas and the race tracks that we have. This is not intended as criticism."[40] He then goes on to compare, with approval, the activities of non-insider speculators to "gambling against someone with loaded dice or marked cards".[41] Manne may not have considered this to be a bad thing, but the US authorities made it clear that the damage to public confidence to which it gives rise is highly detrimental. Arthur Levitt, cited above, closely linked the issue of integrity in the market to public confidence and indeed investment by the public:

> As long as the rules of the game are fair to all, investors' confidence will remain strong. But if there is a perception of unfairness, there'll be no investor confidence – and precious little investment.

Fishman, in his paper cited above, puts the point even more starkly:

---

38 Practice Notes, Council Statements (1974) 71 *Law Society Gazette* 395, cited in Rider, B.A.K. (1978), "The Fiduciary and the Frying Pan" 42 *The Conveyancer* 114, 122. Emphasis added.

39 Rider, B.A.K., Abrams, C., Ashe, T.M. (1997) *Financial Services Regulation* CCH Editions, p. 101.

40 Manne, H., "In Defence of Insider Trading", (1966) 44 *Harvard Business Review*, No. 6, p. 114

41 P. 115

Commercial fraud and insider dealing destroy the investing public's faith that the market presents a level playing field. If the market is rigged, the public will shun investment in securities.[42]

A major reason for the introduction of the Financial Services Act 1986 was that, alongside its privatisation programme, the Thatcher administration wished to encourage the widespread purchase of shares by the general public. It was recognised, however, that this aim was unlikely to be achieved if the stock market was considered to be little better than a casino run by fraudsters. Conversely, it was felt that if the public believed the markets to be characterised by fairness and integrity, they would invest. Levitt, in the speech referred to above, explicitly stated that the requirements under the US securities laws of transparency and honesty were precisely the reason why investors had such confidence in the US markets and hence why those markets were so successful.

The issue of public disapproval applies as much to insider dealing as to any other offence on the securities markets. However much writers such as Manne may rail that to call insider dealing unfair is unreasonable, the fact remains that the public view it as such. Perhaps nowhere is this put better than in Professor Louis Loss' article, "The Fiduciary Concept as Applied to Trading by Corporate Insiders in the United States": "the female law student may have had a healthier reaction to insider trading than her professor when she stamped her foot and declaimed, 'I don't care; it's just not right.'"[43] Rider and Ffrench, who cite this quote, point out that the public view of what is right and wrong on the financial markets is ignored at one's peril. As already seen, courts and regulators would seem to agree with them: the quotes cited above all relate specifically to insider dealing.

Linked to this, it has also been argued that a lack of public confidence in securities markets results in impaired efficiency of the markets themselves. As Zekos has pointed out, "public confidence creates willingness to purchase shares. On the other hand, public distrust creates reluctance to invest in security markets, mostly by small investors."[44] Zekos goes on to argue that the greater the number of investors on a given market, the greater the liquidity of that market. Conversely, the smaller the number of investors, the lower the liquidity of the market, the higher its costs and the greater the difficulty for companies to raise capital through issuing shares. Hence, the less efficient the market. To this, it could of course be argued that individuals in fact contribute a miniscule proportion of the funds invested on securities markets: most, if not all, significant investors are major corporations. Nonetheless, it is very clearly public policy in a number of jurisdictions that individuals should be encouraged to invest on the securities markets. Furthermore, it is not only the very wealthy

---

42 (1993) "A comparison of enforcement of securities law violations in the UK and US" 14 Co. Law 163, 171.

43 (1970) 33 *Modern Law Review* 34, 37. Whether women, as Loss may also suggest by this, have a higher standard of morality than men is perhaps a matter for a separate debate!

44 *Insider Dealing/Trading – An Economic Overview of an Established Offence*, ch. 3. It may therefore be noted that it is not only regulators who take this view.

individuals whom the securities markets sought to attract but also ordinary members of the public. Aunt Agatha in her various guises[45] may be considered by many to be an insignificant figure from a number of perspectives, but her participation is considered highly desirable.[46] It is therefore perhaps not surprising that the Financial Services and Markets Act 2000 states the first regulatory objective of the newly created Financial Services Authority to be promotion of market confidence,[47] defined as "maintaining confidence in the financial system".[48] It is to be noted that two of the other three regulatory objectives are linked to this: protection of consumers and the reduction of financial crime.[49] The latter explicitly includes "misuse of information relating to a financial market".[50]

Although high-profile scandals, underlining the inadequacy of such self-regulation, emphasised the need for controls in order to protect investors and thus the good name of the market, there is, in fact, a third reason for regulation: to assist in the efficient running of the securities industry. While the City of London (and its counterparts overseas) were relatively small, a somewhat flexible system of principles may perhaps have been sufficient. As the industry grew, however, a coherent system of rules became necessary. This was seen not only in the UK, of course, but also elsewhere. In 1966, a report to the Canadian Government stated:

> While the underlying purpose of legislation governing the practices and operation of the securities market must be the protection of the investing public, it is equally true that the character of securities legislation will affect the development of financial institutions and their efficiency in performing certain economic functions. The principal economic functions of a capital market are to assure the optimum allocation of financial resources in the economy, to permit maximum mobility and transferability of those resources, and to provide facilities for a continuing valuation of financial assets.[51]

Eight years later, a similar report to the Australian Government stated that the prime purpose of securities regulation was "to maintain, facilitate and improve the performance of the capital market in the interests of economic development, efficiency and stability".[52]

As markets become larger and more sophisticated, it is important to have a clear regulatory framework, not only in order to maintain the confidence of those who one

---

45 For example, in France she is known as "la veuve de Carpentras" (the widow of Carpentras, a small town in the south).

46 The drive to bring ordinary members of the public into the securities markets has perhaps best been typified by the "Tell Sid" television advertisements in the UK surrounding the privatisation of British Gas in the mid-1980s.

47 s.2(2)(a).

48 s.3(1).

49 s.2(2)(c) and (d).

50 s.6(3)(b).

51 (1966) Report of the Attorney-General's Committee on Securities Legislation in Ontario ("Kimber Report") 1.09.

52 (1974) Report of the Senate Select Committee on Securities and Exchange.

wishes to invest in them, but also to provide clear parameters to the professionals who are required to deal in them.

There remain two specific grounds for controlling insider dealing in particular as opposed to regulating financial markets in general. The first is the theory that it breaches fiduciary obligations; the second, that of misappropriation. Although some, such as R.G. Small,[53] have conflated the two, they are, in fact, separate doctrines and should, as such, be considered separately.

The theory of breach of a fiduciary obligation is a classic common-law theory, originating in England and Wales.[54] Although the general duties of a fiduciary are much wider than this (and indeed could fill a book in their own right), an important aspect is the principle that an employee or agent should not allow a situation to arise where a conflict arises either between their own interest and that of their principal or between the interests of two (or more) different clients.[55] The law on this point is frequently stated to begin with the 18th century case of *Keech v Sandford*,[56] in which a trustee for an infant beneficiary was precluded from renewing the lease of a market stall for himself even though the renewal on behalf of the beneficiary had already been refused. It was then upheld and discussed at length in *Bray v Ford*,[57] in which it was ruled unlawful for a solicitor who was a trustee of a college to charge for his services to the college *qua* solicitor. The House of Lords was unanimous on this, emphasising that this applied even where there was no dishonesty or bad faith. Lord Herschell set out the rule:

> It is an inflexible rule of a Court of Equity that a person in a fiduciary position, such as the respondent's, is not, unless otherwise expressly provided, entitled to make a profit; he is not allowed to put himself in a position where his duty and interest conflict. It does not appear to me that this rule is, as has been said, founded on principles of morality. I regard it rather as based on the consideration that, human nature being what it is, there is danger, in such circumstances, of the person holding a fiduciary position being swayed by interest rather than duty, thus prejudicing those whom he was bound to protect. It has, therefore, been deemed expedient to lay down this positive rule.[58]

---

53 (2001) *Path dependence and the law: A law and economics analysis of the development of the insider trading laws of the United States, United Kingdom and Japan*, PhD thesis, University of London, ch. 2.

54 It is not, however, confined to England and Wales, or even to British-controlled jurisdictions in general: the US Senate in its investigation into the Pecora scandal of the early 1930s, not only described the insider dealing that had taken place as unfair, as mentioned above, but as "a betrayal of fiduciary duties".

55 With regard to conflicts between two or more clients / principals, a number of devices have been approved over the years, such as the "Chinese wall", in order to reconcile fiduciary duties with the requirements of modern commerce. Conflicts between the principal and agent, however, have continued to be viewed with rather less latitude.

56 (1726) Sel. Cas. Ch. 61.

57 [1896] AC 44.

58 *Ibid.*, p. 51.

Lord Watson concurred:

> Your Lordships can entertain no doubt that the respondent was neither entitled to charge profit costs in respect of these services [as a solicitor] nor to retain them when received by him. Such a breach of the law may be attended with perfect good faith.[59]

There were, however, hints that the rule could be overridden by explicit consent on the part of the beneficiary: Lord Halsbury raised the point, but declined to elaborate since he found that there had, in this particular case, been no such consent;[60] as seen above, Lord Herschell qualified the principle with the rider "unless otherwise expressly provided". This is important, since he went on to recognise that a departure from the rule could on occasion not only be made in good faith but actually be in the interest of the beneficiary.

Both *Keech v Sandford* and *Bray v Ford* concerned persons who from the start had been explicitly termed trustees. In the case of *ex p. James*,[61] however, it was made clear that the principle applies equally to others "in a confidential position", a ruling affirmed in *Regal (Hastings) Ltd. v Gulliver*:[62] "The rule, however, applies to agents as, for example, solicitors and directors, when acting in a fiduciary capacity".[63] Again, it was emphasised that the presence or absence of good faith was irrelevant:

> The rule of equity, which insists on those, who by use of a fiduciary position make a profit, being liable to account for that profit, in no way depends on fraud or absence of bona fides ... The profiteer, however honest and well-intentioned, cannot escape the risk of being called upon to account.[64]

Where a person is in a fiduciary position vis-à-vis their employer or client, therefore, they are not to make a private profit through that position. Any profit they make through their work should rightfully go to the person on whose behalf they are working. They are rewarded by a salary (or, in the case of a non-employed agent, a consultancy or agency fee), agreed in advance, and it is unconscionable for them to go on to make a further profit either directly through their work or through any opportunity which the job affords them.

Insider dealers, it is argued, do, however, precisely that. They come into possession of information to which they would not have been privy were it not for their position. They should therefore not abuse their position by making use of

---

59 *Ibid.*, p. 48. Particular emphasis was given to the possibility of a fiduciary acting unlawfully, but in no way dishonestly, in this regard due to the fact that this case involved not an action to recover the profits but a libel action caused by a governor of the college circulating a letter accusing the trustee-solicitor of unlawfully charging fees for his services to the college and, furthermore, doing so out of dishonest motives.
60 *Ibid.*, p. 49.
61 (1803) 8 Ves. 337.
62 [1942] 1 All ER 378.
63 *Ibid.*, p. 381 per Viscount Sankey.
64 *Ibid.*, p. 386 per Lord Russell of Killowen.

information entrusted to them by their employer or client in order to make a profit. In the *Regal* case, therefore, the House of Lords held that, since a director owed a fiduciary duty to his company, if he came into possession of confidential information through his position, it was unlawful for him to trade on it for his private profit. Further, if he did so, the company could recover the profits even though it itself had suffered no loss. The Court emphasised the link between the means by which the five respondent directors respondents had obtained the information, on the basis of which they bought the shares, and their liability to account for any profits.[65] Viscount Sankey referred to "the general rule that a solicitor or director, if acting in a fiduciary capacity, is liable to account for the profits made by him *from knowledge acquired when so acting*".[66]

An arguably extreme application of this principle is to be found in the subsequent case of *Boardman v Phipps*.[67] Boardman was not a company director but a solicitor who acted regularly (although not on the basis of any permanent retainer) for the trustees of a trust, which included among its property a minority shareholding in a company. The management of this company was distinctly hostile to the trust and Boardman therefore recommended that the trust take it over. This the trustees resolutely refused to do; indeed, doubt was later expressed as to whether they could, within their trusteeship, have done otherwise. Boardman then suggested that he and one of the beneficiaries, Tom Phipps, themselves take over the company: following the trustees' approval, he wrote to all the beneficiaries, asking for their consent. All agreed, save the settlor's elderly widow, who was by now suffering from senile dementia and made no reply. After long and protracted negotiations and not inconsiderable effort, expenditure and indeed risk by Boardman and Tom Phipps, the takeover of one part of a now divided company went ahead and not only the two of them but also the trust itself made a considerable profit. At this point, another of the beneficiaries brought an action against the two to account for their profits.

The House of Lords was divided. All agreed that Boardman[68] had acted in the utmost good faith: his trouble, expense and risk had resulted in considerable benefit to the trust. Further, he had throughout been completely open with both the trustees and the beneficiaries about what he was doing. In a dissenting judgment, Viscount

---

65 The Court suggested that the directors could have retained the profits had they first obtained the approval of the company. This has been questioned, however, by Professor David Hayton: "as *Cook v Deeks* [1916] 1 AC 554 makes clear, no resolution at a general meeting can ratify an act of expropriation of company property by the majority to the detriment of the company" (2003) *Underhill and Hayton: Law of Trusts and Trustees*, 16th Edition., Butterworths, pp. 391–92). Hayton goes on to suggest that, in the light of *A-G for Hong Kong v Reid*, it is the use of property, not just a person's position, that gives rise to a constructive trust. For a general discussion of both *Regal (Hastings) v Gulliver* and the later case of *Boardman v Phipps*, see *Underhill and Hayton*, 16th Edition, pp. 391–95.

66 *Regal (Hastings) Ltd. v Gulliver*, *supra*, p. 382 (emphasis added).

67 [1966] 3 All ER 721.

68 It was explicitly stated that no distinction was made between the positions of Boardman and Tom Phipps.

Dilhorne stated that "it must have been obvious to the recipients of this letter [informing the beneficiaries of the plan] that approval of the proposals must involve, if their efforts were successful, the appellants making a profit for themselves".[69] The majority view was, however, that, however honestly Boardman had acted, he had achieved the takeover, and hence made his profit, through the use of information which he obtained in his position as solicitor to the trust. This he would only have been permitted to do had he obtained the consent of all the beneficiaries – and the elderly widow had not given hers. It was irrelevant that the trustees were not in a position to buy the controlling shareholding themselves: this, after all, was analogous to the position in *Keech v Sandford* and *Regal v Gulliver*.[70] Although it was not explicitly stated, it would appear that it was felt also to be irrelevant that the one beneficiary who had not given her consent was, for reasons of ill-health, incapable of giving any kind of informed consent or refusal on the matter. As Lord Hodson said,

> Nothing short of fully informed consent, which the learned judge found not to have been obtained, could enable the appellants in the position which they occupied, having taken the opportunity provided by that position, to make a profit for themselves.[71]

Boardman and Tom Phipps were therefore obliged to disgorge their profits to the trust. Lord Cohen acknowledged that this was harsh, but ruled that it was the law:

> the respondent is a fortunate man in that the rigor of equity enables him to participate in the profits which have accrued as a result of the action taken by the appellants ... in purchasing the shares at their own risk.[72]

The law of the fiduciary was therefore now clearly being applied to insiders dealing. The use of the phrase "insiders dealing" is a deliberate one. The concept of insiders dealing specifically before confidential information is announced, "striking while the iron is hot" in order to make a greater profit ahead of the rest of the market, is absent from the judgments in *Regal*. So, too, it is from those in *Boardman v Phipps*. The defendants were therefore not insider dealers in the sense now accepted. The point was that they were using their positions in order to make a profit, pure and simple. This was held, on the basis of considerable case-law, to be unconscionable and indeed unlawful.

Professor Barry Rider, in "The Fiduciary and the Frying Pan",[73] adds some additional remarks on the *Boardman v Phipps* case. He comments that "it would seem that the solicitor and the beneficiary[74] were under an obligation to use the

---

[69] P. 729

[70] The dissenting judges disputed the latter: in the *Regal* case, it was originally planned the company would buy the shares ultimately purchased by the directors.

[71] P. 746

[72] P. 744

[73] (1978) 42 *The Conveyancer* 114.

[74] That is, Boardman and Tom Phipps.

information that they acquired, if they used it at all, for the benefit of the trust, apparently in disregard of any other interest."[75] Rider goes on, however, to consider what Boardman, in particular, should have done. As discussed earlier in this chapter, there is a strong body of opinion, and was even in the 1960s, that insider dealing is morally wrong. At that time, however, it was not illegal. That being the case, Rider suggests that to have taken the opposite extreme and refrained from dealing at all, could equally have exposed Boardman to liability for breach of trust:

> It would seem unlikely that trustees possessed of inside information could refrain from utilising such for the trust's financial benefit merely on the ground that insider trading is generally regarded as immoral and that it is in the public interest, and thus directly in the beneficiaries' long-term interest, that such abuse does not occur.[76]

In the present case, Boardman and Tom Phipps might well have avoided liability, given that the trustees had made clear that they were not prepared to approve the trust buying the additional shares. The trustees themselves might, however, have been so liable for this stance. Rider therefore put forward a further reason for insider dealing to be outlawed: not merely because it was immoral, but in order to provide a secure legal ground for trustees and other fiduciaries to refrain from engaging in it on their principals' behalf.

Elsewhere, however, the objection of breach of trust has been applied directly to insider dealing. Although, as noted above, Herzel and Harris devote much of their paper to the economic harm caused by insider dealing, they also express strong views as to its unconscionability:

> There appears to be a growing consensus that the real evil of insider trading is not that it cheats less informed investors, but that it exploits the theft of information and breaches the trust between principal and agent upon which society depends.

Or even more starkly:

> We are really dealing with a form of industrial espionage. Once insider trading is seen in this light, it is difficult to see why anyone would object to making it illegal.

Manne could have argued that the opportunity to make a personal profit through the information that he could gain as a trustee might have been an added incentive to Boardman to accept the post in the first place. But the ruling was: he was not entitled to act as he did and therefore held his own profits, like those of his clients, on his clients' account.

---

75 (1978) 42 *The Conveyancer* 114, 123.
76 *Ibid.*, p. 124.

This argument does, of course, apply only to primary insiders.[77] Secondary insiders owe no fiduciary duty whatsoever to the source of the information.[78] Nonetheless, the argument is likely to be extended to them on the basis that the majority of insiders, in order to cover their tracks, get others to execute the actual deals on their behalf. It could be argued, of course, that were insider dealing not prohibited, they would not have to go to such convoluted lengths, but few, if any, would suggest a regime whereby primary insiders were not permitted to deal themselves but it was open to them to get someone else to deal on their behalf.[79]

Finally, there is the misappropriation theory. This originated in the United States. It holds that information is a type of property, belonging to the corporation that produced it. If a person discloses that information to a third party without authorisation, they therefore take this property from the corporation, appropriating it. In effect, they commit a form of theft. Similarly, where a person uses the information without authorisation, they appropriate it. This is easy to see in the case of other property of the company: where a person takes a company vehicle without authorisation and uses it for their own purposes, they are guilty of stealing it (or at least a theft-related offence). So it is, according to the misappropriation theory, with privileged information.

The theory was first applied in the case of *U.S. v Vincent F. Chiarella*.[80] It may be noted that this case was heard in 1980, 46 years after insider dealing was first prohibited in the United States under section 10b of the Securities Exchange Act 1934 and its accompanying SEC Rule 10b-5 and 12 years after the rather more frequently cited *SEC v Texas Gulf Sulfur Co*.[81] The facts were that a printer successfully deciphered the code of the company for which he worked, discovered details of an imminent takeover and proceeded to buy shares in the relevant company. That he was convicted of insider dealing is not remarkable, not least given the lengths to which he had gone to obtain the inside information; what was innovative was the fact that the court considered him to have misappropriated it. Although this was the first case to take this approach, it was far from the last. The following year, the Second Circuit Court adopted the same principle in *U.S. v Newman*[82] to convict a stockbroker who traded on inside tips:

---

77 For the difference between primary and secondary insiders, see Chapter 2.

78 Subject perhaps to the situation where a primary insider discloses inside information to their spouse (or other close connection) in the context of giving them news from work and trusts them not to disclose it on, let alone deal on the basis of it. But one must suspect that, in most cases of insiders' spouses who deal, both know exactly what they are doing!

79 That said, in a number of jurisdictions, the prohibition on unauthorised disclosure of inside information is not extended to secondary insiders. See Chapter 4.

80 (1980) 445 U.S. 222.

81 (1968) 401 F 2d 833.

82 (1981) 664 F 2d 12.

Had appellant[83] used similar deceptive practices to mulct Morgan Stanley and Kuhn Loeb of cash or securities, it could hardly be argued that those companies had not been defrauded ... By sullying the reputation of Courtois' and Antoniu's employers as safe repositories of client confidences, appellee and his cohorts defrauded those employers as surely as if they took their money.[84]

The principle was finally upheld by the US Supreme Court 16 years later in *U.S. v O'Hagan*,[85] in which the Court ruled:

A company's confidential information ... qualifies as property to which the company has the right of exclusive use. The undisclosed misappropriation of such information in violation of a fiduciary duty ... constitutes fraud akin to embezzlement – the fraudulent appropriation to one's own use of the money or goods entrusted to one's care by another.[86]

It went on to state that the concept that information constitutes property is a core principle on which the prohibition of insider dealing is based.[87] This latter point is perhaps a curious one, given how long insider dealing had been prohibited, and indeed punished, in the United States without reference to information being property. It does mean, however, that it is on the misappropriation theory that the modern US law of insider dealing is now based.

The concept of information as property is a complex one and an entire book could easily be devoted to it. Many jurisdictions accept that it is capable of being property in some senses: the area of law relating to copyright and patents is commonly termed "intellectual property". A number, though, not least England and Wales, stop short of considering information the kind of property that can be the subject of theft.[88] Other jurisdictions have, however, taken a different view. The United States is certainly one, but France is another: a secondary insider who deals on the basis of the inside information is viewed as guilty not of insider dealing but of *recel*, i.e. handling property resulting from a crime.[89] France has, however, not gone as far as to charge the primary insider with theft, possibly because of the separate offence of

---

83 In the context, it seems likely that "appellee" is actually meant, although the text of the judgment is as quoted.

84 *Ibid*, per Van Graafeiland, Circuit Judge, p. 17.

85 (1997) 117 S. Ct. 2199.

86 P. 2208.

87 P. 2210.

88 *Oxford v Moss* (1979) 68 Crim. App. Rep. 183; [1979] Crim. LR 119. In laying down this principle, however, Smith J explicitly stated that he was confining his ruling to the context of the law of theft: he said that the previous cases relating to fiduciary obligations were not of assistance to him. The issue has been taken further in relation to tracing claims, for example in the landmark case of *A-G for Hong Kong v Reid* [1994] 1 AC 324. This, however, is related in turn to the issues surrounding money laundering and the proceeds of crime; further discussion of the point is therefore to be found in Chapter 5.

89 See pp. 115-16.

disclosure of inside information, with its accompanying criminal and civil penalties, will apply to him.[90]

These five grounds have led to the position whereby insider dealing is prohibited as a matter of public policy. This is now the case in most, if not all, of the world's major securities dealing centres.[91] The arguments, back and forth, as to whether it should be prohibited and, if so, why have therefore been overtaken by events. Although, as seen above, some of the arguments still continue – particularly the claim that insider dealing has no victims – it is prohibited. Further, this prohibition is, at least in the foreseeable future, highly unlikely to be lifted. What form that prohibition should take and, in particular, how it should be enforced, is a separate, ongoing debate, examined in Chapter 7. This public policy has led to a sixth ground: that of international pressure. Unlike the other grounds cited, this applies equally to the prohibition of money laundering and is therefore dealt with at the end of this chapter.

Money Laundering

Is Money Laundering a Bad Thing?

In contrast to the position with insider dealing, few serious academic arguments have been advanced that money laundering is beneficial or even that it should be permitted. There do exist theories of legitimisation, suggesting that money laundering enables criminals to come in from the shadows and take their place in the legitimate economy. An example of this was the Seychelles' proposed Economic Development Assistance Act 1995, which would have provided that, where a person invested at least US$10 million in the country, they would be immune from criminal prosecution by any party, the only exception being the Seychelles authorities and then only in the context of a drug trafficking investigation. Further, the funds themselves would be *de jure* "clean" and therefore not liable to confiscation. As seen below, however, the prevailing view, certainly among governments (and hence legislators) is that priority is to be given to targeting criminals financially, an approach that leaves little room for legitimisation of their funds.[92]

Professor Barry Rider and others have also pointed out that it may often be beneficial, to the state[93] as well as to individuals, not only to keep the origin of

---

90 In France, theft carries a higher maximum prison sentence than insider dealing, 3 years rather than 2, but a lower maximum fine: €45,000 rather than €1.5 million. (Penal Code, Art. 311-3; Monetary and Financial Code, Art. L465-1.)

91 For example, the United States, Canada, all EU Member States, Japan, Hong Kong, Singapore, Australia, South Africa.

92 The proposed Seychelles Act was later withdrawn in response to international pressure: see p. 35.

93 For example, in the funding of intelligence operations.

certain funds secret but actually to disguise their provenance.[94] The secret trust, a familiar and entirely legitimate instrument of English law, is but one example of this. Although they are often linked, the issue of financial confidentiality and that of money laundering are, however, distinct. Money laundering is essentially concerned with the enabling of criminals and, on occasion, their associates to retain or recover the proceeds of their offences. It is not concerned with the secret funding of intelligence operatives or the hiding of wealth from the lawyers and private investigators of an ex-spouse or even a judgment creditor.[95] It only comes into play in relation to forms of conduct that the state has deemed, on grounds of public policy, to be by definition so seriously wrong as to be worthy of criminal penalties.[96]

Dr Kris Hinterseer has gone further, arguing that actual money laundering is, on occasion, in a country's interests.[97] He focuses on three specific areas: capital flight, evasion of financial embargoes and the investment of the proceeds of corruption in a secure financial system. It is suggested, however, that only the last of these actually involves money laundering. Although capital flight, i.e. the illegal export of funds in breach of exchange control laws, is a major issue and serious criminal offence in many developing countries, it is not money laundering unless the funds have an illegal source. Further, in the European Union, the focus of this book, any provision restricting the movement of capital, whether between Member States or between a Member State and a third country, is explicitly prohibited.[98] Similarly, although the United States, under the Bank Secrecy Act and USA PATRIOT Act, requires imports and exports of cash with a value of more than $10,000 to be declared to the Financial Crimes Enforcement Network (FinCEN), part of the US Treasury, there is no restriction on the movement of the funds themselves.[99] Indeed, it is a common complaint by many developing countries that developed jurisdictions pay too little

---

94 "Of course, there are many reasons, *some lawful*, why it might be desirable to 'hide' wealth or sever it from its source." Rider, B.A.K., Alexander, S.K., Linklater, L. (2002) *Market Abuse and Insider Dealing*, Butterworths, p. 127 (emphasis added).

95 Frustration of a court order may attract the criminal-style penalties imposed for contempt, but, provided that the origin of the funds is legitimate, hiding them *per se* is not money laundering.

96 For the full definition of money laundering, see Chapter 5.

97 Hinterseer, K. (2002), *Criminal Finance: the political economy of money laundering in a comparative legal context*, Kluwer Law International.

98 EC Treaty, Art. 56 (inserted by the Treaty on European Union). Measures limiting this are permitted, under Art. 60, on grounds of foreign policy or security; for example, French customs regulations require any import or export of cash involving more than €7,600 to be declared (although it may then be imported/exported) while the Bank of England has, in compliance with United Nations sanctions, passed orders prohibiting the transfer of funds to certain jurisdictions. A general ban, or even limitation, on the import/export of capital, is, however, prohibited.

99 Since any transaction involving US dollars is deemed as a matter of law to be cleared through the Federal Reserve in New York, any limitation on the amounts of funds which may be imported/exported to/from the United States would render much of the (legitimate) global commerce unworkable.

heed to the economic impact of large amounts of capital being transferred out of the developing world. Engaging in trade or any kind of financial transaction involving a jurisdiction subject to a financial embargo is a serious criminal offence, but it is not itself money laundering. It was with illegally supplying materials to Iraq, not with money laundering, that the defendants in the Matrix Churchill trial, to which Hinterseer refers, were charged.

As regards the secreting/investment of the proceeds of corruption, or even simple looting, by Heads of State and other senior politicians, this certainly constitutes money laundering, but it is questionable whether it is beneficial to the state that it take place. While General Charles de Gaulle's famous dictum, "L'état, c'est moi",[100] would undoubtedly be echoed by leaders in the mould of Duvalier, Marcos and Abacha, it is debatable whether their secreting of funds is, as a matter of law, carried out in the interests of the state. Indeed, the litigation brought by the successor governments to Marcos and Abacha to recover the exported funds would suggest that it is not.

Money laundering is concerned with the processing of property (often, but not exclusively, money) which derives from a criminal offence. It therefore generally relates to offences that are economically motivated, i.e. which produce a profit and for which that profit is the reason for the offence. Not all offences, of course, fit this description. Almost all offences may, in certain circumstances, involve profit,[101] but not all are economically motivated by definition. Murders and assaults may be carried out by criminal organisations or under a contract with them, but in many cases are motivated simply by anger. Similarly, while there have been well-publicised cases of individuals committing perjury in order unjustly to win damages in litigation, many others simply involve a defendant wishing to persuade the court of his innocence. With other offences, however, not only do they produce a financial reward, but that reward is the sole point of committing them. Although, for many years, the war on drugs highlighted drug-trafficking as being a particular example,[102] it is now recognised that it is by no means the only one.[103] Others are financial

---

100 "The state is me."

101 With the arguable exception of sexual offences. Even road traffic offences can be economically motivated: a salesman who breaks the speed limit can, unless he is stopped by the police, fit in more appointments. Indeed, there is anecdotal evidence that many salesmen are actually expected by their employers to do this as it is the only way in which they can achieve all the meetings required of them in a given day.

102 It is to be noted that, both at national and international level, the laundering of the proceeds of drug trafficking was criminalised before that of the proceeds of other types of offences. The history of money laundering legislation in the UK illustrates this: the proceeds of drug trafficking were targeted in 1986, those of other indictable (i.e. relatively serious) offences in 1993 and those of all offences without exception only in 2002. Similarly, both the Financial Action Task Force Forty Recommendations and the EU Money Laundering Directive in their original forms only covered the proceeds of drug trafficking: other offences were only covered by the EU in December 2001 and by the FATF not until June 2003.

103 Indeed, no drug trafficking offence may in fact be classified as being invariably motivated by profit. It is far from unknown for users of controlled drugs to smuggle a small

crimes, of which insider dealing is a good example. It is motivated by profit, pure and simple. It is for this reason that it is an essential element of the offence, at least in the Member States of the European Union, that the information on the basis of which the insider dealt (or which he passed on) be capable of altering the price of the security concerned.

This being the case, if, as is seen below, the purpose of prohibiting money laundering is to restrict, or ideally prevent completely, an offender from making a profit from his offence, the control of money laundering and that of insider dealing will inevitably be intrinsically linked.

Why Prohibit Money Laundering?

With this starting point, one can now examine the reasons for prohibiting money laundering. At its most basic, the rationale is to support the adage that "crime doesn't pay". Firstly, there is the moral dimension: crime should not pay. It is simply not acceptable to society that a person who does wrong should benefit as a result. As with Professor Loss' student and her view of insider dealing, "it's just not fair". Again as with insider dealing, one could respond, as many a parent has to their children, "Life's not fair." As has already been seen, however, the public are not easily satisfied by this and demand action to stop the unfairness. Some have pointed out that the US President who famously remarked that "nice guys come last" ultimately paid a heavy price for this outlook, but there has been displeasure at convicted criminals later becoming successful even in totally legitimate ways. For example, the then British Home Secretary, David Blunkett, was swift to respond to public outrage at Iorworth Hoare, a convicted rapist, winning £7 million in the National Lottery. Indeed, Blunkett announced plans to "recover the money if a prisoner wins the lottery"[104] even though this money could not in any way be considered to be the proceeds of an offence.[105] The general significance of this view may be seen by the UK government's reference to role models, discussed below.

Aside from the moral dimension, there is the theory that ensuring that crime does not pay will act as a substantial deterrent. If the crime is economically motivated, the theory goes, then, if it is impossible to enjoy the profits, there will be no point

---

quantity for their own personal supply, while, under the current UK legislation, supply of a controlled drug includes not only selling it but any instance of passing it to another. Technically, a person who, at a party, passes a "spliff" to a friend is guilty of supply of a Class C controlled drug. This is admittedly stretching the point and in practice, such a person would be extremely unlikely to be charged with anything other than simple possession. But there have been a number of cases where persons who have given tablets of Ecstasy, a class A drug, to friends have been prosecuted for supply even though it is accepted that they did not receive any money for them.

104 *The Sun*, 12 August 2004.
105 Another example was the complaint by a number of tabloid newspapers in the UK in the 1980s at Leslie Grantham, convicted of murder in Germany some 20 years earlier, being given a starring role in a BBC soap.

in committing it in the first place (and hence the crime will not be committed). It is therefore not at all surprising that in tandem with measures to punish those who handle the proceeds of crime have come measures to deprive the offender of his profits.[106]

This argument was upheld explicitly by the Performance and Innovation Unit of the UK Cabinet Office. In its report, "Recovering the Proceeds of Crime", published in June 2000, the Unit stated that depriving the offender of the proceeds of his offence would deprive him of the motivation to commit it in the first place. The report also, however, focused on certain other, though linked, reasons to control money laundering.

One was already familiar: to deprive criminal organisations (and indeed all career criminals) of their "financial lifeblood". It is well recognised that established criminals do not spend all their profits on a luxurious lifestyle: much of the profit is re-invested into the business. If drug traffickers are to continue to sell drugs, they must buy them to replace the supply which they have just sold. They are extremely unlikely to risk importing them into the market country personally, so they must pay couriers to do so. Similarly, those operating a protection racket will rarely go round with the firearms or baseball bats themselves: they will hire others to do so – and must pay them.

Financial criminals are no different. For an insider dealer to commit the offence, he has to buy the securities. Having made his profit, if he wishes to do so again, he will need to invest some of it in buying more securities next time an opportunity arises. Further, as with all trading, legitimate or otherwise, the greater the profit sought, the greater the amount that needs to be traded.

Other professionals will also be hired, such as lawyers[107] and accountants and, in the case of insider dealers, brokers, dealers and the like.[108] The latter act on commission, but the former charge high fees. It may be the case that a range of shelf

---

106 For details of these, see Chapters 4 and 7.

107 That lawyers are viewed as accessories to criminals is increasingly clear. A European Commission study that led to the Second Money Laundering Directive referred to "the vulnerable professions", of which lawyers were one. The UK Proceeds of Crime Act 2002, while it exempts lawyers from the obligation to disclose knowledge or suspicion that their clients are engaged in money laundering where that knowledge or suspicion is gained in the context of providing legal advice, excludes from this exemption cases where the lawyer is himself instrumental to the committing of an offence. In the United States, the *New York Times*, on 11 August 2003, reported far more sweeping curbs on the traditional attorney-client secrecy, introduced at the behest of not only prosecutors but the Internal Revenue Service. For examples of cases where lawyers have been found to have engaged in money laundering, see Bell, R.E. (2002-3), "The Prosecution of Lawyers for Money Laundering Offences" 6 *Journal of Money Laundering Control* 17 and Morton, J. (2003) *Gangland: The Lawyers*, Virgin Books.

108 Unless the insider is himself a broker or professional dealer, as with Newman: see pp. 19-20.

companies can be set up relatively cheaply, but the services of a lawyer, particularly in certain jurisdictions, will cost rather more.

The theory is that if criminals can be prevented from profiting from their offences, they will not be able to re-invest money in these various ways and hence will be hampered from committing further offences. This links into the strategy, of increasing importance, of disrupting crime rather than formally bringing the offenders to book. It has long been recognised that, although some financial criminals (and indeed organised criminals of somewhat wider-ranging activities) are successfully prosecuted, all too many escape justice. The reasons cited for this have been manifold, ranging from the difficulty for a prosecutor to follow the highly complex trail of activities and obtain the necessary evidence to the requisite standard, through the inability of juries to understand the evidence adequately once it is obtained, to the ability of organised criminals to suborn witnesses and to base themselves in corrupt jurisdictions which decline to co-operate in the delivery of either evidence or the individuals themselves. All of these have some basis, some inevitably more than others in any given case. This has led to a recognition that, although the ideal would be to capture the criminals and subject them to a lengthy prison sentence, in practice this will not always be possible. That led in turn to the creation of a strategy that, essentially, is based on the view that an acceptable alternative in such cases is to disrupt the criminal activities in other ways. There may never be a prosecution and consequent sentence, but one can prevent the commission of further crimes, or at least make it substantially more difficult and expensive. The Report explicitly refers to the policy of disruption as a ground for preventing money laundering.

This certainly holds true for many types of offences. The question, though, is whether it holds as true for insider dealers. It is debatable whether there are career insider dealers in the same way as there are career drug dealers or even career fraudsters. Insider dealing depends on access to the relevant information. This not only means being in a position where one will be among the informed group but also the information coming into being in the first place. Events that significantly affect the price of securities,[109] particularly in connection with a given issuer, will only happen once in a while. Thus, one could argue, insider dealers will not re-invest their profits in the commission of further offences in the same way that other criminals do.

There is, however, no evidence that insider dealers only engage in one-off offences. Some may, but one cannot be confident that all do so. Indeed, there have been cases where career, repeated insider dealing by rings set up for the purpose is precisely what has been established. Some members, located in different issuers and institutions, exchange the information, while others conduct the actual deals and then share out the proceeds. *Newman*, possibly the best-known case, was in the

---

109 Although not all jurisdictions require the potential effect on the securities to be significant, some do – for details, see Chapter 3. In any case, where the price-change is not significant, it is arguable that the relatively small profit will mean a correspondingly low motive to deal.

United States, but similar rings have operated in the UK. A variant on this has been groups that have obtained inside information not through willing accomplices, as in Newman, but through other means, such as extortion of otherwise unwilling insiders or the placing of electronic devices in appropriate offices. Herzel and Harris state that insider dealing is a form of industrial espionage; on occasion, this can literally be true.

The third ground raised by the Report for combating money laundering refers not directly to criminals but to those around them. It is important, it says, that unhealthy role models are not created. This is understandable. It is not only morally wrong for crime to pay, but, if it does, it can encourage others to choose a career of crime. This is perhaps most true of relatively deprived areas where educational standards are low and the consequent opportunities to enter into a career that is both legitimate and well-paid are somewhat limited. If a teenager sees his likely career as being a cashier in a supermarket on a salary of £175 per week gross or, worse, unemployed and receiving a fraction even of that, but also sees his brother's friend wearing designer clothes and driving around in a new BMW, which is he likely to view as the attractive option? It is salutary to consider the following account given by Lenny McLean of Hoxton in the East End of London:

> For working-class people to get a living in those days, you had to be involved in some sort of villainy or be 'at it', so everybody was breaking the law just to put bread on the table. The police were the enemy because there was no money about. Outside the ghettos it was only people with anything worth having who relied on the police, because they were worried about their property or their own skin. Then the police became their friends. People like us knew the police were no good, so they didn't have any time for them. If the streets needed looking after, they did their own policing.[110]

This account is not of the 19th century, but of the 1950s and 1960s, well after the foundation of the welfare state and when the economy was relatively buoyant. Nonetheless, McLean refers to breaking the law "just to put bread on the table". Among the role models he speaks of is Ronnie Knight, a man of whom as a child he knew two things: he was involved in fraud and he was married to a film star.

Equally, if the victims of crime, or even just the law-abiding public, see criminals enjoying a very comfortable life, far more comfortable than their own, this will lead to considerable public disquiet. Just as public opinion regarding the financial markets should not be discounted, nor should it be in relation to offenders enjoying the fruits of their misdeeds.

These are the grounds that governments give for controlling money laundering. There is, however, a further ground, given by commentators such as Professor Rider. This is that, as already seen, the criminals themselves are very difficult to bring to book. Governments and the law-enforcement agencies that serve them, however, are extremely reluctant simply to give up. They therefore pursue the professionals that handle the funds, creating what Rider refers to as "facilitator liability": since

---

110 McLean, L. (1998), *The Guv'nor*, Blake Publishing Ltd. p. 2.

they cannot get the criminals themselves, they are determined to get someone and the professional advisors are the obvious targets. A parallel may be drawn with the prosecution of a number of former soldiers of the Frontier Guard of the GDR for the murder of escapees shot as they attempted to flee across the Berlin Wall; not long before these prosecutions, the former East German leader, Erich Honnecker, had succeeded in negotiating an exile in Chile on grounds of ill-health. As was said at the time, "We can't get Honnecker or any of the other leaders; the soldiers are better than nothing at all."

This is perhaps a telling analogy. The soldiers had not taken part in any of the policy decisions, but they had quite literally pulled the triggers. Nor had they acted under any kind of compulsion: to be stationed on the frontier, particularly on the Berlin Wall, was bestowed as an honour on the most faithful, not imposed on unwilling conscripts. Similarly, the professional intermediaries, the bankers, investment professionals, lawyers, accountants and the like, are not the "big fish" themselves, but they are, at least in the eyes of law-enforcement, not wholly without blame either. They, too, have the choice of not being involved, of refusing to take business that they suspect of being linked to crime.[111] If, therefore, the major players are beyond the reach of the law, it is arguable that they are not a bad substitute.

International Pressure

As public policy in the major financial centres decrees that insider dealing and money laundering are, by definition, bad things and therefore to be prohibited, a further ground arises for controlling them, and indeed to regulate financial markets in general. This is rather different to the previous three: the political reality of international pressure. It applies as much to the control of money laundering as it does to insider dealing, hence it being examined here.

Pressure from One Powerful Jurisdiction

International pressure may take one of two forms. The first is the directly expressed disapproval of powerful jurisdictions. The most common jurisdiction involved has been the United States:[112] it is no coincidence that the first legislation to outlaw insider

---

111 Although this option has now been closed in the UK by the Proceeds of Crime Act 2002, it remains open in a number of jurisdictions. Indeed, neither the EU Money Laundering Directive nor the FATF Forty Recommendations, even in their revised forms, requires it to be closed.

112 It is, however, not the only one: France exercises considerable influence over the legislation passed by its former colonies, particularly in Africa, while the UK has, especially in recent years, successfully influenced the offshore jurisdictions of Jersey, Guernsey and the Isle of Man.

dealing was introduced there[113] and its money laundering legislation is similarly looked to as a model. The pressure that this exerts is, of course, particularly great in developing countries, although even countries as large as Russia are not unaffected. The following quote from the deliberations, specifically relating to Russia and money laundering, of the US House of Representatives Committee on Banking and Financial Services is nothing if not direct:

House Representative Spencer Bachus:

... others are going to launder money. It leads to terrorism, racketeering, tax evasion, drug smuggling, all of this. There is one common denominator in all of this. That is that you have these offshore financial centers that are clothed in secrecy and are poorly regulated and have almost no reporting ... Isn't it time to shut down some of these operations or demand that they be regulated and that they report?

Secretary Summers:[114]

I think this is clearly an issue that has to be addressed ... frankly for two inter-related reasons. One is the abuse that is made possible by these offshore centers. The second is the pressure these offshore centers put on the ability to regulate in our country and other major countries where satisfactory regulation becomes more difficult if there is the threat that it will simply produce recourse to offshore centers.[115]

Two points are immediately of note. Firstly, it is clear from Summers' comments that the US Treasury considered that inadequate financial services regulation in other jurisdictions can have a direct impact on the effectiveness of financial services regulation in the United States. But Bachus' remarks are arguably even more striking: he takes for granted that the United States is quite capable of simply "shutting down" financial centres that it does not like.

This should not seem so surprising. It is often made a condition of aid to a particular country that that country brings in legislation, at the very least, to regulate sectors of its economy along the lines that the jurisdiction providing aid desires. Further, however, the US Treasury has the power to issue an "Advisory", warning US financial institutions not to deal with counterparts in the jurisdiction concerned. Hinterseer points out that it has even done so in the case of Israel, notwithstanding the close political links between the two countries, following Israel's listing by the Financial Action Task Force as a Non-Cooperative Country or Territory.[116]

---

113 Sections 10(b) and 16, Securities Exchange Act of 1934 and Securities and Exchange Commission Rule 10b-5.

114 Lawrence Summers, then Treasury Secretary.

115 US House of Representatives, Committee on Banking and Financial Services, "Russia and Money Laundering", 21 September 1999, cited in Hinterseer, K. (2002), *Criminal Finance: The Political Economy of Money Laundering in a Comparative Legal Context*, Kluwer Law International, pp. 223–24.

116 8 July, 2000.

Even in the case of other jurisdictions, however, comments of the type made in *SEC v Wang and Lee*[117] do little to inspire confidence in potential overseas investors. The provocative title of Forman's article, referred to above,[118] illustrates the increasing pressure that was brought to bear by the United States on Europe in the 1980s to clean up its financial services sector. It was a time when financial markets were becoming increasingly globalised and thus the displeasure in this area of the world's most powerful economic centre could no longer be ignored.[119] It is perhaps no coincidence, therefore, that the European Community's respective legislation on insider dealing and money laundering was passed less than 18 months apart.

In the area of money laundering, the pressure from the United States has been even greater. Section 311 of the USA PATRIOT Act,[120] passed in the wake of 9/11, imposes a legal requirement on US financial institutions only to accept information on customers supplied by foreign institutions if the anti-money-laundering provisions of those jurisdictions match those of the United States, in their detail as well as in their intent. President Bush announced the legislation with the words, "If you do business with terrorists, you will not do business with the United States," but the Act goes far beyond terrorist financing to cover any jurisdiction, or even account which "is of primary money laundering concern". Where the jurisdiction in question does not have such measures, the Secretary of the Treasury may either require the US institution to conduct the full measures itself or simply prohibit it from dealing with that jurisdiction. Since no US institution is likely to be able to conduct such detailed checks on a customer in another jurisdiction, this arguably amounts to the same thing.[121]

It must be stated, however, that the US influence is not always as overt as this. Professor Stephen Vogel points out that it also exerted in other, more subtle ways. Without any diplomatic pressure being applied, US measures can act as a model for governments seeking of their own volition to emulate them. As an example, Vogel refers to Margaret Thatcher instructing the UK Department of Trade and Industry to study the case files on deregulation in the United States. Similarly, he argues,

---

117 944 F.2d 80 (2nd Circuit, 1991). See p. 1.

118 P. 1.

119 The US influence on financial services legislation even in developed, "first world" jurisdictions is examined in detail by Vogel, S.K. (1996) *Freer Markets, More Rules: Regulatory Reform in Advanced Industrial Countries*, pp. 36–37.

120 Uniting and Strengthening America by Providing Appropriate Tools Required to Intercept and Obstruct Terrorism Act, HR 3162, October 24, 2001. Sections 311ff. form part of Title III of the Act, the International Money Laundering Abatement and Anti-Terrorist Act of 2001 and amend 31 USC 53 by inserting new sections 5318A ff.

121 Save, perhaps, where the US institution concerned is one of the major international players and therefore has a branch in the jurisdiction concerned through which it can undertake the checks locally at first hand.

economic factors can compel countries to implement corresponding measures in order to enable their institutions to compete.[122]

Pressure from International Organisations

The second form of pressure applies to those jurisdictions that are part of an international organisation, which may itself pass measures which its members are expected, or even required, to implement. In regard to insider dealing, and indeed the regulation of financial markets generally, the most striking example is the European Union. As Professor Vogel has pointed out, "beginning in the 1980s, the European Community (EC) emerged as a major force in defining regulatory policies in Europe. French and German initiatives were often tied to EC directives."[123] This is not the place for an in-depth study of the EU legal system; suffice to say that the European Union is rather more than a mere international organisation and produces legislation of its own. Its Member States are legally required to implement this in their own national legislation within a specified period of time; indeed, they can now be fined if they do not.[124] Furthermore, the European Commission periodically conducts checks to ensure that they do so: in the area of insider dealing, an implementation study was carried out in 1996–7.

In the area of the regulation of financial markets, the European Union has passed a number of Directives. Those specifically focusing on market abuse include the Insider Dealing Directive[125] and the Money Laundering Directive.[126] These require the Member States to prohibit insider dealing and money laundering respectively and set minimum standards for measures which are to be implemented to prevent them.[127] In the area of insider dealing, many Member States only introduced legislation at all following the Directive and it may be noted that the Greek legislation is virtually a copy of it. Although this is an extreme example, it does highlight the influence that EU legislation has, not just on Greece but on all Member States.

It is also appropriate to mention here the Investment Services Directive.[128] This in essence provides for a single European "passport", under which an investment

---

122 Vogel, S.K. (1996) *Freer Markets, More Rules: Regulatory Reform in Advanced Industrial Countries*, p. 36.

123 *Ibid.*, p. 38.

124 It should, however, also be pointed out that the governments of the EU Member States all agreed to the adoption of the measures discussed here.

125 Council Directive 89/592/EEC.

126 Council Directive 91/308/EEC, as amended by Directive of the European Parliament and Council 2001/97/EC. Although this Directive was replaced by the Third Money Laundering Directive, Directive 2005/60/EC in December 2005, it has yet to be implemented in most of the Member States.

127 For a fuller examination of the definitions of insider dealing and money laundering, see Chapters 2–5.

128 Council Directive 93/22/EEC, to be replaced on 30 April 2007 with the Markets in Financial Instruments Directive. Directive of the European Parliament and Council 2004/39/EC.

firm authorised and regulated by the appropriate authorities in one Member State may, subject to certain conditions, provide services in another Member State without requiring separate authorisation from the host state's regulator. Clearly, such a system can only run satisfactorily if the regulatory systems of all Member States meet certain minimum standards and these are therefore prescribed.

In money laundering also, the European Union has acted, as noted above. In contrast to financial services regulation, however, there have also been several international initiatives from other quarters. The Council of Europe is one: it issued a Convention on the Laundering, Search, Seizure and Confiscation of the Proceeds from Crime in 1990. The Council's legislation, however, except for the European Convention on Human Rights, is arguably of lesser effect internationally than that of the European Union. Other states wishing to join the Council of Europe are obliged to sign and abide by the European Convention on Human Rights but not the other Conventions. Even in the case of the Human Rights Convention, breaches by particularly the newer Member States are often overlooked.[129] In contrast, it is made clear to any country wishing to join the European Union that it is a precondition of accession that that country incorporate into its own legislation the *acquis communautaire*, that is, the Union's legislation in its entirety. Although some transitory concessions are often made, full compliance will be expected and indeed, the progress of the country concerned in implementing the *acquis* is monitored as a major part of the pre-accession negotiations.

That said, it is recognised that most jurisdictions in the world have no prospect of ever being Member States of the European Union, if only because they are not situated in Europe.[130] For them, the most important form of international pressure in the area of money laundering comes from the Organisation for Economic Co-operation and Development (OECD) through its Financial Action Task Force (FATF). This acts in three principal ways. The first is that jurisdictions are invited to become actual members of the FATF. At present, 31 jurisdictions are members, including Hong

---

129 For example, it was openly stated at a conference by Paul Mahoney, Registrar of the European Court of Human Rights, that it was recognised by the Council of Europe that Russia could not financially afford to bring conditions in its prisons up to ECHR standards, but that it was felt that Russia should nonetheless be permitted to be a Member State in the interests of preserving and enhancing both Russia's own stability and that of its neighbours. "Human Rights: Dynamic Dimensions", Institute of Advanced Legal Studies, University of London and Dickinson School of Law, Penn State University, London, 27 April 2002.

130 While, for example, a decision was taken by the Council of Europe, in line with the NATO Partnership for Peace agreement, to treat the former Soviet Union as a block and to admit many of its republics as Member States, the European Union has taken a different approach, recognising that certain of the former Soviet republics (for example Georgia and Azerbaijan) are clearly situated in Asia and therefore *per se* not eligible for admission. Those clearly situated in Europe have been viewed differently: Estonia, Latvia and Lithuania became EU Member States in May 2004, while it was openly stated that a victory for Viktor Yushchenko in the 2004 Ukraine presidential elections would take the country on the path towards EU accession.

Kong but not mainland China,[131] as are two international organisations: the European Union and the Gulf Co-operation Council. Membership enables jurisdictions to be at the negotiating table where new measures to combat money laundering are decided on. A place at this table not only allows the jurisdiction in question to have an influence on policy but also, at least in principle, gives international credibility to its banking and financial sectors.[132]

The second is the promulgation of probably the most significant, and certainly the best publicised, of these measures: the Forty Recommendations. These Recommendations were revised in June 2003 and are considered in Chapter 5, which deals specifically with money laundering: it suffices here to state that they set out what the FATF considers to be the minimum measures that jurisdictions should have in place if their efforts to combat money laundering are to be viewed seriously. Finally, there is the NCCT list, the black list of Non-Compliant Countries and Territories. No jurisdictions are currently listed as NCCTs.[133] Appearance on the list is, however, viewed as a very severe warning that the jurisdiction's anti-money-laundering measures are inadequate and other jurisdictions are urged to think carefully before engaging in any financial transactions involving them. The Report of the FATF's Second Review to Identify Non-Cooperative Countries or Territories in 2001[134] is indicative:

---

131 As part of the "one country, two systems" arrangement put in place when Hong Kong moved from British rule to being a Special Administrative Region of the People's Republic of China in July 1997, Hong Kong has retained its own financial services regulator, the Securities and Futures Commission, its anti-corruption bureau, the Independent Commission Against Corruption, and the laws and regulations against money laundering and corruption introduced by the British administration. It is this structure that has enabled Hong Kong to remain a member of the FATF while China as a whole has yet to join. The more rudimentary anti-money-laundering controls currently in place in mainland China are a major block to the country joining the FATF, although there is also a political barrier in the form of the membership of Taiwan, under the name "Chinese Taipei", of the FATF sub-group, the Asia Pacific Group on Money Laundering (APG). China did, however, for the first time attend the FATF Plenary Meeting in Paris as an observer in February 2005 and the FATF President, Jean-Louis Fort, stated at the meeting that he looked forward to China in time achieving membership. (Press Notice, www.fatf-gafi.org.) Macau, however, like Hong Kong, is a member of the APG, although it is not a member of the FATF itself.

132 This is more true of the FATF itself than of its related regional groupings, each of which enjoys observer status before the FATF. For example, the members of the Asia Pacific Group on Money Laundering (APG) included the Cook Islands, Indonesia and the Philippines even while they were on the NCCT "black list". It also includes Taiwan, described by one leading Western expert as "a legal black hole" and, as such, a popular money laundering centre. Similarly, the Eastern and Southern African Anti-Money Laundering Group (ESAAMLG) includes among its members the Seychelles, which, while not actually on the NCCT list, remains a jurisdiction of concern to those engaged in the fight against money laundering.

133 The last jurisdiction, Myanmar, was removed from the list in October 2006.

134 "Review to Identify Non-Cooperative Countries or Territories: Increasing the Worldwide Effectiveness of Anti Money-Laundering Measures", June 2001, para. 89.

These jurisdictions are strongly urged to adopt measures to improve their rules and practices as expeditiously as possible in order to remedy the deficiencies identified in the reviews. Pending adoption and implementation of appropriate legislative and other measures, and in accordance with Recommendation 21, *the FATF recommends that financial institutions should give special attention to business relations and transactions with persons, including companies and financial institutions, from the non-cooperative countries and territories mentioned in paragraph 88 and in so doing take into account issues raised in the relevant summaries in Sections II and III of this report and any progress made by these jurisdictions listed in June 2000.*

It has been said that whether or not a given jurisdiction is placed on the list is often, at least in part, motivated by political rather than purely legal considerations. The first NCCT list, published in 2000, featured several Caribbean jurisdictions and met with considerable protest from their governments, while Monaco was omitted, due, it was rumoured, to lobbying by the French Government. The lenient treatment of Gibraltar, a British colony, and of Jersey, Guernsey and the Isle of Man, also jurisdictions closely linked with the UK, was similarly said to have been secured by the UK's intervention. In the case of Monaco, this may well be true; as for the British-linked territories, one could point out that the Cayman Islands, also a British colony, were featured on the 2000 list, as were the Marshall Islands, a jurisdiction with close links to the United States.[135] In any case, it has also been reported that pressure for regulatory improvements was imposed by France and the UK in return for their intervention.[136]

The list is frequently reviewed and a jurisdiction which remains for a considerable length of time on it risks severe sanctions or "counter-measures" being imposed. To date, such measures have been imposed on Nauru and Ukraine[137] and were briefly threatened against the Philippines. The details remain, however, a matter for individual states, not the FATF: the FATF's role is merely to recommend that "appropriate countermeasures" be taken.[138] Aside from any concrete measures, however, the fact that the jurisdiction of origin of a given customer/potential customer is on the FATF black list will certainly be considered by financial regulators to be a risk factor that an institution should take due heed of: the result is likely to be that customers from such jurisdictions may have difficulty in conducting business with, at least, the main financial centres.

Emphasis as in the text of the Report. The wording of paragraph 83 of the June 2003 Review Report is virtually identical.

135 The Marshall Islands were a US territory until 1986 and the republic remains in a Compact of Free Association with the United States.

136 See Hinterseer, K. (2002), *Criminal Finance: the political economy of money laundering in a comparative legal context*, Kluwer Law International, pp. 244–45.

137 The counter-measures against Ukraine were in place for less than 2 months, from 20 December 2002 to 14 February 2003; indeed, it may be noted that Ukraine has since been removed from the NCCT list altogether. Those against Nauru, however, imposed on 5 December 2001, remained in place for rather longer.

138 Recommendation 21.

There is therefore considerable pressure on such jurisdictions to take measures to be removed from the NCCT list. An example is the Seychelles, which abandoned the proposed Economic Development Assistance Act, referred to above, to avoid continued "black-listing", although there are several others. The effect of the NCCT list in persuading jurisdictions to change their practices was confirmed by the 2001 FATF President, José Maria Roldán:

> We see that this initiative has triggered significant improvements in anti- money laundering systems throughout the world.[139]

Four main issues emerge, therefore, in the regulation of financial markets in general and insider dealing in particular. This book now examines the approach that the EU Insider Dealing Directive takes to the control of insider dealing and how it has been implemented in the 15 jurisdictions that were Member States prior to the enlargement of the EU on 1 May 2004.

---

139 FATF 2000-2001 Report, 22 June, 2001, cited by Hinterseer, p. 245.

Chapter 2

Who is an Insider?

The question as to who constitutes an insider is crucial to the whole definition of insider dealing. As discussed in the previous chapter, among the rationales for prohibiting insider dealing is that it is an unfair use by persons in a privileged position of that position. Before looking in detail, therefore, at what it is forbidden to do, one has to examine who is forbidden to do it.

This question is more complicated than might at first appear: different jurisdictions have taken different approaches. Some simply define inside information, without any reference to how the person came by it,[1] and then state that anyone in possession of the information, so defined, is an insider.[2] Denmark and, to an extent, Spain are examples. Others, however, distinguish between "primary" and "secondary" insiders: the Directive itself does so. Where it is applied, this distinction is an important one. It will decide, in some cases, whether the person who commits the act in question is guilty of an offence at all. Even where the act is prohibited to primary and secondary insiders alike, as with actual dealing, secondary insiders may be punished substantially more leniently, not merely as a matter of sentencing policy but under the legislation itself. Austria is a notable example.

With possession comes also the issue of knowledge. This is perhaps less true of primary insiders (where they are so categorised): a director of a company or a key employee or adviser, for example, will generally be well aware of the nature of the information which they handle, as will shareholders. With secondary insiders, those who are outside the "inner circle" but nonetheless come into possession of inside information, it can be more complicated. They may know, or at least suspect, that the information is confidential and that they should not use it, but this cannot always be assumed. If they do not know this, it is arguable that they do not abuse their possession of the information, they do not act in any kind of bad faith and hence it is a little harsh to punish them, especially with criminal sanctions.[3]

This is, however, not a universal view. Strict liability is a recognised concept and is applied, even in the criminal law, where it is deemed necessary in order to

---

1 For the definition of inside information, see Chapter 3.

2 For a discussion of the various types of insider dealing offences, see Chapter 4 for the criminal provisions and Chapter 7 for the civil/administrative measures.

3 Particularly for actual dealing, all Member States, with the partial exception of Spain, impose criminal penalties, even where civil/administrative sanctions also exist. See Chapter 4.

protect the public interest. An example in the UK would be the offence of driving a motor vehicle without third party insurance cover. Further, a requirement of knowledge, or at least suspicion, on the part of the defendant can make the offence considerably harder to prove – the view was taken in the Netherlands that it made the task impossible, at least on occasion.[4]

In order to consider the merits of the different approaches, it is helpful to examine in turn the precise definition of an insider, first under the Directive and then in the Member States.

The Directive

Article 2(1) of the Directive defines as an insider any person who possesses inside information, having obtained it in one of three ways. The first is "by virtue of his membership of the administrative, management or supervisory bodies of the issuer". This is fairly uncontroversial. If insider dealing is to be objected to at all, then it is not unreasonable to target the directors and managers of the relevant company. These, above all, have access to confidential information, often some considerable time before it is made public; indeed, much of the information that they receive may never be made public. They are therefore those best placed to make a quick profit ahead of the market, precisely what any kind of anti-insider-dealing legislation seeks to prevent. Furthermore, they, above all, are in a fiduciary position, expected to use their situation for the benefit of their company, not themselves.

The second category is where the person obtains the information "by virtue of his holding in the capital of the issuer". This, aimed at the existing shareholders, is a little harsher. It is far from uncommon for those, from whatever background, who have already demonstrated a degree of commitment to a company by investing in it to be entitled to certain privileges, not least the offer of further securities at preferential rates. It could be argued that the opportunity to buy more shares in the knowledge that a profit will result, is simply an extension of this.

This is not, however, the approach that the Directive takes. It very clearly distinguishes between primary and secondary insiders. This being the case, it is somewhat surprising that shareholders should be singled out. On the one hand, it is certainly true that, by virtue of their membership of the company, they are in a position to receive confidential information that is not available to the public at large. On the fairness argument, it can, therefore, be said to be reasonable to restrain them from abusing this information. But on the other, their position is different in nature to that of directors and officers of the company. An officer of a company is invited by that company to hold a position and is trusted to use that position to work for the company's ends. He should therefore not place his own interests above those of the company and in any event is trusted not to make use of his position to make

---

4   See the discussion of the Netherlands' legislation: p. 71-72.

a personal profit.[5] Furthermore, he is paid a salary (usually a handsome one!): this is his reward.[6]

A shareholder, however, is arguably in a different position. He is not paid by the company; he has invested his own funds in it. The dividends he receives are his entitlement in return for his investment; they are not a reward for services rendered: he renders no services. The same is true for the rise in the value of the shares which he has purchased (i.e. the increase of his capital); it is this rise that is the reward for his shrewd investment since an investor with lesser judgment is liable to see his shares fall in value, or at least not rise to the same extent. These, together with the ultimate profit which he hopes to obtain when he does ultimately sell, are the sole incentive to invest (and to maintain his investment) that he receives.[7] Unless constrained by the insider dealing laws, he can sell his shareholding whenever he pleases, without giving any warning that he plans to do so. In short, he owes the company nothing. It is therefore questionable whether there is any essential difference between him using his position to make a profit by buying more of the company's shares (or avoid a loss by selling those that he already has) and him using it to further his ends at the Annual General Meeting.

An exception to this argument is, however, advanced in respect of controlling shareholders. The shareholders as a body make decisions that determine the entire direction of the company. They may give orders to the directors or even remove them (subject to the constraints of the directors' contracts and of employment legislation), they may even alter the company's constitution.[8] It may therefore be seen that, should a shareholder obtain a controlling interest, he[9] will assume management powers over the company even greater than those of its directors and managers. He will therefore owe a duty to the company, i.e. must look to the interests of the company and its other shareholders, not simply his own.[10]

Whether or not they owe a duty to the company, shareholders do owe a duty to the market. Even minority shareholders have powers and privileges not available to investors at large. They have access to information about the company (both proposed major decisions and the periodic accounts) in advance. By voting at meetings, they even, on occasion, help to create the events to which inside information

---

5   For a fuller discussion of this principle, see the previous chapter.

6   It is true that some directors are unpaid, but they usually receive some sort of benefit in return for their services.

7   It is true that in some cases, persons invest in a particular issuer primarily out of support for the company, or perhaps those behind it, particularly when a company is first set up. But these represent a small minority of investors and therefore do not alter the general principle.

8   It will generally take a specified minimum vote to do this (75% in England and Wales), rather than a simple majority, but it can still be done.

9   Or it, since many controlling shareholders will in fact be companies.

10 English company law, for example, ensures the protection of minority shareholders through the imposition of a number of provisions, some of which may cause decided inconvenience and expense to the controlling shareholder.

may relate (whether to launch a takeover bid, for example, or how to react to a bid made by another company). Further, they have rights of inspection of the company's operations, again something that may elicit highly confidential – and price-sensitive – information. They are therefore, through their position, placed at a considerable advantage in relation to the investing public at large. It therefore follows that they should, like others in privileged positions, be precluded from abusing it.

This is the approach that the Directive takes: shareholders are primary insiders. It must be stated that, not only have several Member States followed it in this respect, certain jurisdictions outside the EU have done so as well. South Africa defines an insider as, *inter alia*, "an individual who has inside information through being ... a shareholder of an issuer of securities or financial instrument to which the information relates".[11] This is in keeping with the stated purpose of the Act, namely "to prohibit individuals who have inside information relating to securities or financial instruments from dealing in such securities or financial instruments", although it should be noted that this wider category of "individuals who have inside information" is not carried through to the actual definitions.

The group surrounded by the greatest debate are those who have access to inside information through their work or, as the Directive puts it, "by virtue of the exercise of [their] employment, profession or duties". It is unclear, however, precisely who this covers. Certainly, it will cover those who professionally handle inside information through working at the company whose securities are in question. It will also cover, for example, employees of the bidder, as well as the target, in a takeover bid.[12] This may be contrasted with some jurisdictions, where it is only employees of the target company who are prohibited from dealing in its shares. It will also cover persons such as lawyers, auditors and accountants, who, although they are not employees of the company in question, work with it and therefore have access to price-sensitive information relevant to its shares.

It may also be seen that the prohibition extends to officials of regulators. Although they may not work directly with the companies in question, they will often have access to information which, when made public, will have a major impact on their securities. Consider, for example, the effect on the price of the securities of a German steel company when it is announced that the Bundeskartellamt (Federal Cartel Office) has just imposed on it a fine of €50 million, amounting to 6.9% of its turnover for the previous year, for anti-competitive practice. In practice, officials of such regulators will be forbidden under their employment contracts to disclose confidential information and may in certain circumstances be prohibited from doing

---

11 Insider Trading Act 1998, s.1.

12 Cf. the South African Insider Trading Act 1998, which prohibits employees of all companies involved in a takeover bid from dealing. The Act was principally inspired by the UK's Criminal Justice Act 1993, although the drafts of what later became the UK's Financial Services and Markets Act 2000 also had a considerable influence.

so under the criminal law,[13] but this in itself will not prevent them from dealing on their own account. Their employer may, however, be able to seek restitution of any profits that they make.

A major topic of debate concerns government officials. They may not have access to information concerning any particular company, but they will be involved in the formulating of policies that can have a marked effect on the price of securities. In much of Europe, farms are owned not by small farmers, or even local landowners, but large agricultural corporations owning, in total, thousands of square kilometres rather than a couple of hundred hectares. A decision on agricultural policy may thus have a very definite effect on their securities price. Similarly, details of a change in taxation levels.[14] Again, the disclosure by a government official of confidential information is a criminal offence in most, if not all, Member States and civil remedies may be available to recover any profits made through its unauthorised use.

Another area that arises is that of pressure groups and journalists. Journalists, by definition, make information public, but they will possess any information they receive for some hours at least before their newspapers hit the streets or their TV or radio reports are broadcast. If they deal during that time, are they guilty of insider dealing? Arguably they are: journalism is a profession and they came by the information through the exercise of it. But precisely which circumstances of obtaining information constitute the exercise of a journalist's profession may prove a difficult question. Some, including many journalists, would say that gathering information is a general description of an integral part of their profession and the means by which they obtain it is secondary. Others would argue that even a journalist comes by some information in a private capacity. The question is all the more blurred since a journalist may enter into a situation in which he is not actively looking for "a story" but nevertheless learns facts he later uses for one.

The question is perhaps focused most sharply in the area of share-tipping. Some newspapers have a column in which they recommend to their readers certain shares as being a particularly good investment.[15] Is the journalist who writes such a column, or indeed any other employee of the newspaper (such as its editor) who sees it before the newspaper is distributed, an insider? This issue is complicated by the nature of the column. The reasons why a given security is a good investment may themselves be inside information: if they are, that will certainly make anyone in the newspaper, TV company or whatever insiders. But separate from this, the very fact that a given security is about to be recommended in the financial pages of a major newspaper could be argued to be price-sensitive. The entire rationale of such a column is, after

---

13 In the UK, officials of government departments who disclose confidential information will commit an offence under the Official Secrets Act 1989, which routinely attracts imprisonment. In many jurisdictions, any breach of professional secrecy is a criminal offence; indeed some, such as Luxembourg, provide for a mandatory prison sentence.

14 See the discussion on this topic in relation to the Irish provisions: pp. 68.

15 An example in the UK in the late 1990s, which attracted considerable publicity, was the "City Slickers" column in the *Mirror*. This column was later withdrawn following allegations against the Mirror's editor, Piers Morgan.

all, to encourage readers to buy the securities featured (or possibly to get out of them if they are about to plunge). Hence it is foreseeable, to say the least, that, whether or not there is any inside information behind what is written, a strong write-up in the column may cause considerable buying of the security.[16] This, in turn, will cause the price to rise as markets can be extremely sensitive to a perceived demand for particular securities. It is therefore suggested that a financial journalist who deals in advance of his column being published or any person who leaks what that column is going to say may well be guilty of insider dealing. An example of the former was the City Press affair in June/July 1973, in which a newspaper itself bought 1,200 shares in a company and shortly thereafter published an article urging their purchase and then a second article, stating that recent price movements showed that "something was afoot". In 1973, insider dealing was not yet a criminal offence in the UK, but the Stock Exchange, on discovering what had taken place, was decidedly displeased, as was the Press Council.[17]

Similarly, "ethical investment" has in recent years become a major issue. If human rights abuses in a given country are highlighted, this may have a detrimental effect on companies known to have substantial commercial dealings in that country. It is a debatable point whether those involved in producing such a report would be prohibited from selling their shares before it was published. The question becomes even more complicated where, as in the UK, the motive for dealing can be relevant.

All the above groups come into possession of inside information as an integral part of their work. There is an additional group, however, who may obtain inside information through their work, but arguably incidentally to it. Frequently cited examples of these are taxi drivers, waitresses, barmaids and even cleaners. All of these may, through their work, overhear or perhaps see information that is confidential. That they are never intended to do so is clear. But, as is generally recognised, people are not always as careful as they might be. Those holding a confidential business discussion in a restaurant will in practice rarely stop as glasses are refilled, particularly by the time they get on to the brandy. Similarly, it is all too easy in the back of a taxi to talk as though the driver were simply part of the engine. Receptionists would probably also come into this category: it is all too natural to continue a conversation while waiting for the lift.

The position of such persons is, however, complex. If a waitress overhears a conversation between a group of customers in the restaurant in which she works, she certainly comes by that information through her employment. The same will apply to a cleaner who sees a confidential document which an officer of the firm carelessly leaves lying on his desk or perhaps open on a desktop computer which

---

16 If there are no grounds for recommending the security, but the journalist, knowing this, does so anyway, it is arguable that he may be guilty of the separate offence of market manipulation (styled in the UK "misleading behaviour").

17 For further details of this case, see: Rider, B.A.K. and Ffrench, H.L. (1979) *The Regulation of Insider Trading*, Macmillan, p. 172 and "The Ugly Face of City Journalism", *Evening Standard*, 13 August 1973 (cited by Rider and Ffrench).

he has forgotten to shut down. Although a taxi driver may be self-employed, it is arguable that he obtains the information through his profession.[18]

The latter case raises a separate question: what constitutes a "profession"? In the UK, or at least in England and Wales, there is no legal definition of the term, but in France, the term "the liberal professions" is very clearly understood as covering certain occupations but not others. The Directive does not define "profession" in terms, but the use of the phrase "by virtue of his employment, profession or duties" would appear to cover all persons who obtain information through their work, regardless of whether they are employees of the source or self-employed agents. It would certainly seem perverse for a waitress, because she is employed by the restaurant, to be covered by the prohibition but for a taxi driver, because he is self-employed and is not considered to be a professional, not to be. In the absence of any clear evidence to the contrary, it would therefore seem rash to infer that this is what the Directive prescribes.

The question remains, however, whether any of these types of persons are covered. The Directive is not entirely clear: the wording is simply "because he has access to such information by virtue of the exercise of his employment or duties". It has been said by the Commission, albeit informally, that this provision of the Directive was only intended to cover those who not only obtain inside information through their work but whose work is such that it by its very nature involves the handling of such information. The national provisions of certain Member States are wider, as seen below, but that of the Directive is not. Directors and other officers, as already seen, are covered by a separate category; the present category includes persons such as those employed in the Research and Development Department, legal advisers and accountants (whether independent or in-house), auditors and indeed secretaries. All of these persons need to obtain inside information in order to do their job. In contrast, waitresses, taxi drivers and cleaners do not. Although it can happen that employees and officers alike may leave sensitive documents open on their desks or computer or discuss the contents openly in the backs of taxis or in restaurants and bars, ideally they will not do so. It could be argued that waitresses are a borderline case in a culture where sensitive discussions frequently take place over lunch meetings. But it could be argued in response that where the topic is highly sensitive, particularly where price-sensitive information is involved, such meetings do not need to take place in public restaurants: they can equally well be held in closed meeting rooms at the firm's premises. One thing at least is clear: if those in possession of inside information do take care not to allow it to be seen

---

18 It could be argued that the position regarding the cleaner, who is an employee of the institution from which the information originates and is therefore trusted not to abuse it, is different from that of the waitress and the taxi driver (whether employed or self-employed), who are not. It is not, however, an inherent part of the cleaner's job, any more than it is a part of the waitress' or taxi driver's, that they come into possession of inside information. Furthermore, the argument is weakened by the increasing trend for cleaners not to be employees of the company itself but of an external contractor.

or overheard, their cleaners, waitresses and taxi drivers will not be hindered in carrying out their jobs. In contrast, although it is in theory possible for officers and employees to produce all their sensitive documents themselves and never to involve their secretaries, to do so, particularly for more senior persons, will make their own job considerably more difficult and that of their secretaries commensurately less effective.

The issue is carried over into those of the Member States that draw a distinction between primary and secondary insiders. It is suggested, therefore, that such a distinction be abolished.[19]

Even if waitresses, taxi drivers, cleaners and the like do not qualify as primary insiders, they will, however, definitely be included in a separate class of so-called "tippees" or "secondary insiders", who are also prohibited from dealing (although not from certain other insider dealing offences).[20] A secondary insider is defined in Article 4 of the Directive as:

> any person other than those referred to in Article 2 who with full knowledge of the facts possesses inside information, the direct source of which could not be other than a person referred to in Article 2.

This is the counterpart to the prohibition on a primary insider, as defined above, not only from dealing but from disclosing the inside information to a third party (other than in the normal course of their duties). If such a person defies the ban and discloses it anyway, the person who is tipped off is then themselves prohibited from dealing on the basis of the information. The Directive does not, however, prohibit secondary insiders from disclosing the information, although they are prohibited from encouraging others to deal in the affected securities.[21] Although some Member States do not differentiate between primary and secondary insiders, those that do so tend to follow the Directive in not prohibiting secondary insiders from mere disclosure of the information.[22]

Given the wide definition of secondary insiders under the Directive, this is in many ways a more suitable term than "tippees". A person who is deliberately tipped off by an insider in breach of the prohibition will indeed be covered. So, however, will a person be who overhears insiders talking or sees a confidential document, despite the fact that they were not intended to do so. This need not even be through the carelessness of an insider. A computer hacker, if he discovers inside information in the course of his activities and then makes use of it, will be guilty not only of an offence under the computer security laws,[23] but also of insider dealing as a secondary insider.

---

19 For a more detailed consideration of the argument for abolishing this distinction, see pp. 230-31.
20 See Chapter 4.
21 This issue is discussed at greater length in Chapter 4.
22 There are exceptions, however, such as Finland, Italy and the UK.
23 For example, in the UK, ss. 1 or 2 of the Computer Misuse Act 1990.

The taxi driver, waiter, etc, discussed above will generally come into this category if the direct source of their information is an insider as defined in Article 2. But a short glance reveals that this is not necessarily the case. The two people talking need not be primary insiders: they could themselves be secondary insiders. Even if they are primary insiders (and this will be far from easy to prove), there is the additional hurdle of "with full knowledge of the facts". The taxi driver or waiter may well have worked out that the information they heard was price-sensitive; indeed, if they deal on its basis, they almost certainly will have done. It is questionable, however, whether it will be possible to prove that they knew that the people they heard talking were directors, employees or shareholders. Clearly, where an insider says to his waiter, "Instead of my giving you the standard 10%, do yourself a favour. X Pharmaceuticals SA are about to announce the discovery of a new drug which will send their share price soaring. Buy some of their shares first thing tomorrow morning and you'll make a tidy sum," the waiter is a tippee and covered as such. Otherwise, however, the matter is far less definite. It is therefore perhaps unsurprising that the Member States in their implementing legislation have tended either explicitly to include such individuals or to make it clear that the acquiring of the inside information must be an integral part of the employment, position or duties.

In contrast to these categories, however, there is one group, arguably tippees in the general if not legal sense, who would not seem to be covered by the Directive. These are those who are encouraged to deal, but who do not actually receive any inside information. The position of the waiter who is tipped off about the new drug is clear. But suppose the customer is less candid and simply says to him, "Buy shares in X SA first thing tomorrow morning and you won't regret it." The customer will certainly commit an offence – of encouraging to deal.[24] But the waiter is still not in possession of any actual information. It could be argued that he is, the information being that the shares in X SA are about to rise in value. But it is questionable whether that information, in the terms in which the waiter has received it, is sufficiently precise to be covered.[25] As such, he is free to act on the tip, buy the shares, pass the word, encourage his friends and family to do the same, indeed do all the things that are forbidden to insiders under the Directive.

It could be argued, of course, that this is fair enough. A tip such as the one described, with no explanation attached to it, does not necessarily put the tippee on notice that he now possesses inside information. He may be aware in some vague sense that he is receiving an unfair advantage and that to make use of it would be morally wrong, but this falls far short of the clarity that is expected of the law in a democratic state. Nonetheless, if, as is claimed, the purpose of outlawing insider dealing is to ensure that the securities markets are fair places to deal and that no one

---

24 For the discussion of this offence, see Chapter 4.
25 For the requirement that inside information be precise, see Chapter 3.

can secure an unfair profit on them, this loophole does mean that the measures are not as effective as they might be.[26]

Finally, the position of legal entities needs to be considered. In some Member States, such as the UK, the principles of criminal law allow a company or other legal entity to be prosecuted in its own right; in others, they do not.[27] The Directive does not require one approach or the other; it simply states that, where the insider is a company or other legal entity, the prohibition applies to "the natural persons who take part in the decision to carry out the transaction for the account of the legal person concerned". This may be a director, the entire board or, alternatively, a more junior employee who is authorised to deal on behalf of the company (such as, for example, a trader).

The aim of this provision seems clear: no one should escape liability on the basis that, technically, the transaction was conducted by their company, not by them, and that in their jurisdiction, a company may not be held liable. Whether this is strictly necessary is debatable. Whether or not shares are bought or sold by a legal entity, the transaction is actually carried out by an individual and that individual, it would seem, will come within the provisions of the Directive. It may be, therefore, that it is a simple case of a "belt and braces" approach.

It is debatable, however, whether this is adequate. Where individuals, in any position, commit acts that contravene the criminal law, it is entirely right and proper that they should personally be brought to account for them. But there are cases where they do so to further not only their own ends but also those of their company or institution. It cannot be overlooked that directors, officers and sometimes employees of a company do frequently act as that company not only in name but in fact as well. If they do so, it is arguable that the company should not escape liability. This enters into the territory of a fundamental legal issue: whether or not a corporation or other legal entity should, as a matter of principle, be subject to criminal liability. Since criminal law at an EU level remains in its infancy, it is perhaps not appropriate to discuss this in the context of the Directive, although the prescription of criminal sanctions in the Money Laundering Directive perhaps supports the argument to the contrary. The issue is, therefore, considered below as part of the discussion of the legislation of the individual Member States, particularly that of Austria. It is therefore helpful to turn to these now.

---

26 It is just possible that in England and Wales, a robust judge in the mould of Lord Denning might rule that for this kind of tippee to deal is inequitable and compel him to disgorge the profit, but it is hard to envisage this in any other Member State. In any case, to whom should the disgorged profit be paid? For further discussion of this issue in the context of the UK's market abuse provisions, see pp. 220-21.

27 All Member States provide for criminal penalties for insider dealing, albeit to varying degrees. See Chapter 4.

Austria

The Austrian legislation, the Securities Supervisory Act (*Wertpapieraufsichtsgesetz* or WAG[28]) of 1996,[29] follows the Directive fairly closely. Austria is, however, the only Member State explicitly to use the terms "primary" and "secondary insiders" and to distinguish between them in terms of penalties. Section 48(a)(3) defines a primary insider as a person who, by virtue of his profession, employment, duties or his holding in the capital of the issuer, possesses inside information. A secondary insider is defined in subsection 2 as a person who, not being an insider as referred to subsection 3, takes advantage of inside information, being fully aware that it is inside information.

The first point to make is that no reference is made to directors, managers and the like. They are persons possessing inside information by reason of their position, just as is a lawyer, auditor, or any employee. There are arguments both for and against this approach. In favour of it is the view that the essential point of prohibiting insider dealing is to prevent those who receive inside information for entirely legitimate purposes (be it to prepare accounts, advise on a takeover, consider that takeover or prepare background reports) from using it for their own, illicit ends. On this view, it makes no significant difference whether the person is the managing director, negotiating a major contract, the junior assistant who drafts the proposal or the secretary who takes notes of meetings. Each of them has an unfair advantage in that they possess information in order to carry out their duties and they should not be permitted to abuse that in order to steal a march (and a profit) on the general investing public.

On the other hand, it may be argued that the different positions in and associated with a company do not all carry the same responsibility. A junior assistant holds a less trusted post and should therefore not be penalised to the same extent as a director. Although external professionals, such as lawyers and accountants (and, arguably, even more so auditors) similarly hold a considerable degree of responsibility and trust, they may still not be compared to the decision-makers at the top of the corporate structure. In addition, such external professionals, if they do abuse their positions, can expect not only to be forced, through civil proceedings, to recompense the company that trusted them but also to face disciplinary proceedings before their professional body that may well permanently deprive them of their livelihood.

Although this argument has some weight, it is suggested that it is not strong enough to justify singling out directors and others in a senior management capacity for special attention under the insider dealing laws. They do have a greater overall responsibility than the more junior employees; this much is clear. But that does not imply that the junior employee is under a lower degree of trust not to abuse his position or use information passed to him in the course of his work in ways that are

---

28 Austria and Germany have official abbreviations for their statutes, by which legislation is regularly referred to, not only by commentators but in official documents and literature.

29 BGBl. 1996/753.

not authorised. To argue that a cashier in a bank, who stole cash from the drawer, betrayed the bank's trust only in a mild way because he was only a very junior employee is clearly absurd: in placing him in a position where he routinely handles large amounts of cash, the bank clearly places very considerable trust in him not to misappropriate it! In the same way, the junior laboratory employee who discovers that trials of a given product are successful is trusted to keep that information within the authorised channels of the company and not to deal on the basis of it (until it is formally announced) every bit as much as is the Director of Research and Development or even the Managing Director.

If, therefore, one is to distinguish between primary and secondary insiders at all, the Austrian approach of placing all three in the same category of primary insider is therefore to be welcomed, although it is suggested that it would be better still to go further and remove the distinction between primary and secondary insiders altogether.

Secondly, the definition of a secondary insider is wide: anyone, other than those covered as a primary insider, who knowingly takes advantage of inside information. This is rather stricter than the Directive in that there is no requirement for a "direct source". A tippee who receives the information from a primary insider and one who receives it from someone who himself was a tippee are both secondary insiders and, as such, restrained from dealing on the basis of the information.

The wider definition also serves to cover some of the less clear categories discussed above, such as the journalist, the activist and the waiter. It may not be clear whether they are primary or secondary insiders, but they are in principle covered, provided that they knew that the information was inside information. Whether this is so will vary from case to case, although proving it may be difficult.

As for legal entities, Austria does not impose criminal liability on these. Where, therefore, insider dealing is committed by a legal entity, it is the directors who are held liable. While this approach is taken by a number of Member States, it must be questioned. It is recognised that, historically, the common-law system has tended to impose criminal liability on legal entities (the United States, like the UK, is famous for doing so) while the civil-law system has tended not to do so. As someone from a common-law background, I should perhaps, therefore, tread particularly carefully here. But this does not mean that the issue can, let alone should, be ignored. In any case, certain civil-law jurisdictions, notably France, have altered their criminal law to allow for criminal liability for legal entities and hence the divide is not as sharp now as it once was.

The fact is that, as mentioned above, directors, managers and sometimes even employees do frequently act not as mere individuals but as their company or institution.[30] The fact that their letters routinely carry, below the signature, not only

---

30 The European Union currently comprises 27 different Member States, each with different principles of company law allowing for different corporate forms. Community legislation generally, therefore, adopts the term "undertaking". This term is, however, unhelpful for the present discussion since it can include, for example, a sole trader or professional who has

the author's name but their position is an indication of this. In England and Wales, solicitors' firms often take this still further by signing letters simply in the name of the firm, not that of the individual solicitor who wrote it. Furthermore, the fact that a legal entity has a legal personality separate from those of its officers is fundamental not only to its nature but to its purpose.

Following on from this, it is a well-established principle that if a legal entity commits a civil wrong, it can be sued for it (just as it can sue if it is the victim). Similarly, legal entities, whether companies or partnerships, may be held to account by regulatory bodies: a bank or an investment firm, for example, may only operate under authorisation from a regulator, which may fine it or even withdraw that authorisation if it commits a breach of the rules. If, therefore, a corporation which commits a wrong may be held to account civilly and, where appropriate, administratively, it seems strange that it should be immune from criminal liability.

A further argument for extending criminal liability to legal entities is that, if it is not, corporations can too easily separate themselves from the illegal act. Where, as with insider dealing, the illegal act results in a profit, the issue becomes particularly stark. A company can allow one or more of its senior officers to commit a criminal offence, or at least authorise an employee to do so, it can reap the benefits of that offence and yet, if it is discovered, it can allow a director, or possibly a couple, to be sacrificed while it itself simply walks away scot free. This, it is suggested, cannot be right; if a legal entity is capable of benefiting from a criminal offence, it should be capable of being punished for it.

In response, two main arguments can be put forward against criminal liability of legal entities. Firstly, it may be claimed that it is simply unreasonable to place a corporation at risk of criminal proceedings simply because some employee, in the course of his work, committed an illegal act. Secondly, it is impossible to impose criminal sanctions on a legal entity: how can a company be sent to jail? It is helpful to examine these in turn.

The first argument raises the spectre of a junior employee in the course of his work committing a criminal act, quite possibly unbeknownst to the management, let alone to the board itself. It is all very well, this argument would run, to allow a civil principle of vicarious liability because the stakes are rarely as high. Further, it can be conceded that where, for example, fraud is perpetrated by an employee of a financial institution, there is a public policy reason to permit the clients who have lost out to seek recompense from the firm. Quite possibly, the individual fraudster will no longer have everything he has stolen – or if he has, he may have successfully hidden it – and therefore the alternative would simply be to abandon the victims to

---

no separate legal personality. This book therefore uses either the term "legal entities", which are generally understood to be distinct from natural persons, or "companies and institutions", the latter intended to be sufficiently broad to include partnerships and other legal entities which for one reason or another cannot be described as "companies". For convenience, the latter phrase is sometimes shortened to "corporations", which again is intended to cover all corporate forms.

their loss. In contrast, in the case of criminal proceedings, there are no personal victims who need to be compensated: this is not what the criminal law is designed to do.[31] This being the case, since there is not a choice between two parties, one of which must inevitably lose out, it is simply not right that one bad apple should put the corporation at risk, particularly when the corporation's officers never had any reasonable chance of detecting and stopping him.

The claim that there are no public policy grounds for imposing criminal liability on a corporation in the way that civil liability is imposed does not stand up. Its rebuttal is linked to that to the argument that insider dealing is a victimless crime. If a corporation commits a criminal act and is then permitted to get away with it, society loses out. It is in the interests of a fair society in which the rule of law is upheld that those who break the criminal law are brought to book for it. Nor need this mean one employee placing the entire corporation at risk of criminal proceedings. This can be addressed simply by specifying very clearly the circumstances under which a legal entity may be criminally liable. The approach of England and Wales seems commendable: someone in a senior managerial capacity, part of the "directing mind and will", must have been involved in the offence.[32] One trader who commits an offence of insider dealing will therefore only lead to his institution being prosecuted if it transpires that the management knew what he was doing and approved it.[33]

The second argument, that criminal sanctions are not appropriate for legal entities may be rebutted equally simply. It is of course true that a company cannot be sent to prison. But imprisonment is only one of a number of criminal sanctions. Fines are another well-established weapon, as common in the criminal courts as they are in the hands of regulatory or administrative bodies. Indeed, so closely are they associated with the criminal law that H.M. Treasury, when drafting Part VIII of the UK's Financial Services and Markets Act 2000, decided against the use of the word "fine" to describe the administrative sanctions that were to be introduced to combat market abuse and substituted the term "financial penalty".[34] For these to be effective, they must, of course, be relatively high: corporations tend to be rather wealthier than individuals and hence a fine that will hurt an individual may cause barely a blip on a company's balance sheet. In Austria, the maximum fine for insider dealing, depending on the defendant's income, is just over €78,000. For a fine to be effective against a corporation, this will clearly need to be raised. The model of the

---

31 This is less true of civil-law jurisdictions such as France, where victims are represented and compensated at criminal trials.

32 *H.R. Bolton (Engineering) Co. v Graham* [1957] 1 QB 159, 172 per Denning LJ, affirming *Lennards Carrying Co. v Asiatic Petroleum Co.* [1915] AC 705. For a general discussion of this issue, see Archbold: Criminal Pleading, Evidence and Practice (2005), para. 17–30.

33 It has been explicitly stated that not every "responsible agent", "high executive" or "agent acting on behalf of the company" may render their company criminally liable: *R v Andrews Weatherfoil Ltd.* [1972] 1 WLR 118; (1972) 56 Cr. App. R 31, cited in Archbold: Criminal Pleading, Evidence and Practice (2005) para. 17–30.

34 See pp. 215-17.

unlimited fine, found, for example, in the UK and certain Scandinavian jurisdictions, need not be adopted: a maximum fine of €200 million would probably suffice to make an impact on even the largest institutions.

Belgium

The Belgian provisions are to be found in Articles 175 ff. of the Law of 22 December 1995. The position is complicated slightly by the fact that there are two texts of the legislation, one in French and one in Flemish, and, as can often happen where translations are involved, the two are not quite identical. The difference in the definition of an insider is, however, not significant.

Articles 182 and 184 of the Law, which define an insider, follow the Directive almost exactly. A primary insider (although the terms "primary" and "secondary" are not used) or "inside source" is a person who possesses information which he holds on the basis of his membership of the administrative, management or supervisory bodies of the issuer of the securities concerned, his holding in the capital of the issuer or because he has access to it through the exercise of his employment, profession or duties.[35] It is a requirement, however, that he either know or at least ought reasonably to know that it is inside information The ambiguities discussed in the context of the Directive are, however, retained: what kind of people are covered by the phrase, "because they have access to such information in the exercise of their employment, profession or duties"? The situation regarding the taxi driver, waiter or barman is as unclear in Belgium as it is under the Directive.

The problem is made worse by the fact that, unlike the European Commission, the Belgian legislator has not stated whether it intended to cover such persons. In any case, it is not clear whether, even had it done so, this would have been conclusive: it is what laws state that counts, not what the government which happened to have introduced them is held to have intended. National governments change in political character rather more than the European Commission, or even the Council of Ministers, does and a law originally intended to achieve one purpose can be quite capable of being used by a subsequent government for another. It is for this reason that the argument, advanced on occasion, that even if certain categories are in fact covered by a particular law, no prosecution would in fact be brought in those circumstances, is questionable.[36]

A secondary insider is defined in Article 184 as any person, other than those mentioned above, who possesses information which he knows or ought reasonably to know to be inside information and that it comes from an inside source. It is a defence for such a person not to know that the information was confidential;

---

35 Art. 182.
36 For example, a leading UK prosecutor has stated, albeit informally, that although the Proceeds of Crime Act 2002 could in theory be used to charge with money laundering those who break the alcohol licensing laws, this would never in fact happen, if only because of limited resources. See pp. 239-40.

however, the burden of proof is on the defendant. It is difficult to establish whether a waiter or barman could rely on this. He might argue that if the persons he overheard were prepared to discuss the information in a public place like a restaurant or a bar, it clearly cannot have been that confidential. On the other hand, the court may take the view that he must have realised from the nature of the conversation that it had to be confidential. One may suspect that this is an area in which each case is likely to be decided on its own facts, including, quite possibly, the perceived intelligence of the defendant! The fact that Belgium, like a number of the Member States, does not have juries as part of its criminal justice system and that therefore such matters will be weighed by a judge may also have an influence.

As primary and secondary insiders are dealt with under separate Articles, it is important for the prosecution to establish into which category a given defendant falls. A case in 1997 concerned Quick, a Belgian chain of fast food restaurants – comparable to McDonalds or Burger King – which now covers a number of other countries. Like many restaurant chains of its type, it suffered a marked effect from the BSE crisis. Information concerning the crisis was passed from the parent company to a subsidiary. A number of directors of the subsidiary dealt on the basis of this information shortly before the share price fell. While in some Member States, such as the UK or Denmark, this would have been enough to secure a conviction, it was necessary in Belgium to establish whether the directors were primary or secondary insiders. Ultimately, the court decided that if the directors also sat on the board of the parent company, they were primary insiders; if not, they were secondary insiders.

It is, however, clear that financial analysts are by definition primary insiders.

It is important to recognise that for the prohibition to apply, the dealing must be on the basis of the information: no-one is prohibited from dealing merely by virtue of their position.[37] This was illustrated by the case of *Office of Public Prosecutor of Ghent v Bekaert and Storme*.[38] This case involved a husband and wife. The husband bought shares in his own company shortly before the company for which his wife worked launched a bid to take it over. The couple were then prosecuted, the husband for insider dealing, the wife for unauthorised disclosure of inside information, and convicted. Their convictions were, however, overturned by the Court of Appeal on the basis that it had not been proven that the wife actually disclosed the information; the prosecution had been wrong to presume that, simply because they were married, she must have done so. Clearly, if it could not be proven that the wife had disclosed the information to her husband, it could consequently not be proven that he had dealt on the basis of it.

The case is a striking example of how difficult it is, in general, to deal with insider dealing through the criminal law, particularly where it is suspected that

---

37 This may be contrasted with the position in, for example, the UK, where the Companies Act 1985 places very definite restrictions on directors, in particular, dealing in the securities of their own company.

38 Trial: Ghent Criminal Court, 27 September 1995. Appeal reported in *Le Soir*, 5 May 1997.

secondary insiders are involved. Short of a confession, or perhaps a third party giving evidence, it will be almost impossible to prove that the information was divulged: circumstantial evidence, that a person closely linked to a known insider dealt in the relevant securities shortly before the information in question was made public, is all that the prosecutor is likely to have. One possible solution, to impose a reverse burden of proof in such circumstances, would seem unreasonable. Even if the primary insider did, in fact, respect the confidentiality of his position and the information that went with it, it will be next to impossible to prove that: the difficulty of proving a negative is well known. It may be that a workable solution would be the French approach of imposing on primary insiders an additional duty to take all reasonable measures to prevent the inside information being abused.[39] In the context of the *Bekaert and Storme* case, this would have enabled the prosecutor to argue that even if the wife did not, in fact, inform her husband about the planned takeover, she should have taken care to see that he did not, albeit in ignorance, deal in the shares. She might still have claimed that she did not know, until it was too late, that he had bought the shares, but it would have been down to her to show what efforts she had made to prevent him from doing so.

The position of legal entities is covered by Article 182(2) of the Law, which follows the Directive very closely. Where the insider is a legal entity, liability is imposed on the natural persons who take part in the decision to carry out the transaction in question. The French version of the paragraph copies the Directive exactly. The Flemish version, however, refers to the natural persons "who co-decide to carry out the transaction". This would suggest that the Law focuses not on an individual director, but on the board as a whole, or at least presumes that it will be a group of persons, not merely one acting alone, that will decide to carry out the transaction on behalf of the company. Collective responsibility is very definitely envisaged.

There is something to be said for this: if one is considering the liability of a corporate entity, it does make sense to focus on the management, as a whole, who steer it. Such an approach will not in any way preclude one or perhaps a few individual directors or managers being prosecuted as individual insider dealers. But if it is established that there was a collective decision to engage in insider dealing, or indeed to commit any other criminal offence, it does seem perverse not to recognise that the offence was committed not only by a group of individuals but by the corporation itself. If that is the case, the corporation itself should be held liable, possibly along with the guilty managers. The arguments set out above in relation to the Austrian legislation apply equally here. Indeed, the concept of co-decision found

---

39 The Spanish civil provisions (although not the criminal measures) also impose this duty. Since, however, they, like all civil or administrative provisions, are not subject to the high standard of proof required by the criminal justice system, it is unlikely that they would have been necessary in the *Bekaert and Storme* case: it is most likely that, had the balance of probabilities been the standard, the initial finding that the wife had disclosed the information and her husband had dealt on the basis of it would have been upheld.

in the Flemish version of the Law would provide an admirable safeguard against the perceived risk of one renegade employee, or even director, bringing down the wrath of the criminal justice system on the entire corporation.

Denmark

The Danish legislation, the Securities, etc, Consolidated Act,[40] is extremely wide-ranging, far more so than its Austrian or Belgian counterparts. Anyone who possesses inside information, irrespective of how or in what capacity they came by it, is prohibited to buy or sell securities on the basis of the information or to encourage another to do so. Nor may they disclose the information to any other party except in the normal course of their employment, profession or duties.

The principal consequence of this is that no distinction is made in Denmark between primary and secondary insiders. There is therefore no variation in which acts are prohibited to which types of insiders.

Although it goes considerably further than the Directive actually requires, it is suggested that this is an admirable approach. At a stroke, it solves several problems. Firstly, there is no need, as under the Belgian legislation, for the prosecutor to decide whether the defendant was a primary or secondary insider and prosecute under the consequent provision – with the risk of an acquittal if he gets this wrong. The difficulty of a prosecutor having, against a decidedly unclear background, to choose between two offences which are very similar in nature but contained in distinct legislative provisions was demonstrated all too clearly in the UK for many years in the context of the money laundering provisions.[41]

Secondly, there is no need to wrestle with the question as to what is meant by persons obtaining inside information in the course of their employment, profession or duties. It does not matter whether the position was one that inevitably involved the obtaining of inside information or whether it was simply happenstance: if the person obtained inside information and either dealt in the relevant securities, encouraged another to do so or passed the information on in any circumstances other than those authorised through their work, they are guilty. The waitress and cleaner are covered just as plainly as the laboratory technician or lawyer.

Thirdly, it deals with the problem under the Directive of, where the defendant was not himself closely connected to the inside information, having to show that the direct source of the information was. By neatly side-stepping the whole question of where the information came from, the prosecutor is given a far simpler, and therefore easier, task.

Finally, it means that all insider dealers are liable to the same penalties, in contrast to the position in Austria. As seen above, it is far from clear that secondary insiders are any less culpable than primary insiders; further, primary insiders may arrange for others to do the actual dealing for them. While it was held that Bekaert and

---

40   Consolidated Act No. 168 of 14 March 2001.
41   See pp. 237-38.

Storme had not done this, there is certainly evidence that others have. A system, as in Denmark, under which, should this occur, both will be considered equally guilty and sentenced accordingly would seem nothing less than reasonable.

The term "any person" covers natural and legal persons alike. The drawbacks, considered above, to excluding corporations from criminal liability are therefore avoided.

Finland

As in Denmark, the Finnish legislation, the Securities Market Act (*Arvopaperimarkkinalaki*),[42] is very wide-ranging. The emphasis is not on the relationship between the insider and the issuer of the securities concerned, but rather on that between the insider and the information they possess. Officers and employees of the issuer are certainly covered, as is made clear in the guidance notes on the Act issued by the Financial Supervision (*Rahoitustarkastus*), the authority charged with supervision of the Finnish financial markets. This states that:

A person might have inside information because of his position or tasks, for example:

- member of the board of directors or a member of the supervisory board;
- managing director or deputy managing director;
- auditor or deputy auditor;
- employee of the issuer;
- employee of the business partner of the issuer;
- fiduciary of the issuer (i.e. lawyer or consultant).

The legislation also, however, covers the traditional "secondary insiders": anyone who knows or has reason to suspect that the information has been disclosed to them either without authorisation or inadvertently. These will include the classic "tippee" as well as those who overhear the information or come by it accidentally. Although the Financial Supervision guidance notes would seem to follow the European Commission's view that such persons are not considered to obtain inside information through their work, they will clearly be secondary insiders. This does not present the problems that it does in some Member States, however. Firstly, it is clear into which category the cleaner, waitress, etc, fall. But also, as in Denmark, all insider dealing offences cover all types of insider, primary or secondary. Being a secondary insider does not, therefore, in Finland, mean incurring only secondary liability.

Unlike Denmark, however, Finland does not extend liability to legal entities: only those individuals who actually conduct the transactions, or encourage another to do so, will be liable. (Unauthorised disclosure by its nature tends to be committed by individuals rather than legal entities in any event.) For the reasons considered

---

42 Act No. 1989/495 of 26 May 1995.

above, this is less than ideal. The Finnish provisions do, however, in other respects provide a preferable model to those of, for example, Austria or Belgium.

France

Unlike the other Member States considered thus far, France does not address insider dealing through criminal provisions alone, but also through civil/administrative provisions. That said, the administrative fines imposed can be severe.[43] The two approaches are contained in separate measures. The criminal provisions are found in Article L465-1 of the *Code Monétaire et Financier* (Monetary and Financial Code), while the civil/administrative provisions are found in COB[44] Regulation 90-08. It is helpful to examine these in turn.

Article L465-1 of the Monetary and Financial Code defines insiders in terms of three categories. The first consists of those with a senior management role in a company.[45] All Member States, and indeed the Directive, consider these to be insiders and their inclusion seems fairly uncontroversial.

The second category consists of those who handle inside information through "the exercise of their profession or functions". As in other Member States, the question arises whether these includes such persons as taxi drivers and waiters. This is not entirely clear, but it would seem that it does not. Firstly, it will be noted that the phrase is "through their profession or functions": unlike in the Directive or the legislation of certain other Member States, the word "employment" is not used. In French parlance, the term *profession*[46] does not extend to all occupations and will certainly not be generally considered to cover taxi drivers or menial workers such as waiters and cleaners. Furthermore, the fact that this category is linked closely to the previous one (they are contained in the same sentence) would imply that a close nexus is envisaged with the issuer of the securities in question. This will also, of course, follow the intention as stated by the European Commission.

As to whether legal entities are covered, the wording of the Article is not explicit: it refers merely to "persons" (*personnes*). Guidance may, however, be drawn from the legislation that preceded the Article, Article 10-1 of Ordinance 67-833 of 28 September 1967 (as amended).[47] This, defining an insider, referred to "legal or natural persons", making it explicitly clear that legal entities were covered. This

---

43 See pp. 204-5.

44 The *Commission des Opérations de Bourse* (Stock Exchange Operations Commission) or COB is the body responsible for regulating the French financial markets.

45 The term *dirigeants* covers not only directors in the English sense but anyone with a controlling role in the company: President / Chairman / Chief Executive Officer (CEO), members of the board, etc.

46 It should be noted that the term used in the French text is *profession*, referring to professional groups, rather than the more general term, *métier* (occupation).

47 This Ordinance prohibited insider dealing, with criminal penalties, from 1970 and was therefore the first provision in any Member States to do so. It was, in fact, amended

was a relatively recent development: it was only with the introduction of the new Penal Code in 1992[48] that legal entities could be subject to criminal liability: before this, as in a number of other Member States, this was reserved to individuals. The change did, however, merely permit criminal liability to be so extended: legal entities even now are only covered if the provision dealing with the offence in question so prescribes. As noted, the amended Ordinance did so prescribe and the wording of the current Code is certainly open to the interpretation that it does. This makes an interesting contrast to the approach taken by South Africa, where the general rule is that legal entities may be held criminally liable for offences committed not merely by their directors but by their servants,[49] but, as an exception to this, the Insider Trading Act 1998 defines an insider as "an individual" rather than the more usual "person".[50]

The third category is the widest, consisting of all persons, other than those covered above, who knowingly possess inside information. The way that such persons are dealt with is very similar to the Austrian provisions relating to secondary insiders, considered above, although the terms "primary" and "secondary" are not used. For the main offences of dealing or permitting another person to deal, they are subject to lower penalties than those in the previous two categories: a maximum of one year's imprisonment instead of two years and a maximum fine of €150,000 instead of €1.5 million.[51] As in Austria, but in contrast to the Directive, there is no requirement for a direct source: all that is required is that they knowingly possess inside information (and do not come under either of the previous two categories). But, unlike Austria, France does extend to this group the prohibition against unauthorised disclosure. Furthermore, for this offence, the penalty is the same for all three categories: up to one year's imprisonment and a fine of up to €150,000.

A comparison may therefore also be drawn with Spain: the French intention is that all persons knowingly in possession of inside information are to be prohibited from any of three activities in relation to it, but severe criminal penalties are only to be imposed on persons closely connected with the company concerned. As discussed

---

several times, up to as late as 1996, before it was finally replaced by the Law and (new) Ordinance creating the current provisions in the Monetary and Financial Code.

48 For some time after its introduction, this Code was termed "New Penal Code" in order to distinguish it from the Penal Code which had preceded it. The old Code having now passed into history, however, the simple term "Penal Code" is now used to refer to the post-1992 version.

49 Criminal Procedure Act 1977, s. 332(1). Conversely, any director or servant of a corporation held to have committed a criminal offence may himself be held criminally liable unless it is proved that he did not take part in the offence (s.332(5)). See Burchell, J.M. and Milton, J. (1997) *Principles of Criminal Law*, 2nd Edition, Kenwyn: Juta, pp. 386–87.

50 Cf., for example, s.120(1), (2), Firearms Control Act 2000. The fact that the term "person" is used even of offences which, by their nature, are more likely to be committed by individuals than by legal entities underlines the emphasis in the Insider Trading Act 1998.

51 The fine may, however, be increased – for all categories – if the profit realised would otherwise exceed the maximum fine.

above, in relation to the Austrian and Danish legislation, the ideal would be to draw no distinction whatsoever between particular classes of insider. If, however, one is to make such a distinction, the French approach would seem to be best way of doing so.

What is striking is that, in contrast to the position in other Member States, and indeed under the Directive, shareholders are not covered in the main categories, but as, essentially, secondary insiders. Since the Directive merely requires that those who possess inside information as shareholders be prohibited from unauthorised disclosure as well as from the actual dealing offences, France complies, since all insiders, primary and secondary alike, are prohibited from doing so. Nor does the difference in penalty contravene the Directive, which does not make any specific prescription regarding this. But although France complies, it is clear that, in this respect, its approach is very different. As discussed above in the context of the Directive's provisions, however, it is questionable whether to impose insider liability on shareholders is appropriate in any event. Given that it arguably is not, other than in a context, such as that in Denmark, in which all persons who possess inside information are covered, irrespective of how they came by it, France's approach in this area could well provide a model that other states could follow in the future.

Prior to 2002, under Ordinance 67-833, shareholders were not covered at all: as now, they did not qualify as primary insiders and there was no additional category of secondary insiders. The general legal opinion in France was, however, that secondary insiders, if they made use of the information, would be covered by the offence of *recel* under Article 321-1 of the Penal Code. This offence still exists and remains important in this context, not least because the sentences prescribed for it are considerably more severe than those for insider dealing: 5 years' imprisonment and/or a fine of €375,000.[52] The offence has been compared to the English offence of handling stolen property, although *recel* is in fact wider than that, applying to the proceeds of any crime, not just theft. It is defined as:

> ... the act of concealing, withholding or transmitting a thing, or assuming the rôle of intermediary in order to transmit it, knowing that this thing derives from a *crime* or a *délit*.[53]

> The act of knowingly benefiting, in any way, from the product of a *crime* or a *délit* also constitutes *recel*.[54]

---

52 Although this is substantially less than the €1.5 million fine provided for in respect of persons closely linked to the company, it remains over twice that to which a secondary insider is liable.

53 Criminal offences in France are divided into three categories: *crimes*, *délits* and *contraventions*, *crimes* being the most serious and *contraventions* the least serious. Insider dealing is a *délit*.

54 Probably the closest English equivalents would now be the money laundering offences of concealing, etc, criminal property or use of it under ss. 327 and 329 respectively of the Proceeds of Crime Act 2002. See Chapter 5. The French offence is, however, somewhat

It has been established that inside information qualifies as "a thing" for the purposes of the Article.[55] Since it is a criminal offence for an insider to disclose inside information, the information, once in the possession of the secondary insider, is the proceeds of a criminal offence.

The situation with regard to inside information accidentally disclosed is, however, more complicated. Deliberate disclosure of information by an insider, other than in the course of his professional duties or employment, is certainly an offence, but it is debatable whether criminal liability will attach to persons who, for example, hold a completely legitimate business discussion in a restaurant, but fail to notice every time that the waiter approaches. If it does not, the information the waiter overhears as a result will arguably not be the proceeds of any offence and thus, if he uses it, he will not be guilty of *recel*, merely of insider dealing. The opposing argument could be advanced that the information that the waiter overhears (or which the cleaner happens to see) is the product of an offence, if not of unauthorised disclosure of inside information, of failure to take due care to safeguard it.[56]

Where, however, a tippee[57] does receive inside information through a disclosure that does constitute a criminal offence, he must use it in order to commit the offence: mere receipt (even knowing and deliberate receipt) is not sufficient to constitute *recel*. The Criminal Division of the Cour de Cassation held in the case of *Pechiney* that the tippee must actually deal on the basis of the information. This, of course, is the second limb of *recel*, the knowingly benefiting from the proceeds of an offence. Until the tippee has actually dealt, he has not yet benefited. The question remains, however, whether a tippee would commit *recel* if he passed on the tip that had been passed to him. This is something that is not covered in the Directive, but it is at least arguable that it meets the definition of "transmitting a thing or assuming the role of intermediary for its supply, knowing that this thing is the proceeds of an offence". To date, the French courts have not ruled on this point, but it would certainly seem open to them to hold that it does. Mere encouragement by the tippee of another person to deal in the securities in question would seem not be covered, since it is neither transmitting the information nor using it, unless he then benefits from the third party's dealing, for example by sharing in the profits. The latter would, of course, constitute use, but it would also be far from easy to prove: it should be borne in mind that the French *juges d'instruction* can be far more ruthless than English magistrates in refusing to allow prosecutions to proceed if the evidence is less than

---

older: although its current form came into force on 1 January 2002 (still over a year before Part 7 of the Proceeds of Crime Act 2002), it has been in place in its essential form since the introduction of the New Penal Code almost 10 years earlier.

55 *Pechiney*, Cour de Cassation, Criminal Division, 26 October 1995.
56 For a discussion of this, and indeed all insider dealing offences, see Chapter 4.
57 Here, the term "tippee" is probably appropriate, since he will generally be the beneficiary of a deliberate disclosure.

robust. In such cases, therefore, a prosecutor would be rather better advised to proceed with a charge of insider dealing.[58]

In addition to the above provisions, cases of all types of insider dealing offences may be dealt with under the COB Regulation. Like Article L465-1 of the Monetary and Financial Code, this focuses, in the first instance, on those closely linked with the issuer. Articles 2 and 3 of the Regulation list three categories of insider: members of the administrative, management or supervisory bodies of the issuer, persons who have access to inside information by virtue of the exercise of their profession or duty and all persons holding privileged information as a result of the preparation and performance of a financial operation.

The wording is more expansive than the Code's provisions, but it is doubtful whether the actual scope is any wider. The first category will come within the management (*dirigeants*) class considered above, while the second is identical to its criminal counterpart. The third category has no immediate counterpart, but it is arguable that it is a specific category of the second. If a person holds privileged information as a result of the preparation and performance of a financial operation, does this not by definition mean that they hold it by virtue of their profession or duty: financial operations tend, by their very nature, to be prepared and performed by professionals who are engaged to do precisely this. It would appear, therefore, that the Regulation in this respect does not so much add a further category as highlight a group on whom, although they are already covered, it is considered appropriate to place particular emphasis. It may also be that, should such persons be discovered engaging in insider dealing, higher penalties may be imposed on them than on certain other types of professional: the penalties prescribed are the maximum and there will therefore often be variations between the levels actually imposed in particular cases. There have, however, as in many Member States, to date been relatively few cases brought in France (under either the criminal or the civil provisions) and this must therefore inevitably remain for the time being a matter of speculation.

As with Article L465-1 of the Monetary and Financial Code, shareholders are not immediately covered. They are, however, again as under the Code, covered by a further catch-all provision. Article 5 of the Regulation follows the Directive in bringing within its scope "persons who, with full knowledge of the facts, possess inside information, the direct or indirect source of which could not be other than a person referred to in Articles 2, 3 and 4". This will clearly include shareholders since they receive their information in one of two ways: in announcements and other presentations made at shareholders' meetings or from written statements sent to them in their capacity as shareholders. The presentations will often be made by members of the company's senior management; where they are not, they will certainly be made by close professional advisers. Similarly, the written statements will be compiled by professional assistants (accountants, analysts and the like).

---

58 Since in France, the prosecutor works closely with the investigating magistrate, this is likely in any event.

Who is an Insider? 61

This much is fairly unremarkable. What is rather more notable is that the Regulation's definition of secondary insiders follows the Directive in referring to a direct source. This was originally an extension from the criminal provisions, since the 1967 Ordinance did not cover secondary insiders at all. It is, however, narrower than its new counterpart under the Monetary and Financial Code, which, as noted above, not only does so but in general terms of possession, with no reference to how that possession came about. This creates a highly unusual situation: civil / administrative provisions tend deliberately to be drafted more widely than their criminal counterparts since their purpose is to catch those who cannot so easily be brought to book through the criminal justice system.[59] The record in France, however, is that the Regulation did not prove substantially more effective than the 1967 Ordinance in penalising insider dealing: although there were cases in which substantial penalties were imposed, a relatively low overall number were brought. Furthermore, where insiders were successfully prosecuted, the sentence that followed tended to be a fine rather than imprisonment.[60] It may therefore be that in the future, the Code and the Regulation will operate in parallel, with a decision made on a case by case basis as to which is more appropriate.[61]

The COB Regulation closely follows the Directive in that all insiders, primary or secondary, are prohibited from dealing, while only primary insiders are prohibited from disclosing the information to third parties. Again, the Regulation is in this respect narrower than the new Code. The two run in parallel, however, in providing that liability for insider dealing extends to natural persons and legal entities alike.

Germany

Until very recently, the definition of an insider under the German legislation, the *Wertpapierhandelsgesetz* or WpHG (Securities Trade Act) of 9 September 1998, as amended by Article 9 of the Act of 15 December 2003,[62] followed the Directive very closely indeed. Like the Directive, it divided insiders into two categories: "insiders" and "third parties with knowledge of an insider fact".[63] Although these are the terms

---

59 See pp. 201-4.

60 The *Delalande/Synthélabo* case was a notable example. See pp. 125, 218-19, 234..

61 There is, in fact, no actual requirement to use one or the other: unlike in, for example, the UK, both can be used in respect of the same case. The practice in France to date, however, has tended to be that a person proceeded against under one system is not then also dealt with under the other. See p. 234.

62 The provisions relating to insider dealing, i.e. paragraphs 12–14 of the Act, were, in fact, virtually identical to those found in the previous edition of the WpHG, that of 26 July 1994.

63 Paragraph 14(1) and (2). The Act did not refer to "inside information" as such, but rather to an "insider fact", emphasising that the information must be precise. See pp. 99-100 and page 99, note 29.

used in the Act, not "primary" and "secondary insiders" as in the Austrian legislation, the distinction is the same.[64]

This has now changed with the further amendment of the Act by Article 3 of the Act of 15 December 2004. The terms "insider" and "third party with knowledge of an insider fact" have been removed. Under paragraph 14(1) of the amended Act, all who are in possession of inside information[65] are forbidden to use it in order to acquire or dispose of securities, encourage another person on the basis of it to acquire or dispose of securities or disclose it without authorisation to another person. Although the phrase "in possession of inside information" is not used, it would seem to follow that to use the information, one must be in possession of it. Similarly, one can only disclose information which one possesses in the first place.

The paragraph does not, as paragraph 13(1) of the previous version of the Act did, make any reference to how the person acquired the information. This does not, however, mean that Germany has gone over to the Danish approach. Distinctions are still made as to types of insider, but in terms of the penalties imposed.

These are contained in paragraph 38(1). It begins by reference to the actual dealing offence, contained in paragraph 14(1).1. No distinction is made in relation to this: any person[66] committing it is criminally liable and faces up to 5 years' imprisonment.[67]

The distinction between different categories appears in relation to the other two offences: encouraging to deal and unauthorised disclosure. Here, although the term "insider" is not used, reference is made to the circumstances in which the offence was committed. Four categories are set out, each referring to the circumstances in which the insider possesses the information. In effect, the concept of primary insider is retained; indeed, the first three categories are copied from paragraph 13(1) of the previous version of the Act. Firstly, there are the members of any managing or supervisory organ or as a personally liable partner of an issuer or of an enterprise connected with an issuer. Secondly, there are those who possess the information by reason of their participation in the capital of the issuer or of an enterprise connected with the issuer. Thirdly, there are those who possess it by reason of their profession, business or function and when executing their appointed activities.

---

64 It may be noted that the prohibitions applying to "insiders" and "third parties with knowledge of an insider fact" respectively were identical to those applying under the Austrian legislation to "primary insiders" and "secondary insiders". Similarly, unlike under the Directive, but in common with the Austrian provisions, secondary insiders in Germany were not defined with reference to the source of their information.

65 The term "inside information" (*Insiderinformation*) has replaced the former term "insider fact" (*Insidertatsache*), although in practice, the meaning has remained the same. See pp. 98-100.

66 As is common in German legislation, the Act simply states "*Wer*" ("who" or "whoever") – there is no further qualification such as "a person who …".

67 Paragraph 38(1).1.

The fourth category is new and consists of those who have come into possession of the information through the preparation or commission of a criminal offence.[68]

Those in all four categories who commit the offences of encouragement to deal or unauthorised disclosure are criminally liable and punishable in the same way as those who actually deal.

The first three categories broadly follow the line of most Member States and, indeed, the Directive. Directors, managers, etc, are "classic" insiders and their inclusion is not controversial. Shareholders are similarly covered by the Directive, although one might point out that the arguments against this are given further weight by the French approach of considering shareholders to be at most secondary insiders and dealing with them accordingly.

In any case, in Germany, shareholders are not insiders *per se*: it is necessary for the prosecution to prove not only that the shareholder possessed the information and that the dealing or disclosure took place, but also that he obtained the information through being a shareholder. It could be asked where else he would have obtained it. He may, perhaps, also be a director or employee of the company and have come by the information by this means, but in such a case he will be an insider by virtue of the other two limbs. Alternatively, however, he may have obtained the information through its illicit disclosure by an insider (such as a director or employee). In such a situation, he will not be a primary but a secondary insider; that he happens to be a shareholder will not alter this. The consequence of this is significant, given the lower penalties applicable to secondary insiders other than in relation to dealing itself. The potential confusion that the approach causes is a further ground either to exclude shareholders from the category of primary insiders or, preferably, to abolish the distinction between primary and secondary insiders altogether.

In one respect, however, the Act goes further than the Directive: a person will not only be an insider if he obtains inside information through being a director, manager or shareholder (as the case may be) of the issuer itself but also if he does so through holding such a position in relation to "an enterprise connected with an issuer". This is defined in paragraph 15 of the *Aktiengesetz* (Stock Act) as a company in which the company in question has a majority shareholding, where the relationship of controlling and dependent company exists, which is of the same group as the company in question, in which the company in question has a participation coupled with supervision rights or with whom the company in question is a party to a special contract between business enterprises.

The first four of these broadly extend the application of the Act to companies in the same group: parent companies, holding companies and subsidiaries. The fifth, however, goes further: companies with whom the issuer is a party to a special contract between business enterprises. What this means in practice is not clear.

There remains the third category of insider: those who possess inside information through their profession, business or function or through executing their appointed activities, i.e. their employment. This clearly includes those who, although they play

---

68 Required by Art. 2(1)(d), Market Abuse Directive, 2003/6/EC.

no part in the management of the issuer, are its employees, although it is not confined to these. Lawyers, accountants, notaries, etc, will also be covered since the nature of their work involves the handling of inside information. Consider, for example, a lawyer who is asked to advise a company on a potentially extremely damaging lawsuit or an accountant who prepares accounts revealing heavy losses over the past financial year. Members of an advisory body are not, however, considered to be insiders.[69] In Germany, however, the question of which persons qualify as insiders through their work, is answered by a threefold test. Each of the three elements must be proven if a prosecution is to succeed.

First, there must have been a causal link between the person's profession, business or function and their obtaining of the information. A continuing relationship, contractual or otherwise, between the insider and the source of the information is not necessary, but there must be a definite nexus. The professional activity, business, etc, must have been the means by which the person came by the information. A comparison may be drawn with the shareholder considered above: an employee, lawyer acting for the issuer or whatever, to whom inside information is disclosed other than in the context of their work, will be a secondary insider.

Secondly, it must have been foreseeable that the person's profession, business, employment, etc. would result in their receiving confidential information.[70] This draws a clear distinction between the employee, lawyer or accountant engaged by the issuer (or related company) on the one hand and the barmaid, cleaner or taxi driver on the other. It would seem less than clear that the mere fact that someone works in a bar means that it is foreseeable that they will be given confidential information.

It is conceivable that there may be exceptions. There are bars and restaurants located in the financial quarter of Frankfurt, and indeed the business districts of other German cities, where it is well-known that the business community socialises. It could be argued that it is highly foreseeable that an employee of such a bar might overhear price-sensitive, but confidential, information. Even if this is the case, however, the barmaid will fall at the third hurdle: the information must be *bestimmungsgemäß*, i.e. it must have been directed at the recipient. This is, in fact, a twofold test. First, the recipient must have been intended to receive the information; it is not sufficient if they merely happened to overhear it or (as in the case of the cleaner) happened to come upon it. Second, they must have been intended to receive it in their professional capacity or in the course of their work. Even if an insider

---

69 Under the German system of corporate governance, in contrast to, for example, the English one, a company has two separate boards. One exercises a management function and may be compared to an English board of directors. The other, however, exercises an advisory function and is quite separate from the management. It has no real counterpart in the English system.

70 The general assumption seems to be that this means a person to whom confidential information is given in the course of their work, such as a lawyer. But it would seem clear that this category will also cover those who, in the course of their work, discover confidential information in other ways, such as the research scientist who may well be the first to know that a trial of a new product has been successful.

deliberately passes confidential information to a barmaid at his favourite watering hole in order to do her a favour, he can hardly be said to have intended that she receive the information *qua* barmaid. She will therefore be a secondary insider.

A situation that is less clear, however, is that regarding journalists. In the case of employees, lawyers, accountants, etc, it is understood that the passing to them of the confidential information is legitimate and authorised – not only does the person who actually passes the information to them intend them to receive it in their professional capacity, but so does the company. Consider, however, an employee at a chemical factory who knows that his company has been deliberately dumping toxic waste into the local river in flagrant breach of environmental laws. This is clearly confidential information (insofar as his company will certainly not wish it to become public knowledge!). It is also price-sensitive: its publication is likely to result in a sharp fall in the company's shares. Investors, particularly in a country like Germany, whose population views environmental issues extremely seriously, are likely no longer to choose to invest in the company and may well sell any shares they already hold.[71] Moreover, the heavy fines that the company may expect following the revelations will not improve the value of its securities. If the employee makes a quiet telephone call to a newspaper, he clearly intends the journalist to whom he speaks to receive the information in his capacity as a journalist. But it is equally clear that the disclosure is totally unauthorised. The question therefore arises whether the journalist is a primary or secondary insider.

Although the passing to the journalist of the information was without authorisation (and indeed would most certainly never have received authorisation), there are strong grounds for arguing that the journalist is a primary insider. As set out above, all the explicit tests of a person being a primary insider through their professional activities are satisfied; the requirement that the disclosure to them be authorised is merely implied. In addition, public policy suggests that it is desirable for the journalist to be a primary insider; to hold otherwise would mean that the firm's employee, in passing the information on to him, commits the criminal offence of unauthorised disclosure to a non-insider of inside information and is therefore liable to up to 5 years' imprisonment. It would seem very unlikely, to say the least, that any German court would take this view.[72]

Secondary insiders are no longer specifically referred to in the Act. Since, however, the three offences are forbidden to all persons, any person will be a secondary insider

---

[71] The seriousness with which companies view the public reaction to scandals is illustrated by the case of Medtronic, which in 1996 sought to recruit personnel specifically to handle enquiries from the public following revelations that employees in Germany had bribed doctors to buy Medtronic equipment. Although the company immediately dismissed the employees involved, it nonetheless remained extremely concerned about the publicity that had resulted.

[72] To hold the journalist as a primary, not secondary, insider would not expose him to any liability when he then publishes the article because, firstly, he discloses the information in the proper course of his work and secondly (and more fundamentally), the disclosure will by its very nature constitute an announcement to the public at large.

if they come to be in possession of inside information in any circumstances other than those set out in paragraph 38(1).2. This is considerably wider than the Directive, which defines a secondary insider as "anyone who, with full knowledge of the facts possesses inside information, the direct source of which could not be other than [a primary insider]". Under the Act, the only knowledge required of a secondary insider is the inside information itself. Unlike in France, he need not know that it is inside information, let alone that it came directly from a primary insider. This is draconian, but may be compared to the legislation of some of the other Member States, some of which make no distinction between primary and secondary insiders whatsoever. The Danish legislation and the Spanish administrative legislation apply to "anyone possessing inside information"; although the latter admittedly does not carry a potential prison sentence,[73] the former does.[74]

For such persons, the offences of encouragement to deal or unauthorised disclosure are punishable only with a regulatory fine[75] of up to €200,000. The position is therefore comparable with that in Spain[76] and marks a definite step towards a more civil approach, which did not exist prior to December 2004.

Legal entities may be held liable for insider dealing in Germany just as individuals can: the Act covers both. This reflects the general principle that imposes liability on legal entities in the same way as on individuals, as laid down in paragraph 14 of the Criminal Code and also paragraphs 9 and 14 of the Regulatory Offences Act (*Ordnungswidrigkeitengesetz* or OWiG).

Greece

The Greek insider dealing legislation, Presidential Decree 53/1992, is virtually a copy of the Directive. The definition of an insider in Greece is therefore precisely the same (indeed, the wording is identical) as under the Directive. The comments that may be made in relation to the Greek legislation are therefore the same as those made above in relation to the Directive.

---

73 Prison sentences are available under the insider dealing provisions of the Spanish Penal Code, but these are of very restricted application and only cover primary insiders.

74 Under the Danish legislation, knowledge that the information is inside information, particularly if the circumstances are especially serious, will be regarded as an aggravating factor and therefore result in a higher sentence: see p. 124-25. The inference is that insider dealers who do not intend to commit the offence, for example because they do not realise that the information they possess is inside information, may nonetheless be sent to be jail, albeit for a shorter term.

75 *Geldbuße*. The German legal system distinguishes between a criminal fine (*Geldstrafe*) and a regulatory fine (*Geldbuße*).

76 In Spain, however, secondary insiders are not criminally liable even if they deal.

Ireland (Republic) [77]

The definition of an insider found in the Irish legislation, the Companies Act 1990, broadly follows the Directive, although not as exactly as that of Greece. Sections 108(1) and (2) of the Act define an insider as a person who is either connected with a company at the present time or who has been within the previous 6 months. A person "connected with a company" is defined in subsection 11: it includes an officer of, or a shareholder in, the company or a related company. The former, as has been seen, is in common with all Member States and the latter with most of them. It also includes a person who:

> occupies a position (including a public office) that may reasonably be expected to give them access to [inside information] by virtue of
>
> (i)　any professional, business or other relationship existing between himself (or his employer or a company of which he is an officer) and that company or a related company or
>
> (ii)　his being an officer of a substantial shareholder in that company or a related company.[78]

A "substantial shareholder" is defined for these purposes as having a holding of 5% or more in the company. A "related company" is defined in section 140 of the Act as one which is a holding company or subsidiary of the company concerned, holds more than 50% of its share capital (or whose members do so) other than in a fiduciary capacity, and is entitled to exercise more than 50% of the voting rights or whose management is so closely linked to that of the company in question as to be indistinguishable from it.

The effect would seem to broadly the same as that under the German legislation, insofar as members of any company with either a substantial (let alone controlling) interest in, or which is in the same group as, the issuer will be covered as insiders as

---

77　Northern Ireland is, of course, part of the United Kingdom. Although, like Scotland, it is a separate legal jurisdiction from England and Wales, the insider dealing provisions of the Criminal Justice Act 1993 apply to Northern Ireland as they do to the rest of the UK. Although, until 1999, Article 2 of the Irish Constitution stated that "the national territory" covered "the whole island of Ireland", i.e. including Northern Ireland, Article 3 limited the applicability of Acts, "pending the re-integration of the national territory", to the *Saorstát Éireann* (Irish Free State, later Irish Republic) unless otherwise specified. Exceptions were made, in s.2 of the Criminal Law (Jurisdiction) Act 1976, in respect of certain offences, but insider dealing was never one of them. The Republic's jurisdictional claim to Northern Ireland was repealed, however, in 1999 as part of the Good Friday Agreement and, in any case, Northern Ireland is not in practice a significant centre for securities dealing. All references to "Ireland" in this book therefore refer to the Irish Republic.

78　s.108 (11)(c).

will those with access to inside information through a relationship between them or their company or employer and the issuer concerned.

The application to officers of, and shareholders in, the company follows the Directive and is thus fairly straightforward. What is striking is that the emphasis that the definition of persons who have access to inside information through their work includes persons in public office, not merely those in the private sector. Certain types of public officials will be covered by the legislation of at least most Member States, since they will have access to information which may have an impact on the value of securities of certain issuers. It may be suspected that the emphasis in the Irish legislation is a response to unease at perceived abuses of public office under previous administrations.

The requirement of a specific relationship with the company concerned is also noteworthy. Merely to focus on persons who occupy a position that may reasonably be expected to give them access to inside information would be broadly in line with the Directive and not dissimilar to the approach taken by, for example, Germany. To require, however, that that access must be by virtue either of a relationship between their employer and the issuer or a related company or of the person's being an officer of a company with a substantial shareholding in the company in question will mean that certain categories who clearly do have access to inside information because of their work will not be covered. Journalists will clearly not be covered since it is unlikely that a relationship will exist between a newspaper, TV company or radio station and the issuer concerned. The scenario of a journalist receiving a tip-off from an employee, considered above in relation to Germany, will therefore fall outside the definition.

Similarly, despite the reference to those in public office, most officials, at either central or local government level, will not in fact be covered for the same reason: the lack of a relationship with the issuer. They may, however, possess confidential information which, when made public, will have a direct effect on the price of securities of certain companies but is nonetheless too general in its application for a relationship with any one particular company to be held to exist. A notable example is a decision on altering levels of tax. An alteration to the tax on fuel will have an immediate impact on the profitability, and therefore securities price, of every road haulier, bus company, etc, in the country, while a rise or fall in the level of excise duty imposed on alcohol will have a direct impact on the brewery and distillery sectors. It could, of course, be argued that many of the companies affected by such measures are not, in fact, publicly listed,[79] but some may well be. Nonetheless, although the disclosure of such information by officials may well be prohibited as a breach of confidentiality or secrecy, it is not prohibited under the Companies Act. Nor will such officials be prohibited from dealing on the basis of the information since they do not fall within the definition of secondary insiders either.

---

79 To be classified as inside information in Ireland, the information must be capable of affecting the price of securities quoted on a recognised stock exchange. See pp. 102-3.

A secondary insider is defined in section 108(3) of the Act as a person who has received inside information from another person and is aware, or ought reasonably to be, of circumstances which render that other person an insider and, as such, prohibited from dealing. This goes further than the Directive in two respects. Firstly, the (primary) insider need not be the direct source of the information: if the secondary insider received it indirectly from an insider (and knew or should have known this to be the case), they are liable. In itself, this is unremarkable: it follows the approach of Austria and France, considered above. But secondly, whereas the Austrian and French legislation, like the Directive, requires that a secondary insider know what they are doing, under the Act, negligence is sufficient.

This is tempered somewhat, however, by the requirement that the secondary insider know (or at least be in a position where they should have known) not only that the source of the information is an insider but also the circumstances which make them so. The question may therefore be raised as to the position of a person who hears information which common sense tells them must come ultimately from an inside source purely on the basis that how else could the person(s) from whom he hears the information know of it. An example could include a person who has a friend who is an executive in Dublin, but who does not know the details of what that friend does: what is his position if the friend suggests to him that he would be well advised to buy (or indeed sell[80]) shares in a particular company? Whether he knows, or ought reasonably to know, of the circumstances that make his friend an insider is uncertain, since the Act does not make it clear how precise these circumstances need to be. To date, there have been no prosecutions, let alone convictions, for insider dealing in Ireland and it may be that this will therefore remain a grey area for some time.

The situation with regard to the liability of legal entities is also unclear. The prohibition is considered to be restricted to natural persons, but nowhere does the legislation state that this is the case. It may be that here, too, it will take a test prosecution to establish the position.

Italy

Like France, and indeed a number of other Member States, Italy deals with insider dealing by means of two provisions. Criminal sanctions are imposed by Legislative Decree No. 58 of 24 February 1998 (as amended by Legislative Decree No. 61 of 11 April 2002). This is then supplemented by administrative measures in the form of Regulation No. 5553 of 14 November 1991 of the *Commissione Nazionale per la Società e la Borsa*[81] (CONSOB). The supplementary nature of the CONSOB

---

80 Although, in discussions of insider dealing, it is common to think of persons who buy ahead of the announcement and thus make a profit, it should not be overlooked that the offence also applies to those who sell in advance of bad news being announced in order to avoid a loss. See Chapters 1 and 4.

81 National Company and Stock Exchange Commission.

Regulation is to be noted: the criminal and administrative provisions in Italy are not as distinct as their counterparts in France and Spain. Rather, the Regulation allows the CONSOB to take action where the criminal justice authorities fail to do so.

Under Article 180(1) of the Decree, three specific categories of insider are listed: those who receive inside information through holding an interest in a company's capital (i.e. shareholders), exercising public or other duties or exercising a profession or office. The first of these mirrors the Directive and thus the points raised above concerning shareholders apply equally here. The second, the reference to public officials, is arguably a specific sub-group of those exercising a profession or office and could be construed, as with the similar Irish provision, as merely emphasising that public officials can in certain circumstances be insiders. It is, however, of note in that it represents a widening of the previous Italian provision, Article 4 of Law No. 157 of 17 May 1991, which covered "Ministers or Vice-Ministers of the Government who possess inside information deriving from decisions taken by the Council of Ministers or inter-departmental committees."

This reflected the increased concern in Italy during the 1990s, when the Law was drafted, at corruption in political circles. It also arguably acted as a counterpoint to the corporate exemption of the government, the Banca d'Italia and the Ufficio Italiano dei Cambi (Italian Exchange Office): the point was made that while government departments were permitted to deal while in possession of inside information (in order to carry out acts of, particularly, monetary policy[82]), this did not extend to their officials making a private profit.

All public officials, regardless of their rank or position, are now considered to be insiders if their duties lead them to obtain inside information. Furthermore, there is not the additional requirement, as in Ireland, that there be an actual relationship between the public official and the company. The civil servants involved in the drawing up of new tax legislation, etc, are therefore firmly covered.

The third category, those exercising a profession or office, is very similar to that in the French legislation: as in the French Monetary and Financial Code, the term "employment" is not used. The waitress, taxi driver, etc, are therefore not covered, nor are journalists. Such persons will, however, be covered by the extremely wide Italian definition of secondary insiders.

This is found in Article 180(2), which extends the prohibition on dealing, encouraging to deal or unauthorised disclosure to "any person ... having obtained, directly or indirectly, inside information from a person referred to in paragraph 1". This catch-all addition reflects the intention of the Law as interpreted: the question is not, what was the insider's position but did that position provide them with means of access to inside information? That therefore, as in certain other Member States, no real distinction is drawn in the Italian legislation between primary and secondary

---

[82] This exemption is expressly permitted in Article 2(4) of the Directive and is found in the legislation of all the Member States.

insiders may be seen from the fact that the two categories are subject to identical penalties.[83]

The question arises whether this, in effect, places the position in Italy on a par with that in Denmark. It is arguable that it does. All inside information comes, directly or indirectly, from a person closely connected with the issuer of the securities in question: one of the drawbacks to the Directive's definition is that it requires the source actually to be a direct one. Thus, the Italian definition of secondary insiders will in practice be anyone who possesses inside information and who is not already covered as a primary insider: a parallel may be drawn with the new French legislation. Similarly, the fact that the Italian legislation, unlike the Directive (and certain Member States), prohibits all three insider dealing offences, i.e. including unauthorised disclosure, to primary and secondary insiders alike, would suggest that the focus is on all persons who possess inside information, not on how they obtained it. The provision of identical penalties for both categories, unlike in Austria or France, for example, is a further indication of this. It would, however, provide a measure of certainty if the wording of the legislation followed the simplicity of the Danish provisions, referring to "all persons in possession of inside information".

The Law applies equally to both natural persons and legal entities.

Luxembourg

As in Greece, the definition of an insider in the Luxembourg legislation, the Law of 3 May 1991, is identical to that in the Directive.

Netherlands

The definition of an insider under the Netherlands legislation, the Securities Trade Supervision Act (*Wet toezicht effectenverkeer*) of 1995 is very simple: any person in possession of inside information. No distinction is made, therefore, between primary and secondary insiders.

Since the Act was passed in 1995, considerable disquiet was expressed as to its effectiveness. The doubts focused particularly on the ending of the first prosecution for insider dealing, *HCS*[84] in 1995, in acquittal[85] and the fact that there has only been one conviction since.[86] The Act was therefore amended in 1999. Among the aims

---

83 The penalties provisions do not refer to particular categories of insiders. See pp. 127-29.

84 Hoge Raad, 27 June 1995, Netherlands Jurisprudence (NJ) 1995, 662.

85 It is perhaps interesting that, in financial services cases in particular, an acquittal so often gives rise to the view that the law and/or the criminal justice system has failed rather than that the defendant was not guilty! One may compare the reaction to the HCS case to the criticism levelled in the UK at the Serious Fraud Office and the calls for fraud trials no longer to be tried by jury following the acquittals of such defendants as Kevin and Ian Maxwell.

86 *Weweler*, Rb. Amsterdam, 3 January 1997.

of the amendments was to make insider dealing easier to prove, since it was felt that the difficulty of proving all the elements required under the Act in its 1995 form was a major reason for the low conviction rate. Prior to April 1999, it was necessary to prove not only that the defendant possessed inside information but also that it was reasonably foreseeable that the dealing would result in a profit or, alternatively, in an avoidance of loss (although it was not necessary to prove that any profit was actually realised or loss avoided). This requirement has now been abolished: if a person in possession of inside information deals in the securities to which it relates, they are guilty.[87] In this respect, it follows the Danish approach and, for the reasons discussed above in relation to other Member States, provides a very useful model.

Portugal

The Portuguese legislation, Article 378 of the *Código dos Valores Mobiliários* (Securities Code) of 13 November 1999,[88] does not use the term insider dealing as such but rather "information abuse". The phrase demonstrates, perhaps most clearly of all the Member States,[89] that insider dealing is a form of market abuse: it consists of a person abusing their possession of inside information by profiting from it. Like the Directive, the Code distinguishes between primary and secondary insiders. Curiously, however, the term used for primary insiders is "a person who has information from an inside source"; as discussed above, it is arguable that all insiders, primary or secondary, have information that ultimately comes from an inside source. Articles 378(1) and (2) of the Code give, however, a clear definition of what is covered: a person has information from an inside source if he has it by virtue of his membership of the administrative, management or supervisory bodies of the issuer of transferable securities, of his holding in the issuer's capital, of the exercise of an employment or profession (whether occasional or permanent), to the mentioned issuer or to another entity or of the exercise of a civil service or public duties.

The first two of these categories follow the Directive fairly closely: persons with access to inside information through being either a director or manager of the issuer or a shareholder. The third, persons who obtain inside information through their work, is similar, but has some important differences. The Directive, at least implicitly, requires the work to be such as has a connection with the issuer; as seen above, the Irish legislation goes further and explicitly requires this in decidedly restrictive terms. In contrast, the Portuguese legislation makes it expressly clear

---

87 The amending law of 1 April 1999 has also introduced other changes, among them the definition of inside information: see pp. 106-7.

88 Last amended by Decree-Law No. 66/2004 of 24 March 2004.

89 At least in their criminal legislation. The civil/administrative provisions in Part VIII of the UK's Financial Services and Markets Act 2000 explicitly use the term "market abuse"; indeed, the UK's civil counterpart to insider dealing is termed "misuse of information": see pp. 212 ff.

that an insider's profession or employment need not be linked to the issuer but may be for "another entity". Furthermore, it need not be long-term in nature: the Article refers to it being "occasional or permanent". Casual work, if it leads to the obtaining of inside information, is therefore covered. This will therefore cover such non-employed advisors as a lawyer who acts for the company in relation to a specific deal or an accountant whose sole function in relation to the company is to prepare its annual accounts. Also covered, however, will be, for example, a temporary secretary, taken on for a week or perhaps only a day. There is little doubt that Portugal is not unique in this respect: the Directive and indeed the legislation of all the Member States hold such persons to be primary insiders. But it is the Portuguese legislation which states their position most explicitly.

Furthermore, the paragraph stresses that, where the access to inside information is through the insider's work (of whatever kind), that work need not be linked to the issuer but to "any other entity". In the classic scenario of the takeover, therefore, an employee of the bidding company who buys shares in the target company will be covered just as much as the target's staff. A more distant link would be an employee in the research and development department of a company, who owns shares in one of the firm's competitors.[90] If he discovers a breakthrough that will place his firm as the established market leader and therefore sells the shares before the breakthrough's announcement causes their value to fall, he will be liable as an insider.

The combination of the reference to "occasional" workers, the inclusion of the term "employment", not merely "profession or office", and the fact that the work need not be for the issuer concerned but for any entity will also mean that waitresses will be covered: if they overhear information from customers, they obtain it through their employment. That that employment is casual and not for the company in question is irrelevant. It is even more evident that cleaners will be covered: their employment, even though it is possibly only 2 hours per night, is directly linked to the issuer.

An interesting point on this concerns taxi drivers. They are often self-employed; where they are, they therefore do not obtain information which they may overhear through their "employment". But is driving a taxi a "profession"? It is arguable that it is not: it is an occupation, but some might claim that it is not a profession on the same level as an accountant or lawyer. Portugal may not have the clear class distinctions that France does,[91] but, like many civil law jurisdictions, the concept of the "professions" is not entirely absent. The point is a difficult one and since, as in a number of Member States, there have been no actual cases in Portugal, one cannot look to the courts for guidance. It is suggested, however, that to exclude

---

90 This would hardly be considered by the firm's management as a demonstration of loyalty, but the scenario is not totally unthinkable, particularly where skilled staff move from firm to firm within a fairly specialist sector.

91 It is notable that, after well over 200 years under the banner of not only liberty but equality and fraternity, French society still has a clear class-consciousness with a definite concept of "professions": see pp. 43 and 56.

all but a small group of the self-employed would be absurd. It would mean, for example, that a taxi driver employed by a company who overheard a conversation would be covered but one working for himself would not. Although the extremely wide phrasing of the rest of the paragraph would indicate that this is not what the legislators intended, it must be accepted that carelessly drafted legislation can lead to just such a result. It is therefore suggested that the use of the term "occupation" (*ocupação*) rather than "profession" (*profissão*) would provide a welcome degree of certainty, as well as ensuring that all those who obtain information through their work are covered in the same way.

Interestingly, though, the provisions relating to directors and managers are far more restrictive than those for employees and professionals. In contrast to these, those in a management position are only prohibited from using inside information to deal in the securities of their own firm. Yet in the above scenario, the capacity of a member of the company's board to sell shares in a competitor and thus avoid loss will be as great as that of the employee. Indeed, since board members tend to have higher incomes, and thus own greater numbers of shares, than many of their employees, their capacity is arguably greater. This provision also creates a contradiction: many senior managers are in fact employees of their firm. Persons such as the Chief Executive Officer (CEO) and the members of the Board of Directors will not be employees, but others, such as the Managing Director, are. The same applies where a large firm has a number of branches, offices or factories: all members of the management of these will almost certainly be employed by the company since the external directors will be located at the head office. If a manager of such a branch comes into possession of inside information, as he well might, does he obtain it by virtue of being a manager or by virtue of his employment? On this will hang the extent to which he is restricted from dealing on the basis of it.

The fourth category is those with access to inside information by virtue of their holding public office. This is very similar to the reference to public officials in the Italian legislation. It should, however, be noted that while, in Italy, the original legislation referred specifically to ministers of the national government, other public officials only being included as from 2002, its Portuguese counterpart extended from the start to all ministers, officials and civil servants, at national and local level alike.

Secondary insiders are covered by Article 378(3) of the Code. The definition is very similar to that in the Directive:

> any individual, not covered by the previous sub-articles, who having knowledge of any privileged information received from any individual described in sub-articles 1 or 2.

It is not clear whether the source need be direct. Guidance may, however, be drawn from the previous legislation, Article 666(3) of the Securities Market Code, which referred to information "the direct or indirect source of which could not be other than a person referred to in paragraph 1". If this meaning is retained, it will be a welcome improvement, adopted also by a number of other Member States. A departure from the previous Code, however, is that the new provision no longer states that a secondary insider is "fully aware that the information is inside information".

Since insider dealing, whether by a primary or secondary insider, carries criminal penalties in Portugal, the prohibition only applies to natural persons. It is a general principle of Portuguese criminal law that no criminal liability may be imposed on a legal entity.[92] An exception may be made to this rule, but only where the relevant legislation explicitly states this. There is no such explicit statement in the Code.

Spain

Like France, Spain has two separate pieces of legislation relating to insider dealing, one criminal in nature and the other administrative. They are striking in their contrast to one another: the administrative legislation is very wide-ranging while the scope of its criminal counterpart is extremely narrow.

The criminal provisions are found in Article 285 of the Penal Code. In terms of its application, it is more restricted than that of every other Member State. Not only does it apply only to primary insiders (secondary insiders do not incur any criminal liability in Spain), but there is also a threshold profit requirement: the dealing must result in a profit of at least €450,759.08.[93] Insider dealing which does not meet both of these conditions, is covered solely by the much more extensive administrative legislation.

The definition of an insider under the Penal Code is a person who has obtained inside information through his employment or professional or commercial activity. Shareholders are therefore not covered. They will, of course, be covered where they are also directors or employees or have some other professional or commercial link, but they must have received the inside information through their professional or business status, not *qua* shareholder. No distinction is, however, made between directors and employees, although it could be argued that the minimum profit requirement means that only quite highly paid employees will have an income that allows them to deal on this scale. Non-employed advisors, consultants, etc, such as lawyers or accountants, are also covered, as are members of the government and civil servants, whether at central, regional or local level, and journalists.

In contrast, the administrative legislation, the *Ley del Mercado de Valores* (Securities Market Law), defines an insider as "any person who possesses inside information".[94] As in the Danish and Dutch legislation, there is no distinction between primary and secondary insiders: the same prohibition applies to all, save that it only carries civil/administrative, not criminal, penalties. The one exception is that, under

---

92 Cf. the position in France before the introduction of the New Penal Code.
93 Previously Pts. 75 million. Where the information is disclosed to a third party, the insider must similarly intend a profit of at least this amount to result. An alternative intention to cause profit or loss to another will, however, also suffice, although the same minimum threshold applies.
94 Article 81.2.

Article 81.1 of the Law, those who, through their profession, employment or duties (especially where the work or professional activity is linked to the securities markets), possess information relating to the securities markets are under an additional duty to safeguard that information. In particular, they may not allow others to misuse it.[95]

As regards the position of legal entities, criminal liability is not applied to the company itself. Article 95 of the Penal Code, however, provides that in certain circumstances, where an offence is committed by a legal entity, the directors and managers may be held to be liable.[96] In contrast, the administrative provisions apply equally to both natural and legal persons. Article 81.1 of the Law refers to "any person or entity", while "any person" in Article 81.2 similarly means any natural or legal person. Where the circumstances justify it, however, a legal entity and individuals may incur joint and several liability for the offence. The fines available under the Law where a company is held liable can be severe: up to 5% of the capital of the company or, where the company forms part of a group, of the entire group and thus the effect of such joint and several liability may be considerable.[97]

Sweden

The definition of an insider under the Swedish legislation broadly speaking follows the Directive. Paragraph 4 of the *Insiderlagen* (Insider Act) defines a primary insider as a person who:

> 1) has access to information by virtue of the exercise of his employment, assignment or other position from which knowledge of circumstances of importance for the price of financial instruments normally follows; or
>
> 2) owns shares in the company concerned.

The latter category is in line with the Directive and hence common to most Member States. Although, as seen above, there is a strong argument that shareholders should only be held to be insiders if the focus, as in Denmark and the Netherlands, is solely on whether a person possesses inside information, not how they obtained it, there is no comment on this specifically in relation to the Swedish provisions that has not already been made more generally.

The former category, although also similar to the Directive, makes clear that only those types of work are covered that may be expected to give rise to access to inside information. As seen above, this has been held to be the intention of the Directive and is the approach taken by several, although not all, other Member States. Bar staff and the like will therefore fall outside the definition, as will receptionists. Secretaries, however, because they work that much more closely with those members

---

95 See pp. 210-11..
96 Cf. the concept of the "directing mind and will" in English criminal law.
97 The minimum fine under the Law for insider dealing is €30,050.60 (previously Pts. 5 million). For more details of the penalties available under the Law, see pp. 209-11 and 227.

of the company who handle inside information, may well be covered. Much will depend on who they work for: the PA to a director will almost certainly be covered, the secretary to a junior employee may not be.

The definition of secondary insiders is set out at paragraph 4(3): they are persons who possess information which they either received from a primary insider or which otherwise came into their position without authorisation. Although, as under the Directive, secondary insiders are not prohibited from disclosing the information, the latter heading, "which otherwise came into their position without authorisation", will mean that, where a person is passed information (whether deliberately or not) from a person or persons who themselves are secondary insiders, they will be prohibited from dealing on the basis of it. The uncertain position that pertains in some Member States, where a waiter overhears two people discussing what is clearly inside information but does not and cannot reasonably know the position that they hold, does not therefore exist in Sweden: anyone who holds inside information that they should not have is prohibited from dealing just as much as the primary insider who obtained the information legitimately.

Legal entities are dealt with obliquely: the emphasis is on the individuals who personally conclude the transaction. An insider, primary or secondary, is prohibited from dealing either on his own account or on behalf of another. That other may be a natural or legal person: dealing by an insider on behalf of either is prohibited. This approach does mean, however, that it will be the individual, not the legal entity for whom he deals, who will ultimately be punished.

United Kingdom

In the UK, insider dealing has, since December 2001, been dealt with by means both of criminal legislation, Part V of the Criminal Justice Act 1993, and civil/administrative provisions contained in Part VIII of the Financial Services and Markets Act 2000.[98]

The introduction of the 2000 Act does not, however, alter the criminal provisions of the 1993 Act.[99] It is therefore helpful, as with the other Member States with a "twin-track" approach to insider dealing, to deal with each in turn.

Very much in line with the Directive (which it was introduced to implement), section 57 of the 1993 Act defines a primary insider as a person in possession of inside information which they have received either through being a director,

---

98 Although the Act was passed in June 2000, much of it, including the provisions relating to "misuse of information", only came into force some 17 months later. It was said at the time that the main reason for the delay was to give the new Financial Services Authority time to consult and then draw up its new regulations.

99 Part VIII of the 2000 Act (the Part dealing with market abuse) supplements Part V of the 1993 Act: it does not replace it. The criminal insider dealing provisions, contained in the 1993 Act, remain in force; indeed, there is every prospect that they will remain so for the foreseeable future.

employee or shareholder of an issuer or through their professional activities, office or employment.

A secondary insider is any person who has received inside information from a primary insider. The primary insider need not, however, be the direct source of the information; to have received it indirectly from such a person will suffice. As discussed in relation to, for example, Italy, it could be argued that the net effect is the same as in those Member States where an insider is defined, without any further qualification, as any person in possession of inside information. Certainly the UK, in common with these Member States, imposes the same prohibitions (and indeed penalties) on primary and secondary insiders alike. In this respect, it may therefore be advocated as a model, although the simplicity of the Danish and Dutch legislation would still be welcome.

It should be noted, however, that to incur liability as an insider (primary or secondary) in the UK, a person must know both that the information is inside information and that it came, directly or indirectly, from an inside source. It has been suggested that the requirement for the prosecution to prove this knowledge beyond reasonable doubt is a major reason why there have been so few convictions for insider dealing in the UK. Although the UK's record for successful prosecutions of insider dealing is admittedly less than impressive,[100] it does remain better than that of any other Member State, including those where mere dealing when in possession of inside information is sufficient to incur liability.

As regards legal entities, it is an established principle of criminal law in the UK that liability extends to them just as it does to natural persons. In such cases, however, the directors, or at least the managing director, will invariably be liable as well. This is not merely in order to comply with the Directive – it is a general principle, not one applying to insider dealing alone – but due to the doctrine according to which a legal entity may be held criminally liable. This requires that the "directing mind" of the company take the decision to commit the criminal act; the rationale is that a legal entity by definition does not have a mind of its own and therefore its mind is that of the person who controls or directs it.[101]

The Financial Services and Markets Act 2000 introduced, for the first time, financial penalties (effectively civil or administrative fines) for market abuse, a new term itself created by the Act, although it has since been taken up by the European Commission in the creation of the new Market Abuse Directive.[102] Market abuse includes insider dealing, together with two other principal categories, but, to distinguish it from the criminal provisions, a separate term, "misuse of information"

---

[100] Insider dealing was first criminalised in the UK under the Companies Act 1980. Since then, a period of over 25 years, there have been less than 30 convictions despite the 250,000 transactions reported by the London Stock Exchange each year as giving rise to a suspicion of insider dealing. Of those convictions which have been secured, the majority have followed pleas of guilty.

[101] See p. 50 and notes 32 and 33.

[102] Directive 2003/6/EC, implemented by Directive 2004/72/EC.

is used.[103] This is not mere semantics: although the criminal and civil/administrative offences overlap considerably, they are not identical.

Perhaps more strongly than in any other Member State, the definition of an insider under the 2000 Act is inextricably bound up with that of the substantive offence itself, considered in detail in Chapter 7.[104] This is because the focus of the provisions is on the behaviour, not the person who engages in it. In essence, the definition follows the Spanish approach: any person who possesses inside information will be considered to be an insider. In a departure from the old SRO regime, which only applied to authorised persons, the market abuse provisions apply to all persons, whether authorised or not.[105] Section 123(1) states:

> If the Authority is satisfied that a person is or has engaged in market abuse ... it may impose on him a penalty of such amount as it considers appropriate.

The use of the term "a person" indicates that all are covered. Other than this, however, little is said in relation to the position of the offender. Section 118(2)(a) of the Act simply says that market abuse may be based on inside information, as defined.[106] This is linked to the regular user test: if a regular user of the market in question would consider the behaviour to fall below the standard generally expected on that market, it will, provided it comes within one of three categories in section 118(2), constitute market abuse.[107] It is possible, therefore, that the FSA may hold that a regular user of the market would take the view that persons in certain positions should be restrained from dealing on the basis of information they acquire but persons in others should not. This is, however, a matter of speculation: virtually nothing is actually said. Further definition of market abuse, including misuse of information, is given in the FSA's Code of Market Conduct, which it is required under section 119 of the Act to publish in order to add detail to the general provisions found in Part VIII of the Act. Section 1.4 of the Code, however, says nothing about the position of the insider, focusing entirely on the definitions of inside information and the actual behaviour, including the "safe harbours" which, the FSA holds, will bring it outside the definition of market abuse. Even its remarks on the regular user test are concerned solely with the information and the behaviour. In the light of this, the only safe conclusion is that an insider, for the purposes of Part VIII of the 2000 Act, is any person in possession of inside information.

---

103 This term is not found in the Act itself, which does not provide any titles for the different categories of market abuse. It is, however, that used by the FSA in their Code of Market Conduct, part of their Regulatory Handbook.

104 See pp. 212-15.

105 If it so happens that the person concerned is an authorised person, they may, in addition, be subject to disciplinary sanctions under the FSA regulations. In no circumstances, however, may a person against whom proceedings for market abuse have been brought also face a criminal prosecution: see pp. 218-19.

106 See pp. 212-14.

107 S.118(1)(c). For a discussion of this test, see pp. 213-14.

It is submitted that this is decidedly unsatisfactory. The definition of an insider is crucial to the understanding of the offence itself. The Directive recognises this, as does the legislation, both criminal and civil, of each of the other Member States. The Financial Services and Markets Act 2000 should be no different. True, it could be argued that Part VIII of the Act merely sets the framework and that it is up to the FSA, in their Code of Market Conduct to provide the details; section 119 certainly suggests this. But, as seen, the Code is no more informative as to the definition of an insider than is the Act itself. In any case, an issue as fundamental as who qualifies as an insider should be dealt with explicitly in the legislation. If, as would appear to be the case, any person who possesses inside information will be an insider for the purposes of the 2000 Act, it is submitted that the Act should say so.

In the meantime, the FSA can swiftly amend section 1.4 of the Code of Market Conduct to make clear that any person in possession of inside information (which the Code does comprehensively define) will, if they either deal in securities to which it relates or disclose it other than in properly authorised circumstances, be engaging in market abuse.

There will be no need to add a provision relating to encouragement since section 123(1)(b) of the Act already states that persons who encourage others to engage in behaviour which, were they themselves to engage in it, would constitute market abuse, may be penalised in the same way as those who act directly.

Conclusion

In conclusion, therefore, certain Member States define insiders quite simply as any person who possesses inside information. Denmark and the Netherlands are notable examples; Finland takes a similar approach but does not include legal entities, while Spain, although it takes the same approach in its civil/administrative legislation, has, in contrast, a remarkably restrictive definition in its criminal legislation. The simple approach has much to commend it, not only because of its simplicity and clarity but because it best answers the fundamental objection that it is unfair that a person who possesses price-sensitive information ahead of the rest of the market should be able to profit from it.

Most Member States, however, take a more complex line, following the Directive. Directors and managers invariably qualify as insiders, as do others whose work inevitably results in the handling of inside information. But those who overhear or see inside information in the course of their work but whose work does not, of its very nature, inevitably lead them to do so, generally will not be covered. There are, however, Member States, such as Portugal, where it may be inferred that all types of employee are covered but it is not explicitly clear: hardly an ideal state of affairs from the point of view either of the prosecutor or of the employee. The Italian and Portuguese legislation makes particular reference to public officials, but it is arguable that these are merely a specific example of persons who obtain inside information through their work and therefore will be covered in any event.

Except in France, shareholders also qualify as insiders, although it is rather harder to justify their being singled out for particular attention. Although they do owe certain duties to the company and indeed the other shareholders, especially if they have a controlling shareholding, they are, unlike officers, employees and professional advisers, not placed in a particular position of trust. Further, far from receiving compensation for their involvement in the issuer (other than in the form of dividends and a raise in the value of the securities, neither of which is especially predictable), they invest their own funds and, if the securities fall, rather than rise, in value, stand to lose money in absolute terms. They should therefore only qualify as insiders under the regime just outlined, under which all liability is imposed on all who possess inside information, regardless of where they came by it.

The final point concerns the distinction between primary and secondary insiders. Not all Member States make such a distinction, but most do so, as does the Directive itself. This raises a number of problems. The definition of a secondary insider as a person who receives the information directly from a primary insider clearly leaves a considerable loophole: it allows a person who holds the information at second remove from the primary insider to do as they please. Although not all Member States take this approach, a number do. It is also common for secondary insiders not to be prohibited from passing on the information further and in any case to be subject to rather more lenient penalties. Given that primary insiders rarely deal themselves but arrange for others to do so on their behalf, this is a charter for abuse. The simple definition of an insider as anyone who possesses inside information and the provision for all such to be penalised alike if they either deal, encourage another to deal or without authorisation disclose the information is therefore the model that is to be commended.

Chapter 3

Inside Information

The Directive

The definition of inside information is to be found in Article 1.1 of the Directive. It is information:

- which has not been made public;
- of a precise nature;
- relating to one or several issuers of transferable securities;
- which, if it were made public, would be likely to have a significant effect on the price of the transferable security or securities in question.

This goes to the heart of insider dealing: making illicit use of information concerning an issuer or issuers of securities, which is not available to the public at large, in order to make a swift profit ahead of the crowd.[1] The first and third elements are therefore straightforward. The second and fourth, however, are more complicated. The information must be "of a precise nature". How precise and what is meant by this is not immediately clear and the Member States have therefore taken different approaches in implementation; the most radical being perhaps that of the German *Wertpapierhandelsgesetz* (Securities Trade Law), which until recently rejected the term "inside information" altogether, using instead the term "insider fact". As the term implies, only actual facts are covered: anything else, including opinions, falls outside the ambit of the Law. The Luxembourg legislation takes a similar approach.

This is perhaps surprising, given that the opinion of a respected expert, for example, can have as great an impact on the market, and hence the price of the securities in question, as actual facts. It could be argued that the opinion is based on facts and that if these are not in the public domain, the analyst's report will contain material that comes within the provisions and will therefore still be covered. This is all very well, but the problem still remains that the impact may still lie not in the facts themselves but in the analyst's assessment of them. Similarly, a report

---

1 The offences covered by the term "insider dealing" are, of course, more complex than this. See Chapter 4.

may contain predictions, which, while they are not yet facts (and indeed may never become facts), are certainly capable of influencing the value of certain securities. Suppose, for example, a financial institution has made large loans to a developing country; indeed, an important part of the institution's income derives from the interest paid on these loans. A report compiled by someone widely respected as an expert on the region that states that there is likely soon to be a change of government in that country and that the predicted new government will default on the loans in order to free revenue for internal spending, will be more than capable of causing a fall in the value of that institution's securities.[2] (It will also markedly affect the value of government bonds produced by the country concerned.) Nonetheless, a person who sees such a report before it is published and promptly sells his holdings of the relevant securities will, within the terms of the Directive, commit no offence.[3]

The fourth criterion, that the information must "if it were made public, ... be likely to have a significant effect on the price of the transferable security or securities in question" is also worthy of comment. Given the purpose of the prohibition, it clearly makes sense for information which is not likely to have any effect at all on the price of securities to be excluded from the prohibition. But once the information is required to be likely not only to have an effect but a "significant" effect, the question immediately arises as to how great an effect is significant. Is the test to be subjective or objective? If subjective, in whose eyes: the defendant's, the court's, the "reasonable investor's"?

The Directive itself does not address this issue and, of the Member States, only Sweden does so explicitly, laying down a 10% threshold.[4] It may be that the lack of clarity in this area is one reason for the general lack of success, experienced by all Member States, in prosecuting insider dealers.[5]

Another potential area of uncertainty surrounds the term "likely" to affect the price of securities. Once again, the question arises: likely in whose opinion? Generally speaking, the approach is that of the reasonable investor, although in Spain, the test is subjective: did the defendant know the likely effect of the information? It could be argued that where the offence was actual dealing or encouraging to deal, as opposed to mere unauthorised disclosure of the information, the practical difference is small: the very fact that the defendant dealt within a short time of obtaining the information goes to suggest that he knew its likely effect. But this nonetheless remains another area in which the Directive is unnecessarily uncertain.

---

2   During the 1990s, precisely this happened in both Brazil and Peru. The Brazilian default caused heavy losses to Midland Bank and led to the bank's takeover by HSBC.

3   The Directive does not itself prescribe that breach of the prohibition against insider dealing is to be a criminal offence. Insider dealing does, however, attract criminal penalties in all Member States with the partial exception of Spain. See Chapter 4.

4   Denmark follows this, albeit not in its legislation but as a matter of prosecution practice. See p. 93.

5   See Chapter 7.

Closely linked to the definition of inside information itself is the range of securities to which it is to relate. Article 1.2 of the Directive sets out the various types. They are:

(a) shares and debt securities, as well as securities equivalent to shares and debt securities;
(b) contracts or rights to subscribe for, acquire or dispose of securities referred to in (a);
(c) futures contracts, options and financial futures in respect of securities referred to in (a);
(d) index contracts in respect of securities referred to in (a).

The Directive goes on to specify that these are only covered when they are "admitted to trading on a market which is regulated and supervised by authorities recognised by public bodies, operates regularly and is accessible directly or indirectly to the public." In other words, unlisted securities, of whatever type, do not come within the Directive's remit. There is, however, provision in Article 6 for the provisions of the Member States to be stricter than those actually required by the Directive. The legislation of a number of the Member States (for example the Netherlands) does therefore cover information likely to affect the value of both listed and unlisted securities.

Austria

The Austrian definition of inside information is to be found in section 48(a)(1) of the Stock Exchange Act (*Börsegesetz* or BörseG[6]) of 1993.[7] It is very similar to that in the Directive:

> Inside information" is information which has not been made public of a precise nature relating to a security or to an issuer of securities, which, if it were made public, would be likely to have a significant effect on the price of the security in question.

The principal difference is that the Austrian legislation refers to information relating not only to issuers of securities, but also the securities themselves. Whether this makes any significant difference in practice is debatable. It could be argued that any inside information held by a primary insider,[8] at any rate, is likely to relate primarily to the issuer and only indirectly to its securities. For example, advance

---

6 Austrian and German statutes have official abbreviations, to which they are referred not merely for convenience, as UK statutes sometimes are, but also in legal literature and official documents.

7 BGBl. 1993/529.

8 Like that of certain (but not all) other Member States, the Austrian legislation distinguishes between primary insiders (*Primärinsider*) and secondary insiders (*Sekundarinsider*). See p. 47.

knowledge of a takeover bid will of itself relate to the companies concerned. It will also indicate, of course, that the share price of the target company is likely to rise sharply, but this is merely in consequence of the bid. Where the distinction could, perhaps, be of greater relevance is in the context of a secondary insider being tipped off. Where a director or manager of the company intending to make a takeover bid informs an unauthorised third person of the plans, this is clearly passing on inside information relating to an issuer (the target company).

But another path is, of course, for the (primary) insider to tell the third party that the share price of X AG is certain to rise sharply in a few days' time, without giving further details and leaving the tippee to draw his own conclusions rather than, as in the above example, spelling them out. Again, it could be argued that the Directive's text will cover this. Telling a third party that the share price in a given company is about to rise is tantamount to encouraging them to buy the shares, particularly if the insider knows or believes them to be in a position to do so. (If they do not, one may ask what the point is of passing on the information at all.) Moreover, it could equally be argued that information relating directly to the securities of a given issuer is a specific type of information relating to the issuer.

Nonetheless, the Act has adopted a "belt and braces" approach and such constructions are unnecessary to secure a conviction for insider dealing in Austria: both information relating to the issuer generally and that relating specifically to its securities is covered.

The types of securities covered by the Act are listed in section 48(a)(4) of the Act. As in the Directive, four categories are given, the first consisting of "primary securities" covered and the following three consisting of contracts, rights, etc, relating to them. Unlike the Directive, however, the list of "primary securities" is rather more detailed; instead of the general "shares and debt securities, as well as securities equivalent to shares and debt securities" of Article 1(2), the Act refers to:

- shares and stock;
- scrips;
- participating certificates;
- bonds;
- mortgage bonds;
- municipal bonds;
- deposit certificates;
- investment fund certificates.

The list then ends with a catch-all "and other transferable securities".

The second and fourth categories are identical to those in the Directive: subscription, acquisition and disposal contracts or rights and index contracts respectively (both in relation to the securities listed in category 1). The third, however, relating to futures contracts, etc, is more detailed: rather than referring simply to "futures contracts, options and financial futures", as the Directive does, it covers "financial instruments with a definite period in respect of securities referred to in (1), financial futures and options".

Belgium

Inside information is defined in Article 181 of the Law of 20 December 1995:

> For the purposes of this Book, "inside information" shall mean information which has not been made public of a sufficiently precise nature relating to one or several issuers of transferable securities or other financial instruments or to one or several transferable securities or other financial instruments which, if it were made public, would be likely to have a significant effect on the price of this/these transferable security/securities or other financial instruments in question.

This is very similar to the Directive, although the securities covered are expressed as "transferable securities or other financial instruments" in keeping with the aim of those who drafted the Law that the definition of inside information should be as wide as possible. It is, however, to be noted that the Article refers to information that is "sufficiently precise", not merely "precise" as in the Directive. The distinction is clearest when one compares the wording of the Flemish edition of the Law and that of the Dutch edition of the Directive.[9] The latter states that the information should be "*concreet*", i.e. concrete or definite, while the former uses the term "*voldoende duidelijk*": "sufficiently precise". The French wording is identical: "*un caractère suffisament précis*".

The securities and financial instruments to which the Law applies are now set out in Article 175(1) of the Law of 6 April 1995. The list is extensive:

1. a) shares and other similar securities, bonds and other debt instruments that can be traded on the capital markets, and
   b) all other securities that are traded regularly and which allow the acquisition of such financial instruments by subscription or giving rise to a cash settlement,

---

[9] For the purposes of legislation, Belgium has two official languages: Flemish (a dialect of Dutch) and French. The third language, German, only official received official status comparatively recently and German editions of legislation are therefore rare.

but not including legal tender;

2. parts in a collective investment entity;

3. the categories of financial instruments which are traded on a regular basis on the monetary market, called hereafter "monetary market instruments";

4. futures, including equivalent financial instruments giving rise to a cash settlement;

5. future rate agreements;

6. interest rate swaps, currency swaps and equity swaps;

7. options to buy or sell financial instruments referred to in this paragraph, including equivalent financial instruments which give rise to a cash settlement; currency options and interest rate options are included in this category.

In addition, Article 1(2) of the Law provides that other rights and titles may also be designated as financial instruments in the future.

No further qualification on the nature of the information is given. It has therefore been said that a mere rumour, provided that it passed the precision test, would be covered. This is, of course, important, since not only actual facts but mere rumours may be capable of having a significant effect on the price of a company's securities. Suppose, for example, a rumour is put out (perhaps by one of the company's competitors) that a senior manager of a company is being investigated for fraud. Or that the government of a country in which a company has major mining interests is about to nationalise its mineral resources (perhaps less likely now than in the past, but still not inconceivable). Both of these are likely to make the companies concerned less than attractive to investors, causing the value of their securities to fall. Indeed, this will be the case even if the rumours are not in fact true. Once it transpires that they were not, the value of the securities may well return to its previous level, but it may still have altered sharply in the meantime.

As mentioned above, the information must not have been made public. It is considered that this means that it must not have been made generally known to the "interested community". Precisely what is meant by "the interested community", however, is unclear. One practical definition that has been suggested is those persons who, if they possessed the information, might be likely to make investment decisions on the basis of it. This may be viewed as those in general whom it is foreseeable might deal in the securities to which it relates. This suggestion is not, however, in any way official; indeed, no official guidance exists. There has also been very little case law on the point and the courts have therefore been compelled to choose whatever interpretation seems appropriate. In the two cases that have dealt with the point, the Belgian courts have sought assistance in the case law of the US Federal courts, which is rather greater.[10] These cases define inside information simply as information which, if it were made public, would encourage the purchase or sale of securities. Given that this approach was adopted in both the Belgian cases, it would seem likely that it will be the standard definition in Belgium in the future.

There is, however, one major exception in the Belgian provisions: the "holding exception". This states that information which a holding company comes to possess by virtue of its management of companies in which it participates is not considered inside information, although this exception does not apply where separate legislation relating to the listing of securities on an exchange obligation requires that the information be published.

Here again, concern has been raised by a discrepancy between the French and Flemish texts of the Law. The Flemish text refers to a "*holding maatschappij*", which simply means "holding company". The French text, however, uses the term "*société à portefeuille*". This would seem to mean "portfolio company" and, in any case, it is specifically defined in an earlier piece of legislation, Article 1 of Royal Act No. 64 of 10 November 1967. The Flemish text of the Article uses the term "*portefeuille vennootschap*" and thus "*holding maatschappij*" remains without any statutory definition unlike its French counterpart.

The problem has transpired, however, to be one of theory rather than practice: the terms "*société à portefeuille*"/"*portefeuille vennootschap*" and "*holding*"/"*holding maatschappij*" are viewed as having the same meaning. In the case of *Office of Public Prosecution v Bekaert and Storme*,[11] the Ghent Criminal Court, located in the Flemish-speaking part of Belgium, used the term "*holding maatschappij*" without any reference to linguistic difficulties and Belgian legal opinion has taken the same view. Indeed, a Belgian multi-lingual legal dictionary lists "*société à portefeuille*" and "*holding*" as synonyms.

Linguistic discussions aside, however, considerable debate has surrounded the holding exception itself. Some argue that it is incompatible with the Directive, others that it is not. Essentially, Belgian legal opinion on this issue has divided into three schools of thought.

When the Law was before Parliament prior to being enacted, it was argued that the holding exception was justified by considerations 11 and 12 of the Preamble to the Directive. These state:

> Whereas, since the acquisition or disposal of transferable securities necessarily involves a prior decision to acquire or dispose taken by the person who undertakes one or other of these operations, the carrying out of this acquisition or disposal does not constitute in itself the use of inside information.

---

10 While Belgium only criminalised insider dealing in 1995, it has been a criminal offence in the United States since 1934.

11 Trial, Ghent Criminal Court, 27 September 1995; Appeal, Court of Appeal, reported *Le Soir* 5 May 1997.

> Whereas insider dealing involves taking advantage of inside information, whereas the mere fact that market makers, bodies authorised to act as contrepartie, or stockbrokers with inside information confine themselves, in the first two cases, to pursuing their normal business of buying or selling securities or, in the last, to carrying out an order should not in itself be deemed to constitute use of such inside information, whereas likewise the fact of carrying out transactions with the aim of stabilising the price of new issues or secondary offers of transferable securities should not in itself be deemed to constitute use of inside information.

The first of these two would seem to say no more than that the mere decision to conduct a given securities transaction does not constitute inside information. This would not seem a controversial approach and it is in any case difficult to see its direct bearing on holding companies: it will apply to any person, natural or legal, who has simply decided to buy or sell securities.

As for the second consideration, most of it will likewise not apply to holding companies, since their normal business is not buying and selling securities in the way that that of market makers is. Similarly, the qualified exemption given to stockbrokers does not seem to apply. It appears simply to say that, where a stockbroker is asked by a client to execute, on that client's behalf, a securities transaction, the mere fact that the stockbroker happens to possess inside information regarding those securities (or their issuer) should not prevent him from executing the order. Again, this is not controversial. If the stockbroker had previously passed on the inside information to his client, thus inducing the order, that would be another matter, but this is not what the Preamble is referring to.

The one aspect that may be relevant is the reference to the carrying out of transactions in order to stabilise the price of new issues and the like. Where a holding company does this, the Preamble clearly grants an exemption. It is, however, questionable whether most purchases or sales by a holding company of securities of companies in which they participate will be conducted with this aim.

Others argue that Parliament was wrong and point to consideration 5 of the Preamble. This states:

> Whereas the factors on which such confidence [ie. investors' confidence in the market] depends include the assurance afforded to investors that they are placed on an equal footing and that they will be protected against the improper use of inside information.

The holding exception flies in the face, they say, of such equality of investors: it means that, far from being dealt with on the same basis, holding companies are placed in a special, privileged category. On the surface, at any rate, this would seem to be true: they are being permitted to deal, albeit only in the shares of companies in which they participate, in circumstances where others would either be prohibited from doing so (because they possess inside information) or would not possess the requisite information that would enable them to take an informed decision to deal.

On the other hand, there is some considerable force in the argument that a holding company, whose sole activity is the possession of shares in the companies in its group, should not be restricted under the insider dealing laws from dealing in those shares. The Preamble makes clear that the object of the Directive is to prevent abuse, i.e. persons in a privileged position taking advantage of that position at the expense of those who are not "in the know". It is hard to see how the buying or selling of shares by a holding company could constitute such abuse – effectively, it is a variant on a company buying or selling its own shares. There are reasons to control this, but they properly belong in the realm of company law rather than financial services regulation.[12] Indeed, even those of the view that the holding exception is inconsistent with the Directive acknowledge that it is necessary (see below).

The third school of thought maintains that the holding exception is virtually meaningless anyway and therefore not worthy of concern. There would seem to be a certain amount of force in this, particularly as regards not dealing itself but the disclosure of information. Both Article 3 of the Directive and Article 183 of the Law make clear that the prohibition on the disclosure of inside information does not extend to disclosure made in the normal course of a person's employment, profession or duties.[13] Arguably, the passing of information, even confidential, sensitive information, between a holding company and other companies in its group will be made "in the normal course of a person's employment, profession or duties".

Dealing is of course more complicated. It can, however, be argued that, in the context of insider dealing, there is no real difference in practice between a holding company buying or selling shares in companies in its group and a company buying or selling its own shares. There may well be other consequences (for example, tax avoidance or even evasion) and there are certainly good reasons to control a company's dealing in its own shares, but, as mentioned above, these properly relate to matters of company law rather than insider dealing or financial services.

All schools of Belgian legal thought are, however, agreed that, whether or not it conforms to the Directive, the holding exception is necessary. The reason put forward is the definition of insider dealing under the Law, which covers a wider *mens rea* than does the Directive. Article 2 of the Directive prohibits an insider from taking advantage of that information "with full knowledge of the facts". In contrast, Article 182(1) of the Belgian Law refers to a person possessing information "which they know or ought reasonably to know" to be inside information. It is said that, unless special provision were made, this would prevent a holding company from doing anything. A holding company's sole business is to hold shares in and to manage the companies in which it participates. Furthermore, if it is to play an effective management role, it will routinely hold inside information on which its decisions will be based. There was a concern, when the Law was being drafted, that holding companies should not be prevented from continuing their role and thus specific provision was made to allow them to do so. In the case *of Bekaert and*

---

12   For example, in the UK, these restrictions are found in the Companies Act 1985, not in the Criminal Justice Act 1993 (which controls insider dealing) or the Financial Services and Markets Act 2000 (which more generally regulates financial services).

13   For a discussion of this exemption, see Chapter 4.

Storme,[14] the Ghent Criminal Court specifically upheld this view: both the defendants' convictions and the subsequent overturning of these convictions on appeal were on other grounds.[15] It would therefore appear that the Belgian holding exception is here to stay.

Denmark

Section 34(2) of the Danish Consolidated Act Act No. 168 of 14 March 2001, very much in line with the Directive, defines inside information as non-published information on issuers of securities, securities themselves or market information relating to securities which "would be likely to have an effect on the pricing of one or more securities if such information was made public".

Unlike the legislation of some Member States, the Act provides a definition of "published". Section 34(2) goes on to state that information is made public when "a relevant and general conveyance" of it has been made to the market. This is, however, not necessarily that helpful: what constitutes a "relevant and general conveyance"? The only guidance the Act contains is that information submitted to a stock exchange shall be deemed to have been made public once the stock exchange has disseminated it. This in itself is unsatisfactory: how is an insider to know, once he has fulfilled his obligation by disclosing the information to the stock exchange, when precisely the exchange has disseminated it? The issue is an important one. While it is right and proper that insiders should not be permitted to steal a march on other investors by dealing in the securities before the information is publicly known – this, after all, is the entire point of insider dealing legislation – it must also be recognised that legitimate trading is an extremely fast-moving business. The insider may well, therefore, wish to trade the moment that the information is in the public domain. Furthermore, in Denmark, as in certain other Member States, insider dealing is punished exclusively by means of criminal penalties: up to 18 months' imprisonment[16] or an unlimited fine. It is therefore not unreasonable that the time of publication of the information should be in the control of the issuer, if only so that insiders within the issuer know where they stand.

The information will also be "published" if it is available through the "established channels" used by traders operating on the markets. These will include the general and financial press and other media as well as electronic information systems such as Reuters, Bloomberg and the like.

---

14 Trial, Ghent Criminal Court, 27 September 1995; Appeal, Court of Appeal, reported *Le Soir* 5 May 1997.

15 For a discussion of this case, see pp. 52-53.

16 S.94(1). In particularly serious cases, this sentence may be increased to 4 years: see pp. 124-25. It is at least arguable, however, that an insider who believed, on the basis of his disclosure to the stock exchange, that the relevant information was already in the public domain when he undertook the dealing would be a less serious, rather than more serious, offender.

"Market information" is also defined: it refers to knowledge of the expected purchases or sales of securities by a third party. This may clearly have a considerable effect on the price of those securities. Suppose, for example, it becomes known that a major investment company plans to sell its entire holdings in a given petroleum company. If the holding is large enough, the mere act of placing such a quantity of securities on the market may well depress their value.[17] In addition, investors may well draw their own conclusions, which may or may not be accurate, as to the investment company's reasons. At the very least, the action will not demonstrate great confidence in the petroleum company concerned. Similarly, of course, news of a large purchase of a given security is likely to drive the price up. For this reason, many jurisdictions provide for an offence, separate from insider dealing, of market manipulation, which can in some cases carry prison sentences.

Finally, there are guidelines concerning the price sensitivity of the inside information. This is not found in statute, but in practice, a prosecution will only be brought by the Danish authorities if the impact of the information results in a change in price of the securities concerned of over 10%.

Section 2 sets out at considerable length the types of securities covered by the Act. These are:

(1) shares and other similar transferable securities;
(2) bonds and other similar transferable securities;
(3) other securities which are traded and whereby securities as listed in 1 or 2 above can be acquired by subscription, exchange or against payment in cash;
(4) shares in investment funds;
(5) money market instruments which are listed at a stock exchange as well as certificates of deposit and commercial papers;
(6) financial futures and similar instruments;
(7) future rate agreements (i.e. FRA contracts);
(8) interest and currency agreements as well as swaps relating to shares or share indices;
(9) commodity instruments, etc, including similar instruments which are traded against cash payments;
(10) options to acquire or dispose of a security which are covered by numbers 1–9 above and options on share and bond indices, including similar instruments

---

[17] A salutary illustration of this is provided by events on the Madrid Stock Exchange at the end of 1995. In the final 10 minutes of trading on 27 December 1995, two major European banks placed a considerable amount of capital on the Madrid market. The consequence was a fall of the Madrid index by over 2%.

which are traded against cash payment;
(11) transferable mortgage deeds conveying a security in real property or movables;

There is also a final, catch-all provision similar to that in the Belgian legislation: "such other instruments and contracts as may be specified by the *Fondsrådet* (Securities Council)".

Under section 34(1) of the Act, in order for such securities to be "transferable" and therefore covered by the insider dealing provisions, they must come into one of two categories:

(1) securities listed or traded on any stock exchange or traded in an authorised market place or in a similar regulated market for securities in a country within the European Union or in countries with which the Community has made a co-operation agreement

(2) unlisted instruments which are associated with one or more securities listed on a stock exchange or traded in an authorised market place.

Although the requirement that the securities be at least linked to a regulated market is standard, the Danish provisions are wider in scope than their counterparts in some other Member States. It is to be noted that the exchange concerned does not need to be in Denmark: securities listed on an exchange anywhere in the EU and even in certain third countries are covered. In contrast, the insider dealing legislation of most Member States, including Austria and Belgium, but also, for example, Ireland, applies only to securities listed on a domestic market. The same is true, albeit to a lesser extent, of the Swedish legislation and the wider approach taken in Denmark is an example of how the Danish legislation, although modelled on its Swedish counterpart, differs from it.

In addition, it is to be noted that certain unlisted instruments are also covered, provided that they are linked to securities which are listed or traded on an authorised, regulated market. Examples of these will be certain derivatives, which may be traded on too small a scale to warrant an official listing but which relate to shares that are traded much more widely and on a recognised stock exchange.

Finland

The Finnish insider dealing legislation, the *Arvopaperimarkkinalaki* (Securities Market Act), Act No. 1989/495 of 26 May 1995, is supported by explanatory Guidelines issued by the *Rahoitustarkastus* (Financial Supervision). Chapter 5, section 1 of the Act defines inside information as information which:

- relates to securities that are traded publicly and/or their issuers;

- has not been made public; and
- if were made public would be likely to have a significant effect on the price of securities.

The information may relate to either one or several issuers or to one or several securities. Furthermore, its potential effect need not be on the securities to which the information relates: if it is capable of having a significant effect on the price of any security, this will suffice.

That information regarding a given company may have an impact on the value of securities of other companies is not difficult to see. Suppose a report on a company (A) recommends the closure of one of its factories. The factory is a major customer of a local supplier (B), which, although relatively small, is listed on the stock exchange. Although the loss of its customer will not threaten B's viability, it will impact on its profits. The announcement of the factory's imminent closure will therefore be very likely to affect the share price of not only A but B as well. If the impact is likely to be significant, a person with advance access to the report who sells his shareholding in B, or who advises another to do so, will be guilty of insider dealing just as much as if he deals in the shares of A.

The securities covered by the Act are set out in Chapter 1, section 2. They are:

- shares and other interests in the equity capital of a company;
- rights to dividends, interest or the right to subscribe for shares;
- an interest in a bond or equivalent;
- shares in unit trusts.

Chapter 10, section 1 of the Act also provides that options and futures are covered by the Act (provided that they are traded on an exchange).

As mentioned above, in order to be covered by the Act, securities, of whatever type, must be "publicly traded". Clearly, securities traded on the stock exchange will come within this definition. As in Denmark, however, certain off-exchange transactions are also covered. Chapter 1, section 3 provides that this will be the case where either an intermediary is contractually bound to notify the issuer of any binding offer made outside the stock exchange to buy or sell the securities or the securities are traded by an intermediary on the basis of a public and binding offer to buy or sell.

France

As noted in Chapter 2, insider dealing is dealt with in France under two separate provisions; criminal measures in Article L465-1 of the *Code Monétaire et Financier* (Monetary and Financial Code) and civil/administrative measures in Regulation No. 90-08 of the Stock Exchange Operations Commission (*Commission des Opérations de Bourse* or COB). The term "inside information" as such is not used in either provision, which instead use the term "privileged". The kind of information covered by each of the provisions is, however, essentially the same. The pattern is that the definition in the COB Regulation is the more detailed, but the French courts have referred to it when interpreting the criminal provisions.

Article L465-1 of the Code refers to "privileged information on the prospects or situation of an issuer whose securities are traded on a regulated market or on the prospective price-movement of a financial instrument listed on such a market". As far as it goes, this is broadly in line with the Directive. Although the Article does not give a definition of the term "privileged", guidance may be drawn from that in the COB Regulation, namely information that has not been made public. This is the definition that the Cour de Cassation, France's highest court,[18] adopted in its interpretation of the previous criminal insider dealing legislation.[19] Such an interpretation certainly fits with the Code, which refers to the three offences of dealing, encouraging another to deal and unauthorised disclosure as taking place "before the public has knowledge of the information".

Similarly, the Code, like the Ordinance before it, does not state that inside information must be precise. The Regulation does, however, do so and, in interpreting the Ordinance, the Paris Cour d'Appel[20] has ruled that information must be precise if it is to be regarded as privileged.

Possibly the greatest divergence between the Code and the Regulation is that the Code does not refer to privileged information being price-sensitive. It is the only

---

18 The Cour de Cassation cannot, however, be termed the "Supreme Court". Firstly, unlike a Supreme Court, which typically sits in one location, serving the entire country, the Cour de Cassation sits regionally. Secondly, and perhaps more significantly, France has two sets of courts, the "judicial order" and the "administrative order", which run in parallel, neither superior to the other. The Cour de Cassation is the highest court of the judicial order; its counterpart in the administrative order is the Conseil d'État. There is no tribunal superior to either.

19 *La Ruche Méridionale*, Cour de Cassation, Criminal Division, 26 June 1995, considering Ordinance 67-833 of 28 September 1967 (as amended). This is the principal case in France in which the definition of inside information has been examined. Because the provisions of Article L465-1 of the Monetary and Financial Code are relatively new, only having come fully into force on 1 January 2002, no cases on it have yet come before the higher courts. In any case, because of the similarities between the former Ordinance and the Code, the judgments on the Ordinance do apply equally to the new provisions.

20 France has a two-tier appellate court structure. The Cour d'Appel is a regional court: there is a Paris Cour d'Appel, a Rennes Cour d'Appel, a Rouen Cour d'Appel, etc. It may therefore be compared to the German Oberlandesgericht rather than to the English Court of Appeal. The Cour de Cassation is a national court and is the highest court in France. Unlike, for example, the English House of Lords, however, the Cour de Cassation does not render a final decision as such; rather, in the case of a successful appeal, it overturns the decision of the Cour d'Appel, but then returns the case there for a final judgment. The judgment of the Cour de Cassation will, however, give a strong indication to the Cour d'Appel in question as to the decision it is expected to reach; should the Cour d'Appel simply repeat its earlier decision (as has sometimes occurred), a further appeal may be brought to the Cour de Cassation.

definition of inside information in any of the Member States which does not do so. The Ordinance did require, as the COB Regulation still does, that the information be "likely to have a significant effect on the price of the transferable securities in question". It would appear likely that, at least for the time being, this will continue to be the rule. The price-sensitivity of the information, after all, goes to the heart of insider dealing: the essence of the offence is that a person takes advantage of their privileged knowledge in order to make a profit (or avoid a loss). The wording has, however, been criticised as being too subjective a test. What does "likely" mean (and according to whom) and how likely need the effect be? Forecasts are by definition imprecise, at least until the time is reached when the forecast event either has or has not taken place. In practice, however, this has proved relatively straightforward: in deciding the likely effect of the information, the courts have looked to the experience and expertise of the defendant. This would seem to be correct. Certain information, regarding such things as a planned takeover bid or particularly good (or bad) end of year accounts are highly likely to affect the value of a company's securities, as may news of a breakthrough regarding the development of a new product.

The definition of "a significant effect" has, however, proved more problematic. What is significant is highly subjective. Again, extreme cases will be simple: if the price of a given security doubles in a single day's trading, it will not be controversial to say that this is a significant rise. Smaller rises and falls, which are nonetheless marked, are, however, harder to place on one side or the other of the line. It has therefore been suggested that a threshold should be prescribed along the lines of the Scandinavian 10% provision. This could be achieved by a guidance statement by the COB or by an amendment to the Code (or indeed both, given the dual regulation of insider dealing in France). Neither would be complicated. The Code's provision is, after all, itself a replacement of an Ordinance that was frequently amended between its initially being passed in 1968 and its final repeal at the end of 2001. The insider dealing provisions were only incorporated in 1970 and were amended as recently as 1996. As for the route of a simple guidance statement by the COB, this, too, would be effective: in Denmark, the 10% rule does not formally exist in the legislation but is rather the practice adopted by the authorities.

The Article uses the terms "securities" (*titres*) and "financial instruments" (*instruments financiers*) effectively interchangeably. "Financial instruments" were formerly defined as: shares and other securities conferring direct or indirect access to capital and voting rights, transferable by registration on account or by remittance, bonds representing a debt on their issuer, transferable by registration into account or by remittance, however, excluding commercial notes and treasury bonds, equity interests or shares of mutual funds and financial futures.[21] The simple phrases "securities traded on a regulated market" and "financial instruments listed on such a market" clearly cover these, but also, in their non-specific nature, all other transferable securities: if it appears on a regulated market, it is covered.

---

21 Law No. 96-597 of 2 July 1996.

Further, the Article simply refers to "a regulated market"; it does not prescribe where that market is, or by whom it is regulated. It therefore covers, in addition to those issued and traded in France, any securities that are issued under foreign laws or traded on foreign markets. The local terminology applied to such securities will similarly be irrelevant, although, even under the Ordinance, it was held that they would be covered if they were in nature equivalent to the categories described above. This illustrates the wide jurisdiction of the French provisions when compared to those of most other Member States: indeed, it is the widest of any Member State except Sweden. One of two criteria must, however, be satisfied; both are found, however, not in the Article itself, or indeed in the Monetary and Financial Code in general, but rather are general provisions of French criminal law under the Penal Code.

The first is that the offence have some connection with France. Under Article 113-2 of the Penal Code, a criminal offence is deemed to have been committed on French territory if a constituent act of that offence is committed there. That act may, however, only be a minor element of an operation, every other aspect of which is located abroad. This was demonstrated in the case of *Pechiney*,[22] one of France's best known insider dealing cases. This case involved securities listed in the United States and much of the dealing operation took place in Switzerland. There was, however, one telephone call made to Switzerland from a public call box in France. The Cour de Cassation ruled that this telephone call constituted a constituent act of the offence and that the French courts therefore had jurisdiction.

Even if no element of the offence is committed in France, the offender will often still be liable if he is a French national. Under Article 113-6 of the Penal Code, the French criminal law extends beyond France to any *crime* or *délit*[23] committed by a French national abroad. The one proviso is that, where the offence is a *délit* (such as insider dealing), it must also be a criminal offence in the jurisdiction where it was committed. Thus the Monetary and Financial Code will extend to insider dealing committed by a French national in any EU Member State (except, in certain circumstances, Spain[24]) as well as, for example, the United States or Australia.

The COB Regulation, in the scope of the securities covered, very much follows the provisions of the old Ordinance.

---

22 Cour de Cassation, Criminal Division, 26 October 1995.

23 Under French criminal law, there are three categories of offence: *crimes*, *délits* and *contraventions*. *Contraventions* are the most trivial, including such things as most road traffic offences. *Crimes* and *délits* are more serious and may respectively be compared to felonies and misdemeanours in the United States. Insider dealing is a *délit*: the French term for it is *délit d'initié*.

24 Insider dealing is only a criminal offence in Spain if, *inter alia*, it results in a profit (or avoidance of loss) of at least €450,759.08 (formerly Pts. 75 million). In other circumstances, it is merely a regulatory offence, punishable with administrative fines only.

Germany

The German legislation, the *Wertpapierhandelsgesetz* or WpHG (Securities Trade Act) of 9 September 1998, as amended by Article 3 of the Act of 15 December 2004, now refers to "inside information". This is defined in paragraph 13(1) as:

> a concrete piece of information concerning circumstances which are not publicly known, relating to one or several issuers of insider papers or to insider securities themselves and which is liable, if it were to become publicly known, significantly to effect the price of the insider securities.

The term "insider papers" covers "financial instruments". This includes securities and derivatives, but also money market instruments, in turn defined as claims, other than securities, which are commonly traded on the money market, as well as rights to subscribe for securities.[25] The securities themselves which are covered are:

- shares, certificates representing shares, bonds, bonus shares and options certificates;
- other securities equivalent to shares or bonds;
- shares in investment opportunities offered by capital investment firms or foreign investment firms.[26]

Derivatives, within the meaning of the Act, are futures and options instruments whose price depends, either directly or indirectly, on:

- the exchange or market price of securities, money market instruments, commodities or precious metals;
- interest rates or other returns;
- the price of foreign exchange.[27]

In addition, these securities must be capable of being traded on a regular basis on a market that is regulated and supervised by state regulated authorities and to which the public has direct or indirect access. They must further be listed on a stock exchange either in Germany or another EEA Member State[28] or be included in a free market.

The legislation makes clear the precise nature of inside information under German law. Anything that cannot be confirmed or established is therefore excluded. A person who deals on the basis of a rumour, or who passes such a rumour on to a third party, will therefore not be guilty of insider dealing, although they may in certain circumstances be guilty of market manipulation. The position of forecasts

---

[25] Paras. 2(1a), (2b).
[26] Essentially the equivalent of the UK collective investment scheme.
[27] Para. 2(2).
[28] The European Economic Area (EEA) consists of all 27 EU Member States plus Norway, Iceland and Liechtenstein (although not Switzerland).

and analysts' reports is, however, more complicated. Until confirmed, they are not yet facts: facts are, by definition, true.[29] Under the pre-2004 legislation, they were therefore not covered and dealing on the basis of them was not an offence. The new term "information" (*Information*) is, however, broader: in German as in English, information may be inaccurate. The Act itself recognises this: among the market manipulation offences is the "publication of untrue inside information".[30] This admittedly relates to information which is definitely untrue; the fact, however, that inside information is not necessarily true would suggest that information whose truth or falsehood has yet to be determined could be covered by the separate insider dealing provisions. If this is how the new provision is interpreted, forecasts and analyses will come within the definition.

In any case, forecasts and analyses may be based on facts. An analyst, for example, may write a confidential report to the effect that the securities of a given issuer are likely to rise by a certain amount, which he predicts. Arguably, this is mere prediction until the said securities do rise (or fail to do so!) But he may well have reached these conclusions on the basis of specific, though confidential, information relating to the company's expansion plans.[31] That specific information will certainly constitute inside information. In these circumstances, the report itself will similarly constitute inside information and it is generally considered that the analyst will therefore commit the offence of insider dealing if, possessing such information, he advises his client to deal in the relevant securities.

It has also been suggested that the very fact that an analysis has taken place may constitute inside information and thus that dealing on the basis of this, even where one does not know the report's contents, could be an offence. It is difficult, however, to see how such dealing could be an offence where the person has no knowledge whatsoever of the contents. Certainly, it may be possible to guess whether or not the report was favourable, but until one knows, this would seem to be too imprecise to be a fact and to fall into the category of rumours and forecasts. This may be distinguished, however, from the situation where the insider knows that the report is favourable,[32] although they do not know the details. Such information will indeed be inside information, since it is sufficient for the person to know, as opposed to guess, in which direction the securities price will move.

Precision aside, there remains considerable debate on what is meant by the terms "relating to an issuer or issuers or security or securities" and "liable to have a significant effect". It is not clear whether information relating to the market as

---

29 The previous version of the Act referred not to "inside information" (*Insiderinformation*) but to an "insider fact" (*Insidertatsache*), emphasising the precise and accurate nature of the information concerned. Compare the approach to this issue taken in the French legislation: p. 96.

30 Para. 37c.

31 Where the report is based solely on information which is publicly available, paragraph 13(2) explicitly states that its evaluations are not considered to be inside information, even if is capable of having a significant effect on the price of securities.

32 Or unfavourable, as the case may be.

a whole, rather than to specific issuers, will be covered. Given the emphasis on precision just discussed, it is certainly a point of view that a fact relating to an entire market will not be specific enough in its application to fall within the definition. On the other hand, a fact that affects an entire market sector, or even the national economy, will also affect specific securities and issuers.[33]

As for the term "significant effect", in Germany, as in many other Member States, there have been calls for a specific definition. The Deutsche Börse AG (German Stock Exchange) has issued guidelines indicating a threshold of 5% of market value or, in cases of fixed interest securities, 1.5% of nominal value, a rather stricter level than the Scandinavian 10%. Two objections have, however, been raised to this, both along the lines that it is inadequate. The first has been that a defendant could claim that they did not anticipate that the value of the securities would rise (or fall) by the amount that they did. This would seem to be a simple question of evidence: in the circumstances, is the court of the view that a person of the defendant's expertise is likely to have realised the probable impact of the information concerned?[34] The second objection is that the guideline is merely that and that actual legislation, or at least a clear indication from the courts, is required. This, too, is debatable. The Danish 10% threshold is also simply a matter of prosecution practice, not legislation, but would seem to be workable in practice. For the moment, however, the approach of the courts in the several cases that have been brought in Germany since insider dealing was outlawed has been to deal with each case on its own facts rather than either to set down or to endorse any principles.

Finally, the information must not be publicly known. This is a change from the 1994 wording, which referred to it being "publicly available". The revised term, "known" (*bekannt*) is a clarification, although the added description, "publicly" (*öffentlich*) remains. The information must therefore be in the public domain, but not necessarily widely publicised. Publication through a press agency such as Reuters or dpa[35] is certainly sufficient, as is publication on a market-orientated system such as Bloomberg. Moreover, the information need not even be available to all investors, provided that it is known to the market in general. It has been said that this reflects the aim of the legislation (and indeed the Directive[36]) to protect the market, not individual investors. It is likely, however, that the rationale is more one of practicalities than legal theory. However information is published, it is always possible for a given individual investor to miss its announcement. A requirement that every potential investor be informed before the information is considered to be

---

33 For examples, see the consideration of government officials in the context of the Irish legislation: p. 68.

34 Indeed, the same issue arises in relation to the "with full knowledge of the facts" provision in the Directive.

35 Deutsche Presse-Agentur: German Press Agency.

36 See, in particular, consideration 6 of the Preamble to the Directive: "Whereas, by benefiting certain investors as compared with others, insider dealing is likely to undermine that confidence [i.e. investors' confidence in the market] and may therefore prejudice the smooth operation of the market."

publicly available and thus dealing on the basis of it permitted would be virtually impossible to meet. An obligation to publish it through a medium that will reach the market as a whole is, however, not too onerous and is a practical way of ensuring that dealing is conducted on a playing field that is at least reasonably level.

Greece

The definition of inside information in the Greek legislation, Article 2 of Presidential Decree 53/1992, is identical to that in the Directive. The list of securities covered by the Decree is likewise identical to that contained in the Directive.

Ireland

The Irish definition of inside information, section 108 of the Companies Act 1990, is one of the simplest: information relating to securities which is not publicly available, but, if it were, would be likely materially to alter the price of the relevant securities. Again, the phrase "materially" is not defined further. Nor have the courts been of any assistance on the matter as yet since no insider dealing cases have as yet been brought in Ireland.

Section 107 sets out the securities to which the Act applies. They are:

(a) shares, debentures and stock issued or proposed to be issued, whether in Ireland or elsewhere, for which dealing facilities are or are to be provided by a recognised stock exchange;
(b) any right or option in relation to securities referred to at (a);
(c) any right, option or obligation in respect of an index relating to any securities referred to at (a);
(d) such interests as may be prescribed.

It is to be noted that the Act only requires the securities to be issued (or proposed to be issued) on a recognised stock exchange: the dealing itself may be on- or off-exchange. The definition of "proposed to be issued" is, however, less clear and until cases before the courts settle the issues that this raises, it is likely to remain so. One prominent lawyer in the field in Ireland has said that it is unlikely that securities would be covered whose listing is pending but not yet approved. It will surely depend, however, on by whom their issue is "proposed". If it means proposed by the recognised stock exchange to be issued, the view will be correct: an exchange cannot propose the issue of shares until it has approved their listing. The wording is, however, also capable of the interpretation, proposed by the issuer. On this reading, securities whose listing is awaiting approval will be covered, at least unless and until a decision is taken by the stock exchange not to approve it.

Similarly, the view has been expressed that the Act will apply to securities whose listing has been temporarily suspended, although not where the suspension is for an indefinite length of time. The latter would certainly seem to be the case: where there is no prospect of the suspension being listed at any given date, the issue of the securities cannot be "proposed". As for where the suspension is indeed temporary, the crucial question would seem to be when it is to be lifted. If the suspension is due to end in a week's time, it would seem straightforward enough to say that the securities are proposed to be issued next week. But if the listing is suspended for, say, 6 months, to argue that it is proposed to issue them in 6 months' time would seem to be stretching the point. On the other hand, construction of the wording of the section to say that the securities' issue is proposed to take place in 6 months (or a year or whenever) and therefore that they are covered by the Act would arguably be possible. Again, however, until the Irish courts are given the opportunity to decide on these points, they will remain matters of conjecture.

Although section 108 makes clear that securities issued both inside and outside the Republic of Ireland are covered by the Act, the Companies Act, 1990 (Insider Dealing) Regulations, 1992[37] state that the dealing itself must take place inside the Republic.

Italy

Article 180(3) of Legislative Decree No. 58 of 24 February 1998 (as amended by Legislative Decree No. 61 of 11 April 2002), defines inside information as:

> specific information having a precise content concerning financial instruments or issuers of financial instruments that has not been made public and that, if made public, would be likely to have a significant effect on the price of such instruments.

All but the first of these criteria are straightforward enough and indeed found not only in the Directive but in the legislation of all the Member States. The first, however, that the information be "specific, having a precise content" raises the same issues as have been discussed in relation to Germany, in particular the question: will information of general application be covered? The test applied is: whatever other impact the information may have, is it capable of having a specific effect on the securities in question? Suppose, for example, the United Nations imposes economic sanctions, prohibiting all trade or even financial transactions with a jurisdiction in which a given Italian company has a major interest. Although the sanctions are of general application and will affect many companies, not merely the one in question, the fact that the continuation of one of that company's important commercial operations has been rendered illegal will of course specifically affect its profitability and consequently the value of its securities. This being the case, the Decree will apply.

It was said in relation to the previous legislation, which referred to "specific and determined information" that in cases involving general information of this

---

37 SI 131/1992.

type, the view could have been taken that the prosecution was obliged to prove that it was of specific application to the securities or issuer concerned. Certainly the wording would admit this interpretation, as would that of the current Decree. The construction adopted, however, was that the criteria were defences, not elements for the prosecution to prove. Given the similarity between the wording of the two provisions, this would appear to continue to be the case. As such, if the defendant is to avail himself of them, it is for the defence to prove that they do not apply (for example, that the information in question did not specifically concern the securities in which he dealt). The choosing of this construction was a practical one: it was felt that the alternative would place the prosecution under an impossible burden. It is certainly true that in some Member States, notably the Netherlands and the UK, the view has been expressed that insider dealing is too difficult to prove and that this is the reason why so few convictions are secured.[38] In most Member States, however, the view remains that the definition of inside information is an essential element of the offence of insider dealing and that it is therefore for the prosecution to prove that the information to which the charge relates falls within it.

Under Article 183, the Decree applies to financial instruments traded on a regulated market, either in Italy or in another EU Member State. Article 183(1) explicitly states, however, that, provided that the instruments are traded on such a market, the Decree will apply even if the offence is committed "abroad". The broadness of this term would suggest that, as with the French legislation, the act in question need not even be committed in another EU Member State: transactions in the United States, Japan or wherever will equally be covered. Off-exchange transactions will not be covered, however, unless the instruments are also available for trading on a regulated market.

The term "financial instruments" is not defined, unlike in most Member States. It would, however, seem likely that those types of securities which are listed in Article 1(2) of the Directive (and covered in the legislation of the other Member States) will also be covered by the Decree.

Luxembourg

Article 1 of the Law of 3 May 1991 defines inside information in identical terms to those of the Directive:

> information which has not been made public of a precise nature relating to one or several issuers of transferable securities, which, if it were made public, would be likely to have a significant effect on the price of the transferable security or securities in question.

---

38 See, for example, Rider, B.A.K. and Alexander, R.C.H. (1998), "The Regulation Of Financial Markets With Particular Reference To Market Abuse", Report of Criminal Law Session of Fifteenth World Congress on Comparative Law. In the Netherlands, the legislation has been amended specifically in order to make insider dealing easier to prove.

A number of points are worthy of note here. "Not been made public" means only available to a restricted group of individuals. This would seem fairly clear, but for the Law to apply, the information must lie outside the public domain in all its respects. For example, a confidential report will not be covered if its contents are entirely drawn from sources that are publicly available. The question of course arises as to the status of a report which contains material both from public and non-public sources. In principle, the public material will not be covered, while that which is non-public will be. In a case where a person dealt on the basis of the report, however, it is not difficult to see the problems of establishing on which part of the report they dealt.[39]

A further problem with such a narrow definition arises in relation to wide-ranging reports. Consider a report on a company with holdings in other companies in several different jurisdictions in various parts of the world. All of the material on which it is based may be publicly available – it may, for example, be drawn from the press in the jurisdictions concerned. It is, however, unlikely that many investors will have access to the entire jigsaw even if between them they hold all the pieces. The whole picture, revealed by such a report, may therefore be extremely price-sensitive. But it is at least arguable that it will nevertheless not fall within the definition of non-public.

Linked to this is the issue of opinions, particularly those of analysts. It is clear that the assessment of information by a respected analyst will have a very definite impact on the market, quite possibly as great as certain types of non-public information. Nonetheless, under the Luxembourg provisions, analyses and the like are not covered on the basis that they are not sufficiently precise. A comparison may be drawn with the German definition: an opinion is not concrete information and therefore, in itself, is not covered.

In passing, it is worth noting the requirement that the information must relate to "one or several issuers of transferable securities". Among the areas that this covers are information relating to:

- the issuer, whether internal (for example an increase in the issuer's capital) or external (for example, a takeover bid against the issuer by another company);
- the issuer's situation
- the prospective development of one or more securities;

Similarly, information capable of having an impact on the market in general will be covered. Such information will include a decision by the central bank to change

---

39 Where the report was disclosed without authorisation (see Chapter 4), it could be argued that the non-public material was disclosed along with the public. In any case, since it would generally only be a professional who would be in a position to disclose a confidential report of this kind, a successful prosecution could normally be brought for breach of professional secrecy under Article 458 of the Penal Code.

interest rates or by the government to advise against financial services transactions with certain jurisdictions.[40] A decision to take a measure against another state which is likely to provoke a trade retaliation will likewise be covered, although this would seem of lesser importance given the relatively small size of Luxembourg's international trade in manufactured goods.

The list of securities covered by the Law is identical to that in the Directive. Unlisted securities are therefore not covered, even those periodically sold on a regulated exchange. Those sold on secondary exchanges are, however, covered. To date, no such secondary exchanges exist in Luxembourg itself. The Law does, however, cover securities listed not only in Luxembourg but in any EU Member State. It therefore extends to securities sold on such exchanges as the Alternative Investments Market (AIM) in the UK

Netherlands

The Netherlands legislation covering insider dealing, the *Wet toezicht effectenverkeer* (Securities Trade Supervision Act),[41] has undergone a number of amendments since it was first introduced in 1995. The most recent amendment came into force in 1999 following public perception that the Act was ineffective in bringing insider dealers to book.[42] Inside information is now defined in broadly the same terms as under the Directive:

- specific information which relates to particular securities or particular issuers; which
- is not public; and which
- if it were made public would be likely to have a significant effect on the price of the relevant securities.

Before the 1999 amendment, the Act required that the information not only be non-public but actually confidential and, furthermore, that the defendant know this.[43] Following the lack of successful convictions under the 1995 regime, however, it was felt that this resulted in a charge of insider dealing being too difficult to prove and

---

40 As an example of the latter, the UK Treasury in 1999 advised strongly against any transactions with financial institutions located in Antigua and Barbuda. The effect of such an advice on any company with holdings there is not difficult to imagine!

41 As the name implies, the Act does not cover insider dealing alone: it was introduced in order to implement several EU Directives, including the Insider Dealing Directive, but also, *inter alia*, the Investment Services Directive (Council Directive 93/22/EEC) and the Capital Adequacy Directive (Council Directive 93/6/EEC).

42 See p. 71-72.

43 Several, although not all, Member States explicitly require that the defendant know that the information on which he deals (or which he discloses) is inside information. See Chapter 2.

therefore the requirement of confidentiality was removed. It is now sufficient for the information not to be in the public domain.

Similarly, the range of securities covered has been widened. Whereas previously the securities in question had to be traded on a recognised exchange, the Act now covers unlisted shares, shares that may be listed at some point in the future (arguably merely a category of unlisted shares) and certain unlisted derivatives, such as options and warrants. The range of securities now coming within the ambit of the Act is therefore:

- instruments, profit sharing certificates and founders' shares, traded options, warrant and similar negotiated paper;
- participation rights, options, futures contracts, registrations in share and debt registers and similar rights, whether conditional or not;
- certificates and receipts issued for instruments as referred to above.

A further important change is that the information must merely be capable of influencing the value of the relevant securities. The direction in which the information will push the value is irrelevant. This in itself is not new: as in all Member States, the prohibition against insider dealing is designed to prevent insiders from unfairly avoiding a loss as much as it is to prevent an unfair profit. What is new is that the direction need no longer be foreseeable, provided that it is foreseeable that the information is capable of having some effect.

This is, of course, controversial. If it is not foreseeable whether the securities will move up or down, the insider is arguably in no better position than any other actual or potential investor. Nonetheless, as of 1999, such an insider is still caught by the Act. The intention would seem clear: to prevent insiders from dealing at all (just as company directors are in many jurisdictions severely restricted from dealing in their company's shares). The question must be asked, however, whether the Dutch Parliament, in its eagerness to give prosecutors a realistic chance of success in insider dealing cases, has not moved the pendulum too far the other way.

Portugal

Inside information is defined particularly widely under the Portuguese legislation. Article 378(4) of the *Código dos Valores Mobiliários* (Securities Code) of 13 November 1999[44] refers to:

> all non-public information that, being accurate and with respect to any issuer or securities or other financial instruments, would be capable, if it was given advertising, of influencing in a sensitive manner its price in the market.

---

44 Last amended by Decree-Law No. 66/2004 of 24 March 2004.

"Securities" are not defined in terms, but guidance may perhaps be taken from the previous Portuguese legislation, Article 666(5)(c) of the *Código do Mercado dos Valores Mobiliários* (Securities Markets Code), which referred to the catch-all "any other securities, of whatever nature and form, titled or untitled". The range covered is among the widest in any Member State: only that in the Spanish legislation, which does not require that the securities be listed on an exchange, is wider.

Spain

Inside information is defined under Article 81.3 of the Securities Market Law (*Ley del Mercado de Valores* or LMV) as information which

- is specific;
- relates to one or more securities or issuers of securities;
- has not been made public;
- if made public, would be likely to have a significant effect on the price of those securities.

Like much of the Law, the provision is extremely wide ranging. The term "securities" is not defined and all types of securities are therefore covered. These include not only shares, bonds, options and the like, but also, *inter alia*, promissory notes, shares in *cajas de ahorro* (savings banks) or in the Confederación Española de Cajas de Ahorro (Spanish Confederation of Savings Banks), mortgage-backed certificates and securities, bills of exchange and all investments in mutual funds. It may be questioned whether quite such a wide-ranging definition is necessary. It is perhaps a positive step to extend the net wider than the traditional company stocks, shares and debt securities and their derivatives, since highly price-sensitive, non-public information could arise in relation to, for example, investments in mutual funds. The series of demutualisations of building societies in the UK provide a particular case in point: a person with advance knowledge of the decision to demutualise would arguably have been well-placed to make a considerable profit by increasing their investment and could equally have encouraged friends and the like to do so as well.[45] But other securities on the Spanish list, such as bills of exchange, do not rise and fall in value in the way that shares, bonds, options, etc, do.

The test of whether or not it was foreseeable that the information was price-sensitive is, however, a subjective one: to be covered by the Law, the insider must have known what he was doing.

---

[45] In the UK, at least, there is of course also the counter-argument that the very high degree of speculation in relation to building societies that followed the first demutualisations meant that an insider would in fact not be in any more significant a position to make a "quick profit" than any other potential investor.

Sweden

Paragraph 4 of the Insider Act (*Insiderlagen*) covers information or knowledge of a fact which:

- concerns a circumstance which has not been made public;
- relates to financial instruments or issuers of financial instruments generally;
- if it were made public would be likely to have a significant effect on the price of any financial instruments;

At first glance, this does not appear very different from the Directive. There are, however, some important differences. The first is that there is no explicit requirement that the information be specific or precise. The second is that "not been made public" is interpreted strictly. Although the information need not actually be made known to the entire investing public (it is difficult to see how this could ever be guaranteed), it must be available to them.

Nor, significantly, is it sufficient to release the information to the media: it must actually be published. The phrase "which has not been made public" without further clarification would seem definitely not to include any information which has been released to the press or other media. But in the nature of things, with all but the most dramatic news, there is an interval between the information being released to the media and it being broadcast, the newspapers being available for purchase or whatever. This highlights the fact that financial journalists may qualify as insiders,[46] although it also raises another important issue. Many pieces of price-sensitive information are broadcast on radio and television and published in the press some hours after they are announced, but appear on news services such as Bloomberg far sooner. In terms of availability to institutional investors, this makes no difference, since all traders constantly scan the screens on which Bloomberg and other such services publish their information. In terms, however, of availability to non-institutional investors, the difference is considerable. To date, the holding of securities by private individuals has been very limited in Sweden and thus the practical importance is perhaps not that great. This is, however, changing, particularly with the demutualisations of insurance companies, more prevalent in Denmark but increasing in Sweden as well. Thus, one can foresee that, on occasion, there may be two separate periods of increased dealing in the securities of a particular issuer following the respective appearances of news on wire services and the general media.

It may be, therefore, that in the future, the question of when information is deemed to be in the public domain will have to be revisited. To hold that it only becomes public with the availability on sale of the next national newspaper or the broadcast of the next major television or radio news programme would clearly be impractical. Traders and their employers make their living by being the first to make a purchase or sale once a news item hits the screens. But if it is to continue to be the position

---

46 See also the discussion of journalists in Chapter 2: pp. 41-42, 65.

in Swedish law that given information does not become public immediately on its release to the media but only once it is announced to the investing public in general, the means by which that is deemed to be done will need to be settled.

Finally, the information's likely effect on the price of the securities must be "significant". This is interpreted as achieving a threshold limit of 10%. This limit, need only, however, be reached by the likely effect: the actual effect of the information may be less. It is therefore no defence to show that, in the event, the price of the securities only moved by, say, 7%: if, at the time of the deal or unauthorised deal or disclosure, it was foreseeable that it could well have risen by rather more, this will be sufficient to secure a conviction.

The Act refers not to securities, but to "financial instruments", a reference to the *Lagen om Handel med Finansiella Instrument* (Financial Instruments Trade Act). This defines financial instruments as "market papers (*"fondpapper"*) and any other rights or commitments designed to be traded on the securities market". "Market papers" in turn cover:

- share and debt securities and other rights to shares (*"delägarrätter"*);
- rights to claims (*"fordringsrätter"*) issued for general trade;
- share in a securities trust (*"värdepappersfond"*);
- shareholders' rights towards persons holding share certificates in a foreign company on their behalf.

The Insider Act adds to this list, however, by including

- issue certificates;
- interim certificates (*"interimsbevis"*);
- option certificates (*"optionsbevis"*);
- convertible debt instrument (*"konvertibelt skuldebrev"*);
- debt instruments connected with an option to subscription (*"skuldebrev förenat med optionsrätt till nyteckning"*);
- participating debentures (*"vinstandelningsbevis"*);
- stock options;
- futures.

United Kingdom

Inside information in the UK is defined in section 56 of the Criminal Justice Act 1993. The definition is similar to that found in the Directive, but the information must not only be precise but refer to specific issuers and/or securities. Information likely to affect the price of securities across the entire market is therefore not covered. Such information will even include a report by Sainsbury's stating that purchases of British beef have risen sharply. While it could be argued that the latter relates to a specific issuer of securities, i.e. Sainsbury's, it is not difficult to see that the news will be highly relevant to the British beef sector in general, as well as to all butchers and supermarket chains (not just Sainsbury's), who will be able to raise their prices to reflect the increased demand.

The restriction of the Act's application to information relating to specific issuers or securities certainly reflects the Directive's requirement that inside information be precise. It does, however, ignore the point that information relevant to the market in general can be as price-sensitive as that relating to specific securities or issuers. The market in general is, after all, made up of individual issuers: what affects all of them therefore by definition affects each of them.

The range of securities covered by the Act is listed in Schedule 2. The securities are:

- shares and stock;
- any instrument creating or acknowledging indebtedness (e.g. bonds);
- any right to subscribe for shares or debt;
- rights under depository receipts (as defined);
- options to acquire or dispose of any security;
- futures;
- contracts for differences.

H.M. Treasury, however, reserves the power to add to this list by Order should it see fit. To date, it has not done so. It is, however, instructive to compare the list to that of "specified investments" set out in the Financial Services and Markets Act (Regulated Activities) Order 2001.[47] Many of these are not immediately applicable to insider dealing, while others are covered by the 1993 Act either explicitly or by implication: government securities may be argued to be merely a specific sub-group of shares or, more commonly, debt securities. One which is, however, worthy of note is rights to or interests in investments. These are defined as "any right to or interest in anything that is specified by any other provision of this Part (other than article 88 [i.e. mortgage contracts])".[48] It may be seen that an interest in a security can be as valuable as the security itself. Given that other forms of derivatives, such as futures, options and contracts for differences, are included in the 1993 list, it is therefore a little strange that rights to and interests in securities are not included. It is perhaps arguable that these, although transferable, are not as easily such as the securities themselves, but it is submitted that their inclusion would be desirable to close an unnecessary lacuna, particularly given the ease with which a very short amending Order could achieve this.

---

47 SI 2001/544.
48 Article 89.

Chapter 4

Criminal Offences of Insider Dealing

Introduction

The Directive prohibits three types of conduct: dealing (i.e. buying or selling securities) on the basis of inside information, encouraging another to do so and the unauthorised disclosure of inside information. Encouraging another to deal and unauthorised disclosure may often, of course, go together, although they need not do so, as is discussed below. Two Member States, France and Spain, add a further offence of failing to protect inside information, although they are currently alone in doing so.[1] Since insider dealing is an acquisitive crime, i.e. property derives from it, another offence which needs to be considered in this context is money laundering. This is, however, a complex topic of its own and is therefore dealt with separately in the next chapter.

This seems straightforward enough, but there are a number of complexities. All persons in possession of inside information are prohibited, both under the Directive and in the national legislation of the Member States, from dealing on the basis of it. In respect of the other offences, however, only certain types of persons are covered.

A second issue is the way in which insider dealing, in any of its forms, is dealt with. The Directive explicitly leaves this up to the Member States. Article 13 states:

> Each Member State shall determine the penalties to be applied for infringement of the measures taken pursuant to this Directive. The penalties shall be sufficient to promote compliance with those measures.

In particular, there is no specification as to whether insider dealing is to be criminalised. In practice, however, insider dealing in its various forms is a criminal offence in all Member States with the partial exception of Spain.[2] A direct consequence of this is that in certain Member States, for example Portugal and, until recently, France, legal

---

1 The offence arguably exists also in Greece by extension: a general principle of Greek criminal law imposes a liability to prevent, insofar as one is able to, another from committing a criminal offence. Insider dealing is a criminal offence in Greece and therefore a person who allows another to engage in it will themselves be criminally liable.

2 Many Member States also provide for civil penalties: see Chapter 7.

entities do not incur liability, since the criminal law in those States only extends to natural persons. Many Member States (although not all) also impose civil or administrative sanctions. Since, however, the civil/administrative offences in some cases differ from the criminal ones not only in terms of sanctions but also in their nature,[3] they, too are dealt with separately, in Chapter 7.

Dealing

The prime insider dealing offence is, of course, dealing itself, i.e. buying or selling securities on the basis of inside information. Article 2 of the Directive prohibits a primary insider[4] from:

> taking advantage of that information with full knowledge of the facts by acquiring or disposing of for his own account or for the account of a third party, either directly or indirectly, transferable securities of the issuer or issuers to which information relates.

Article 4 extends the prohibition to:

> any person other than those referred to in that Article who with full knowledge of the facts possesses inside information, the direct source of which could not be other than a person referred to in Article 2.

At first glance, it would therefore appear that anyone knowingly in possession of inside information is prohibited to deal on the basis of it. Closer analysis reveals, however, that this is not in fact the case. For the Directive's prohibition to apply, a primary insider must be the direct source of the information. If the person who deals is even two steps removed, they will be excluded. This is impractical, not least because many insiders (primary or secondary) arrange for another person (a friend, partner, whoever) to carry out the transaction in order to cover their tracks. One may thus consider the following two scenarios.

Alison, the marketing director of Buckinghamshire Construction plc, informs her friend, Deborah, that the company has just secured the contract to build a road tunnel under the Simplon Pass to supplement the existing rail tunnel. The news of such a major contract will certainly, when it is announced, increase the share price of Buckinghamshire Construction. If Deborah then, before the announcement, buys shares in the company, she will be guilty of insider dealing.

If, however, instead of Deborah buying the shares herself, her husband, Edward, buys them instead, he will not be guilty, within the terms of the Directive, of any offence. Edward's direct source of the information is Deborah and she is not a primary insider. Nor, within the terms of the Directive, will Deborah have committed any offence, since both encouraging another to deal on the basis of inside information

---

3   This is particularly true of the legislation of Spain and the UK.
4   For the distinction between primary and secondary insiders, see Chapter 2.

and unauthorised disclosure of that information may only be committed by primary insiders.[5]

This is not only bizarre but absurd. It is one thing for the use of another person to obscure the evidence and make any case more difficult to prove: this is inevitable. But it is another for such a simple manoeuvre to circumvent the prohibition altogether.

It is perhaps not surprising, therefore, that not all the Member States reflect this dichotomy. Many Member States[6] make no distinction between primary and secondary insiders. Of those that do, only Greece and Luxembourg follow the approach of the Directive in requiring that a secondary insider, in order to be prohibited from dealing, must have received the information directly from a primary insider. This is in keeping with the particularly close way in which the Greek and Luxembourg legislation follows the Directive. Indeed, the Greek implementing legislation, Presidential Decree 53/92, is virtually a carbon copy of the Directive.

One Member State which does not fit neatly into either category is Spain. Like many of the Member States, Spain addresses insider dealing with both criminal and civil measures. The civil measures, contained in the *Ley del Mercado de Valores* or LMV (Securities Market Law), do not make any distinction between primary and secondary insiders. Those in the Penal Code, however, are very specific in their application. They only apply to primary insiders and even then only where the dealing results in a profit of at least €450,759.08.[7] Spain is unique in this respect: although other Member States provide for civil as well as criminal penalties for insider dealing, none of them exclude criminal liability completely for all secondary insiders. Furthermore, no other Member State prescribes a threshold profit (or avoided loss) that must be realised in order for the criminal provisions to take effect.

It should be noted that it is the actual profit realised that is the decisive factor: the Penal Code makes no reference to foreseeability or intention. A primary insider who finds that the price of the securities rises more than he expected may thus find himself criminally liable even though he never intended to be. Similarly, one who deliberately decided to take that risk may escape criminal liability if the result of his actions is, in other respects, disappointing. On the other hand, the provisions are clearly targeted at large-scale, quite possibly organised, offences. In order to make a profit of the equivalent of nearly £300,000, the amount invested will often be close to £1 million, possibly even more. There will be few, if any, individual company directors, let alone mere employees, who will have access to these kinds of amounts.

Other than Greece and Luxembourg, all Member States prohibit all persons who possess inside information, irrespective of how they came by it, from dealing in the securities concerned. That said, the French legislation concerning secondary insiders, or tippees, who deal is complex. Only primary insiders are covered by

---

5   See below for discussion of these offences.
6   Belgium, Denmark, Finland, Ireland, Italy, Netherlands, UK and, for the purposes of the offence of actual dealing, Germany.
7   Formerly Pts. 75 million.

the insider legislation itself, Article L465-1 of the Monetary and Financial Code. Secondary insiders who make use of the information, however, although they are immune from a charge of insider dealing *per se*, may find themselves charged with the separate criminal offence of *recel*. This is defined in Article 321-1 of the Penal Code as:

> the act of concealing, withholding or supplying a thing, or assuming the rôle of intermediary for its supply, knowing that that thing is the proceeds of a crime.
>
> The act of knowingly benefiting, in any way, from the product of a crime also constitutes *recel*.

In contrast to the English legal position, established in *Oxford v Moss*,[8] inside information in French law qualifies as "a thing" or indeed "the product of a crime".[9] This is the closest that any of the Member States come to the position taken in the United States, where insider dealing is viewed as a form of fraud and, as such, is covered by a fraud statute, section 10(b) of the Securities Exchange Act 1934 and Rule 10b-5 of the Securities and Exchange Commission, which legally forms part of the Act. Since *recel* is an offence related to theft (and indeed also, now, to money laundering), it is punished accordingly. It is perhaps ironic that in consequence, secondary insiders who deal on the basis of the information may therefore be punished more harshly than primary insiders.[10]

Exemptions Relating to Dealing Offence

National and Regional Authorities

Although dealing, whether by a primary or secondary insider, is prohibited, there are certain exemptions. One is to be found in the Directive itself. Article 2(4) states:

> This Directive shall not apply to transactions carried out in pursuit of monetary, exchange-rate or public debt management policies by a sovereign state, by its central bank or any other body designated to that effect by the state, or by any person acting on their behalf. Member States may extend this exemption to their federated states or similar local authorities in respect of the management of their public debt.

The term "federated states" is clear: four Member States, Austria, Belgium, Germany and Spain, have a federal structure within which the state[11] governments

---

8   (1979) 68 Crim. App. Rep. 183. This case is limited, however, to the proceeds of theft. See p. 20, note 88 and pp. 160-62..
9   This was established by the Cour de Cassation, France's highest criminal court, in the case of *Pechiney*, Cour de Cassation, Criminal Division, 26 October 1995.
10   For the sentences available for both insider dealing and *recel* under the French legislation, see pp. 125-26.
11   *Land* in Austria and Germany, region in Belgium and Spain.

have considerable autonomy. The term "similar local authorities" is perhaps more complicated. It would not seem to apply to such authorities as the French *départements* or British or Irish counties. It could, however, arguably now apply to the Scottish Executive and Northern Ireland Assembly (should it be re-convened), although not, in view of its somewhat more restricted powers, to the Welsh Assembly. Similarly, it would seem to apply to the Italian autonomous regions of Valle d'Aosta, Trentino – Alto Adige and Sicily; although Italy has to date not extended the exemption in this way, it certainly remains open to it to do so. The Italian position is, in fact, carefully balanced: the exemption covers the Italian State, the Banca d'Italia and the Italian Foreign Exchange Office (Ufficio Italiano dei Cambi or UIC).[12] It does not, however, cover any of the regional governments.

As mentioned above, the exemption is applicable to the regions of Belgium. It has also been applied, however, in Belgium to the provinces and even municipalities as well as to the communities, reflecting the highly federal structure of the country. This structure is the most complex certainly of any Member State and arguably anywhere in the world. There are three "state regions", but then several provinces,[13] equivalent to British counties or French *départements*. These are divided into municipalities and, in the cities, communes, comparable to British boroughs or district council areas. In addition, there are three "communities", based not on geography but on language: they represent the French, Flemish and German speaking groups.[14] Finally, language and geography are combined in the four "language regions": Flemish, French, German and Bilingual (the last being Brussels). Each of these entities, from regions (both state and language) down to communes, enjoys the local authority exemption under Article 2(4).

In contrast, the exemption does not exist at all in the French and Spanish legislation. In France, this is perhaps not surprising. As mentioned above, French *départments* would not seem in any case to be similar local authorities to federated states and even though the regional governments have rather greater powers, the main seat of decision-making remains Paris. In the case of Spain, however, the omission is rather more interesting, since the country's federal system devolves considerable autonomy to the regions. One might therefore have expected to see the Spanish implementation of the Directive make use of the exemption offered in Article 2(4). Nonetheless, like Italy, it has not chosen to do so.

Similarly, Austria has not chosen to exempt its *Bundesländer* from the prohibition against insider dealing: only the Federal Government and the Österreichische Nationalbank (Austrian National Bank) are exempt, as a matter of general legal

---

12 Article 180(6), Legislative Decree No. 58 of 24 February 1998, as amended by Legislative Decree No. 61 of 11 April 2002.

13 It is inaccurate to describe the regions being "divided" into provinces since a number, notably Brabant, straddle the regional boundary of Flanders and Wallonia.

14 Notably, their titles are national/ethnic: the French-speaking community, for example, is not the *communauté francophone* but *française*.

principle. In contrast, the German *Bundesländer* were exempt[15] until the amendment of 15 December 2004.

Belgian Holding Exception

Belgium is also noteworthy for another important exemption: the "holding exception". This is, however, discussed at length in the previous chapter[16] and need not, therefore, be considered further here.

Dealing not Motivated by Information

The UK provides a defence that the person, although he possessed inside information and dealt in the relevant securities, would have carried out the transaction in any case.[17] This certainly solves the problem of holding companies and is entirely within the spirit of the Directive that it is only those who take advantage of inside information in order to deal that should be penalised. Indeed, the legislation of many other Member States in effect contain the same defence by mirroring the Directive's reference to taking advantage of the information. The German legislation, for example, explicitly states that the prohibited dealing is "through use of inside information",[18] while an insider is only forbidden to encourage a third party to deal if his encouragement is "on the basis of his knowledge".[19]

Such a defence does, however, present a serious obstacle to the prosecution. Consider a lawyer advising the bidder on a takeover. The target company has enjoyed considerable success over the previous few months; indeed, this is a major reason why the bid has been made. Two days before the bid is announced, the lawyer's boyfriend buys 200 shares in the target company. Given the timing, one may suspect that he had been tipped off by his girlfriend; indeed, she may well even have overtly suggested that he buy the shares. But how easy will it be to satisfy a jury beyond reasonable doubt that, even if the lawyer did pass him the information, he would not have bought the shares anyway given the information available to him, together with the rest of the investing public, in the *Financial Times*? The same problem, of course, will apply in any of the Member States which, following the Directive, require the defendant to have "taken advantage of", "used" or "misused" inside information in order to deal. Indeed, this may be one reason for the relative lack of success in prosecuting insider dealers across the European Union, although such an argument is perhaps rebutted by the fact that the two Member States which

---

15 *Wertpapierhandelsgesetz*, para. 20.
16 See pp. 89-92.
17 Criminal Justice Act 1993, s. 53(1)(c). Note that, as with the subsequent defences in the UK legislation, it is for the defendant to prove the defence, albeit to a rather lower standard.
18 *Wertpapierhandelsgesetz*, para. 14(1).
19 Para. 14(3).

Specialist Defences in the UK

The UK provides certain other, more specialist defences. The first is where the person dealing did not expect the transaction to result in a profit (or avoided loss) to him, attributable to the inside information.[20] It is to be noted that the test is not whether or not he in fact made a profit (although where he did not, he will be unlikely to be prosecuted), but his state of mind: did he believe that he would not make an attributable profit? An example that has been cited of where this defence would apply is where a person receives information suggesting that the market price of a given security is lower than its real value, but sells at the market price anyhow.

The second defence is where the person dealing believed on reasonable grounds that the information had been sufficiently widely distributed for neither party to the transaction to be prejudiced.[21] In many cases, it could be argued that, where this is the case, the defendant did not realise that the information was inside information; he believed that it had been made public. But an example has been cited where the insider discloses the information to another person and then enters into a transaction with him, hence the term, "equality of information". It is questionable, however, how often this in practice occurs. In any case, if one subscribes to the view that insider dealing is a crime against the market as a whole, such a defence is hard to justify; on the contrary, it could be said that it allows a small coterie to continue to make profits at the expense of the investing public at large.

Market makers also have a defence. These are persons who hold themselves out at all normal times in accordance with the rules of a regulated market or approved organisation as willing to acquire or dispose of securities and are recognised as such under those rules. Where such a person can show that their dealing was done in good faith in the course of their employment, or, as the case may be, their own business, as a market maker, they do not commit an offence.[22]

Two further defences concern the use of market information, defined in Schedule 1, paragraph 4 of the Act as information about past or future dealings, including whether or not they will actually take place. The first is that "it was reasonable for an individual in his position [i.e. that of the defendant] to have acted as he did despite having that information as an insider at the time"; the second, more complex, is discussed below. As with so many examples of the "reasonable man" defence, which indeed is common to English criminal law in general, no guidance is given as to what is or is not to be regarded as reasonable. One must suspect, therefore, that, as with other offences, this is a question to be decided by the jury on the day.

---

20 Criminal Justice Act 1993, s. 53(1)(a).
21 Criminal Justice Act 1993, s. 53(1)(b).
22 Criminal Justice Act 1993, Schedule 1, para. 1.

It has been suggested that, following the introduction of the concept of market abuse in the Financial Services and Markets Act 2000, the Code of Market Conduct, issued by the Financial Services Authority (FSA), is likely to be taken into account when considering this defence to the criminal offence of insider dealing as well as for its explicit purpose of assessing what conduct does or does not amount to market abuse.[23] This must, however, be questioned. Nowhere is it stated in the 2000 Act that the Code of Market Conduct is to be used, or even that it can be, for this purpose. Nor has the 1993 Act been amended to indicate this. It is possible that the defendant may wish to cite the Code to support his defence. Similarly, the prosecutor may wish to cite it in order to rebut it, particularly given that the prosecutor, since the coming into force of the relevant parts of the 2000 Act on 1 December 2001, will generally be the FSA.[24] But what is not clear is whether the Code will actually be admissible as evidence in such proceedings (in contrast to civil proceedings for market abuse, where it is not only admissible but often conclusive). It may well be up to the individual trial judge to rule whether or not to admit it, at least until specific guidance comes, either in the form of further legislation or, more likely, that of a ruling on the point from the Court of Appeal or possibly even House of Lords.[25] Even if the Code is admitted as evidence, the question of what is or is not reasonable will be one for the jury, not the judge;[26] as such, it may or may not be heeded. This is such a fundamental principle of criminal law, at least in England and Wales, that only legislation would be sufficient to override it.[27]

The second, more complex, market information defence applies where the defendant shows:

(a) that he acted -
   (i) in connexion with an acquisition or disposal which was under consideration or the subject of negotiation, or in the course of a series of such acquisitions or

---

[23] For a discussion of the market abuse regime, including the role of the FSA's Code of Market Conduct, see pp. 212-21.

[24] Among the specific objectives given to the FSA under the 2000 Act is the reduction of financial crime. As such, it is given the power to prosecute a number of economic crimes, including insider dealing.

[25] Or a Guidance Notice from the Attorney-General.

[26] Although insider dealing is a triable either way offence, i.e. may be tried either on indictment, in the Crown Court, or summarily, in the Magistrates' Court, it is generally tried in the Crown Court before a judge and jury. This is partly because its complexity makes it difficult to prove to a lay jury (see Chapter 7) and thus a defendant is likely to opt for a Crown Court trial, where he has a greater chance of acquittal. Also, however, the maximum sentence which a magistrate may pass, i.e. 6 months' imprisonment and/or a £5,000 fine, is unlikely to be seen as adequate in most cases.

[27] It is possible, of course, that such legislation may be introduced as part of the abolition, under current Government consideration, of jury trials for economic crime cases.

disposals, and
(ii) with a view to facilitating the accomplishment of the acquisition, disposal or series; and
(b) that the information which he had as an insider was market information arising directly out of his involvement in the acquisition, disposal or series.

This is aimed to facilitate takeovers. Clearly, the fact that there is about to be a takeover bid is not only confidential but also highly price-sensitive: the announcement of a takeover bid, especially where it is hostile, invariably has a marked effect on the price of all securities connected with the target company and often of the bidder as well. But without a defence, this could be argued to mean that, once a decision has been taken by a company to launch a takeover bid, for that company to buy shares in the target company – which, of course, it has to do in order to make the takeover – will constitute insider dealing. In fact, however, it is questionable whether such a special defence is necessary. It would seem fairly clear that the bidder would have bought the shares anyhow; because the taking over of a company by definition involves the bidder buying the target's shares (and indeed other securities), the decision to deal is simultaneous with the decision to launch the bid. To argue that buying the shares in these circumstances constitutes insider dealing would seem a particularly fine form of legal sophistry. Nonetheless, as a "belt and braces" approach, the special defence has been incorporated.

It should be noted, however, that the defence only applies to dealings in furtherance of the takeover itself; those dealings that merely serve to prepare the ground will not be covered. These, too, however, would seem to be covered by the general defence that the dealing would have taken place in any event.

Finally, a defence is afforded to those who deal in order to conform with price stabilisation rules made under section 144 of the 2000 Act. This avoids the situation where a person is placed in a "no win" situation whereby he commits a criminal offence if he does deal, but commits a regulatory offence (which, although it does not carry a prison sentence, certainly carries sanctions capable of putting him out of business) if he does not.

Penalties for Dealing

All Member States punish actual dealing with imprisonment and/or a fine. It is interesting, however, to see the divergence in the actual levels (length of maximum prison sentence or amount of fine) between the different Member States. This is, however, entirely in keeping with the Directive: Article 13 explicitly leaves it up to each state to decide what sanctions to impose, providing only that "The penalties must be sufficient to promote compliance." Before looking at each Member State in detail, a number of general points can usefully be made.

Firstly, several Member States view dealing by a primary insider as more serious than that by a secondary insider or tippee.[28] Accordingly, separate penalties are provided. Although there may be cultural reasons for this, it does mean that a primary insider with a little foresight can easily reduce his liability by persuading someone else to make the deal on his behalf. He is in any case likely to do this in order to obscure the trail back to him; it seems odd that he should be rewarded for it by lower penalties in the event that he is brought to book. Some Member States, such as Austria, avoid this problem by providing for identical punishments for all insider dealing offences (even if not for all offenders), but in those that do not, further action would appear to be called for.

Secondly, it must also be stated that in all Member States, the number of convictions for any insider dealing offence is relatively low. In some cases, there have been none at all. This has led to increased use of civil and administrative penalties; the possible reasons for the low conviction rate are therefore discussed in Chapter 7.[29]

Thirdly, 12 of the Member States are now members of the "eurozone"[30]. The levels of fines in those states were, however, for the most part fixed when they still had their own national currencies. The euro amounts of these fines are therefore hardly rounded.[31] In a number of Member States, they have now been adjusted, either through general revisions, such as in Belgium,[32] or through specific new insider dealing legislation, such as in France and Germany, not only modifying the definition of the offence but also stating the fines in euros. In others, however, the old pre-euro levels are maintained. In Greece, for example, both judges and lawyers have electronic euro-converters: the judge decides the level of the fine in drachmas, as before, and then converts it into euro. Perhaps more surprisingly, Ireland enacted a Euro Changeover (Amounts) Act in 2001 in order to make the necessary

---

28 For the distinction between the two classes, see Chapter 2.

29 See pp. 201-3.

30 Austria, Belgium, Finland, France, Germany, Greece, Ireland, Italy, Luxembourg, Netherlands, Portugal and Spain. As the provisions for economic and monetary union were part of the *acquis communautaire* which the twelve new Member States were obliged to accept as a condition of accession, these Member States will also adopt the euro in time, although, to date, none have done so.

31 In Finland, however, no maximum (or indeed minimum) fine is prescribed and therefore the problem does not arise.

32 In Belgium, the fines set in the Penal Code were subject to a multiplier, which was increased from time to time. (A comparison may be made with the system in the English Magistrates' Courts, where the fines are set as levels, 1 to 5, with the actual monetary amount for each level raised from time to time by legislation.) At the time when the Belgian franc was abolished, this multiplier was 200. On the introduction of the euro, the figures of the original fines were maintained, but stated in euro, and the multiplier was set at 5. Thus, the Penal Code set the minimum fine for insider dealing offences as BF50; this was increased by the last pre-euro multiplier (200) to BF10,000. This was then converted to €50 multiplied by 5, i.e. €250.

arrangements for the conversion to the euro, but this does not cover the provisions of the Companies Act 1990! Similarly, Italy introduced new insider dealing legislation in 2002 but continued to state the levels of fines in Italian lire. Even where the levels are adjusted, any change is unlikely to be substantial (particularly as an increasingly civil approach is preferred) and in any case, the current figures do reflect the approach taken by each Member State.

Finally, it should be noted that, just as many Member States deal with insider dealing by means of civil and/or administrative measures as well as criminal ones, so too they provide for civil as well as criminal penalties. These are dealt with separately in Chapter 7. Linked to this is the issue of parallel proceedings, i.e. whether a person can be pursued under both the criminal and the civil provisions or whether the authorities must choose one or the other. This is a complex matter also dealt with in Chapter 7.

Austria

Austria, in common with a number of Member States, punishes dealing by primary insiders more severely than that by secondary insiders, although it does balance this by not distinguishing in its penalties between actual dealing and encouraging to deal or unauthorised disclosure of inside information. Section 48(a) of the *Börsegesetz* (Stock Exchange Act) punishes all three offences with up to 2 years' imprisonment for primary insiders and 1 year for secondary insiders. In each case, a fine may be imposed instead of, or in addition to, the prison sentence. The level is, however, complicated. Like those of Germany and Portugal, the Austrian criminal justice system directly links fines to the offender's income: fines are expressed in terms of "days". A comparison may be drawn with the ill-fated unit fines system briefly introduced in England and Wales in the early 1990s.[33] In Austria, the value of one "day" is nominally equal to the defendant's salary for 1 day; in fact, it varies between €2 and €327.[34] For insider dealing offences, the maximum fine is 360 days, i.e. an absolute maximum of €117,720.[35]

As regards sentences actually imposed, no convictions for insider dealing offences have to date been reported. This is, however, in common with a number of Member States.

Belgium

In Belgium, the penalties for dealing on the basis of inside information are strict. Article 189 of the Belgian Law of 20 December 1995 provides for a mandatory

---

33 Contained in the Magistrates' Courts (Unit Fines) Rules 1992, SI 1992 No. 1856 (since repealed).

34 *Strafgesetzbuch* (Criminal Code), para. 19. The maximum was previously the rather lower Sch. 3,000 (equivalent to just over €218).

35 Previously Sch. 1,080,000 (€78,486.66).

prison sentence for insider dealing: minimum 3 months. That said, the maximum sentence is relatively short: only 1 year. The main reason for this is that the main penalty is a financial one. In addition to the prison sentence, a fine of between €250 and €50,000 is imposed.[36] The comparative leniency of the prison sentence has, however, another reason. Under the Belgian company and financial services laws, any person who receives a prison sentence of 3 months or more is automatically disqualified from a range of positions, including that of company director or any kind of employment in the banking or financial services industry. It has therefore been said that the real purpose of the mandatory imprisonment is not in fact to put those guilty of insider dealing behind bars, but rather to guarantee that they are banned from the financial sector.

A further fine may also be imposed of up to three times the profit attributable directly or indirectly to the offence. This provision bears similarities to measures in other jurisdictions, including some other EU Member States, but there are also significant differences. Many Member States link the level of the fine directly to the profit made as an explicit provision in their legislation, but such penalties are generally civil or administrative in nature, not found in criminal legislation as here.[37] Similarly, the power to make a restitution order under the UK's Financial Services and Markets Act 2000 is civil (or sometimes administrative) in nature.[38] There are Member States where a link is made in the imposition of a criminal fine, for example France (see below), but such criminal fines are not described as being in addition to other criminal fines for the same offence. Perhaps a more useful comparison is with confiscation orders, found, for example, in a number of UK criminal statutes, most recently the Proceeds of Crime Act 2002. Such orders are, however, defined as recovering the profit actually made from an offence, not, as here, a multiple of it.

Denmark

Under section 94(1) of the Danish Securities, etc, Consolidated Act,[39] insider dealing is punished with up to 18 months' imprisonment or an unlimited fine. It should be noted that relatively few Member States, such as the UK and, as just discussed, Belgium, allow their courts to impose both imprisonment and a fine for the same act. There is provision for a harsher prison sentence, however, in aggravating circumstances. Where the offence is both committed intentionally and is particularly serious, the maximum sentence is increased to 4 years. Examples of particularly serious offences would be those involving an especially high volume or

---

36 Previously BF10,000 to BF 2 million.

37 A comparison may also be made with the fines imposed by the South African Financial Services Board under the Insider Dealing Act 1998. These are three times the profit where the offender settles, i.e. confesses his guilt, or four times the profit where he does not. They are, however, explicitly civil/administrative fines, imposed as an alternative to criminal prosecution.

38 For a discussion of this power, see pp. 219-21.

39 Consolidated Act No. 168 of 14 March 2001.

value of securities or a flagrant breach of trust by an employee. Where a series of intentional offences has been committed, this, too, will be regarded as an aggravating circumstance. It might be considered that a maximum sentence of even 4 years' imprisonment is very lenient compared to, for example, 7 years in the UK or 10 years in Ireland. This should, however, be seen in the context of a more lenient sentencing culture generally in the Scandinavian jurisdictions than is found in some other Member States.

Finland

Finland provides for similar penalties. Chapter 8, section 1 of the *Arvopaperimarkkinalaki* (Securities Market Act)[40] imposes, where insider dealing is committed either intentionally or through gross negligence, a maximum prison sentence of 2 years or an unlimited fine.

France

France's criminal statute relating to insider dealing is now Article L465-1 of the Monetary and Financial Code.[41] This provides for a sentence for insider dealing of up to 2 years' imprisonment and/or a fine of up to €1.5 million.[42] The fine may, however, be increased to up to ten times the profit realised from the offence and should in any event not be less. France is, however, one of the few Member States where a number of insider dealing cases have been brought and these show that the practice is rather different to the theory; in the case of *Delalande/Synthélabo*, a director of Delalande was found to have profited from insider dealing to the tune of FF69.5 million,[43] but in the event only fined FF10 million.[44] Overall, there has been considerable variety in the sentences imposed in France for insider dealing: the most severe to date have been in the case of *Pechiney*,[45] where two defendants, in contrast to the previous practices of only imposing suspended sentences, were sentenced to 2 years' imprisonment, of which 1 year was suspended. Fines of FF20 million were also imposed, compared with the most lenient sentence imposed under the Ordinance: a fine of FF5,000.

Recel, with which secondary insiders who deal may be charged, carries the rather harsher prison sentence of a maximum 5 years, although the maximum fine is rather less: €375,000.[46]

---

40 Act No. 1995/495 of 26 May 1995.
41 France also provides for civil sanctions: see pp. 204-5.
42 In fact, these are almost identical with the previous legislation, which similarly imposed a 2 year prison sentences and/or a fine of FF10 million.
43 Equivalent to approximately €10.6 million.
44 This was, in fact, a civil fine, but in the criminal proceedings that were also brought, no additional fine was imposed, even though it was open to the court to do so.
45 Cour de Cassation, Criminal Division, 26 October 1995.
46 Previously the slightly higher FF2.5 million (equivalent to €381,122.54).

Germany

Under paragraph 38 of the German *Wertpapierhandelsgesetz* (Securities Trade Act), insider dealing, by any person, carries up to 5 years' imprisonment and/or a fine. As in Austria and Portugal, fines in Germany are defined in terms of "days", 1 day nominally representing the defendant's income for 1 day. In fact, under paragraph 40 of the German *Strafgesetzbuch* (Criminal Code), the value of 1 day ranges from a minimum €1 to a maximum €5,000.[47] The maximum fine for insider dealing is 360 days, i.e. on the maximum value of a day, €1.8 million. Although a number of cases have been brought, relatively few have resulted in a conviction, partly because of the difficulty in proving an insider dealing case to a criminal standard, but also because of the use of the option of a gift to charity. This is a provision under section 153 of the *Strafprozessordnung* (Criminal Procedure Code), whereby the state prosecutor may, in less serious criminal cases, give the defendant the option of paying a specified sum to charity. If he does so, the case is dropped and no conviction results. Among the major cases that have resulted in a conviction was that of *Weru*.[48] In this case, the defendant was found to have bought shares in his own company on the basis of inside information, later selling them at a profit of DM1.22 million.[49] He was fined DM1 million,[50] which the court calculated his profit to be once tax had been allowed for, and a further suspended fine of the maximum 360 days at the then maximum day-value of DM10,000 was imposed. This was considered a lenient sentence, reflecting the defendant's plea of guilty.

Greece

Like those of Belgium and Spain, the Greek criminal provisions for insider dealing provide for a mandatory prison sentence. Under Article 30 of Law 1806/1988, dealing carries between 1 and 4 years' imprisonment as well as a fine of up to three times the profits realised. That said, there have to date been no criminal prosecutions for insider dealing in Greece, civil proceedings being preferred.

Ireland

In Ireland, section 114 of the Companies Act provides for insider dealing to be punished with a maximum 12 months' imprisonment and/or a €1,269.74[51] fine on

---

47 Previously DM 2 and DM 10,000 respectively.
48 Amtsgericht Frankfurt am Main, January 1997. Reported, *Frankfurter Allgemeine Zeitung*, 27 February 1997.
49 Equivalent to €623,776.10.
50 Equivalent to €511,291.88.
51 Previously IR£1,000.

summary conviction or 10 years' imprisonment and/or a €253,947.62[52] fine on indictment.[53]

Italy

Under Article 180 of the Italian Legislative Decree No. 58 of 24 February 1998 (as amended), insider dealing offences are punishable with up to 2 years' imprisonment and a fine of between 20 million and 600 million lire.[54] In aggravated cases, the fine may be trebled to a maximum of 1.8 billion lire.[55] Since, however, there have been very few criminal prosecutions (as opposed to civil/administrative proceedings) of insider dealing in Italy, precisely what kind of cases will be considered to have aggravating features is unclear. The Decree simply refers to cases "where, in view of the particular seriousness of the offence, the personal situation of the guilty party or the size of the resulting gain, the maximum appears inadequate".[56] The latter reference to the size of the profits would appear straightforward; as to the other two, some guidance may, perhaps, be found in the legislation that preceded the Decree, Law No. 157 of 17 May 1991. Article 2(3) of that Law reserved especially severe sentences for cases involving information derived from resolutions in board meetings. Where such a resolution was price-sensitive (clearly, if it was not, it by definition did not qualify as inside information), those falling into one of six specified categories, if they dealt in the relevant securities before the resolution was made public, could receive a sentence of double the normal levels. Since this provision was supplementary to a provision allowing for penalties to trebled in "particularly serious cases", this meant, in a particularly serious case, a sentence of six times the normal level, i.e. up to 6 years' imprisonment and a fine of up to 1.8 billion lire. The relevant categories were: directors, officers, supervisory board members, controlling shareholders, auditors and liquidators. It may well be, therefore, that dealing in such circumstances would continue to qualify as a "particularly serious offence".

The scope of that paragraph was remarkable and remains worthy of note, given that it could in the future be used to interpret the new provision. It did not require that the defendant actually have attended the meeting; auditors, in particular, are unlikely to attend all board meetings. Nor was it explicitly stated that the defendant must have dealt on the basis of the resolution or indeed any inside information. It is possible, therefore, to envisage a situation where a board meeting passes a highly

---

52 Previously IR£200,000.

53 As in the UK, insider dealing in the Ireland may be tried either summarily, i.e. in the District Court before a judge sitting alone, or on indictment, i.e. in the High Court before a judge and jury. Again as in the UK, the sentencing powers of the District Court are considerably less than those of the High Court.

54 This is between €10,329.14 and €309,874.14. Interestingly, although the Legislative Decree was amended by a Decree dated 11 April 2002, some 3½ months after the introduction of the euro in Italy, the levels of the fine remain stated in Italian lire.

55 €929,622.42.

56 Article 180(4).

price-sensitive resolution (for example, to mount a takeover bid) and an auditor, with as yet no knowledge of this, deals in the securities of either the bidding or target company. Since the provision relating to board meeting resolutions comes within the context of insider dealing in general, the penalties being expressed as a multiple of those normally imposed for this offence, it is at least arguable that a person who comes into one of the above categories but is not in possession of any inside information at the time that they deal will not be guilty of any offence.

The situation will be more complicated, however, where such a person is in possession of inside information, but it does not relate to the board meeting resolution. For example, if the profits of a company in the financial year just ended were very good, that company's auditor will know this before the accounts are published. But he may not know that the board has just decided, in view of the company's strong financial position, to launch a takeover bid. This news will affect the securities not just of the target but of the bidder as well. In such a case, if the auditor deals in the company's securities, he will clearly be guilty of insider dealing but is questionable whether or not the increased sentence would be applicable. This could, and very possibly would, be an issue hotly contested at trial, but the discretion given to the judge could well in these circumstances provide a useful way of resolving it.

There were also explicit provisions prohibiting senior government Ministers from dealing.[57] One may conclude, therefore, that a public official, particularly one in a senior position, who dealt on the basis of inside information deriving from his office would similarly be liable, "in view of his personal situation", to the increased penalties. But one must equally suspect that only a number of such sentences passed following convictions will confirm for certain what is covered.

A feature that has been retained from the old provisions is judicial discretion. Article 180(4) states that in aggravating circumstances, "the judge may increase the fine ..." He is not obliged to do so. It may well be, therefore that, where the issues discussed above would have led to a conclusion that was especially controversial, the judge would simply exercise his discretion either to consider that the offence was not particularly serious or, even if he felt it was, not to impose an increased fine.

Any conviction for insider dealing, however, will result in the sentence being published in the national press. Under the former legislation, this was something the judge merely had a discretion to order and then only in particularly serious cases. Article 182 of the Decree, however, now makes such publication mandatory and furthermore applies it to all cases:

> Conviction for any of the offences referred to in Articles 180 and 181 [i.e. insider dealing or market manipulation] shall entail ... the publication of the judgment in at least two daily newspapers having national circulation, of which one shall be an economic newspaper.

This latter sentence highlights the different cultures in the various Member States regarding the press reporting of criminal trials and their outcomes. In the UK, it is accepted that the press attend any court case that they wish and report on much of

---

57 See p. 70.

the detail, including, in criminal trials, the eventual sentence.[58] In any case, should a conviction result, the sentence will be released to the press since it is a matter of public record. In many other Member States, however, a far more discreet approach is taken and it is far from standard practice for even the sentence to be reported in the press.

Finally, the judge may also order the defendant to be suspended from office for a period of between 6 months and 2 years.

Luxembourg

Article 9 of the Luxembourg Law of 3 May 1991 provides for insider dealing to be punished with between 1 and 5 years' imprisonment and/or a fine of between €123.95[59] and €1,239,467.62.[60] In addition, any profits made from the offence may be confiscated as the proceeds of crime under Article 34 of the Penal Code. Unusually, however, the Luxembourg legislation also provides for the sentence to be reduced where there are extenuating circumstances. Under Article 75 of the Law of 13 June 1994, in such circumstances, the prison sentence imposed must not be greater than the minimum prescribed and fine may be reduced to a figure below €247.92[61] but in no event less than €24.79.[62] Such a provision is rare among the Member States, although it derives at least in part from the fact that the Luxembourg legislation, like that of some, but by no means all, other Member States, prescribes minimum as well as maximum sentences for insider dealing.

Netherlands

Under the Dutch Law on Securities Trade, insider dealing carries up to 2 years' imprisonment and/or a fine of up to €11,344.51.[63] Additional penalties are provided for, however, where the offence results in large profits. Under 1,3° and 6,2° of the Economic Offences Act, where the profits accruing from the transactions are more than 25% of the maximum fine, i.e. amount to more than €2,836.13,[64] the maximum fine is increased to €45,378.02,[65] and, in addition, the profits may be confiscated. This also applies where the value of the securities traded exceeds that amount.

The legislation is unusual in two key respects. Firstly, confiscation is provided for only where the profits, or the value of the securities traded, are above a stated

---

58   There are exceptions to this rule, but these do not apply to trials of insider dealing or indeed any kind of economic crime.
59   Previously LF5,000.
60   Previously LF50 million.
61   Previously LF10,001. The impact of this is debatable given that the minimum sentence for insider dealing is only half this.
62   Previously LF1,000.
63   Previously Fl. 25,000.
64   Previously Fl. 6,250.
65   Previously Fl. 100,000.

threshold. Most Member States, if they provide for confiscation at all, do so regardless of the size of the proceeds: the amount confiscated may be €1 or €100 million. The practice may be closer to that of the Netherlands than the theory would suggest; it is doubtful, for example, whether a prosecutor in the UK would in fact seek a confiscation hearing if he believed the benefit to the defendant to be £5 (although he may do so in order to make the point). But only in the Netherlands is confiscation barred if a threshold is not reached.

Secondly, the Netherlands is unique in considering the value of the securities to be a criterion for sentence, separate to the size of the actual profits. In most cases, of course, the two will be linked: dealing in a package of securities worth €10,000 on purchase is likely to lead to higher profits than in one worth €50. But it is far from inconceivable that the price of the securities may for some reason move rather less dramatically than the dealers had planned. In such a case, it would perhaps be surprising if an especially high fine were imposed. In the UK, for example, the judge would in all likelihood be more concerned, when passing sentence, about the actual profits made rather than the volume of the securities that led to them.

Portugal

Article 378 of the *Código dos Valores Mobiliários* (Securities Code) of 13 November 1999[66] distinguishes, for the purpose of penalties, between primary and secondary insiders, but not between the different offences. Under paragraphs (1) and (2), a primary insider who either deals, encourages another person to do so or discloses inside information without authorisation is liable to up to 3 years' imprisonment or an unlimited fine. Secondary insiders who commit any of these offences are subject to the slightly lower sentence of up to 2 years' imprisonment or a fine of up to 240 days.[67] To date, however, there have been no convictions for insider dealing in Portugal and therefore it has yet to be seen what sentences will actually be imposed in practice.

Spain

In Spain, as discussed above, only primary insiders (and indeed only certain categories of primary insider at that) are liable to criminal penalties at all.[68] Both primary and secondary insiders are, however, liable to civil/administrative penalties under separate legislation. There is the additional requirement, in order for the criminal provisions to apply, that the profit made or loss avoided be at least €450,759.08.[69] Where this is the case, Article 285 of the Penal Code imposes on qualifying primary

---

66 Last amended by Decree-Law No. 66/2004 of 24 March 2004.
67 Like that of Germany, the Portuguese criminal justice system expresses fines in terms of "days", 1 "day" being nominally 1 day's salary for the person concerned.
68 See p. 75.
69 Previously Pts. 75 million.

insiders who deal a sentence of between 1 and 4 years' imprisonment and a fine of up to three times the profit realised. In view of the threshold profit that must have accrued in order for these provisions to be applicable, it may be seen that the fine will generally be extremely high.

Sweden

Under the Swedish criminal justice system, a criminal act falls into one of three categories: "serious", "of normal degree" and "slight". At first glance, this may appear analogous to the French *crimes, délits* and *contraventions*. What sets the Swedish categories apart from these, however, is that it is not offences that are categorised (so that in France, murder is a *crime*, insider dealing a *délit* and most traffic offences *contraventions*); rather, it is the specific act of which the defendant is accused: how serious an example of the offence is it? The category into which a given act falls will decide the range of sentences available. A comparison may perhaps be drawn with aggravating or mitigating circumstances in the English system, reflected to a greater or lesser degree in the legislation of a number of other Member States, such as Italy, Luxembourg or the Netherlands.

As in other Member States, no precise definitions are laid down: "serious" means a particularly serious example, "slight" the other extreme and "of normal degree" quite simply one that is neither "serious" nor "slight"! It has been suggested, however, that in the case of insider dealing, the following factors will apply:
"Serious".

- a large profit is made;
- the offence results in a major change in the price of the security/securities concerned, regardless of the actual profit made by the offender;
- a series of acts have been committed;
- the offence has involved an organised group of persons well placed to assist each other in its commission
- there has been a deliberate delay in the publication of the information in order to allow greater opportunity for the insider dealing to take place.

"Slight": the act has no effect on public confidence in the market in question.

The Insider Law adds two other criteria: whether the offence was committed intentionally or through gross negligence. Cases of insider dealing through gross negligence will include those where the defendant, before dealing, did not bother to ascertain whether or not the information was publicly known or, alternatively, considerably underestimated its effect on the price of the securities. In such cases, the experience (or lack of it) of the defendant in the market in question will be taken into account.[70]

Where there has not even been gross negligence, no offence is committed. Sweden in this regard follows the doctrine that a significant *mens rea* or mental element must be present in order for insider dealing to constitute an offence. This is also the approach taken in the UK, where not even gross negligence is sufficient for the criminal provisions: the offence must be intentional.[71] It contrasts, however, with the doctrine that no mental element should be required: those who possess inside information must not deal in the relevant securities. This is the approach taken in certain other Member States, notably Denmark, and also in South Africa.

The actual sentences are laid down in paragraphs 19–28 of the Insider Law in conjunction with chapter 9(9) of the Criminal Code. Where the offence is committed intentionally, a sentence of between 6 months' and 4 years' imprisonment may be imposed in serious cases and up to 2 years' imprisonment (no minimum prescribed) in those of normal degree. Alternatively, an unlimited fine may be imposed. Where it is committed rather through gross negligence, the sentence is up to 1 year's imprisonment or a fine. (An offence committed merely through gross negligence will never be regarded as serious.)

Where the offence is slight, only a fine is imposed; furthermore, no criminal conviction results. It therefore becomes a civil offence in all but name.

United Kingdom

The UK has among the most severe sentences for insider dealing of any Member State; only Ireland provides for a longer prison sentence. Under section 61(1) of the Criminal Justice Act 1993, all insider dealing offences carry up to 7 years' imprisonment on indictment and/or an unlimited fine. If tried summarily, the maximum sentence for any offence tried before the Magistrates' Court will apply, i.e. 6 months' imprisonment and/or a fine of up to £5,000. In practice, however, few, if any, insider dealing prosecutions are brought before the Magistrates' Court.

This approach is in keeping with the rather harsh UK sentencing culture in general compared to those in much of the rest of Europe. Although there have been few actual convictions, those that there have been have resulted in severe sentences, at least by the standards of other Member States. Imprisonment of at least 1 year has been the norm and in one high-profile case, the so-called Guinness Four in 1990,[72] sentences of 4 and 5 years' imprisonment were imposed.[73]

---

70 Cf. the defence to market abuse in the UK that the person did not realise that what he did would generally be considered by regular users of the market as abuse: see p. 218.

71 Recklessness may, however, be sufficient for the civil offence of market abuse: see pp. 217-18.

72 Ernest Saunders, Gerald Ronson, Jack Lyons and Anthony Parnes.

73 These also covered convictions for false accounting, theft and conspiracy and were in any event halved on appeal. The case does, however, illustrate the fact that a person convicted

There remains, however, a widespread view amongst the public and commentators that sentences imposed in the UK for insider dealing – and indeed most types of financial crime – are too lenient. This is partly because the length of time actually served is considerably less than that actually imposed by the court. Unless an offender's behaviour in prison is seriously bad (for example, they are involved in major drug trafficking or serious violence against prison staff or, in some cases, other prisoners), they are entitled to release, albeit on licence, after two-thirds of their sentence, or even only half where the sentence was less than 4 years. Parole will often mean release earlier still. Since few "white-collar criminals" receive more than 4 years[74] and fewer still "behave badly" while in prison, this means that their actual prison sentences are relatively short.

A further penalty is that of confiscation. The term "confiscation" is used in different contexts to mean different things; indeed, its meaning varies from Member State to Member State. In this book, however, it is used in its UK sense: the means under the criminal justice system of depriving a convicted offender of the proceeds of his offence or offences. There are separate civil and administrative means, notably civil recovery under Part 5 of the Proceeds of Crime Act 2002 and restitution orders under sections 382–384 of the Financial Services and Markets Act 2000.[75]

Many of the Member States provide for the proceeds, at least of the more serious offences, to be removed. The UK's provisions are, however, of particular interest for three reasons: the way in which confiscation is viewed, its links with the civil and administrative measures and its use, in certain circumstances, of assumptions.

A number of Member States deprive insider dealers of the profit from their offences by means of a fine. In France and Greece, for example, the fine imposed is calculated as a multiple of the profit obtained. In the UK, however, confiscation is not and has never been a fine. It is not intended as a punishment, an expression of the state's disapproval of the conduct in question; rather, it is designed simply to ensure that the offender does not profit from his wrongdoing. Thus, it is quite possible for a convicted offender to have imposed on him a fine and, in addition, a confiscation order. In fact, this is of little consequence in cases of insider dealing, since they are almost invariably dealt with by means of imprisonment rather than a fine, but the principle still holds. Nonetheless, confiscation, unlike its civil counterparts, is a criminal sentence. In consequence, it only applies after a criminal conviction. Should

---

of insider dealing in the United Kingdom may expect a prison sentence of years rather than months.

74 For comparison, in recent high-profile perjury cases, Jonathan Aitken was sentenced to 18 months' imprisonment and therefore released after 9 months, while Lord Archer was sentenced to 4 years and released after 2 years. In Archer's case, his chances of parole were compromised through breach of prison rules while on day release (he took the officers guarding him out for an expensive meal). The maximum sentence for perjury is 9 years.

75 The latter are considered in Chapter 7 (pp. 219-21), since they are directly linked to the market abuse provisions under the 2000 Act. The former, since they are not a criminal sentence but are viewed as a way to recover the proceeds of crime in general, fall outside the scope of this book.

a prosecution therefore fail, no confiscation order may be made. It has been said that, because of this, relatively few offenders have actually suffered a confiscation order; this view, in turn, has led to new civil measures being introduced.

Confiscation has been available in the UK for some considerable time; it now operates, however, under the Proceeds of Crime Act 2002. This was introduced following a Cabinet Office report,[76] in which it was perceived that the existing mechanism to deprive criminals of the proceeds of their offences was simply not effective. The new measures are designed specifically to address this problem.[77]

Confiscation operates through one of two routes. As with any other sentence, both follow conviction.[78] The first route is the simplest: where a person is convicted of a criminal offence and is shown to have obtained an identifiable financial benefit from it, that financial benefit is confiscated.[79] Thus if, for example, a person engages in insider dealing and, in consequence, makes a profit of £1,000, that £1,000 is confiscated. In such cases, it is, however, for the prosecution to prove firstly that the accused has benefited from his offending at all and secondly how much.

The second route is more complex. This is where the court determines that a person has what is termed "a criminal lifestyle", defined in section 75 of the Act as, *inter alia*, where the conduct forms part of a course of criminal activity, i.e. he has committed other offences within a specified time from which he also benefited.[80] Where this is established, it is assumed that everything he owns, as well as every item of property, he transferred and every payment that he made in the previous 6 years was obtained from crime. It is also assumed that any property he holds is held free of any other interest in it. These assumptions may be rebutted: for example, the defendant may show that he had a legitimate salary, from which he paid for much of his property,[81] or a bank may show that it has an interest in a house (in the form of a mortgage). The burden of proof is, however, on the defendant or third party.

The Proceeds of Crime Act 2002 is still quite new; it remains to be seen how it will work in practice. As mentioned above, however, its explicit purpose is considerably to improve the system's record on recovering the proceeds of crime. It

---

76 *Recovering the Proceeds of Crime*, Performance and Innovation Unit (PIU), June 2000. An analysis of the system of civil recovery may, however, be found in Bell, R.E. (2004-5), "Justifying the Civil Recovery of Criminal Proceeds" 12 *Journal of Financial Crime* 8.

77 As mentioned elsewhere in this book, the United Kingdom is in fact made up of three jurisdictions: England and Wales, Scotland and Northern Ireland. In each of the three, the system of confiscation is different. The principal securities exchanges are, however, located in London and this book therefore examines the system in England and Wales.

78 In contrast to a restitution order.

79 S.7(1).

80 S.75(2)(b). There are two other tests for a criminal lifestyle, but neither applies to insider dealing. It should be noted that it is not necessary for all the convictions to be for the same offence: a person may, for example, be convicted of one count of insider dealing, one count of false accounting and two counts of smuggling alcohol.

81 Since most insider dealers are professionals, they will generally have had well-paid legitimate jobs.

may therefore be expected that, particularly to start with, its implementation will be more draconian rather than less.

Encouraging to Deal

At first glance, the offence of encouraging to deal is simply an example of incitement, as with any criminal offence. Closer analysis, however, shows this is not in fact the case. The principal offence that has just been examined is not dealing in securities *per se* but dealing in them on the basis of inside information. It is quite possible for someone with inside information to encourage someone else to deal in the securities to which it relates without actually divulging the information itself.[82] Where the insider does divulge it (except in specified authorised circumstances), this is a separate offence from encouragement. The two may go together, but they need not.

Nonetheless, the loophole that would be left if mere encouragement to deal were not prohibited to insiders would render the entire measure pointless. Any insider could simply, without further explanation, ask a friend or relative to buy or sell the requisite securities for them and they would be immune from any kind of sanction. It is not sufficient to argue that such conduct would constitute dealing through another: the relative or friend could simply buy and later sell the securities and quietly split the profits with the insider. That such an arrangement had taken place would, in the case of all but the most careless and foolhardy insider dealers, be impossible to prove, certainly beyond reasonable doubt. For the measures to have any kind of meaning, it was clearly necessary to prohibit this.

Encouraging another to deal is therefore prohibited in Article 3(b) of the Directive:

Each Member State shall prohibit any person subject to the prohibition laid down in Article 2 [i.e. primary insiders] who possesses inside information from ...

recommending or procuring a third party on the basis of that inside information to acquire or dispose of transferable securities admitted to trading on its securities markets as referred to in Article 1(2) in fine.

It should be noted that, in contrast to the offence of actual dealing, the Directive does not extend the prohibition to secondary insiders. Member States that so choose are, however, authorised to do so by Article 6. This is a broad provision that simply states that it is open to Member States, if they choose, to enact stricter measures than those laid down in the Directive. In this area, some have done so, while others have not. In fact, the division between the Member States is not quite as simple as this; there are not two but several groups.

The first group is those Member States that make no distinction at all, for any purposes, between primary and secondary insiders. These are: Denmark, Finland,

---

82 See the discussion of tippees in Chapter 2.

Ireland, Italy, Netherlands and the UK.[83] In these Member States, any prohibition imposed on primary insiders, including encouragement of another to deal, is therefore by definition imposed on secondary insiders as well.

The next group may be described as an intermediate group, where a distinction is made between primary and secondary insiders, but, nonetheless, secondary insiders are prohibited from encouraging another to deal just as primary insiders are. These are Belgium, Greece, Portugal and Sweden. This is perhaps not particularly noteworthy in the case of Belgium and, especially, Sweden. The insider dealing legislation of all three Scandinavian Member States is very similar, that of Denmark and Sweden most strikingly so[84] but also Finland for the most part. It would therefore be surprising if Denmark and Finland both prohibited secondary insiders to encourage a third party to deal, but Sweden did not. That Greece also takes this approach is more striking. The principal Greek insider dealing statute, Presidential Decree 53/1992, is almost a photocopy of the Directive; in most places, not only the substance but even the wording is identical. It is therefore interesting that, where the Directive imposes on secondary insiders only "the prohibition provided for in Article 2" (i.e. actual dealing), the Presidential Decree goes further and imposes on them "the prohibitions provided for in Articles 3 and 4", i.e. encouraging to deal and unauthorised disclosure, as well.

The third category consists of only one Member State: France. Here, secondary insiders are not explicitly prohibited from dealing, but it should not be assumed that they are therefore free to do so. Although in France, secondary insiders are not as such covered by the criminal legislation (in contrast to the civil provisions), if they encourage another person to deal, it has been suggested that they could be held liable as accomplices under the general principles of French criminal law.

Finally, Austria and Luxembourg do not prohibit secondary insiders from encouraging to deal. The same position is taken in the German and Spanish criminal legislation, although not their civil provisions. To date, the principal insider dealing offences in Austria and Luxembourg are dealt with by criminal measures only, although this will change with the implementation of the EU Market Abuse Directive.[85]

Penalties

In most Member States, primary insiders who encourage another to deal are liable to precisely the same sentences as those who engage in actual dealing. This must be qualified, however, by pointing out that the legislation inevitably prescribes maximum

---

83 Although Part V of the Criminal Justice Act 1993 does follow the Directive in setting out separate categories, all three offences are prohibited to all and the same penalties are prescribed.

84 It has been said, albeit informally, that the Danish legislation was strongly influenced by that of Sweden.

85 See pp. 245.

sentences; although some Member States also prescribe a minimum, there is still considerable discretion left to the sentencing judge. The most extreme example of this is perhaps Sweden, where how seriously an offence is punished depends on which of three categories of seriousness it is deemed to fall into. This applies to all criminal offences, not just those related to insider dealing, but for the present discussion, it could well be that a judge might consider encouraging another to deal to be, in principle, a less serious offence than actual dealing. If this rationale were adopted, it may be seen that an offence of encouragement could never fall into the "serious" category. This is certainly the approach taken by Luxembourg and Spain, as discussed below. Such a rigid approach at least appears, however, to exclude cases of simple collusion. If A, who possesses inside information, encourages B to deal in the relevant securities and they then split the profits, is this not as equally serious as where A simply deals in the securities himself? There is the argument that in such a case, A will be guilty not just of encouraging B to deal but of actually dealing, albeit indirectly. But unlike its counterparts in some other Member States, for example Austria, the Swedish Insider Act does not explicitly state that dealing both directly and indirectly is prohibited. It may well be that judicial discretion will prove the solution to this problem, although, as so often in the area of insider dealing offences, until there have been more convictions, one can merely speculate.

Luxembourg does differentiate between primary insiders who deal and those who merely encourage a third party to deal. (Secondary insiders, as mentioned above, are not covered by the prohibition on encouragement.) In contrast to actual dealing, which carries between 1 and 5 years' imprisonment, the prison sentence for mere encouragement to deal is between 3 months and 3 years.[86] In addition, or as an alternative, a fine may be imposed: the minimum is the same as for actual dealing, i.e. €123.95, but the maximum is much lower: €24,789.35 as opposed to €1,239,467.62.[87]

In Spain, there is no criminal liability whatsoever for encouraging to deal, although there is, in certain circumstances, for unauthorised disclosure.

A number of Member States do not prohibit secondary insiders from encouraging a third party to deal. Of those which explicitly do so,[88] the penalties are the same as those for dealing, with the possible exception of Sweden. In France, if a secondary insider were held to be guilty as an accomplice (as in the example considered above), they would be liable to the same penalties as a primary insider, i.e. the same as for dealing. In the UK, since encouraging to deal is considered to be simply a form of insider dealing, there is the possibility of a confiscation order in addition to any other sentence imposed. It may, however, be more difficult for the prosecution to prove that the defendant gained at least some benefit (always a prerequisite for a confiscation order). Not every tip by an insider actually results in an identifiable

---

86 Law of 3 May, 1991, Article 10, p.245.

87 Formerly LF1 million as opposed to LF50 million.

88 Belgium, Denmark, Finland, Greece, Ireland, Italy, Netherlands, Sweden and the UK.

benefit to him and while it is far from uncommon for insiders to arrange for someone else actually to buy the securities and then split the profits, this can be extremely difficult to prove.

Allowing to Deal

Separate from the offence of encouraging to deal is the wider one of allowing to deal. This is not actually found in the Directive; Article 3 only covers actual encouragement. Two Member States, however, France and Spain, do place this additional burden on primary insiders. In Spain, the provision is civil only and is therefore discussed in Chapter 7.[89] In France, however, Article L465-1 of the Monetary and Financial Code imposes criminal penalties on a primary insider who allows the realisation of operations on the basis of privileged information unknown to the public. This can be justified on one (or indeed both) of two bases: first, that permission (in the sense of knowing that a criminal act is about to be committed and doing nothing about it) amounts to encouragement and, second, the wider basis that everyone has a duty to uphold law and order.

It is helpful to take these in turn. The first basis raises a wider question. If I know that a criminal offence is about to be committed and do nothing to prevent it, do I in practice encourage the perpetrators to go through with their crime? If they are unaware of my knowledge, clearly not; something of which they are not aware cannot influence them. But if they are aware, this may be different. It may be useful to draw a comparison with English law. If I stand across the street from a store one evening and watch two men throw a brick through the window and prepare to climb in, does my standing there and watching them encourage them to go through and burgle? The English position is that it does not unless I go further and actually call out, "Go on, lads, go for it!"[90] But in other circumstances, mere knowing inaction may indeed constitute incitement. Consider the following scenario. Adams is in his office, making a telephone call in which he is explicitly passing on inside information. Part-way through the call, his boss, Brown, walks in. Instead of expressing any kind of disapproval or attempting to cut short the call, he simply says, "Oh, you're on the phone. Don't worry, nothing urgent – come and see me when you've finished." Adams may well swiftly recover from his alarm and take Brown's attitude as a nod and a wink. While, to take the first example, it could be argued it is not any of my business whether or not John Lewis gets burgled, it is clearly Brown's concern whether or not his staff commit criminal offences from their workplace, especially

---

89 See pp. 210-11.
90 "Mere continued voluntary presence at the scene of a crime, even though it was not accidental, does not of itself necessarily amount to encouragement." Archbold: Criminal Pleading, Evidence and Practice (2005), para. 18-18, citing *R v Coney* (1882) 8 QBD 53 and *R v Clarkson and others* (1971) 55 Cr. App. R 445, pp.210-11.

ones with a direct bearing on the company. Since Adams knows that, he is likely to take his boss' inaction as tacit encouragement.[91]

This leads on to the second argument; that there is a duty to uphold law and order. It is to be noted that the criminal penalties for allowing a person to deal on the basis of inside information are not imposed on the public at large, only on primary insiders. This may be compared to the far more draconian approach of Greece which obliges every citizen to report any crime. The French position is that the possession of confidential information through one's employment, profession, etc, or through being a shareholder is a privilege (hence the use of the phrase, "privileged information") which carries with it certain responsibilities. It may be compared to the duties placed, primarily on the financial services sector but also increasingly on certain others, to prevent money laundering.[92]

Under the Code, the offence of knowingly allowing another to deal is punished severely, carrying identical penalties to those for actual dealing: up to 2 years' imprisonment and/or a fine of up to €1.5 million or 10 times the profit realised, whichever is the greater.[93]

Unauthorised Disclosure

As seen above, the offence of unauthorised disclosure is closely linked to that of encouragement to deal. Indeed, it could be said that, although an insider may encourage another to deal without disclosing any information to the tippee, unauthorised disclosure of price-sensitive non-public information will almost invariably be tantamount to encouragement to deal. Why else, one might ask, would a person pass on such information, other than in authorised circumstances, unless he expected his confidant to do something about it?

In any case, the offence will often overlap with another offence, the more general one of breach of official or professional secrecy. In all Member States, as in most other jurisdictions, unauthorised disclosure of official government information is a serious criminal offence. Some Member States, such as Luxembourg, go further and punish any breach of professional secrecy, whether in the public or private sector, with a mandatory prison sentence. But in other Member States, such as the UK, breach of secrecy or confidentiality in the private sector generally gives rise only to civil

---

91 Although the point has not to date been raised in relation to insider dealing offences, it has more generally been established, particularly in the context of a manager / employer and employee, that "knowledge of the principal's offence, plus an ability to control his actions, coupled with a deliberate decision not to exercise such control, may constitute aiding and abetting." Archbold: Criminal Pleading, Evidence and Practice (2005), para. 18-19, citing *R v J.F. Alford Transport Ltd.* [1999] 2 Cr. App. R 526.
92 See Chapter 5.
93 Article 465-1.

liability or occasionally administrative liability as well.[94] The criminal law is only involved where confidential government information is concerned or, occasionally, some other very specific category.[95] Although the non-criminal sanctions available are not inconsiderable – substantial damages and/or, in certain cases, suspension or expulsion from the profession – this marked dichotomy does at least in part explain why unauthorised disclosure is dealt with as a specific offence under the Directive, whether or not it may also constitute some other offence.

In addition, some examples of unauthorised disclosure of inside information will not, in fact, constitute a breach of professional secrecy even in those jurisdictions with the strict confidentiality laws. Consider the CEO whose company has just received legal advice that a takeover of a planned target company will not raise any competition law problems. If he then tells his brother of the planned takeover before it is formally announced, whose confidentiality has he broken? Certainly no client: he has no client. Nor his employer: he is the CEO. If the company is a public company, it could be argued that he has breached the confidentiality of the company, as personified by its shareholders. Has he, however, caused them any quantifiable loss? Unless such a loss can be shown, they, too, will have no cause of action.

To avoid such loopholes, as well as to provide a more or less uniform position across the Member States, the Directive in clear terms prohibits the unauthorised disclosure of inside information. Article 3 states:

> Each Member State shall prohibit any person subject to the prohibition laid down in Article 2 who possesses inside information from:
>
> (a)   disclosing that inside information to any third party unless such disclosure is made in the normal course of the exercise of his employment, profession or duties.

The first point to be noted is that it is unauthorised disclosure that is prohibited. This is perhaps obvious, but is worth stating. It is of course recognised that certain types of employment/professions inevitably involve the disclosure to specified persons of confidential information. The Finance Director of a company, on receiving the annual accounts, will need to share them with the Board before they are published. There are also occasions when confidential information is shared informally with colleagues in the context of one's employment or profession. Thus, what is prohibited is disclosure of inside information outside the normal course of a person's employment, profession or duties. Secondly, as with the prohibition on encouragement to deal, the Directive only imposes the prohibition on primary insiders. Secondary insiders are not covered. As with encouragement to deal, the

---

94   For example, an English lawyer divulging confidential information commits a serious disciplinary offence under the Solicitors' Guide to Professional Conduct or the Bar Council Code of Conduct and will almost certainly be "struck off" or "disbarred", i.e. lose his authorisation to practice.
95   For example, in the United Kingdom, disclosure of confidential medical information.

prohibition is extended to them in the legislation of some, but not all, Member States and the breakdown is similar. There are, however, certain important differences and it is therefore worth going through the categories.

Denmark, Finland, Ireland, Italy, Netherlands and the UK make no distinction between primary and secondary insiders and this offence therefore applies to them. Furthermore, they may be liable for breach of confidentiality or secrecy.

Belgium, Greece, Portugal and Sweden, although they do distinguish between primary and secondary insiders, extend to the latter the prohibition on unauthorised disclosure.

France does not explicitly do so. However, the issues of liability as an accomplice and of joint enterprise apply to an even greater extent here than they do with encouragement to deal. Where unauthorised disclosure takes place, the tippee does not merely encourage the third party to deal, he provides them with the material on which to do so. Consequently, the likelihood of the third party actually dealing is higher. Compare the two scenarios. In the first, the secondary insider says to the third party, "I suggest that you buy securities in X SA." In many cases, the secondary insider does not have a clear connection to the company, although in some cases, they may do: the third party may know them to be a friend (or even close friend) or relative of someone who works for or advises the company concerned. If they do not, their recommendation may not carry much weight. In the second, however, the secondary insider lays the situation on the line: "My next-door neighbour's law firm is advising X SA on a planned takeover of Y SA. The bid will be announced next week and when it is, Y's shares will go through the roof." Even if the hint is not as strong as that, the mere information that X is about to make a bid to take over Y will provide a strong incentive for the person informed to deal now.

Austria and Luxembourg do not extend to secondary insiders the prohibition on unauthorised disclosure in their insider dealing legislation, nor, in their criminal legislation, do Germany and Spain.[96] Furthermore, secondary insiders will not be liable for any kind of breach of professional secrecy, since they did not obtain the information through their profession: had they done so, they would be primary, not secondary, insiders. Professional advisors are nonetheless strongly advised to take care in this area. All four Member States have strict legislation on professional confidentiality: its breach may carry a prison sentence, which in Luxembourg is mandatory. Given this background, the only safe approach is not to divulge.

---

[96] Until recently, Germany did not extend the prohibition on unauthorised disclosure to secondary insiders at all. The December 2004 amendment of the Securities Trade Act now does so, but only imposes a regulatory fine.

Chapter 5

Money Laundering: The EU Directive and the UK Statutory Response

Introduction

Money laundering is an issue easily overlooked in the context of insider dealing. It is, however, nonetheless an important one, not least for financial intermediaries, particularly stockbrokers, who buy and sell securities on behalf of their clients. The laws and regulations relating to money laundering would fill a book in their own right; indeed, many have been published on the subject. For the present purposes, therefore, it suffices to state that, generally speaking, the offence of money laundering consists of, *inter alia*, disguising the origin of the proceeds of (generally) a serious criminal offence,[1] assisting another to do so or, perhaps most importantly in this context, assisting another to retain the benefit of such an offence. As regards the more detailed provisions, this book will examine the EU Money Laundering Directive[2] and the legislation of the UK but only passing reference will be made to that of other Member States. Following a consideration of the Directive itself, it will then turn to the two UK money laundering statutes, the Proceeds of Crime Act 2002 and the Terrorism Act 2000.[3]

With the exception of the UK, no Member State's money laundering legislation covers the proceeds of all criminal offences and that of some, for example

---

1   Under the UK's Proceeds of Crimes Act 2002, the offences of money laundering apply to all criminal offences, however serious or minor they may be. All the other Member States, however, continue to confine the definition of money laundering to the proceeds of relatively serious offences.

2   As the Third Money Laundering Directive, although now in force, is as yet largely unimplemented by the Member States, this chapter focuses on the First and Second Money Laundering Directives: see p. 145.

3   The Money Laundering Directive is also implemented in the UK by the Money Laundering Regulations 2003, SI 2003/3075, which themselves replace the Money Laundering Regulations 1993. These contain not money laundering offences per se, but measures which financial institutions and certain other businesses are required to take to prevent money laundering. For a detailed discussion of the Regulations, see Alexander, R.C.H. (2004) "The Money Laundering Regulations 2003" 8 *Journal of Money Laundering Control* 75.

Luxembourg, does not extend to the proceeds of insider dealing. That of others, however, including the UK, France and Germany, does. In the light of this, it is salutary to consider the following scenario. Lest one think that it is too fanciful, it is based on the facts of an actual incident that took place in the late 1990s.[4]

A stockbroker, Alan Brooks, has a long-standing client, Colin Davies. Over the years, Brooks has frequently bought and sold securities for Davies and now receives instructions to buy 200 shares in Edmundsons plc. This he does and is pleased to see the price of Edmundsons' shares rise sharply 2 days later. Brooks is given considerable pause for thought, however, when he discovers the following week that Davies is a neighbour of Frank Grayson, Edmundsons' CEO.

It is clear that Brooks is not guilty of insider dealing, although one may suspect that Davies may well be. At the time at which he bought the shares, Brooks did not possess any knowledge that could remotely be termed inside information. Nor was he aware of anything to make him suspect that Davies might and hence he will not be guilty as an accessory either. So far, therefore, he has not committed any criminal offence. The situation will change, however, should Davies instruct Brooks, as he is likely to do, to sell the shares and then re-invest the proceeds. At this point, Brooks – and indeed his firm – will have a problem. If he carries out Davies' instructions, he will be assisting him to retain the benefit of a criminal offence and thus will commit the offence of money laundering. This will not, of course, be the case if Davies' purchase of the shares was in fact innocent, but this is unlikely to be a gamble that Brooks or his firm will wish to take. Brooks will therefore be compelled to notify the police, in the form of the Serious Organised Crime Agency, preferably before the second transaction or, at the latest, as soon as is practicable thereafter.[5]

Making a report, however, will not mean that Brooks is free of risk. In England, where our scenario takes place, legislation protects those who fulfil their duty to report suspicions of money laundering from any liability for breach of confidentiality. It does not, however, protect them from an action for breach of contract, should it transpire that the suspicion was unfounded.[6] Many Member States, such as France and Germany, deal with this problem by protecting those who report suspicious transactions from "all legal liability arising from the disclosure"; the UK does not. Even in these Member States, however, the outraged Davies will be free to complain widely that Brooks accused him, without foundation, of insider dealing and money laundering. The certain impact resulting to Brooks' business is all too clear.

Brooks' problem simply underlines the fact that the offence of insider dealing, like many financial crimes, is not one that can be viewed in isolation: its consequences

---

4   The names of the parties concerned have, to protect client confidentiality, had to be changed. For the same reason, the precise date of the incident cannot be given.

5   The option which would have been open until recently, namely simply declining to execute the transaction and severing the relationship, has now been closed: see below.

6   Until relatively recently, a defamation action was an additional risk. It has now been established, however, that a report to law enforcement, or indeed a regulator, enjoys the protection of absolute privilege: *Taylor v Serious Fraud Office* [1999] 2 AC 177; 219 [1998] 4 All ER 801, 818; *Mahon v Rahn (No. 2)* [2000] 4 All ER 41. See pp. 197-98.

are such that the possible money laundering implications need to be considered as well.

The EU Position

The European Union has introduced a total of three Directives to combat money laundering: Council Directive 91/308/EEC of 10 June 1991, Directive 2001/97/EC of the European Parliament and of the Council of 4 December 2001 and Directive 2005/60/EC of the European Parliament and of the Council of 26 October 2005. The third of these replaced the other two and came into force on 15 December 2005. The deadline for Member States to implement it, however, is not until 15 December 2007 and the majority have to date not yet done so. The anti-money-laundering regime in the EU therefore remains, for the time being, that of the 2001 Directive and it is therefore proposed to focus on this for the purposes of this chapter. This came into force in December 2001[7] and was to be implemented by the Member States no later than 15 June 2003.[8]

The bulk of 2001 Directive, however, simply amends the Directive that preceded it. References here shall, therefore, unless otherwise stated, be to the 1991 Directive in its amended form.

It should, incidentally, be made clear at the outset that the term "money laundering" is rather misleading. It is not simply money, but property of virtually any kind, which is covered. Article 1(C) states that "money laundering" means the committing of various acts in relation to "property" that is derived from a serious crime,[9] while Article 1(D) defines property as:

> assets of every kind, whether corporeal or incorporeal, movable or immovable, tangible or intangible, and legal documents or instruments evidencing title to or interests in such assets.

In essence, the amendments have had two major areas of impact. The first is the range of originating offences covered by definition of money laundering, while the second is the range of institutions that are now required to implement measures to combat money laundering. It should be noted, however, that Article 15 of the

---

7 This is in common with all EU Directives. Unlike UK Acts of Parliament, which may come into force as soon as they receive Royal Assent (e.g. Anti-Terrorism, Crime and Security Act 2001) or alternatively may await an implementation order months – or even longer – in the future (e.g. Financial Services and Markets Act 2000), EU Directives come into force as soon as they are published in the *Official Journal*, unless they contain an explicit provision stating otherwise. The Directive itself prescribes a date by which Member States must have implemented it, although, almost invariably, some Member States miss this deadline!

8 2001 Directive, Article 3(1). The UK was well ahead of this deadline: Part 7 of the Proceeds of Crime Act 2002 and the Money Laundering Regulations 2003 came into force in the early part of 2003.

9 For the definition in the Directive of "serious crime", see below.

original Directive (i.e. in its 1991 form) provided that "The Member States may adopt or retain in force stricter provisions in the field covered by this Directive to prevent money laundering." This Article remains unaltered. Thus, although the 1991 Directive originally only covered the proceeds of drug trafficking offences, the national legislation of the Member States covered those of a rather wider range even before the 2001 Directive was signed, let alone published.

It is nonetheless helpful to consider the changes brought about since the Directive's amendment. As mentioned above, the Directive in its original form applied only to the proceeds of drug trafficking. In the years that followed its introduction, however, the horizon expanded beyond the "war on drugs". It was increasingly seen that society is threatened by a wider range of serious crimes than drug trafficking alone and that the financial system is used just as effectively to launder the proceeds of these other crimes. A number of Member States therefore responded, at a national level, by passing so-called "all crimes legislation". In fact, this did not cover all criminal offences: the approach taken by the different Member States varied. That of France, for example, covered the proceeds of *crimes* and *délits*, although not *contraventions*;[10] Germany, which classifies criminal offences in much the same way, took a similar approach.[11] In contrast, the legislation of Luxembourg covered only a fairly short list of specified offences, although this list did, and still does, include any offence committed by a criminal organisation.

A wider list at Community level, and hence a new Directive, was therefore called for. This received added impetus and not inconsiderable publicity in the wake of the events of 11 September 2001, but in fact, as many have pointed out, it had been the subject of serious discussion since at least July of that year. The amended Directive, as of 28 December 2001, now covers the proceeds of, in addition to drug trafficking, the following range of other offences:[12]

- serious fraud against the EU budget;
- corruption;
- any offence committed by a criminal organisation;

---

10 *Crimes* are the most serious offences, attracting a prison sentence of at least 5 years, *délits* are less serious offences while *contraventions* are the least serious, comparable to the English summary offences.

11 *Verbrechen, Vergehen* and *Ordnungswidrigkeiten*. These are not to be confused with the term *Straftat*, which is a general term denoting any criminal offence of whatever category. The German money laundering legislation applies to the proceeds of all *Verbrechen*, and certain (although not all) *Vergehen*, but no *Ordnungswidrigkeiten*: Strafgesetzbuch (Criminal Code), para. 261.

12 The term "general crimes" has often been used by commentators in the UK to distinguish drug trafficking offences from those not linked to drug trafficking. In a discussion of the legislation of the different EU Member States, however, this is unhelpful, since in French, Belgian and Luxembourg criminal law, the word *crime* has, as seen above, a specific meaning: the more serious criminal offences. (A comparison could be made with "felony" in the United States.) In this book, the term "other offences" is therefore preferred.

- an offence which may generate substantial proceeds and which is punishable by a severe sentence of imprisonment in accordance with the penal law of the Member State.

It is helpful to take these in turn. Serious fraud against the EU budget would not seem to be applicable to the context of insider dealing: whoever is determined to be the victim of insider dealing, it is unlikely to be the finances of the European Union.[13]

Corruption is similarly unlikely to apply, at least at first glance. That said, it is to be noted that corruption is not defined in the Directive. The common definition is broken down into two categories: (1) receiving some kind of gift or favour in return for abusing one's office, or (2) using one's position to perform an act inconsistent with one's duties in that position or requiring such a gift or favour in order to perform an act that one has a duty, under one's office or position, to perform in any event. In the context of insider dealing, the second category would not apply: the Directive and the implementing national legislation refers to various things that an insider is not permitted to do. The first category might, however, apply. Suppose a person working in the research laboratory of a pharmaceutical company leaks the positive results of experiments to a third party in return for some kind of favour. They will certainly be guilty of unauthorised disclosure in the terms of the Directive. But they are also abusing their office, in return for a favour, to commit an act (leaking the information) inconsistent with their professional duties, something that does arguably fit within the definition of corruption.

In contrast, the third category, any offence committed by a criminal organisation, will certainly be covered: Newman and his associates, considered in Chapter 1,[14] would, at least on some definitions, be argued to be a criminal organisation.[15]

The most complex category is perhaps the final category. Two questions immediately arise. What are "substantial proceeds"? And what constitutes a "severe sentence of imprisonment"? As to the former, just how subjective this may be illustrated by the definition in the UK of "serious fraud" in terms of the jurisdiction of the Serious Fraud Office. When this was set up in 1987, it was given jurisdiction over fraud involving at least £1 million. The threshold has since been raised to £5 million, although it has been reported that, in practice, the SFO will only deal with cases involving at least £10 million. In contrast, in Spain, the profit threshold for insider dealing to be considered sufficiently serious to warrant criminal penalties is the equivalent of less than £300,000.

---

13 It is perhaps noteworthy that only where the victim is the EU budget is the inclusion of fraud on the list mandatory!

14 See p. 19-20.

15 They were a group of three persons, formed for the purpose of committing a series of criminal offences (obtaining and dealing on the basis of inside information). The details of their activities are set out in the judgment of Van Graafeiland, Circuit Judge in *U.S. v Newman* 664 F 2d 12 (2nd Circuit, 1981).

"Severe sentence of imprisonment" is similarly subjective. In Belgium, a sentence of three months is deemed *per se* to indicate that the offence is sufficiently serious to warrant automatic disqualification from holding a company directorship or working, in any capacity, in the financial services industry. In contrast, in England and Wales, a sentence of twice this length is deemed to be sufficiently light for three lay magistrates, with very little legal training,[16] to be able to impose it. The range of maximum sentences for the same offence shows a similar diversity. As seen in the previous chapter, insider dealing may be punished with up to 10 years' imprisonment in Ireland but only 1 year in Belgium. This could be interpreted as suggesting that insider dealing is viewed very seriously in Ireland but as a rather trivial offence in Belgium. A more likely explanation, however, particularly in view of the mandatory disqualification rule, is that prison sentences in Belgium generally tend to be much shorter than those in Ireland.

The 2005 Directive does, inspired by the revised FATF Recommendations, partially solve this problem. It removes the subjective "severe sentence of imprisonment", although the replacement is somewhat complicated. In principle, all offences carrying a maximum sentence of more than one year are covered. Where, however, the Member State in question provides in its criminal justice system for minimum, as well as maximum, sentences of imprisonment, it is offences carrying a minimum of more than six months that are to be regarded as predicate offences.[17]

Even without this complication (an unnecessary one, it is submitted), these revised provisions only partially resolve the question as to whether or not insider dealing constitutes a predicate offence. While most Member States impose a maximum sentence of more than one year's imprisonment (and/or a minimum sentence of more than six months), not all do. In Belgium, as noted above, although insider dealing carries a mandatory prison sentence, the minimum sentence is only three months.[18] Spain, as discussed elsewhere, is a special case as insider dealing is, save in very restricted circumstances, not a criminal offence at all and hence its proceeds will not constitute the proceeds of crime.[19]

Whether insider dealing is therefore covered by the Directive itself is therefore debatable. This may or may not be viewed as a serious problem. There is an argument

---

16 Lay justices are assisted and advised by a Magistrates' Clerk, who is required to be legally qualified. They are, however, under no obligation to follow the advice given. Lay justices are, in fact, now increasingly being phased out and replaced by professional District Judges, although they still remain for the moment, endowed with their full powers.

17 Article 3(5)(f). To take account of the different terms used in the various Member States, the term "imprisonment" is not in fact used, but rather "deprivation of liberty or detention order".

18 Even taking the maximum sentence as the criterion will not assist: the maximum sentence in Belgium is 12 months, while the Directive refers to a maximum sentence "in excess" of this.

19 Perhaps ironically, given this context, in those cases where insider dealing does attract criminal penalties in Spain, those penalties include a minimum of one year's imprisonment. See Chapter 4.

that Directives are merely designed to lay down guidelines and minimum standards; it is for Member States to fill in the details in their national legislation. Such an argument is, of course, strengthened by the importance given in recent years to the principle of subsidiarity. But this approach has one serious problem: the Member States make clear in their legislation that no heed is to be given to where the act from which the property is derived was carried out. Article 1(C) of the Directive requires this draconian approach, as does Article 1(3) of the 2005 Directive, which in this respect is identical. The lack of a uniform list of originating offences therefore creates a situation whereby a person in one Member State may perform an act that is not a criminal offence at all there, but a bank or other financial intermediary in another Member State, which invests the proceeds for him, may commit a serious criminal offence. This issue is discussed in greater detail below in the context of the UK's money laundering legislation.[20]

In the wider context, a completely uniform list of originating offences may be difficult to achieve due to the different approaches taken in relation to, for example, pornography and cannabis. In the present context, however, the problem may be surmounted by arguing that insider dealing, like most, if not all, acquisitive offences, is at least capable of producing unlimited profits and therefore comes within the fourth category mentioned above. After all, the only real limit on the profits made is the number of securities bought or sold. Alternatively, there is scope for taking the Spanish case-by-case approach. Were this adopted, cases of insider dealing where large profits are realised would come within the Directive, while relatively minor cases would not.[21] Such an approach would, however, require a minimum threshold to be set, which would need to apply across the entire European Union. There is, however, a precedent for this in the provisions dealing with identification requirements in Article 3 of the current Directive, again carried over to the 2005 Directive.[22]

The level of the threshold would inevitably be the subject of debate and quite possibly negotiation. The current Spanish threshold for criminal insider dealing is just under €450,760; a money laundering threshold of €450,000, necessitating only a small amendment of the Spanish Penal Code, might therefore be appropriate. Alternatively, since the threshold for triggering the identification requirements imposed on banks and most other financial institutions is the rather lower €15,000, this could be adopted. For the sake, however, of a consistent approach to insider dealing across the European Union, the higher threshold might in fact be preferable.

---

20 See p. 159.
21 Looking beyond Europe, a comparison could perhaps be drawn with the approach taken in the Chinese legislation relating to financial crimes: cases involving more than RMB 1 million (approx. £76,700 or €121,000) are capital crimes, carrying the death penalty, those between RMB 10,000 and RMB 1 million are non-capital criminal offences, while those involving less than RMB 10,000 are (generally) merely administrative offences.
22 Chapter II.

As mentioned above, the other key respect in which the Directive has been amended is the scope of institutions that are required to carry out measures to prevent them being used as unwitting accomplices in money laundering. All persons are prohibited from actually laundering money (or indeed any property) which they know[23] to be derived from serious crime. Certain designated professionals are, however, in addition required to carry out these preventative measures. Before examining the changes regarding their application, it is useful to outline the preventative measures themselves, which have not in fact changed since 1991.[24]

The Directive imposes two key obligations, identification of customers and reporting of suspicious transactions, plus an ancillary one: training of staff. Identification is often referred to as "know your customer". Under the Directive, when an account is first opened or a business relationship commenced, the institution must obtain evidence of the client's identity. The Directive does not state what form the evidence is to take. Originally, a national identity card or passport was generally required. Although this worked well in most Member States, it did create a potential problem in the UK and Ireland, which did not (and still do not) have a compulsory national identity card as other Member States do.[25] Frequently, however, a second form (at least) of identification would be asked for: in Germany, for example, where foreign nationals apply for a bank account, the bank asks not only for their national identity card or passport, but also for the stamped counterfoil of the police registration form.[26] Once the account is opened, identification must be obtained each time a transaction takes place involving €15,000[27] or more; this also applies where there is a series of transactions, each of which is less than this figure but which appear to the institution to be linked and which in total amount to €15,000 or more. In addition, identification must be obtained in relation to any transaction where money laundering is suspected. Where it is doubted that the customer is acting on their own account (or indeed where it is known that they are not!), the institution must take "reasonable measures to obtain information as to the real identity of the person or

---

23 Under the legislation of certain Member States, notably the UK, suspicion, or in some cases, mere negligence, is sufficient to incur liability for money laundering. The Directive, however, requires actual knowledge.

24 Save that the threshold amounts are now stated in euro rather than ECU; the amounts themselves, however, have not changed.

25 In the United Kingdom, compulsory national identity cards have at various times been proposed over the last 10 years. To date, however, although the Government has clearly expressed the intention to do so in the future, no legislation to create them has actually been introduced.

26 In Germany, all persons, German citizens as well as foreigners, are legally required to register with the police if they move to a new address for more than 3 days. Registration is done on a form, the counterfoil of which is stamped and retained by the person registering. Although this requirement is widely ignored for temporary moves of just a few days or weeks, it remains an important provision for changes of address lasting longer than this: it is impossible, for example, to open a bank account without producing the stamped counterfoil.

27 Approximately £10,335. Slightly different provisions apply to insurance business.

persons on whose behalf they are dealing". In all cases, copies of the evidence of identification must be kept on record for a period of at least 5 years.

Institutions are also under a duty to assist the authorities responsible for combating money laundering.[28] This involves co-operating with any investigation launched by those authorities but also, on the institution's own initiative, reporting any suspicions of money laundering to them in accordance with the national legislation.

Finally, they are under a duty to ensure that all relevant employees receive training, both in the current money laundering legislation and in how to recognise the modi operandi frequently used at the time to launder money. "Relevant employees" will mean any member of staff who in any way handles client money or processes transactions. It will not just mean the Account Manager who opens a new customer's account; it will also include the cashier who subsequently receives a payment by or for that customer.

In its original, 1991 form, the Directive imposed these measures on two types of institutions: credit institutions (in essence, banks) and financial institutions. The latter referred to undertakings[29] other than banks, which, *inter alia*, deal in or manage securities on behalf of their clients or give investment advice, etc; it also included insurance companies and undertakings offering money transmission or remittance services. As regards geographical scope, all such institutions located within the EU were covered; this explicitly included branches in an EU Member State of an institution whose head office was located in a third country. Thus, for example, Dresdner Bank was covered, but so was the London branch of the Bank of China.

Since the 2001 amendments, the reach of the Directive goes much further. All institutions (including EU branches of third-country banks and investment firms) which were previously covered remain so. That the term "financial institution" includes investment firms is made more explicit with reference both to the Investment Services Directive[30] and to collective investment schemes. It also now explicitly includes bureaux de change.

Considerable publicity has been given to inclusion of money transmission offices and bureaux de change in the 2001 Directive. It is arguable, however, that they were included in the Directive's original scope; indeed, money transmission offices certainly appear to have been covered. The 1991 text referred to financial institutions which, although they were not credit institutions (which by definition were covered), had as their principal operation the carrying out of "one or more of the operations included in numbers 2 to 12 and number 14 of the list annexed to Directive 89/646/

---

28 These vary from Member State to Member State: in the UK, it is the Serious Organised Crime Agency (SOCA) in the first instance and law enforcement agencies such as the police, H.M. Revenue and Customs or the Financial Services Authority thereafter; in Luxembourg, it is the Public Prosecutor for the City of Luxembourg.

29 The term "undertaking" is frequently used in EU legislation: it covers all business entities. The term was chosen in order to avoid a word which fitted some, but not all, corporate entities under the laws of the various Member States.

30 Directive 93/22/EEC.

EEC".[31] This list, now Annex 1 to the Consolidated Banking Directive,[32] includes "money transmission services". It also includes "trading for own account or for account of customers in ... (b) foreign exchange" (number 7). This could, of course, be taken as referring to buying and selling large amounts of foreign currencies as investments and also to future rate agreements. But if "trading" is interpreted simply as buying or selling, then not only will such operations be covered, so will bureaux de change. After all, their principal business is to buy and sell foreign currencies from/to customers. They may not do so on the same basis and the amounts involved in any one transaction are much less, but they still buy and sell currencies for their own account. Furthermore, when, as they frequently do, they order an amount of a given currency for a customer, it is at least arguable that they buy that currency for the account of a customer. The explicit reference to bureaux de change in Article 1(B)(1) of the amended Directive does, however, remove all doubt.

The Directive's reach is also extended to cover:

- auditors, external accountants and tax advisors;
- real estate agents;
- notaries, lawyers and other independent legal professionals;
- dealers and auctioneers in high-value goods, such as precious stones or metals, or works of art;
- casinos.

In fact, some Member States had already included some of these categories in their national legislation: the UK's Money Laundering Regulations 1993, for example, covered lawyers, while those in Finland were amended in 1997 to cover casinos. But the Directive itself, in its original form, only covered banks and related firms.

Interestingly, however, a qualification is placed on dealers and auctioneers in high-value goods. The Directive only applies to them where the value of the goods bought or sold is more than €15,000 and, furthermore, payment is made in cash. Thus, if a person walks into a jeweller's and buys a pendant worth £12,000 and pays for it in cash, the jeweller will be required to go through the full anti-money-laundering procedures. But if that person buys the same pendant with a Visa card issued by a bank in Nauru,[33] the Directive will not apply. Nor will it apply if another customer walks in and sells a diamond necklace, very possibly acquired in a third country, to the jeweller and is either paid by cheque or receives one or more other pieces of jewellery in exchange.

Also interesting is the threshold of €15,000. This is also used to trigger a further identification check for transactions involving financial institutions (in the widest sense). Such a threshold has its uses: it would be burdensome to impose such

---

31 That is, the Second Banking Directive.
32 Directive 2000/12/EC.
33 Nauru featured for some years on the Financial Action Task Force (FATF) list of Non-Cooperative Countries and Territories (NCCTs).

requirements in relation to each and every transaction, however small, by each and every customer. Indeed, it would be unworkable. But identification requirements are imposed when a new customer opens an account, regardless of the opening transfer. In practice, the opening transfer will often be the payment of the customer's next monthly salary. When one considers that a monthly salary of €15,000 equates to €180,000 (approximately £124,000) per annum and that in the UK, £30,500 per annum is sufficient to trigger the higher rate of income tax, it may be seen that many, indeed probably the majority, of the customers at an average bank branch will open their account with a transfer of far less.

There is, of course, the argument that when an account is opened, this prepares the way for many transactions over a period of time, not merely a one-off transaction such as takes place when a customer buys or sells a piece of jewellery. But this is not entirely satisfactory. Firstly, there are persons (generally legal entities rather than individuals) who do trade with dealers in high value goods on a regular basis. No identification check, however, will be required in relation to them unless they deal in cash. Secondly, unlike with credit and financial institutions, there is no reference in the Directive to transactions being covered where, although they involve less than €15,000, they appear to be linked to others in a series that totals more than this amount. Indeed, how could this be applied to dealers and jewellers? If the customer of a bank issues an instruction to transmit, each week, €14,000 to the same account in Nauru, these transactions at least appear at first glance to have a clear link. But if the same individual comes into a jewellers each week and buys, even for cash, jewellery worth €14,000, on what basis is there a clear link? Each purchase might have a completely different purpose. Whatever the rationale, however, no identification check will be required. It is true that if the jeweller in this scenario persists in asking no questions, he will risk falling foul of the national legislation of certain Member States (such as the UK), but it is not clear that he is covered by the Directive.

The 2005 Directive amends the reference to high value dealers: it covers any person providing any goods or services with a value of €15,000 or more for cash.[34] Although such a provision has the advantage of taking the particular spotlight off specific sectors (while not actually diminishing their obligations), the essential objections discussed above remain. If, as is submitted, certain credit cards are as capable as cash of being used for money laundering, it would seem strange to require identification where payment is in cash but not where it is by credit or debit card.

The deadline for implementation of the Directive by the Member States was 15 June 2003. The regime is therefore still quite new and it remains to be seen how it will work, particularly in practice.[35] It may be suspected that bureaux de change and casinos will continue to give cause for concern. Banks, investment firms, etc, have a range of checks that they can adopt in order to establish a new customer's true identity. A passport or national identity card is, of course, one, but then there are

---

34 Article 2(3)(e).
35 Since the 2001 and 2005 provisions in this area are quite similar, the introduction of the new Directive does not affect this point.

secondary forms of identification: possibly a driving licence, more likely something proving the person's address, such as one or more of the following: bank statements, credit card bills, utility bills, etc. In addition, most new customers will have had some form of relationship with a financial institution in the past and hence references can be asked for and confirmed.[36] But in a bureau de change or a casino, such detailed and complex checks are unworkable.

In the past, it was a standard requirement that anyone seeking to change currency had to produce their passport. In some cases, this is now returning.[37] This is, however, as far as one can reasonably go. In bureaux de change, above all, an important market is foreign visitors, often in the country only for short stays. Such persons do not carry utility bills or bank statements with them and even if they did, the bills/statements would often be in a language that the staff of a small bureau de change cannot read. It may be reasonable to ask them for a credit card, but these are easily forged or simply stolen. A driving licence is another possibility, although again, a person who visits another country for only a short time and has no intention of driving a car there may well leave this at home. Bank references are also impractical: the business of a bureau de change is that of a fast, over-the-counter service and customers expect this.

A passport on its own, however, is now widely recognised to be inadequate in establishing a customer's identity for anti-money-laundering purposes. It could be stolen or forged and, all too often, only an expert would be able to tell. In researching this book, it transpired that even genuine documents were not correctly recognised.[38] It is debatable, therefore, whether an employee of a financial institution, particularly one that is relatively small or located in a small provincial town, will recognise a genuine passport from a forged one. To an extent, this is addressed by the requirement under the Directive that staff should be trained in anti-money-laundering procedures – but experience suggests that there is no guarantee that this will always be adequate. It is for this very reason that the banks go further than a mere passport check. As has

---

36 The exceptions are minors and indeed young adults, who in themselves present money laundering risks: it is far from unknown for criminals to open accounts, sometimes with considerable sums in them, in the names of their infant children. Where it is suspected that the account is in fact simply a sham and the true beneficiary will be the adult opening it, that adult can be checked out in the normal way. But where the institution is faced with, say, an 18 year old opening their first bank account (a category, incidentally, which all the retail banks regard as a highly important market), it is a problem.

37 Save where the transaction is in a bank of which the person is an established customer. This is, however, not universally the case.

38 A bank teller in a small Portuguese town, when asked to change currency, required to see a passport, but was confused by the words "United Kingdom of Great Britain and Northern Ireland" and therefore noted the customer's nationality as Irish, not British. Similarly, an immigration officer training a junior colleague at Berlin Tegel airport, when presented with a passport bearing the words "People's Republic of China", confused this with "Republic of China" and informed his colleague that this was what a passport from Taiwan looked like.

been seen, however, what is practical for a bank is not always practical for a bureau de change.

It could be argued that the threshold of €15,000 prevents such problems from arising: the legitimate businessman, over in London for just a few days who wishes to buy £100 to cover those small transactions for which he will not use a credit card may continue as before. Unfortunately, however, the wording of the Directive does not make this clear. Article 3(1) states:

> Member States shall ensure that institutions and persons subject to this Directive require identification of their customers by means of supporting evidence when entering into business relations ...

A bureau de change, as has been seen, is certainly an institution or person subject to the Directive and it arguably enters into business relations with its customers. The threshold appears in Article 3(2):

> The identification requirement shall also apply for any transaction with customers other than those referred to in paragraph 1, involving a sum amounting to EUR 15,000 or more, whether the transaction is carried out in a single operation or in several operations which seem to be linked.

It could be argued that "business relations" means an ongoing relationship and the reference in the latter part of Article 3(1) to "particularly, in the case of institutions, when opening an account or savings accounts, or when offering safe custody facilities" demonstrates this. On that interpretation, those institutions specialising in one-off transactions with customers with whom they will never deal again are covered by Article 3(2) and hence the €15,000 threshold. The provisions are, however, also open to a wider interpretation: that "particularly" does not mean "solely" or even "primarily" and that one-off business types are therefore, at least prima facie, covered by Article 3(1), not 3(2). On this analysis, the role of Article 3(2) is to cover transactions of more than €15,000 carried out by (or on behalf of) existing customers. In other words, its purpose is to prevent institutions from simply identifying a customer once, when he first opens his account, and then regarding that as its full anti-money-laundering procedure in relation to that customer for the rest of time. Bureaux de change and the like are therefore subject to the full identification requirements, regardless of the amount of money the customer wishes to change.

The view may, of course, be taken that small bureaux de change are themselves a bad thing, prone to money laundering that is all too often deliberate;[39] hence, if they go out of business and currency exchange becomes the preserve of the banks, so much the better. If, however, one believes that Travelex and even its smaller

---

39 A senior police officer in one major European city claimed in the mid-1990s that over 50% of the bureaux de change in the centre of that city were fronts for criminal organisations.

competitors provide a service that, in at least a reasonable number of cases, is both legitimate and useful, this is an issue that needs to be considered.

United Kingdom

Just as the UK had in place legislation prohibiting insider dealing before the Insider Dealing Directive was introduced, so too it was ahead in the area of money laundering legislation. Drug money laundering became a criminal offence under the Drug Trafficking (Offences) Act 1986, 7 years before the original Money Laundering Directive, while the roots of the Proceeds of Crime Act 2002 can be traced to a Cabinet Office report published in June 2000.[40]

It is therefore perhaps unsurprising that in one aspect, at least, the UK was ahead of the Union as a whole in its enhanced money laundering legislation. On 12 November 2001, a few weeks before the new Directive was signed and over a month before it was published, the Money Laundering Regulations 2001[41] were introduced. These amended the Money Laundering Regulations 1993 to cover bureaux de change, cheque cashiers and money transmission agents. It is, however, perhaps an indication of the focus of this move that its enforcement is placed in the hands of H.M. Revenue and Customs. Not only is Customs to be the regulator, at least for these purposes, of these three types of business but it is also empowered to prosecute both actual money laundering (which it already prosecuted) and also breaches of the Regulations. This despite the fact that it was to be less than three weeks before the Financial Services Authority took up its full powers and responsibilities for the regulation of financial services as a whole, including, notably, the power to prosecute money laundering offences. One is inclined to suspect that the Government's aim in producing the 2001 Regulations was to combat international terrorism and drug trafficking; this was, after all, the time of the war in Afghanistan, where the Taliban were not only supporting Al Qaeda but were believed to be producing heroin as a cash export crop.[42] Since it is Customs that lead the fight against drug trafficking and also guard against the importation of terrorist weaponry, it would have been logical that they should also be the agency that combats the financing behind these. But this mere speculation; it is equally possible that in the rush to pass through legislation in the wake of 9/11, the potential for overlap and indeed conflict between the roles of Customs and the FSA was simply overlooked.

---

40 (2000) Cabinet Office Performance and Innovation Unit Report, "Recovering the Proceeds of Crime".

41 S.I. 2001/3641.

42 Even with the fall of the Taliban, little has changed here: it was recently stated that 85% of the heroin imported into the UK is produced in Afghanistan. *Independent*, 19 November 2004.

There were plans to introduce further Money Laundering Regulations in 2002, but these only reached draft stage and were superseded by the Money Laundering Regulations 2003, the bulk of which came into force on 1 March 2004.[43]

The substantive money laundering offences are, however, found in the Proceeds of Crime Act 2002, which came into force in early 2003, although this is supplemented by separate provisions relating to terrorist property under the Terrorism Act 2000, as amended by the Anti-Terrorism, Crime and Security Act 2001.[44] It is useful to consider these in turn.

Proceeds of Crime Act 2002

For the first time, the proceeds of drug trafficking and other offences are brought together under the same piece of legislation. The remit is also widened. The previous "all crimes legislation", the Criminal Justice Act 1988 as amended by the Criminal Justice Act 1993, did not in fact cover the proceeds of all offences but only indictable offences, i.e. offences either triable on indictment, in the Crown Court before a judge and jury, or triable either way. Summary offences, those triable only before a Magistrates' Court, were, with a few technical exceptions, not included.[45] They are now, however, included in the 2002 Act, which refers to "criminal conduct". This is defined as "conduct which constitutes an offence in any part of the United Kingdom" or which would do so if it had occurred there.[46] "An offence" means precisely that: any offence is covered. This has, however, little impact for the purposes of the current study, since insider dealing, being triable either way, is an indictable offence.

What is new is the extent of the new money laundering provisions. At first glance, they are similar to the old regime. The laundering offences all relate to criminal property, a concept defined in section 340 of the Act as property which constitutes or represents a person's benefit from criminal conduct and, crucially, which the defendant knows or suspects to be such. This latter provision is important. Unlike their counterparts in the previous legislation, most of the provisions of the 2002 Act setting out the money laundering offences do not directly refer to any state

---

43 A detailed consideration of the 2003 Regulations may found in Alexander, R.C.H. (2004) "The Money Laundering Regulations 2003" 8 *Journal of Money Laundering Control* 75.

44 At first glance, the issue of terrorism and terrorist funding might appear to have little connection with that of insider dealing. There have been allegations, however, connecting the two, hence its inclusion in this book.

45 Very broadly, the three categories may be compared to the *crimes, délits* and *contraventions* of the French system or the *Verbrechen, Vergehen* and *Ordnungswidrigkeiten* of the German.

46 S.340(2). An identical definition is provided, for the purposes of the confiscation provisions, in s.76(1) in respect of England and Wales, s.143(1) in respect of Scotland and s.224(1) in respect of Northern Ireland. S.340(2) applies, however, to the entire United Kingdom.

of knowledge or suspicion on the part of the defendant. The reference is indirect, through the definition of criminal property, found elsewhere. This is perhaps not the most useful means that the draftsmen could have chosen, but, contorted though it may be, it does mean that, for the laundering offences, the state of knowledge required of the defendant is the same as it was before.

Further, criminal property includes mixed property. Section 340(7) states:

> References to property ... obtained in connection with conduct include references to property ... obtained both in that connection and some other.

That other connection can be an entirely legitimate one. Thus, where a person engages in insider dealing and pays the profits into his bank account, into which his salary is also paid, the entire contents of that bank account, for the purposes of these provisions, constitute criminal property. From the point of view of law enforcement, this is essential. While there are persons whose entire income is derived from crime, there are also many who commit offences from which they derive property but who also receive genuine payments for activities quite legally performed. This is perhaps especially true of insider dealing. The concept of the "primary insider", found both in the Directive and the legislation of many Member States, is a person who obtains inside information through his employment, profession, duties, etc.[47] Even though the UK does not distinguish between primary and secondary insiders, in practice, most, if not all, insider dealers will either have accessed the inside information through their work or be closely connected with someone who has. Further, where the insider does arrange for someone else (typically a partner or friend) to conduct the actual deal for him, that associate will generally have a professional position of their own if their transactions are not to arouse comment. A housewife who suddenly buys shares worth £10,000 is likely to attract the interest both of the stockbroker and the Financial Services Authority, particularly if events shortly afterwards cause the price of those shares to rise sharply. Where, in contrast, a lawyer or an employee of a major investment bank buys the same shares at the same time, it is rather more likely that it will be considered firstly that they are buying them on their own behalf rather than for someone else and secondly that the purchase is due simply to their own investment judgment.

If the definition of criminal property is to be confined to property (such as the contents of a bank account), 100% of which is derived from crime, it will therefore be virtually impossible to prosecute successfully the financial intermediary who conducts transactions in relation to it. It may be shown that they knew or suspected that the account contained the proceeds of crime. But they could argue that the funds which they transferred represented only a relatively small proportion of the total in the account (very possibly true) and that further, they believed that those funds were drawn from the legitimately-obtained portion. The legislation can therefore only be workable if a mixed fund is included in the definition.

---

47 For the full definition of an insider and the issues that this raises, see Chapter 2.

Now to the offences themselves. It is an offence for a person to enter into or become concerned in an arrangement which they know or suspect facilitates another person to acquire, retain, use or control criminal property, either directly or through an intermediary.[48] It should be noted, incidentally, that it is nowhere stated that the other person need be the person who committed the offence, or even anyone linked to them in some way. Facilitating any person, regardless of who they are, to acquire, retain, etc, criminal property is an offence.

It is similarly an offence to conceal, disguise, convert, transfer or remove criminal property from the jurisdiction[49] as well as to acquire, use or have possession of it.[50] As under the previous legislation, a defence is afforded where the person makes a report of their knowledge or suspicion either before undertaking the action or as soon as is practicable thereafter, or, alternatively, they intended to make such a report and had a reasonable excuse for not actually doing so. Clearly, where the action is undertaken after the report is made, the person receiving the report must consent to it.[51]

A number of points immediately arise. The first is that the jurisdiction is firmly based in each part of the United Kingdom rather than the UK as a whole. Removal from the jurisdiction is explicitly stated to be from England and Wales, Scotland or Northern Ireland.[52] In other words, a person who moves criminal property from London to Belfast commits an offence just as much as if he moves it from London to Panama. Similarly, criminal conduct, which gives rise to criminal property, is an act which is, or would be, "a criminal offence in any part of the United Kingdom". Thus, it need not be an offence in all of it. Again, this has no impact currently on insider dealing offences (although it would have done prior to 1993) or the proceeds that derive from them. It is nonetheless worthy of note that, in principle at least, a person in, for example, Edinburgh, could be guilty of money laundering when they carry out a transaction in respect of proceeds of an act which was committed quite legally there but was an offence in England.[53]

Of much wider application is the removal of the requirement that, in order to be an offence, the concealment, disguise, etc. of the proceeds of crime must have a specific purpose. Under the former legislation, an element of the offence was that the transfer, etc. of the property was "for the purpose of assisting any person to avoid prosecution for an offence [or a drug trafficking offence] or the making or

---

48 S.328(1).

49 S.327(1).

50 S.329(1).

51 For the system of reporting knowledge or suspicion of money laundering, see below.

52 S.327(1)(e).

53 For example, trading on a Sunday outside the restricted hours permitted in England. An example of the reverse would, until February 2005, have be a hunt with hounds for which participants paid but which did not fulfil the requirements now required in Scotland but not, at that time, in England and Wales.

enforcement of a confiscation order".[54] Unless this could be proven, the prosecution would fail. This provision has been removed; it is now immaterial what the purpose of the transfer is. A banker who transfers funds, part of which derive from insider dealing, from his client's account to a building society as his regular mortgage payment – or even to H.M. Revenue and Customs in settlement of his VAT bill – will be guilty of an offence. All that the prosecution need prove is that the transfer took place, it was of criminal property and the bank had the requisite knowledge or suspicion.

An innovation that has been widely publicised is that all these offences apply not simply to those handling property on behalf of someone else but equally to those dealing with it on their own account. This is frequently expressed in terms of dealing with one's own property; as some have stated, "A person can now be guilty of laundering their own money as well as someone else's." This is misleading, however, since the immediate proceeds of some offences, for example those under the Theft Acts 1968 and 1978, consist of property which most would agree is not the property of the person handling it. In the context of financial crime, it might be the contents of a pension fund, or perhaps simply company assets, that have been misappropriated; it is not unduly controversial to argue that these still remain the property of the fund's contributors or of the company as the case may be. (Whether the company is considered as the legal entity or as the shareholders is immaterial for these purposes.) The terms "on behalf of another" and "on one's own account" are therefore probably more helpful.

This also raises an important point about the nature of the property itself (wherever it is derived). In this section, and indeed this chapter in general, the money laundering provisions are generally discussed in relation to money, typically the contents of a bank account. It should be noted, however, that, although criminal property of course includes money, it covers far more than that. Section 340(9) of the Act states:

Property is all property wherever situated and includes –

(a) money;
(b) all forms of property, real or personal, heritable or moveable;
(c) things in action and other intangible or incorporeal property.

It may be seen that this covers essentially all types of property. For almost 25 years, the case of *Oxford v Moss*[55] has been cited as establishing that, under English law, information does not constitute property.[56] The definition of information in the Proceeds of Crime Act 2002 questions this, however. What is meant by "intangible and incorporeal property"? It is clearly not confined to choice in action and rights, since category (c) above clearly refers to "things in action *and other* intangible and

---

54 Criminal Justice Act 1988, s.93C; Drug Trafficking Act 1994, s.49(2).
55 (1978) 68 Cr. App. R 183, discussed [1979] Crim. LR 119.
56 In contrast to the US theory of insider dealing as misappropriation of information.

incorporeal property".[57] Other jurisdictions have certainly accepted information as property. In the United States case of *Diamond v Oreamuno*,[58] the New York Chief Judge Fuld referred to "potentially valuable information" as "that asset".[59] Similarly, in France, secondary insiders who deal on the basis of the inside information that they have received are guilty of *recel* or handling the proceeds of crime.[60] In the UK, although it has yet to be seen how the phrasing of the definition in the 2002 Act will be construed, it would certainly seem to allow for such an interpretation. US cases have persuasive authority in the UK, while the French provisions are an implementation of an EU Directive and inspiration might therefore be drawn from them.

Indeed, the classification of information as property is already not wholly alien to English law. In the civil law, although the opinion has not been unanimous, some judges have considered it to be such, sometimes in quite strong terms. Lord Hodson, in the case of *Boardman v Phipps*,[61] stated:

> I dissent from the view that information is of its nature something which is not properly to be described as property ... I agree ... that the confidential information acquired in this case, which was capable of being and which was turned to account, can be properly regarded as property of the trust.[62]

Lord Guest concurred:

> If Mr. Boardman was acting on behalf of the trust, then all the information that he obtained ... became trust property. ... I see no reason why information and knowledge cannot be trust property.[63]

Lord Upjohn made it clear that he felt otherwise, but his judgment proved, ultimately, a minority one. Further, even in the case of *Oxford v Moss* itself, Smith J stressed that his examination of the question whether information did or did or not constitute property was confined solely to the context of a charge of theft; indeed, he said that the case law on fiduciary obligations was "of little assistance".[64] Insider dealing is an offence that has throughout its history been dealt with in quite separate legislation

---

57 Emphasis added.
58 24 NY 2d 494 (1969). For a discussion of this case, see Rider, B.A.K., Ashe, T.M. and Counsell, L. in Rider and Ashe (ed.) (1995) *The Fiduciary, the Insider and the Conflict*, Brehon Sweet & Maxwell, p. 181.
59 P. 496
60 For a discussion of *recel* in this context, see pp. 58-60 and pp. 115-16.
61 [1966] All ER 721.
62 Pp. 745–46.
63 P. 751.
64 (1978) 68 Cr. App. R 183, 186.

to theft and therefore the ruling in *Oxford v Moss* could be argued to have little application to it.[65]

Whatever the view on the status of the inside information itself, what is clear is that the securities bought on the basis of it constitute property within the meaning of the Act. Debt securities, options and the like are things in action. It is arguable that shares are, also, but in any event, since they represent a part of a legal entity, i.e. a company, they definitely come within the phrase "all forms of property".

The effect of this is that it is not just dealing with the profits from insider dealing that is prohibited: it is also an offence to deal with the securities themselves. In order to make the profit, the insider dealer needs to sell the securities; this will constitute transferring criminal property (since he transfers them to the person to whom he sells them). This carries a maximum prison sentence not of 7 years for insider dealing but 14 years for money laundering.

Even before he sells them, he will be guilty of other offences. In addition to simplifying the laundering offences which existed under the previous legislation, the Act adds three more: acquiring, using and having possession of criminal property. To be liable, it is no longer necessary to do anything with the securities; merely receiving them or having possession of them will suffice. At first glance, it may seem unnecessary to have two offences: receipt and possession. One cannot have possession of something unless one has first received it; equally, as soon as one receives something, one has possession of it. For the insider dealer himself, this is indeed the case. But the situation is different for the intermediary. Property is only criminal property if the defendant knows or suspects that it is derived from an offence. Consider the scenario with Alan Brooks, depicted at the beginning of this chapter. When he bought the shares on Davies' behalf, he had no suspicion that anything was amiss. He therefore did not receive criminal property, although Davies did.[66] But once he discovers the connection between Davies and Grayson and suspects that Davies, when he instructed him to buy the shares, did so on the basis of inside information, he immediately becomes guilty of having possession of criminal property. This puts Brooks in a very difficult position; despite the fact that he has acted with complete propriety throughout, he finds himself guilty of a serious

---

65 In *A-G for Hong Kong v Reid*, Lord Templeman appears to confirm that information does constitute property: "*Boardman v Phipps* ... demonstrates the strictness with which equity regards the conduct of a fiduciary and the extent to which equity is willing to impose a constructive trust on a property obtained by a fiduciary by virtue of his office ... the solicitor obtained the information which satisfied him that the purchase of the shares in the takeover company would be a good investment". [1994] 1 All ER 1, 10-11; [1994] 1 AC 324, 338. His Lordship's remarks are merely persuasive, since they are firstly a Privy Council decision and secondly, arguably *obiter dicta*, given that *Reid* concerned the proceeds of bribes, rather than misuse of information. They have, however, been taken to settle the point: see Hayton, D.J. (2003) *Underhill and Hayton: Law of Trusts and Trustees*, 16th Edition, pp. 391–92.

66 This analysis assumes that Frank Grayson did indeed pass on inside information to Davies; if in fact he did not, it is of course clear that neither Davies nor Brooks will be guilty of any offence.

criminal offence. The only way in which he can avoid such liability is to make a report.

Under the previous system of the Criminal Justice Act 1988, Brooks had the alternative option of simply closing Davies' account and asking him to take his shares elsewhere. The regime of the 2002 Act, however, closes this. If he does so, Brooks will be guilty of the offence of transferring criminal property (transferring the shares either to Davies or whichever intermediary he is instructed to send them to) and, in addition, of a further offence of failing to report a suspicion of money laundering.

Before examining the provisions relating to the making of reports, the offence of use of criminal property should be further considered. It could be argued that it is unlikely to apply to insider dealing, but this will not always be the case. The insider may not simply make a quick profit by selling immediately after the price goes up; indeed, if he wishes to avoid investigation and quite possible detection, he may well keep the securities for a time. If they are shares, they entitle the person holding them to attend shareholders' meetings and, moreover, vote at them. If the insider dealer does so attend and vote, or even puts a question, he will have committed the offence of using the shares within the meaning of Act.

Furthermore, the profit derived from shares is not only the price for which they are sold. While the shareholder retains them, they entitle him to a dividend. If the shares have been bought on the basis of inside information, this is further criminal property. Hence, when the insider receives the dividend cheque, he is guilty of a further offence of receipt. The full indictment sheet of a person who had carried out one act of insider dealing could therefore contain counts such as the following:[67]

1. Insider dealing, contrary to section 52(1) of the Criminal Justice Act 1993. Particulars of Offence: that, being in possession of information as an insider, he did on Thursday 6 January 2005 purchase 1,200 shares in Edmundsons plc, the price of which was affected by that information when it became publicly available.

2. Acquisition of criminal property, contrary to section 329(1)(a) of the Proceeds of Crime Act 2002. Particulars of Offence: that he did on Thursday 6 January 2005 acquire 1,200 shares in Edmundsons plc, a benefit from insider dealing.

3. Use of criminal property, contrary to section 329(1)(b) of the Proceeds of Crime Act 2002. Particulars of Offence: that he did on Monday 28 February 2005 use his holding of 1,200 shares in Edmundsons plc, being a benefit from insider

---

67 The following is, of course, not in the exact format of an indictment, but it does serve to demonstrate some of the counts. It is arguable, in fact, that rather more counts could be brought; these do, however, represent the key offences that he would be likely to have committed.

dealing, in order to vote at the Annual General Meeting of Edmundsons plc.

4. Acquisition of criminal property, contrary to section 329(1)(a) of the Proceeds of Crime Act 2002. Particulars of Offence: that he did on Tuesday 15 March 2005 acquire a dividend of £70 in respect of his holding of 1,200 shares in Edmundsons plc, a benefit from insider dealing.

5. Transfer of criminal property, contrary to section 327(1)(d) of the Proceeds of Crime Act 2002. Particulars of Offence: that he did on Tuesday 22 March 2005 transfer to Harold Ingham 1,200 shares in Edmundsons plc, a benefit from insider dealing.

6. Conversion of criminal property, contrary to section 329(1)(a) of the Proceeds of Crime Act 2002. Particulars of Offence: that he did on Tuesday 22 March 2005 convert 1,200 shares in Edmundsons plc, constituting a benefit from insider dealing, into the sum of £38,400 in money.

The indictments of the financial intermediaries will not be quite as long as this, but, as has been seen, their liability is also complex. In addition to the actual laundering offences discussed above, there is now an additional offence of failing to report knowledge or suspicion of money laundering.[68] This carries up to 5 years' imprisonment. The provision does not go quite as far as compelling a person guilty of such an offence to confess immediately on pain of yet another count on his indictment: it refers explicitly to knowledge or suspicion that "another person" is engaged in money laundering and is further restricted to "the regulated sector". This, however, under Part 1 of Schedule 9 to the Act, covers virtually all areas of financial services activity: banks, those engaged in any kind of investment activity, (whether regulated directly by the Financial Services Authority (FSA) or from other EEA Member States[69], operating under a "passport"),[70] building societies, credit unions, bureaux de change and money transmission offices. Certain non-financial institutions, although they are now covered by the amended EU Money Laundering Directive, are not subject to section 330; these are casinos, auctioneers and dealers in

---

68 S.330.

69 Although the passport is provided under EU Directives, those benefiting from it include not only institutions based in the 27 EU Member States but also the three additional countries which, while not being members of the EU, are members of the European Economic Area (EEA). These are Norway, Iceland and, perhaps most significant from the point of view of financial services, Liechtenstein.

70 Provided under the EU Consolidated Banking Directive, Directive of the European Parliament and Council 2000/12/EC or the Investment Services Directive, Council Directive 93/22/EEC. The latter will be replaced, however, on 30 April 2007 with the implementation of the Markets in Financial Instruments Directive, Directive of the European Parliament and Council 2004/39/EC.

high value goods such as fine art, precious stones and precious metals.[71] It should be stressed that it is not only managers and the like who are covered, but any member of the regulated business: even the most junior cashier.

A similar provision, carrying the same sentence, was contained in section 52 of the Drug Trafficking Act 1994;[72] there are, however, some important differences. Firstly, that provision related solely to knowledge or suspicion of drug money laundering, i.e. where the property concerned was related to drug trafficking. The new provision relates to any kind of money laundering, irrespective of to what kind of offence it relates. But in another sense, the new provision is more restricted: it is confined to where knowledge or suspicion comes to a person in the course of their business in the regulated sector, whereas the Drug Trafficking Act offence applied to a person in the course of any business or employment, regulated or otherwise.

The most controversial aspect of section 330 is, however, its inclusion of those with reasonable grounds to suspect money laundering: these, too, have an obligation to report. Whether or not they actually suspected anything is immaterial. This has caused considerable disquiet amongst the regulated sector and human rights lawyers alike. What constitute "reasonable grounds"? As has been said many times, hindsight is invariably 20-20: how can one tell what were reasonable grounds at the time? Is it fair to ask a jury to decide this? Those on the other side of the argument have pointed out that, where actual knowledge or suspicion is required, the legislation is almost impossible to enforce. Which is more difficult for a jury, they ask: to judge what at the time were reasonable grounds to suspect money laundering or to look inside the defendant's head and discern what his actual state of knowledge or suspicion was? The answer, it has been said, may be found not only from our own judgment but from the record of the UK, to date, of convicting money launderers. The provision's defenders however, frequently explain the extended requirement by use of the phrase, "the Nelsonian blind eye", suggesting that they believe that they are pursuing not so much the negligent as the wilful.

The provision is nonetheless as wide-ranging as it is draconian. Money laundering, for the purposes of section 330, means any of the offences contained in sections 327, 328 or 329.[73] As has been seen, these cover a far greater range of activity than the traditional hiding or disguising of ill-gotten gains. No longer will it suffice to ask whether a given transaction makes commercial sense; the financial intermediary now needs to ask whether he has any reason to suspect that any part of his client's property (money, investments, securities, whatever) may be derived from

---

71 It should be made clear that it is only those who deal in precious metals as objects and artefacts (i.e. jewellers, goldsmiths, silversmiths and the like) who are not covered by section 330. Those trading in the precious metal markets as investments are most certainly covered, as are those who deal professionally in any other kind of investment, since they are subject to the regulation of the FSA. Jewellers and the like are, however, subject to the provisions of the Money Laundering Regulations 2003: see Alexander, R.C.H. (2004) "The Money Laundering Regulations 2003" 8 *Journal of Money Laundering Control* 75.
72 The anti-terrorism legislation also had, and indeed still has, a similar provision.
73 S.340(11).

some criminal offence. This effectively means going back one stage and judging whether his client might have "been up to no good". Moreover, although the section specifically refers to information or matters that come to the person's attention in the context of his work in the regulated sector, this is of little comfort. The financial professional may hear rumours, gossip, etc. outside his work, but it is nonetheless firmly within the context of his work that he is aware that, wherever and however his client obtained his property, he instructs him or at least his institution to handle it.

One effect of this is that the responsibility for preventing financial crime is passing, at least in part, from the traditional law enforcement agencies to the financial professionals themselves. This is something that certain commentators have long been predicting. The record in the UK of detecting financial criminals has not been great and, although civil sanctions are seen as one solution, the concept of "facilitator liability" is seen as another.[74] Some years ago, the strategy was introduced of disruption, of forcing criminals out of the financial system, even if they themselves could not be prosecuted. It has now been supplemented by recruiting financial professionals, under compulsion, as informants and agents of law enforcement.

A further consequence of the legislation concerns how an institution is required to deal with those of its own staff who are suspected of involvement in money laundering (as now defined). The provisions do not refer to "the person's client", but merely to "another person". Where, therefore, an institution comes to suspect, or even has reasonable grounds to do so, that one of its own staff is engaged in money laundering, it is obliged, on pain of criminal penalties, to make a report. In the past, there was widespread anecdotal evidence that the general practice in such cases was for the institution simply to part company with the employee in question. There would be a quiet meeting between a few senior managers or partners and the person concerned, the culprit would be informed that they had been discovered and must leave, but, if they resigned without demur, a good severance package and reference would be provided. The object, above all, was to keep the matter quiet and thus preserve the institution's reputation. This was why the reference was provided: lack of one would swiftly result in the news going round the wine bars of the City of London that Ms X had left PQR "under something of a cloud". It was far better to keep things quiet and the confidence of the clients undisturbed and simply move the problem to a competitor institution.

Such an approach is now explicitly illegal. Any person discovered to have been involved in such a sweeping under the carpet faces up to 5 years in prison. Of course, proving that such a deal took place will be next to impossible, but this is not important: if the manager had reasonable grounds to suspect that his colleague was involved in any money laundering offence and did not report this, either to the

---

74 Professor Barry Rider, for example, for some years before the passing of the 2002 Act, and even the introduction of the Bill that preceded it, warned in several conference papers that facilitator liability was to be the strategy of the future in fighting organised and economic crime. See the comments made relating to facilitator liability in Chapter 1: pp. 27-28.

nominated officer[75] and thence to SOCA or directly to law enforcement, he is guilty of an offence.[76]

There have been those who have raised human rights objections to this. For this reason, it has been suggested that certain Member States may be reluctant to adopt this approach. Germany, whose eastern states have recent memories of the Stasi and its use of informants, has been cited as a particular example; Poland, Spain and Greece are others. But the recent history of the UK, in the perception of the government and much of the population alike, has not so much been of an oppressive state targeting innocent victims, but rather of the unscrupulous, not to say dishonest, abusing the financial services system and a justice system all too often powerless to bring them to book.[77] It is therefore perhaps unsurprising that draconian legislation has been seen as the answer, compelling those who handle other people's accounts to inform of anything suggesting wrongdoing by their clients.

Not only is making a report obligatory in the circumstances considered above, it is also a defence provided to each of the money laundering offences. That defence is phrased in absolute terms. Instead of the wording, "It shall be a defence for the accused person to prove [or show] ...", popularly used to place a burden on the defendant, subsection (2) of each of the three sections states, "But a person does not commit such an offence if ...". This is carried over from the previous legislation. As before, there are two defences, either that the person disclosed his suspicions to the appropriate person or that, although he did not, he intended to do so and had a reasonable excuse for not doing so. What is considered to constitute a reasonable excuse is likely to vary in each individual case. Simple negligence will not be enough; a lack of opportunity, however, for whatever reason, may be, particularly in the context of a short timescale.

The 2002 Act sets out in great detail the process of making a report. Firstly, persons are divided into two categories: nominated officers and others. Nominated officers are those persons who, in the course of its anti-money-laundering strategy, the institution has appointed to receive reports from other members of staff of suspected money laundering. They are therefore what up to now have generally been referred to as Money Laundering Reporting Officers or MLROs.

In practice, the first person in the institution to suspect money laundering is likely to be someone other than the nominated officer: the cashier at the banking counter, for example, the individual trader or the assistant solicitor. They are to make their

---

75   See below.

76   Where the deal can be proved, it is arguable that the reference could give rise to an action by the "successor" institution for deceit; this issue, however, is one for a separate discussion.

77   Perhaps ironically, the provisions introduced to deal with terrorism have caused public perception to start to swing the other way. There are no signs, however, that either the current Labour Government or the Conservative Opposition is likely to question the provisions of the Proceeds of Crime Act 2002.

report to the nominated officer.[78] Provided that they then act in accordance with the nominated officer's instructions, they are then protected.

Alternatively, they may make a report directly to a police or customs officer; section 338 defines an authorised disclosure as one to either a police officer, customs officer or a nominated officer. They then act according to that officer's instructions.

If the report is made before the transaction has been executed, the nominated officer must take a decision whether or not to authorise it. For this reason, the roles of MLRO and Compliance Officer are in many institutions combined in one person (or sometimes, if the institution is a large one, one department or section). If he considers that the proposed transaction is not related to money laundering, he will give the authorisation to proceed. If that judgment turns out to be wrong, it is his responsibility, not that of the person who sent him the report. Where he knows or suspects that it is connected to money laundering, he must make a report to the Serious Crime Agency (SOCA). This also applies, of course, where it is the nominated officer himself who first suspects something is amiss. In either case, the transaction must be halted pending a response from SOCA. Where the report came originally from another member of staff, the nominated officer must therefore not authorise that member of staff to proceed with the transaction; if he does so authorise, he commits a criminal offence carrying up to 5 years' imprisonment.[79]

So far, this is not a dissimilar system to that in place before; in many ways, these provisions state explicitly what was already required. The previous system did not contain separate provisions, as the 2002 Act does, for nominated persons (or MLROs) and others, but it did permit, indeed expect, most staff to make their reports to the MLRO rather than directly to law enforcement, albeit on the understanding that the report would then be forwarded on to SOCA. Similarly, the former legislation merely required a report to be made to "a constable"; it was a tacit understanding that it was in fact sent not to the local police station, but to SOCA.[80] That said, the explicit provision in the 2002 Act that a member of staff other than the nominated officer has a choice of where to make their report is important. Although one would hope that the nominated officer will always be a person of integrity, this cannot be assumed. The Proceeds of Crime Bill, which became the Act, was drafted and debated at a time when the subject of whistleblowers and how to protect them was a topic of major interest amongst government and regulators alike.[81] There is therefore explicit provision for an employee (or indeed other officer), where they do not trust the nominated officer, to report suspicion (or even knowledge) of money

---

78 An assistant solicitor will any case be expected to act in consultation with the relevant Partner. This is, however, separate to the obligation to make a report to the nominated officer unless, of course, the relevant Partner is also the nominated officer, as is often the case in the Financial Services Department.

79 S.336(6).

80 Indeed, from a strictly legal point of view, an institution that did send its report to the local police station would have fulfilled its obligations.

81 The introduction of the Public Interest Disclosure Act 1998 is but one example.

laundering directly either to the police or to H.M. Revenue and Customs. This provision, together with the severe consequences, considered above, for suspecting wrongdoing by a colleague but keeping quiet, may improve instances of whistle-blowing. In the past, the choice was: keep silent and let sleeping dogs lie or risk one's career by speaking out. Now, it is: keep silent and risk up to 5 years in prison or speak out, making use of the possibility of reporting, if necessary, directly to law enforcement rather than through one's employer.

With the exception of the move to objective, rather than subjective, liability, these provisions are merely a clearer statement of what was already the case. What follows the reporting requirement is, however, new. It was a criticism of the old system, expressed by many in the financial services community, that the time they had to wait for a response from SOCA was unduly long. This was, of course, owing to the large number of reports that SOCA had to sift through, but that was of little comfort. They could not process the transaction, but nor could they tell their increasingly impatient client what was going on.[82] Further, if the transaction was eventually authorised, they risked being sued by their client on account of the delay. A prison sentence if they processed the transaction before a reply was received, the risk of their institution suffering an expensive lawsuit and unfavourable publicity if they did not; this was not a choice that financial intermediaries enjoyed having to make.

The 2002 Act therefore introduced strict time limits. If, after 7 working days from when the report is made to SOCA (or, in the case of non-nominated officers, to any police or customs officer), the person making it has not been informed that permission to proceed with the transaction is refused, they may proceed with it in any event.[83] Given that the retail banks in the UK take 4 working days to transfer funds within the country and over twice that if they are to be sent overseas, a delay of 7 working days will often be able to be explained without undue difficulty.

This is of some assistance, but it does not completely solve the intermediary's problem. What if permission to proceed is refused? Section 333 of the Act provides, as did the previous legislation, that where a person knows or suspects that a report of a suspicion of money laundering has been made, they are forbidden to "make a disclosure which is likely to prejudice any investigation which might be conducted". If they do so, they commit the offence of "tipping off", which similarly carries up to 5 years' imprisonment. Despite the name, it may be seen that the offence covers far more than deliberately warning the client that the police are taking an interest in him. It refers to any information "which is likely to prejudice any investigation". This faced intermediaries with a problem: if permission to proceed with the transaction is refused, what do they tell their client? The client notes with displeasure that the transaction has not been executed and asks why not. "We are unable to process it at present?" "Why not?" "Well, there is a delay?" "What kind of delay?" "A delay in the system." Any more specific reply will constitute the tipping-off offence. The

---

82 See below.
83 S.335(2), (3); S.336(1), (3).

intermediary could perhaps take refuge in a lie, but no explanation will hold up indefinitely. The client then asks, "How long will this take?" "I'm sorry, I can't tell you that." At this point, the client will demand that the problem be sorted out immediately or, more likely, he will lose patience altogether and inform the institution that he is closing his account and wishes his property transferred elsewhere. The second option is virtually certain if the client has indeed been involved in money laundering. But then the intermediary is obliged to tell him that he cannot have his property back. It will be a very adroit intermediary who thinks up a way of telling his client he cannot move any of his property without arousing, particularly in the mind of a criminal, any suspicion that law enforcement may be involved.

The Act therefore replaces the indefinite freeze with a moratorium. Once notification has been received that permission has been refused, a period of 31 days begins. Unlike the time limit for notifying permission, or lack of it, to proceed, this is not working days but one calendar month or, at most, 3 days more than this. At the end of this period, the bank may proceed with the transaction unless a court has made a freezing or restraint order in the meantime. It could be argued that informing the client that such an order has been made will constitute a disclosure that could prejudice an investigation into him. This is not, however, necessarily the case. The intermediary may explain, "I'm sorry, sir, we have received a court order prohibiting us to transfer any of this property. It appears that there is some civil litigation taking place in relation to it." In any case, if the funds have been frozen, the client will by then very likely either have been arrested or been the subject of some form of civil action.[84] If the decision has been made rather to leave him at large and track the movements of him and his property, it is likely that permission to proceed with the transaction will have been granted.

A further criticism of the old system was the civil liability that the financial institution might itself incur. The previous legislation made clear that a person making a report under an obligation imposed by the Criminal Justice Act 1988 or the Drug Trafficking Act 1994, as the case may, be could not, on account of making that report, be held liable for breach of confidentiality or, as the legislation put it, "any restriction on the disclosure of information imposed by statute or otherwise". This covered both a civil action by the client and disciplinary proceedings brought by a regulator or professional body. Such protection was, however, far from comprehensive, a weakness that was long the subject of comment. It did not protect against, for example, actions by third parties, since they are not based on a duty of confidentiality – none was ever owed to them – but rather on the loss arising from the transaction not proceeding. Nor did it necessarily protect against actions for defamation.[85] In contrast, the legislation of certain other Member States, notably

---

84 This may be a civil recovery action under Part 5 of the Act or perhaps proceedings for market abuse or a restitution order under Part VIII or ss.382-4, respectively, of the Financial Services and Markets Act 2000. For details of the latter, see pp. 219-21.

85 The House of Lords finally dealt with this issue by applying the doctrine of absolute, rather than merely qualified, privilege to reports made to law enforcement and, latterly,

Germany and Luxembourg, protects in such cases against "any criminal or civil liability" arising out of the disclosure.[86] It is to be noted that both of these are jurisdictions which have, albeit for different reasons, given strong emphasis to the protection of privacy and hence restricted the disclosure of information rather more severely than the UK has generally chosen to do. It is perhaps interesting that, despite this, they ensure that where a financial intermediary co-operates as required with the anti-money-laundering authorities, they have no fear of any legal consequences.

When the 2002 Act was drafted, however, this was not addressed. The phrasing of the provision, in sections 337(1) and 338(4) that the disclosure, i.e. making of the report, "is not to be taken to breach any restriction on the disclosure of information (however imposed)" is almost identical to its counterparts in the previous legislation.[87] The weakness of the previous system has therefore been carried over into the new Act.[88]

In addition to that in connection with the making of a report, two further defences are provided. The first applies to all the money laundering offences. A person does not commit an offence if:

> the act that he does is done in carrying out a function he has relating to the enforcement of any provision of this Act or any other enactment relating to criminal conduct or benefit from criminal conduct.[89]

This provision is essential if those engaged in enforcing the provisions are to be protected. These include a greater range of persons than may at first appear. It clearly covers police officers and those of other law enforcement agencies, such as H.M. Revenue and Customs or the Financial Services Authority,[90] who act in cooperation with a financial institution in order to follow transactions and thus identify those who are behind them. Similarly, it will cover officers at the Serious Organised Crime Agnecy who authorise an institution to proceed with a transaction (or series of transactions) in order that their colleagues may conduct such an investigation. It will also, however, cover a number of other categories.

---

regulators also. See p. 198.

86 The German legislation places a proviso that the report must not be made maliciously or with gross negligence.

87 Criminal Justice Act 1988, s.93A(3)(a), s. 93B(5)(a); Drug Trafficking Act 1994, s.50(3)(a), s. 51(5)(a).

88 The problems of legal liability are considered further in Chapter 6.

89 S.327(2)(c), s.328(2)(c), s. 329(2)(d).

90 Although the FSA is primarily a regulatory organisation, it does have the power to investigate and indeed prosecute criminally certain types of financial crime, including insider dealing, market manipulation and money laundering. It may therefore be considered to be a law enforcement agency for the purposes of these provisions.

One group is receivers, appointed under sections 48-53 of the Act, who manage and then subsequently dispose of property restrained or seized. Criminal property is first restrained, to prevent its dissipation prior to trial, and then, if a conviction and subsequent confiscation order follows, removed and realised. Management receivers are appointed to manage the property at the restraint stage. Certain types of property can decline in value or, in the case of businesses, go bankrupt and lose value altogether if they are simply frozen. If a confiscation order is ultimately made, there will be nothing left to realise; if the defendant is acquitted and hence it is not, he is likely to bring an action for default, arguing that the failure to manage his property in any way constitutes gross negligence. But the reason for restraint in the first place is that the owner (or at least apparent owner) of the property cannot be trusted to manage it in such a way as to keep it available to the court. The appointment of the management receiver gets around this problem. If confiscation does follow, an enforcement receiver (possibly, although not necessarily, the same person as the management receiver) is appointed to realise, i.e. liquidate, the property. They, too, may well manage the property for a while before realising it in order to obtain the highest price for it for the state; it is not particularly helpful to sell an asset immediately after a confiscation order is made if, at that time, the market in that type of property (shares, other types of securities, real property or whatever) is especially low. Both types of receiver clearly acquire and subsequently have possession of criminal property. Similarly, when the enforcement receiver disposes of the property, they convert it (into money); this in turn entails their transferring the original property to another person, the purchaser. And at all times, they strongly suspect the property to be derived from a criminal offence; indeed, to all intents and purposes, the enforcement receiver knows that it is. Were it not for the defence protecting those who undertake their actions in relation to the enforcement of the provisions of the Act, they would therefore be guilty of serious criminal offences.

Another group, easy to overlook, is police custody sergeants. When a person is arrested (for whatever offence), if they are detained at the police station, whatever property they have on them is taken by the custody sergeant, logged and stored. The custody sergeant will know what offence the person has been arrested for and, depending on what it is, may well suspect, or even know, the contents of the accused's pockets to be criminal property.

Receivers and custody sergeants may avail themselves of the defence afforded to those who make a report to their superiors or SOCA. But to force them to do this would burden the system with information that is totally useless. In the case of management and enforcement receivers, the property is already well-known to law enforcement; similarly, the person whose property is entrusted to the custody sergeant has by definition been arrested. Another piece of paper for SOCA, and the time of the relevant receiver or officer filling it out, will achieve nothing. It is important, therefore, that they are afforded this additional defence.

The final defence to be considered concerns the offences of acquisition, use or possession under section 329. No offence is committed if the person acquired, used or possessed the property for adequate consideration.[91] Whether or not the consideration is indeed adequate is specifically linked to the value of the property.[92] There is an additional caveat that the provision of goods or services will not constitute consideration where the person providing them knows or suspects that his so doing may help another to carry out criminal conduct (i.e. any criminal offence). Thus accomplices in money laundering, who buy criminal property in order to help the launderer obscure the trail, are offered no defence. It does mean, however, that those who purchase property from an enforcement receiver are protected. It also addresses the concern, raised by some, that a lawyer who conducts his client's defence, or simply provides him with legal advice, could be barred from receiving a fee unless it is provided from public funds under the legal aid scheme. The adequate consideration defence makes clear that such a lawyer will only be liable if the fee he charges is considerably higher than normal, raising the suspicion that the fee is in fact a money laundering device. Finally, the defence is an added protection for those who in good faith trade with what turns out to be a front for a criminal organisation.[93] That said, such persons should in any case be protected by the definition of criminal property as property which the person knows or suspects to represent a benefit from criminal conduct.

Terrorism

The laundering of terrorist property is, as it has been for some time, covered by separate legislation: the Terrorism Act 2000. This Act was introduced in response to the Omagh bombing of August 2000 and placed, for the first time, the UK's anti-terrorism provisions on a permanent footing.[94] It was amended in the wake of 9/11 by the Anti-Terrorism, Crime and Security Act 2001.

Terrorist property continues to be dealt with separately because it is different in nature. "Traditional" money laundering, covered by the 2002 Act and the legislation that preceded it, concerns property which is derived from crime and efforts to combat it therefore focus on its origin. With terrorist funding, however, the focus is not on where the property has come from but where it is destined: its ultimate purpose. This purpose is distinct from "ordinary crime". Offences such as drug trafficking, insider dealing, fraud, etc. are, at least generally, committed in order to make money. While one can make money by dealing legitimately on the securities exchanges, one can make much more, and at far less risk, by dealing on the basis of inside information,

---

91 S.329(2)(c).
92 S.329(3)(a), (b).
93 If they did not act in good faith, they will be caught by the accomplice provision.
94 Previously, they were contained in provisional Prevention of Terrorism (Temporary Provisions) Acts, which needed to be renewed by Parliament each year in order to remain valid.

knowing for certain, rather than merely making an educated judgment, which way what security is going to move when. There are exceptions: persons who seek to exploit an exchange not in order specifically to make a profit, but merely in order to show it can be done[95] or perhaps to enjoy the sense of power that successfully doing so creates. But these are exceptions, not the rule.

In contrast, the terrorist does not seek to become rich, or indeed any personal gain.[96] His goal, and that of his organisation, is the achievement of a political end:[97] the independence of a territory, a change in governmental order or, as with Al Qaeda, the complete destruction of a given system worldwide. Both the terrorist and the drug dealer devote funds to their activities. Whereas, however, the drug dealer does so in order to make even more money, for the terrorist, the cause is no mere means to an end: it is the entire point.

Since the purpose of terrorism is a political end rather than a financial profit, it has, in addition to "active service units", supporters. This is where the traditional definition of money laundering breaks down. The supporters are a highly important source of funds, but, in acquiring the property which they give to the organisation, they commit no criminal offence. It may be an offence to provide funds to a terrorist organisation or, more generally, to provide them for the purposes of terrorism, but the actual origin of the funds is not "dirty". The £10 put in the collecting tin in the pubs of certain Irish areas of London or the $100 donated to Noraid came from the donor's salary, legally earned. There was often no attempt to disguise its origin either: these were donations from persons sympathetic with the Catholic population of Northern Ireland. It may have been alleged that the funds were to provide financial support for families of persons killed by Protestant paramilitaries (or indeed the security forces), rather than to buy arms, but this is a question of purpose, not origin.

The organisation may also set up legitimate operations in order to raise funds. These are frequently not mere fronts, laundering money obtained elsewhere, but genuine businesses carrying on activities which, in themselves, are entirely legal. A well-publicised example is the companies producing and selling honey, discovered to be funding operations for Al Qaeda. In terms of their activities, they were entirely what they appeared to be: honey producers. It was only the purpose for which their profits were designated, i.e. funding acts of terrorism, that was illegal.

---

95 George Soros, for example, stated that his purpose in forcing sterling out of the European Exchange Rate Mechanism in 1992 was to show that an agreement signed between governments without reference to the markets is ultimately unworkable if speculators choose to oppose it.

96 The ultimate example of this is, of course, the suicide bomber (save to the extent that Islamic suicide bombers believe that they will achieve special status in Paradise for their act).

97 Even where the organisation appears, or even claims, to have a religious basis (for example the Ulster Volunteer Force's strongly Protestant identity or Islamic Jihad's Muslim one), its aim is in fact political: government of the state or territory by those subscribing to that religion and under that religion's laws.

In the face of such operations, the definition of money laundering found both in the EU Directive and the Proceeds of Crime Act 2002 breaks down. The funds' origin, far from being disguised, is openly proclaimed. Assisting another to retain the benefit of the proceeds from the sale of honey is not a criminal offence. Where terrorist organisations do raise money through traditional criminal offences, such as drug trafficking, extortion or armed robbery,[98] these are of course caught by the traditional means. But for the rest, other provisions must be devised.

In the UK, these are found in the Terrorism Act 2000. The problem of the donations was addressed by creating an offence of "fund-raising".[99] This prescribes that a person commits a criminal offence if they

- invite another person to provide money or other property,
- receive money or other property, or
- contribute money or other property

when they either intend it to be used for the purposes of terrorism or have reasonable cause to suspect that it may be. "Terrorism" includes acts committed inside or outside the UK.[100] The first two offences cover those who pass round the tins (or undertake the larger-scale operations), the third those who donate. Any of the three carries, on indictment, up to 14 years' imprisonment, the same as for money laundering.

It should be noted that the fund-raising offence not only covers donations but any activities, including those just discussed, carried out in order to raise money for the cause. All of these produce funds to be used for the purpose of terrorism and hence anyone who receives these funds commits the offence.

It is also worthy of note that the section refers to "the purposes of terrorism", not just terrorism itself. Although, therefore, section 15 is entitled "Fund-raising", it covers much more than the mere raising of funds.[101] Such activities as the forging of passports or the purchase of travel tickets will therefore be covered. Although such documents and tickets are not used directly to commit terrorist acts, they are used for the acts ancillary to them: travelling to the place where the act is to be committed or evading arrest, either beforehand or afterwards, and hence for the purpose of terrorism. Any person who either provides or receives the property (e.g. the travel tickets or procured passport) will therefore be guilty of the offence.

---

98 The importance of these should not be underestimated: "security sources" were recently said to have "revealed that the IRA has become one of the largest and richest organised crime gangs in Europe", while Bill Tupman was similarly quoted as saying., "Successful terrorist groups survive by resorting to funding methods copied from organised crime." O'Neill, S. and Lister, D. (2005) "MI5 given task of boosting intelligence on money making", *Times*, 25 February 2005. The problem of additional funding from legitimate sources, however, still remains.
99 S.15.
100 S.1(4)(a).
101 A comparison may be made with the term "money laundering"; as seen above, it covers all property, not just specifically money.

Separate to "fund-raising" itself, and very much mirroring the general money laundering provisions, there is an offence of entering into a "funding arrangement"; this is where a person enters into or becomes concerned in an arrangement as a result of which money or other property is made available to another, or is to be in the future. The person involved in the arrangement must know or have reasonable cause to suspect that the property will or may be used for the purposes of terrorism. Although the wording of this offence refers to knowledge rather than intention, the test is essentially the same as for fund-raising itself.

Similarly, section 16 of the Act creates an offence of using property for the purposes of terrorism or possessing property, intending that it be so used. Since, however, in order to possess property, one must first receive it, this will be of limited additional impact.[102]

It must, however, be questioned how effective these provisions will be in practice. Where the property consists of arms, explosives and the like, it is relatively simple to show their likely purpose; similarly, several sacks of ammonium nitrate fertiliser supplied to a person who can have no agricultural or horticultural use for it. With money, however, it is more difficult. Even the objective test of "reasonable cause to suspect" places a considerable burden on the prosecution, particularly in relation to the donors. What is "reasonable cause" – and who decides? Suppose A asks B to donate money to a collection for, he claims, relief work in Palestine: building homes, a clean water system, etc. Does B have reasonable cause to suspect that the money is in fact to be used to buy arms? This will often apply to the lower-level fundraisers as well: they may also have been told that they are collecting money for relief work. Do they have reasonable cause to suspect otherwise? Some would argue that they do, that "relief work" and "welfare" have been well-known covers for terrorist organisations for many years. But essentially, it is a judgment call and furthermore, at the end of the day, it will be the jury that are asked to make it.

This raises a further problem. Terrorism, almost invariably, is inextricably linked with a political or ideological viewpoint.[103] Furthermore, that cause is frequently linked to a group that is perceived to be oppressed; indeed, the very aim of many terrorist organisations is to free that group. Where this is the case, there will often be those in the mainstream of society who do not advocate acts of violence but who do sympathise with the group that is supposed to be liberated. Also in the mainstream of society are those whose sympathies in no way lie with the supposedly oppressed group but rather with the government.

---

102 Because of the element of intention, property will not suddenly become transformed into terrorist property on the person possessing it discovering new information or evidence; the practical distinction between receipt and possession of criminal property is therefore not mirrored with terrorist financing.

103 There have been exceptions, such as the Red Army Faction, which operated in Germany in the 1970s and early 1980s, but the overwhelming majority of terrorist movements have a definite ideological cause.

An example is Israel/Palestine; it should be recalled that terrorism, within the meaning of section 1 of the Act, includes acts perpetrated outside the UK.[104] The case was discussed above of a person who donates to a collection that is allegedly to provide for relief and welfare work in Palestinian areas. The position of the Israeli Government has often been made clear: any organisation working to assist the Palestinians is at the very least supportive of terrorism; this has often included the Palestinian Authority itself.[105] Where funds are given to such an organisation, there is therefore, on this view, reasonable cause to suspect that they will be used for the purposes of terrorism. Other groups, however, deny this and claim that there are organisations working in the Palestinian areas that have no involvement in violence and simply undertake genuine relief work. If the donor is charged with an offence under section 15(3) – or, more likely, if a supporter is charged with inviting them to provide money under section 15(1) – it will be for the jury to decide what they had reasonable cause to suspect. If those on the jury are broadly supportive of the Israeli Government, they will convict, not simply on principle but because they are genuinely satisfied that the elements of the offence have been proven. If, however, they have broad sympathy with the Palestinian side, they may well agree that the organisation raising funds exists simply in order to undertake or support genuine relief work; hence they will acquit. The scenario could equally well be painted concerning relief work in any area of conflict, from Chechnya to Sri Lanka.[106]

It could therefore be said that the success or failure of many prosecutions could ultimately depend on the political/ideological sympathies of the jury. It may be that, in the future, such legislation will only be enforceable in a consistent manner if these offences are tried before non-jury courts. In Northern Ireland, the conflict there led to the creation of non-jury "Diplock" courts for terrorist offences, although this was to prevent intimidation rather than the problems outlined above and they were never introduced in mainland Britain. Although the current Labour administration has called for the abolition of juries for certain types of cases, this remains highly controversial; in any case, these proposals have not related to terrorist cases. For the time being, at least, cases brought under the Terrorist Act 2000 will therefore continue (except in Northern Ireland) to be tried before juries.

Whatever the shortcomings, potential or actual, of the legislation, the types of conduct set out in section 15 of the Act are criminal offences and property deriving from them will therefore be covered by the Proceeds of Crime Act 2002. Although

---

104 As the UK, through its strong political relationship with the United States, becomes increasingly associated in many Arab/Muslim minds with the Israeli cause, the dividing line between acts to be perpetrated in the UK and those abroad may in any case become blurred.

105 Although the Israeli Government has, since the election as President of Mahmood Abbas, given greater legitimacy to the Palestinian Authority, it remains to be seen whether this will last, particularly against the background of continued attacks on Israel by other Palestinian groups, on the one hand, and the accusation of the Government of treason by certain sectors of Israeli opinion on the other.

106 Although the prohibition of the LTTE (Tamil Tigers) was lifted in Sri Lanka as part of a ceasefire agreement, they continue to be prohibited in the UK as a terrorist organisation.

that Act was not even in its final draft when the Terrorism Act 2000 was passed, the proceeds were covered by the previous legislation, the Criminal Justice Act 1993, since all three are indictable offences. On this approach, there is no need for an additional "terrorist money laundering" offence; nonetheless one is created in section 18 of the Act. This refers to "terrorist property", a concept defined in section 14(1) of the Act as:

(a) money or other property which is likely to be used for the purposes of terrorism (including any resources of a proscribed organisation),
(b) proceeds of the commission of acts of terrorism, and
(c) proceeds of acts carried out for the purposes of terrorism.

Of these, (a) and (b) are relatively straightforward. Property likely to be used for the purposes of terrorism is, for the most part, property deriving from the offences in sections 15 or 17; acts of terrorism are also fairly clear, although they are precisely defined in section 1 of the Act. But the purpose of category (c) is less clear. As seen above, there are various types of activities that could be said to be carried out for the purposes of terrorism, not least the various kinds of fund raising. But the proceeds of all of them come within the term "money or other property which is likely to be used for the purposes of terrorism" and hence they are already covered by category (a). This being the case, category (c) would seem to be redundant.

The laundering offence in section 18 is both simply and extremely widely drafted. It is an offence to enter into, or even become concerned in, an arrangement which facilitates the retention or control, on behalf of another, of terrorist property. This may be by concealment, removal from the jurisdiction, by transfer to nominees or "in any other way". It should be noted that the arrangement must assist another person to benefit; in contrast to the concealment, etc, offence in the Proceeds of Crime Act 2002, it is not an offence under this section to make such arrangements for one's own benefit. Since, however, it is an offence, under the preceding sections of the Act, to be in possession of terrorist property, this restriction is of limited significance.

No state of knowledge or intention need be proven by the prosecution. Subsection (2) does provide a defence where the accused proves that he neither knew nor had reasonable cause to suspect that the arrangement concerned terrorist property, but the burden of proof is on the accused. A contrast may thus be drawn with the receiving offence in section 15(2), considered above. For that offence, it is a requirement that the accused either intended the property to be used for the purposes of terrorism or had reasonable grounds to suspect that it may be. The burden of proving it therefore lies with the prosecution; if they cannot, the case fails. For the laundering offence, however, the prosecution need only prove two things: that the property in question is terrorist property and that the accused was involved in some sort of arrangement whereby another person was assisted to retain its benefit.

The second of these will generally not be difficult to prove; this is the very purpose of the simple and wide drafting. The task of proving, however, that the property is terrorist property should not be underestimated, particularly where it is category (a) that is relied on. Persuading a jury that property is likely to be used for the purposes of terrorism may well incur the same problems as those discussed in relation to the fund-raising offence: particularly where it is funds rather than other types of property that is at issue, what was it, in fact, to be used for? The burden of answering this question remains, even in a laundering case, on the prosecution.

A further offence is that of failing to disclose a belief or suspicion that a person has committed a fund-raising, possession or laundering offence under sections 15–18.[107] This is, however, identical to those offences relating to the general money laundering ones discussed above. Similarly, the Act affords defences, mirroring those in the general money laundering legislation, where a person carries out an act covered by these sections but does so with the express permission of a police officer or makes a report to the police immediately after he carries it out.[108]

The Act also provides a protection, in section 20, for those who disclose information relating to knowledge or suspicion involving terrorist property. This is essentially the same as that found in sections 337 and 338 of the Proceeds of Crime Act 2002, considered above.

---

107 S.19.
108 S.21.

Chapter 6

Impact on the Financial Services Industry

It is arguable that the impact on the financial services industry of the anti-money-laundering rules is rather greater than that of the insider dealing legislation, at least at first glance. The impact of the insider dealing provisions should, however, not entirely be discounted: here, too, there is a compliance element. In addition, there is a close link for the compliance department between insider dealing and money laundering. The scenario illustrated at the beginning of Chapter 5 demonstrates this all too clearly. The coming into force of the Proceeds of Crime Act 2002 with its new offence of receiving criminal property is a further cause for concern. Despite this link, however, the compliance issues connected with insider dealing on the one hand and money laundering on the other are generally distinct and it is therefore helpful to deal with them separately.

Insider Dealing

To deal with the issues connected specifically with insider dealing first, they may be broken down into three categories: the risk of financial intermediaries themselves engaging in insider dealing, the risk of them attracting liability by dealing on behalf of their clients and finally the potential civil liability that may arise.

It must be remembered that, in certain Member States, liability for insider dealing may be imposed on natural and legal persons alike. Even in those jurisdictions which do not provide for this, the directors of the firm may find themselves personally liable. In this context, it is important to recognise the risk to institutions posed by staff engaging in insider dealing on their own behalf. Although this book is careful to cover all potential insiders, financial intermediaries have traditionally often been overlooked. The Directive may cast the net wider, but, all too often, a primary insider has been conceived as being a director or officer of an issuer, or perhaps a major shareholder. It is salutary to consider that when the US anti-insider-dealing provisions have been considered, discussion has often centred not around SEC Rule 10b-5, applicable to all cases of insider dealing, regardless of the position of the persons who engage in it, but Section 16(b) of the Securities and Exchange Act of 1934.[1] This latter is restricted in its scope to certain specific persons linked to issuers

---

[1] For example, Wu, H.K. (1968) "An Economist Looks at Section 16 of the Securities Exchange Act of 1934" 68 *Columbia Law Review* 260.

of securities: their officers, directors and major shareholders, the latter defined as having a shareholding greater than 10%. Indeed, a major study in the United States of the effect of insider dealing on the price-movement of the relevant securities bases its entire argument on the dealing by these three types.[2] The authors concede that their findings may be skewed by their not having taken into account (because they cannot) spouses and other close relations of persons in the three categories, but they make no comment whatsoever on dealings by other persons, who fall outside the three, but who are nonetheless well placed to obtain inside information.

Under the European provisions, however, such financial intermediaries fall firmly within the category of insiders, even of primary insiders (where such a distinction is made).[3] The lawyer, the accountant, the investment professional who handles the purchase and sale of the shares in connection with a takeover, all these are well-placed to "cash in" on the information that passes across their desks.

But why does this have an impact on the financial services industry? To say that financial and other professional intermediaries have an opportunity, and are therefore vulnerable to temptation, to engage in insider dealing is like saying that a person who works in a shop has an opportunity to steal some of the stock. The difference is the responsibility of financial institutions and professional firms for their staff. If a shop assistant steals from the stock, or even from the till, the only problem for the shop is the losses that this causes. An eyebrow may be raised if it transpires that the thefts occurred through a particular laxity on the part of the shop's management, but there is unlikely to be any official liability.[4] In the case of intermediaries in the financial sector, however, it is another matter. As indicated above, not only the individual dealer but their entire institution may be held liable. The most blatant way in which this could happen would be in the case of a small firm with a similarly small management team, all of whom take part in the dealing. Even in larger firms, however, there is a risk. Many law and accountancy firms are partnerships and, as such, a wrongful (let alone illegal) act by one partner in the course of his professional activities may draw down liability on the entire firm. This has rarely occurred in insider dealing cases (but then, in all Member States, there have been relatively few insider cases in general), but it is not unusual in cases of money laundering.

Furthermore, where the liability is civil, rather than criminal, in nature, it is commonplace for the wrongdoing of one partner to lead to joint and several liability for the other partners of the firm. This is not the place to discuss in detail the

---

2   Lorie, J.H. and Niederhoffer, V. (1968) "Predictive and Statistical Properties of Insider Trading", 11 *Journal of Law and Economics* 35.

3   Although the Directive, and indeed certain Member States, such as Austria, Germany and, to an extent, Spain, make a distinction between primary and secondary insiders, certain other Member States, such as Denmark and Finland, do not. See Chapter 2.

4   Save, of course, where the thefts took place with the actual connivance of managers.

principles of partnership law; suffice to say that the partners of, for example, a law firm, share the profits made but also the liabilities incurred.[5]

A third aspect is the regulatory point. It is expected of financial institutions, and indeed of professional firms such as lawyers and accountants, that staff be adequately supervised. Should they engage in wrongdoing, they will be punished individually, certainly, but their institution is also likely to face sanctions for not having prevented the wrongdoing from occurring in the first place. This liability is especially stark in jurisdictions such as France and Spain, which impose an explicit duty on directors and managers, in particular, not only not to misuse insider information themselves but to prevent others from doing so. In France, breach of this duty leads not only to civil but also to criminal penalties including imprisonment.[6] Although the equivalent Spanish provision is only civil, it does carry a moderate fine, of up to just over €30,000.[7] For a corporation, this is admittedly low, but for an individual, it is decidedly unpleasant, particularly for an offence of mere negligence. The situation can therefore easily be envisaged where a director of a company discloses inside information to a colleague in the quite proper course of their professional activities and the colleague then either passes it on without authorisation (for example to his wife or a couple of friends) or simply deals directly on his own account. The colleague will be aware that he is not supposed to do this and indeed will face not only the wrath of the state but disciplinary action from his institution if he is caught. He will therefore be most unlikely to inform the director of what he plans to do; indeed, he will take care to be discreet about it. But if, after the event, it is found that the director could have done more to prevent the information being misused, he will be liable. As with money laundering, hindsight is by definition 20-20.

In Spain, this will apply not only to directors but anyone who obtains inside information through their employment: thus the above scenario could equally easily apply to a lawyer who works on a takeover bid with a junior colleague or even trainee. The solution could arguably be that one never involves trainees in sensitive cases, but is this practical? It will certainly entail the quality of the traineeship being diminished.[8]

The fourth and final point in this context concerns the actions that an institution is to take should an officer or employee be found to have engaged in insider dealing. It is very often a temptation for a financial institution that discovers that one of its employees, let alone one of its officers, has engaged in any kind of wrongdoing, to attempt to cover things up. It is a watchword of such institutions that such an incident embarrasses the firm and causes at least potential damage to its reputation. The point,

---

5   The introduction of the Limited Liability Partnership in certain jurisdictions has, as the name implies, limited this, but the point still holds.

6   See pp. 138-39..

7   For the details, see pp. 210-11.

8   One possible solution might be to adopt the approach of taken by the European Commission, which requires its *stagiaires* to sign a statement acknowledging legal liability for any misuse of information. It is questionable, however, whether this will necessarily be sufficient to exonerate the supervisor.

it is felt, will not be that the firm discovered a wrongdoer and removed him, but that they appointed him in the first place. What kind of recruitment screening can they have? How can prospective clients be sure that, if such screening is so lax, there are not other officers out there whose misdeeds have not been detected? To this may be added the inconvenience of having time taken up dealing with the police (and indeed regulators, who will certainly also take an interest), the expense of instructing lawyers and, possibly, the risk of lawsuits from clients who have suffered loss. The result of these kinds of concerns is that firms often go to great lengths to hide what has happened. This will even to extend to how the miscreant officer or employee is dealt with. They will frequently be allowed to resign, an agreed statement as to the reason for their leaving will be drawn up and they will even be provided with a good reference.[9]

These points have often been observed in relation to fraud, in which the institution concerned loses considerable sums: how much more will they apply to an offence such as insider dealing, in which it loses nothing, in material terms at least? In most Member States, this may lead to raised eyebrows by the regulator (although even this is not guaranteed), but no greater risks will ensue. In Greece, however, the position is rather different. Under the Greek Criminal Code, any person who becomes aware of a criminal offence having taken place must report it to the police or other authorities. As noted in Chapter 4, although Greece does, like a number of other Member States, have parallel civil/administrative provisions, insider dealing is a criminal offence there, as are encouragement to deal and unauthorised disclosure of inside information. As such, should other members of the institution in question become aware that a colleague as engaged in an insider dealing offence, they will be legally obliged to report this: remaining silent and attempting to cover the matter up will itself constitute a criminal offence.[10]

An issue of equal, if not greater, concern than the risk of staff themselves engaging in insider dealing is the risk of dealing on behalf of a client. The situation may well arise that the client himself is not in possession of inside information, but the firm instructed to carry out the transaction is. Insider dealing itself is defined as a person in possession of inside information taking advantage of it "with full knowledge of the facts by acquiring or disposing of for his own account or for the account of a third party, either directly or indirectly, transferable securities of the issuer or issuers to which information relates."[11] It must be stressed that a person who deals for the account of a third party is as liable as the principal himself. Nor is it anywhere suggested in the Directive that the intermediary must be part of some deliberate conspiracy: if they possess inside information and deal on their client's behalf in

---

[9] This is as true of insider dealing as it is of money laundering, discussed in the previous chapter: see p. 166.

[10] It is arguable that, with the wide ranging definition of money laundering under the Proceeds of Crime Act 2002 this will now also apply in the UK due to the stringent reporting requirements. See pp.166-67.

[11] Art. 2, Directive 89/592/EEC. See Chapter 4.

securities to which the information relates, then, if they are aware of the situation (i.e. that the information (a) is inside information and (b) relates to the securities which they are about to buy or sell), they are guilty of insider dealing.

It could be argued that only an intermediary who was actively conspiring with his client would find himself in such a situation. But little reflection is required to see that this need not necessarily be the case. Financial intermediaries do, in the nature of things, from time to time become privy to inside information. Although mere gossip is excluded from the definition of inside information as being insufficiently precise,[12] certain information can go round the City of London, or its equivalents, that is rather more concrete: which takeovers are being planned, which firms are planning a new issue of shares, or possibly bonds, etc. The City may no longer be the gentlemen's club it perhaps once was, but it remains a village. The results are all too predictable: the Senior Partner of one law firm, on announcing the firm's merger with a major firm in the United States, referred to it as "the worst kept secret in the City".[13]

Linked to this is the problem that financial institutions are growing in size and, as such, one arm may be involved in a takeover while another arm of the same institution may be engaged in private client work. Thus conflicts may easily arise, or at least situations where one department may be asked by its client to undertake a transaction involving the securities of a client of another department. The solution to this has traditionally been the so-called "Chinese wall": a system whereby client work is kept within the particular department that is dealing with it and it is no more permissible to discuss the details with persons in other departments than with persons outside the institution altogether. Experience has shown, however, that for all the good intentions, the term "Chinese wall" is decidedly apt: the inter-departmental barriers are as full of gaps as the Great Wall itself. Firstly, it is, in practice, almost impossible to keep information hermetically sealed: there will often be aspects that other departments will need to advise on. Secondly, there will often be links, whether professional or personal, between colleagues in different departments and, whatever the official rules may say, work will, from time to time, get discussed between them. Thirdly, it is all too easy for the systems to slip. Doors that are supposedly kept locked at all times may, in practice, be left open for convenience, leaving staff from, for example, the legal division to walk through the open-plan consultancy division as a short-cut.[14]

Given such realities, it is easy to see how the rule that no person may deal, even on behalf of another, in securities when they are in possession of inside information relating to them is rather more complicated in practice than it may appear in theory.

---

12 For the requirement of precision and indeed the definition of inside information generally, see Chapter 3.

13 Since the law firm was a partnership, it was not an issuer of securities, but it easy to see that the same scenario could take place in relation to, for example, a bank.

14 In one London group, this literally took place on a regular basis.

It is true that there are often safe harbours to protect intermediaries in such cases. Among those in the UK legislation are where a person was already contractually bound to execute the transaction when he came into possession of the inside information or where he can show that he would have executed the transaction even had he not been in possession of the information in question.[15]

This is all very well as far as it goes, and will certainly protect the broker in cases of actual dealing, but in cases of advice, the situation is different. All persons have an obligation not to disclose inside information unless authorised in the proper course of their work. In the UK, however, as in other Member States (and indeed jurisdictions outside the EU), financial intermediaries are under a regulatory obligation (as well as a civil duty of care) to give their clients best advice. This means that they are required, to the best of their ability and expertise, not only to advise their client on the best means of achieving an investment objective that he has already identified, but also on what particular securities would or would not be a good investment.[16] Both obligations are right, but it may be seen that they will occasionally conflict. In an ideal world, no financial intermediary would ever be party to inside information, but, as seen above, this is not always the case. Tip-offs that go beyond mere rumour or City gossip, although they are forbidden, are in the manner of things made from time to time.

The civil provisions are discussed in detail in the next chapter. In the UK, the Financial Services and Markets Act 2000 creates a regulatory offence of market abuse, of which one category is termed "misuse of information". Although this is wider than the criminal concept of insider dealing, there is a general requirement that, for a given type of conduct to constitute market abuse, it must fall below the standard generally expected by a regular user of the market in question. This does not mean any securities market but the one on which the securities are traded to which the information in question is related. If it is decided that a regular user of that market would take the view that the behaviour in which the person engaged is in keeping with the general standards applicable there, it will not constitute market abuse. It may well be the case that, where an institution had put in place all reasonable measures to prevent insider dealing taking place, it could be held to have kept to expected standards.

---

15 See pp. 118-19.

16 In the UK, the FSA Conduct of Business Rules now require merely that such advice be "suitable" (FSA Regulatory Handbook, COB 5.3.5); it is arguable that to give advice on the basis of inside information would not be suitable, although this has to date not been tested. Professor Barry Rider highlighted the problem of conflicting duties when insider dealing was not yet prohibited in the UK but was soundly disapproved of, to the extent that the Law Society had issued a Practice Statement forbidding it: see Rider, B.A.K. (1978) "The Fiduciary and the Frying Pan" 42 *The Conveyancer* 114. It is arguable that an actual statutory prohibition will override a duty to one's client under the doctrine of illegality (see, for example, *Fibrosa Spolka Akcyjna v Fairbairn Lawson Combe Barbour Ltd.* [1943] AC 32); as Rider points out, however, a merely regulatory obligation may not.

Further safe harbours are given in the Code of Market Conduct, which the Financial Services Authority is required to issue, giving guidance as what, in its view, will and will not constitute market abuse. Under the Act, if the FSA states in the Code that a given form of conduct does not constitute market abuse, this is an absolute defence.

The drawback to both of these is the lack of certainty. As with all "reasonable man" tests, there can be different views. One professional may take the view that the Chinese wall that an institution had in place was adequate. It may not have been totally impermeable, but he may feel that a totally impermeable barrier would in practice have been impossible to create – or that, even if it could, it would have formed an unacceptable impediment to the flow of other types of information which are not only legitimate but important for an institution of that sector to conduct its business effectively. But another may be of the opinion that such a barrier was far from impractical. True, it does present certain drawbacks, even nuisances. But, such a person may argue, such nuisances are a price worth paying in order to ensure that abusive practices cannot take place, even by accident. Which of the two views is adopted by the FSA's Regulatory Decisions Committee will decide whether the institution concerned is held to have acted properly or whether it is to face heavy financial penalties[17] and far from fortunate publicity.[18]

Similar problems attach to the safe harbours in the Code of Market Conduct. The Act not only requires the FSA to publish such a Code, but permits it to alter the Code whenever it sees fit. It is true that if it is amended, the FSA must publish the said amendments. But it does mean that the compliance department of a financial institution will need to monitor the Code on a regular basis: it will not be sufficient merely to master it when it comes out. It is salutary to consider that many of the Manuals making up the FSA's Regulatory Handbook were amended three or even four times in the months following their initial publication. Some of these amendments merely corrected typing errors, but others were rather more substantial and careful consideration was required in every case.[19] The vigilance that will be required in order to ensure that an institution complies with the Code on a continuing basis may therefore easily be seen.

Thus far, it has been the danger of committing insider dealing that has been considered. There is also, however, another danger: an intermediary may, through being excessively cautious, refrain from undertaking a transaction that in fact

---

17 In order to ensure that no court would take the view that the market abuse provisions were in fact criminal, not civil, in nature, those drafting the Act were careful to use the term "financial penalty", not "fine". See pp. 215ff.

18 S. 123(3) of the Financial Services and Markets Act 2000 does allow for a public statement to be made instead of a financial penalty being imposed. Nowhere, however, does the Act prescribe that, where a financial penalty is imposed, the FSA is barred from making a public statement to this effect. Indeed, the FSA's website itself gives details of cases in which it has recently imposed sanctions.

19 In one City law firm, a team of three lawyers was devoted simply to keeping the firm's set of Manuals up to date during this period.

would have been quite legitimate. Although the customer could in theory, in such circumstances, go to another intermediary and get him to execute the transaction, the price of securities in practice all too often moves so quickly that this is impractical: by the time the client has approached another intermediary, the opportunity has passed. In the case of a major commercial client, for whom a single trade will perhaps involve hundreds of thousands of securities, the resulting loss will be considerable. There will then be a substantial risk that the client will seek to recover that loss by suing the firm in question. Even the alternative scenario, where the securities in question are not so volatile and the client is therefore able, without suffering any loss, to go to another institution, is not attractive. The original firm may not be sued but will nonetheless lose a substantial commission: if a transaction is worth £2 million, even 1% of this will be £20,000. The knock-on effect, the loss of an important client, may well cost many times this amount.

Money Laundering

The compliance issues relating to money laundering are closely linked to the EU Money Laundering Directive. While the previous chapter sets out the Directive's requirements, complying with them is rather more complicated. Any doubt that there may have been on this has been dispelled in the UK by the fine of £1.25 million imposed by the FSA on the Northern Bank in August 2003 merely for failure to take the required precautionary measures.[20]

A major issue is that, although substantial duties are placed on the Compliance Officer and/or Money Laundering Reporting Officer (MLRO),[21] it is not just these but every member of staff, from the most senior officer to the most junior employee, whom the duties affect. The officer appointed as Compliance Officer may be fully persuaded of the importance of complying with the anti-money laundering regulations, but his greatest task will often not be discerning whether a given transaction is or is not suspicious or even whether or not a given identity document is or is not adequate, but persuading his colleagues of the importance of compliance. In the past, the main problem was often persuading senior management. Complying with anti-money laundering regulations was seen as a chore and a burdensome one at that and it was therefore all too often handed to a relatively junior employee in order not to waste the time of more senior staff with it.[22] This has changed following a series of pronouncements from government and the courts alike: the practice of

---

20 Contained in the Money Laundering Regulations 1993, since replaced by the Money Laundering Regulations 2003.

21 These may be, indeed often are, in practice the same person: see pp. 167-68. The roles are, however distinct.

22 It is also tempting to take the cynical view that a number of firms felt that such a policy ensured that, if a breach of the regulations were found to have occurred, a relatively junior scalp could be sacrificed, leaving the senior officers unscathed.

one City law firm, where the Money Laundering Reporting Officer is the Head of Financial Services and one of the more senior partners, is now the norm.

While, however, the senior managers are now well aware of the seriousness of the obligations, the more junior staff may not always be. This is highlighted by the reaction to the holding of anti-money laundering training sessions. Such training is an explicit requirement of the Directive and therefore of the national legislation that the Member States have passed in order to implement it; it is also essential if those who deal with clients on a day-to-day basis "at the coal face" are not find themselves involved in money laundering through simple lack of awareness. Yet the efforts of the compliance staff to persuade their junior staff to attend such training can often meet with decided lack of cooperation.[23] It may be in the future that draconian measures, such as disciplining staff for non-attendance, will have to be imposed: after all, in case of a breach, the MLRO can be sent to prison. But for the moment, the climate is such that this would be seen as decidedly controversial.

Before leaving the area of the impact on the financial services sector of the criminal law, a new issue should be considered that has been created by the Proceeds of Crime Act 2002. As seen in the previous chapter, this not only simplifies the money laundering offences which had come before but adds a new offence of receipt of criminal property. It need not be with any illicit purpose: mere receipt of property, which is derived from a criminal offence, by a person who knows or suspects it to be such constitutes money laundering. Further, in the case of persons in the regulated sector, even a lack of suspicion will not serve as a defence if the person had reasonable grounds to suspect that the assets in question were criminal property. This creates a new interface between insider dealing and money laundering, as in the scenario depicted at the beginning of the previous chapter. Under the previous legislation, the broker risked committing a money laundering offence if the securities then rose in value and he was instructed to sell them and re-invest the proceeds (or even simply remit the money to the client in question). But now, his position is even worse: he risks being guilty of money laundering simply by possessing the securities. The securities are, after all, quite clearly property which may derive from a criminal offence, namely insider dealing. True, the broker committed no offence when he purchased them since at that point, he did not even have reasonable grounds to suspect anything untoward. But now he does and his position is precarious indeed. He will in fact have only one way of saving himself and his situation: he will have to make a report to the Serious Organised Crime Agency.

This new development also very effectively removes one of the traditional defences to insider dealing: the defendant, when he came into possession of the inside information, was already contractually bound to execute the transaction. It also removes the linked defence that the defendant would have undertaken the transaction anyway, even if he had not come into possession of the information.

---

23 In one City institution, a substantial number of staff failed to attend training sessions despite repeated requests, which emphasised the importance that all staff attend and indeed stated that it was a requirement of the firm that they do so.

As is seen in Chapter 4, these defences are provided in the UK in respect of the criminal offence of insider dealing;[24] they similarly apply to its civil/administrative counterpart of misuse of information. The offence of receipt of criminal property will, however, at the very least substantially erode it. In some cases, it will remain, but not in all. Two scenarios may be considered.

The first concerns Charlie, a broker who at 10.25 am receives an order from his client to sell 10,000 shares in Peterborough Construction plc and 5,000 shares in Rochester Petrochemicals plc. As he is obliged to, he seeks to execute this transaction in the way most advantageous to his client and hence seeks the best price by contacting a number of dealers. At 10.40, he calls Eddie, a dealer in another firm, who tells him, "I'll give you £4.80 a share for the Rochester lot, but you'll be lucky to get anything for Peterborough. It's being announced this afternoon that they've lost the Solent Bridge contract and they're laying off 200. Mind you, you didn't hear it from me."[25] Charlie has no reason to believe that his client has any links to Peterborough Construction. It, like Rochester Petrochemicals, is typical of the medium-sized British companies in which he tends to invest and, furthermore, Charlie knows he has personal reasons for wishing to realise some of his assets. As for his own position, when he hears the news from Eddie, he is already contractually bound to sell the shares on behalf of his client. If he goes ahead, therefore, he will not be guilty of insider dealing. Nor, for the reasons just outlined, will his client be (in all likelihood – few things are completely certain), hence the proceeds from the shares, when he does manage to sell them, will not represent criminal property and Charlie need have no qualms.

But contrast this with the scenario where, when he hears Eddie's news, Charlie does suspect that his client knew something and that this was the reason for his instruction to sell. He is still safe from a charge of insider dealing or market abuse: it is still the case that he came into possession of the information at a time when he was already contractually bound to sell the shares. The proceeds of the sale may, however, now be criminal property: Charlie suspects his client of insider dealing and therefore suspects that the proceeds will be derived from a criminal offence. He is now in a very difficult position. He cannot sell the shares: if he does, the moment he receives the price for them, he may be guilty of receipt of criminal property. Yet what can he do? He can hardly tell his client that he believes he may be engaging in insider dealing. Certainly he cannot tell him the news he has just heard. If he does, he will be guilty criminally and civilly of unauthorised disclosure of inside information. Furthermore, he will ensure that his client, who possibly was not in fact in possession of the information, cannot now sell the shares and the client will be entitled to sue him for the loss as their price crashes.

---

24 See pp. 118-19.

25 By telling Charlie this, Eddie is, of course, clearly guilty of unauthorised disclosure of inside information. This discussion is, however, concerned with Charlie's position, not Eddie's.

Perhaps the area of impact that has received the greatest publicity, however, is the simple one of financial cost. Of course, a successful legal action against the institution will also involve considerable cost, but what is referred to here is not damages or compensation, nor the fines that may be imposed, but the simple financial cost of implementing, on an ongoing basis, the measures that are required. Various estimates have been given for this, but in the late 1990s, there was a general consensus that the measures that institutions were required to take in order to comply with the anti-money laundering regime cost the financial sector, in the UK alone, in the region of £650 million per year. There is similar consensus that the requirement under the Proceeds of Crime Act 2002 to report suspicions of any kind of money laundering, whether or not the transaction is actually processed, and its imposition of liability on those in the regulated sector, not only where they knew or suspected money laundering but also where they did not but should have done, has led to a considerable increase in the number of reports and consequent expense. The industry has for some time now been protesting that it is being not just asked but required to bear the majority of the burden, in terms of both financial and other resources, of the fight against money laundering. While the official response of the government, law enforcement and regulatory sectors has been that it is in the interests of the state and the financial sector alike to eliminate financial crime, institutions often suspect that the real attitude is: "It is you that cause the problem – you can pay for solving it." Indeed, some in the law enforcement sector have expressed the view, albeit off the record, that the financial sector makes a very profitable living from a business that carries with it an inherent risk of money laundering and it is therefore not entirely unreasonable that they should devote some of their profits to reducing those risks.

Actual compliance is not, however, the only financial cost that an institution faces. There is also the risk of civil litigation. Those risks relating to insider dealing are set out in Chapter 7, but there are also risks relating both to money laundering itself and to the fight against it. The former relate to where actual money laundering has taken place, the latter to where a report is made but it transpires that the suspicion is unfounded. Some of these issues are set out in the previous chapter, but it is helpful in this context to remind oneself of them.

Money laundering, by definition, relates to acquisitive crimes, i.e. offences which produce a financial benefit. In some cases, there is no actual loser (as some argue is the case with insider dealing) and there are others where, while there is arguably a clear victim, that victim is unlikely to make a claim. Drug trafficking, for example causes considerable harm to the addicts it creates, but no addict has as yet sued their dealer.[26] Other offences do, however, have clear victims who are potential litigants.

---

26 Whether the precedent set in the United States by the successful lawsuits against tobacco companies may change this has yet to be seen. It is possible that, on the basis of some of these actions, not least that brought by the State of Mississippi, even if no addict felt willing or able to sue, a state health ministry might do so. See *Mike Moore et al. v. American Tobacco Company et al.*, Case No. 94-1429, Chancery Court of Jackson County, Mississippi; Givel, M.S. and Glantz, S.A. (2002) *Political Reform and Tobacco Control Policy Making in*

Among the more highly publicised have been cases of grand corruption, in which, following a corrupt politician (even head of state) leaving office, the successor government has sought to recover, as the robbed state, the assets that have been misappropriated. The politicians themselves may be unavailable, even deceased, in which case the financial institutions that have handled the assets may well find that it is they who are pursued: the action brought by the Government of the Philippines against the Union Bank of Switzerland is but one example. If the money is still in the possession of the institution, the consequences may not be too dire, although the interest claimed may not be inconsiderable and the publicity is likely to be embarrassing. If, however, it has been transferred out and now either cannot be located or, if it can, is in a jurisdiction which tends not to co-operate in such cases, the institution may find itself liable in negligence and/or as a constructive trustee. Where the appropriate assets run into many millions, or even billions, of euro, let alone pounds sterling, the fall-out from a successful lawsuit could be devastating.

Even where an institution takes scrupulous care to comply with all its anti-money laundering obligations, it may not be free from liability. Firstly, however careful a person or their institution may be, mistakes can happen and laundered property go undetected. Secondly, however, it can happen that an institution suspects money laundering, very possibly with reasonable grounds, but that these suspicions prove unfounded. There can then follow a range of liabilities. In order to encourage institutions to report their suspicions and co-operate with the anti-money laundering authorities, many Member States provide fairly wide protection against these. The Directive requires all of them to provide a defence in such circumstances to a charge of breach of professional confidentiality[27] and many go further, with legislation providing that, where an institution makes a suspicious transaction report in good faith to the appropriate authorities, no liability, either criminal or civil, may ensue as a result.[28] That of others, however, notably the UK, confines the protection to actions for breach of confidentiality. This leaves out a whole range of potential liabilities.

The first arises from the fact that, following the filing of the report, there will almost invariably be a delay before the transaction is permitted to proceed. This will very possibly cause loss to the client. The client may be denied an opportunity to make a totally legitimate profit in a very fast-moving marketplace: investment opportunities are rarely still there days, let alone weeks, after they first arise. Alternatively, the transfer of funds may be in settlement of an invoice: failure to pay this within the requisite time may lead to interest charges at the very least. The client is likely to be far from willing to take these losses "on the chin": they will

---

Mississippi From 1990 to 2001, Center for Tobacco Research and Education, University of California, San Francisco, Paper MS2002. But this is inevitably speculation.

27 Although not all Member States provide for criminal penalties for breach of confidentiality (in the absence of a defence), as, for example, Luxembourg does, in all of them this does provide a civil right of action.

28 France, Germany and Luxembourg are examples, although the German provisions, in order for protection to be granted, require not only that the report be made in good faith but also that it not be made through gross negligence.

seek compensation from the institution that has held up the payment. It will not be the Serious Organised Crime Agency on whose desk the claim form arrives, but the financial institution.

Linked to this is the possible loss that the client's counterparty may suffer: it may be their money that is held up. The possible types of losses will be similar to those listed above; so, therefore, will the potential claims.

The problems are exacerbated by the fact that the institution is criminally barred from informing its client, or indeed anyone else, what is going on. To do so is to commit the offence of tipping off.[29] In a number of cases, notably *C v S and others*[30] and *Governor and Company of the Bank of Scotland v A*,[31] the National Criminal Intelligence Service has emphasised this to the institution concerned in no uncertain terms. In *C v S*, NCIS went further, even informing the bank, which had made a number of suspicious transaction reports, that to comply with a court order that it disclose certain bank documents to a third party in an action against those suspected of having misappropriated funds would constitute tipping off. The bank was therefore in a particularly difficult position: its officers faced the unenviable choice of going to prison for tipping off or going to prison for contempt.[32] NCIS's solicitors were not amenable to being of assistance, taking the view, firstly, that it was the bank's problem and that the Service should not become involved in actions in the civil courts and, secondly, that it was in any event not qualified to give any assurance as to abstention from prosecution, since such matters were the decision of the Crown Prosecution Service,[33] not it. The matter was ultimately resolved by a detailed guidance statement from the Court of Appeal.[34] Since this is now referred to as a general guide to practice, it is useful to outline it here.

The starting point is that the institution should inform NCIS as soon as it becomes aware that an order for discovery has been applied for, or actually obtained, as the case may be. NCIS may then identify the material which it does not wish to be disclosed and indicate how it wishes the institution to deal with the application. It may therefore be possible to comply with the order in part, very possibly with a suitable undertaking as to confidentiality. Although it was recognised that this may not apply where NCIS does not wish the applicant to become aware that an investigation is in progress, Lord Woolf felt that this will not always be the case. Where NCIS does have no such objection, the applicant may be satisfied with partial discovery if it is explained to them that the alternative is for the court to consider the matter. Where NCIS is opposed to any kind of disclosure, however, directions will need to be sought from the court. Circumstances will dictate precisely how this may

---

29 See pp. 169ff.
30 [1999] 2 All ER 345.
31 [2001] 1 WLR 751.
32 Whether a jury would have convicted or, if it had, the trial judge actually imposed a prison sentence had the bank disclosed the information in obedience to the order of a High Court judge is a question which, ultimately, it was never necessary to answer.
33 Or, now, the Financial Services Authority.
34 [1999] 2 All ER 345, 349-50 *per* Lord Woolf MR.

be done. If the order was made in the absence of the other party, there may simply be an application to set it aside; alternatively, a formal application for directions may be made. If extreme confidentiality is required, a sealed letter may be sent to the judge, setting out the circumstances.

The court will then need to decide how to proceed, in particular on the extent to which the applicant for the order may be involved and whether or not the matter may be heard in open court. As far as is possible, however, the normal procedures should be followed. Where this is not possible and, for example, submissions are made in camera and/or in the absence of the applicant, a full transcript is to be prepared and the institution must be required to provide a copy to the applicant once NCIS informs it that secrecy is no longer necessary. Following this, the court will need to decide what evidence it requires to make an appropriate order. In some cases, a mere letter from NCIS may suffice; at the other end of the scale, NCIS may be joined as a party to the proceedings if the interests of justice require this. In any event, it will be for NCIS, or indeed any other investigating authority such as the Financial Services Authority, to demonstrate to the court that there would be a real likelihood of the investigation being prejudiced. It should be noted that Lord Woolf stated that, where NCIS[35] does not co-operate with either the institution or the court, the court may draw the inference that there will be no such prejudice and may make the disclosure order, crucially, "without offending the principle in *Rowell v Pratt*[36] and without putting the institution at risk of prosecution". Not only does this do much to relieve the institution, it also sends a very clear message to the investigatory authorities that they are expected to co-operate not only with the court but also with the institution. The non-cooperative approach taken by NCIS in the *C v S* case itself was very clearly stated not to be appropriate.

Finally, it was stressed that the court must recognise its own responsibility to protect the applicant's interests. This is especially important where the applicant is not represented: the court "must have material on which to act if it is to deprive an applicant of his normal rights". It is submitted, however, that this is more a warning to the court than a matter for the institution.

This, at least, clarifies the situation where an actual disclosure order has been issued (or may be about to be issued). A further problem, however, concerns the bank risking being caught between two liabilities. Where the authorities do decide that money laundering has taken place, they may well wish the institution to proceed with the transaction, or even relationship, in order to gather intelligence and/or evidence.[37] If the institution complies, it will not face criminal liability for money

---

35 Or, presumably, any other investigating authority.

36 [1938] AC 101. That is, a court will not make an order if this would result in a person being compelled to commit a criminal offence.

37 It will not always be possible for the police, or other authorities, to use the information they gather as evidence: procedural rules of evidence may render it inadmissible or its use may jeopardise other operations. The information may, however, still be highly useful as intelligence.

laundering, but this may not be the end of the matter. The funds may turn out to have a criminal origin but it may not be possible subsequently to recover them, either because they are now located in an uncooperative jurisdiction or because the trail is simply lost. In such a case, the victims of the offence may pursue the institution as a constructive trustee on the basis that it assisted in the removal of their assets.[38] If, on the other hand, the institution declines to co-operate, it is within its rights to do so, but this will involve not executing the transaction; this, in turn, will lead to liability to its customer, should the suspicion prove to be unfounded. Much has been said, since *Foley v Hill*,[39] about the bank merely owing an unsecured debt to its customer rather than holding property on his behalf, but even a debtor may be sued by their creditor. Furthermore, it is well established that the banker–customer relationship involves an element of agency: the customer is not only owed his balance by the bank but, in the normal course of things, expects the bank to do various things on his behalf.[40] This includes transmitting funds when requested to do so. It is true that the authorities cannot compel it to co-operate, but if it does not, it will risk being sued by its client. The only defence that it can give, namely that it had reason to believe the transaction to be linked to money laundering, will jeopardise the money laundering investigation that the institution knows to be in progress: the offence of tipping off. Attempts by institutions to obtain the assistance of the courts in navigating their way between the Scylla of criminal liability under the money laundering laws and the Charybdis of civil liability as a constructive trustee have been of little avail. In *Bank of Scotland v A*,[41] the Bank of Scotland requested the High Court to make an order which the bank would then have been legally obliged to obey and which therefore would have protected it from liability for so doing. Although a preliminary order was made in these terms, this was later overturned as inappropriate, a ruling which the Court of Appeal upheld. Lord Woolf, by now Lord Chief Justice, stated that a more appropriate way to proceed in such cases would be for the bank first to seek to come to an agreement with the Serious Fraud Office on behalf of the police and, if this proved impossible, to apply for a declaration (as opposed to injunction) from the court.

Although, as Lord Woolf pointed out, such a declaration may, under the Civil Procedure Rules, be binding, this has been viewed as of little comfort to the institution. This is confirmed by the decision of the court in *Amalgamated Metal Trading Ltd. v City of London Police Financial Investigation Unit and others*[42] not to grant one. In this case, the financial institution, Amalgamated Metal Trading Ltd. (AMT), had come to have serious doubts about the integrity of its client, Wavesmetco, and had

---

38 *Royal Brunei Airlines Sdn Bhd v Tan* [1995] 2 AC 378. For a consideration of the law of the constructive trust, see Hayton, D.J. (2003) *Underhill and Hayton: Law of Trusts and Trustees*, 16th Edition, Butterworths, pp. 391ff.
39 (1848) 2 HL Cas. 28.
40 *United Dominions Trust Ltd. v Kirkwood* [1966] 2 QB 431.
41 [2001] 1 WLR 751.
42 [2003] 1 WLR 2711.

therefore closed off its positions with it. This had, however, left a net balance of some US$450,000 owing to Wavesmetco. Concerned that to pay this could constitute the offence of facilitating the retention or control of the proceeds of criminal conduct under section 93A of the Criminal Justice Act 1988,[43] AMT therefore sought the consent of the City of London Police Financial Investigation Unit to make the payment. This consent was refused, although City Police did not confirm that the funds were derived from crime either. Faced with the prospect of being sued by Wavesmetco if they did not pay over the funds, AMT therefore issued proceedings against City Police and applied to the court for a declaration that the funds were not the proceeds of criminal conduct (and that therefore, by implication, they could release them). The court declined, ruling that, to make such a declaration, it required actual evidence that the funds had a legitimate origin, not simply an absence of evidence that they did not. Such an approach would seem reasonable: to decide otherwise would open the way for criminal proceeds to be transferred with impunity while an investigation is ongoing. Tomlinson J appreciated the difficulty faced by the institution, but referred to the remarks made by Lord Woolf in the *Bank of Scotland* case that, on occasion, the courts could not help and the institution would simply have to take a commercial decision whether or not to defend any action which its client might bring.

This is of little assistance, however. Tomlinson J explicitly did not consider the issue of tipping off, since this was not the offence that the institution was fearful of committing and possibly also because, by the time of the hearing, Wavesmetco had learned of what was going on; indeed, its controlling manager had been charged with offences in India while two others with close links to the company had been arrested in the United States. In other cases, however, it will be a real issue. If the company's sole defence to the action is that it was constrained by the police, but it is barred by the criminal law from saying so, this is a legal issue, not merely a commercial one. The consequence will be that it will lose the action and be ordered to pay over not only the funds but damages for any loss suffered by the client plus, given the rule of English civil procedure, the client's legal costs as well. It could be argued that the institution may limit this by paying over the funds as soon as it receives the claim form, but this will expose it to criminal prosecution for money laundering. Tomlinson J's words are instructive:

> It is to my mind inconceivable that there could be criminal proceedings brought under section 93A against a bank or other financial institution which has taken such steps as are reasonable in all the circumstances to resist proceedings but has none the less been ordered by the court to pay over money which subsequently is proved to be the proceeds of criminal conduct.[44]

---

43 The events took place before the coming into force of the relevant provisions of the Proceeds of Crime Act 2002, but the offences under the Criminal Justice Act 1988 were very similar to their 2002 Act counterparts.

44 [2003] 1 WLR 2711, 2723.

The requirement is that the institution has resisted the proceedings and been ordered by the court to pay over the funds. It is therefore compelled to embark on an expensive and fruitless exercise when, all the time, it in fact had a defence, namely illegality. The option of simply not resisting the action at all and letting the case go quickly and comparatively inexpensively to summary judgment would not seem to be open: it is debatable whether "such steps as are reasonable in all the circumstances to resist proceedings" can mean no steps at all. It remains notable that there has yet to be a case in this area in which the approach taken by the institution has been endorsed by the court.

The situation is now slightly better in respect of the risk of liability as a constructive trustee. A year after the *Amalgamated Metal Trading* case, Coleman J stated, in *Hosni Tayeb v HSBC Bank plc and Al Foursan International Company*,[45] that it was "wholly unrealistic" that an institution that followed the guidelines in *C v S* and *Bank of Scotland v A* would find itself liable as a constructive trustee. This does, however, stop short of actually stating as a matter of law that it will not be so liable, particularly in view of Lord Woolf's comment in the *Bank of Scotland* case that "the law in this area [i.e. liability of financial institutions as constructive trustees] has been developing and continues to develop".[46] Lord Woolf may be proved right: one may need to see how future cases are decided.

Another possible claim that has been the subject of debate is that of defamation. A suspicious transaction report is, after all, a statement to a law enforcement (or, in some cases, regulatory) authority that the financial institution believes that the person concerned may be involved in money laundering. Indeed, it may go further: the suspicion may be that the client is involved not just in the laundering of the proceeds of the offence but in the committing of the predicate offence as well. If this turns out to be true, well and good; if it does not, such a statement is, at least prima facie, defamatory. Certainly a number of recent cases have demonstrated that those who bring such claims, sometimes even invoking "the trusty sword of truth", are not always as innocent as they allege. For some considerable time, the position was therefore unsatisfactory. The truth of allegations might be established, but only after an expensive court case.[47] There have been some, however, who have argued that those who, in good faith and in compliance with the Proceeds of Crime Act 2002, file a suspicious transaction report may be protected by the doctrine of qualified privilege. While, however, such a defence would protect a person who, for example, reports a suspected crime to the police, it is unclear whether a report of a suspicious transaction would fall into the same category. In any case, qualified privilege is a defence, not a bar to action, and, further, is dependent on a number of conditions, such as absence of malice.

---

45 [2004] EWHC 1529 (Comm.).

46 [2001] 1 WLR 751, 767.

47 Although the general principle under English law is that the loser of a lawsuit pays the other party's costs as well as his own, the successful defendant is in practice not always reimbursed, even if the court orders that he should be.

The situation was rectified not, as some called for, by legislation, but by the courts. The first step was taken by the House of Lords in 1998 in the case of *Taylor v Serious Fraud Office*.[48] This related to a report of suspicion of fraud, made to the Serious Fraud Office. Lord Hope stated in terms the limitations to qualified privilege and then went on to rule that absolute privilege was to apply:

> The requirement therefore is to extend to informants, investigators and prosecutors whose statements are revealed by the operation of the disclosure rules the benefit of the absolute privilege in respect of the statements made which is already accorded to witnesses and potential witnesses. And it is necessary to extend to them the same absolute immunity against actions for conspiracy or for negligence based upon disclosed material as has already been recognised in the case of the police.[49]

Although Lord Lloyd disapproved of this view, he, like their other Lordships, dismissed Taylor's appeal and left the absolute privilege point undecided.[50] Their remaining Lordships, in particular Lord Hoffman, ruled, like Lord Hope, that absolute privilege was to be extended in such cases. Although there has yet to be a similar case relating to money laundering rather than fraud, it is submitted that those who report a suspicion of money laundering constitute informants and will therefore be covered by the complete protection of absolute privilege rather than the partial protection of qualified privilege. The extension of the principle to statements provided to a regulatory authority, made two years later in *Mahon and another v Rahn and others (No. 2)*[51] would seem to underline this. The *Mahon* ruling may be of particular importance in this context given the leading role of the Financial Services Authority, under the Financial Services and Markets Act 2000, in investigating and indeed prosecuting money laundering offences.

Finally, one should mention reputational risk. It is very difficult, if not impossible, to put an actual figure on the losses that this can entail, but they are no less real for that. Doug Hopton, at the time Head of Fraud and Money Laundering Prevention at Barclays Bank, commented in a speech in July 2002 that the damage to an institution's reputation was a greater threat even than the risk of imprisonment of some of its officers. Others have made the same point: long after the individuals have gone to prison, their institution remains tarred with their misdemeanours. For an example of the impact of this, albeit in the context of a different type of financial crime, one need only consider the fate of Arthur Andersen after it became embroiled in the Enron scandal.

---

48 [1999] 2 AC 177; [1998] 4 All ER 801.
49 [1999] 2 AC 177, 219; [1998] 4 All ER 801, 818.
50 [1999] 2 AC 177, 203-4; [1998] 4 All ER 801, 804-5.
51 [2000] 4 All ER 41; [2000] WLR 2150. This case related to a statement made to The Securities Association, the predecessor of the Securities and Futures Authority. Since the Securities and Futures Authority has now in turn been replaced by the Financial Services Authority, it is submitted that the same principle will apply to statements made to the FSA.

Nor is it only the guilty who have cause to fear this type of risk. It was well publicised that the Bank of New York was used as a conduit for the laundering of money from Russian mafia groups and also that two of its officers were suspected of being not just careless instruments but knowing accomplices. What was less well publicised, however, was that, at the time that the story hit the headlines, the Bank had, at an institutional level, been assisting law enforcement in their investigation of the launderers for over a year.

Conclusion

In conclusion, therefore, the impact on the financial services sector of both the insider dealing and the money laundering provisions may be seen to be considerable. In many Member States, it is not only individuals but also corporate entities which may be found liable, either criminally or civilly (or conceivably both), for offences of insider dealing. This is only underlined by the legislation in France which includes a duty on primary insiders, under the criminal law, not only not to abuse inside information themselves but also to ensure that others do not do so. In the UK, the enhanced definition of money laundering under the Proceeds of Crime Act 2002 makes the situation decidedly difficult should an intermediary latterly come to suspect that a client, who instructed the purchase or sale of securities, may in fact have done so on the basis of inside information. Similarly, the traditional approach in the UK of a firm dealing with an offender quietly is no longer open; indeed, in some Member States, such as Greece, this option was never available.

Compliance with the money laundering regime is even less simple. It involves considerable financial cost to the institution, which has risen further in the UK as a greater number of reports now need to be filed. Moreover, a number of institutions have now found themselves in the difficult position of holding funds which the investigating authorities suspect, but do not yet know, to be derived from crime, yet being barred on pain of criminal sanctions from explaining their actions. They face potential liability as a constructive trustee to third parties if they do release the funds and, often, criminal liability as well unless they force their client to bring an action which they will be powerless to defend. Invariably, there is also the issue of reputational risk. Some guidance has been given by the courts as to how an institution is to negotiate its way through this minefield, but, at the same time, the courts have yet to endorse as successful any model that has actually been adopted. The tension between the need of society or the state to combat the financing of crime and the need of legitimate financial institutions to be able to conduct their business along clear legal lines may therefore be expected to continue.

Chapter 7

Civil and Administrative Offences

Substantive Insider Dealing Offences

As stated in Chapter 4, the Directive prohibits insider dealing, but it does not prescribe how Member States are to penalise it. Article 13 merely states that it is up to the Member States to decide the penalties and that these are to be "sufficient to promote compliance" with the measures set out. The approach taken by the Member States has, with the partial exception of Spain, been to start from a basis that the three principal offences of dealing, encouraging another to deal and unauthorised disclosure of inside information are criminal offences and punished accordingly. The additional requirement, under Article 7, that undertakings publish significant, price-sensitive information has, in contrast, been addressed by means of a regulatory requirement.

Some Member States left it at that, notably most of the northern Member States: Belgium, the Netherlands, Luxembourg, Germany,[1] Austria, Denmark, Sweden, Finland and the UK. Alone of the southern Member States, Portugal also adopted this approach. France, Greece, Italy and Spain, as well as Ireland, however, although they introduced criminal provisions for insider dealing, supplemented them with civil or administrative provisions. In some cases, these were in essence no more than an additional means of dealing with what were identical offences, but often there were important differences. Nowhere was this more so than in Spain, where the criminal offence of insider dealing was extremely restricted in its scope, but, in contrast, its civil counterpart was extremely wide-ranging.

In time, however, there was an increasing recognition that the criminal justice system is ill-suited to deal with offences of insider dealing. Some took the view that insider dealing should not be a criminal offence at all, that it is something which, if it should be opposed at all, should be a regulatory matter for the markets: it should not attract the opprobrium of a criminal conviction. Others, although they took the view that insider dealing should be dealt with extremely seriously, to the extent of a criminal prosecution with accompanying penalties, felt that the criminal justice system simply did not work. Professor Barry Rider, for many years Head of the Commercial Crime Unit of the Commonwealth Secretariat, has frequently

---

1 Until the reform to the provisions in December 2004.

commented on the record in the UK. In the 25 years in which insider dealing has been a criminal offence in the UK, there have been less than 50 prosecutions and less than 30 convictions. Some might argue that a success rate of around 60% is not unreasonable, but the statistics go on to reveal that of those convictions, the overwhelming majority followed pleas of guilty. In any case, the London Stock Exchange has, since 1980, reported an average of 250,000 transactions each year that it considered gave rise to a suspicion of insider dealing. Over 25 years, this comes to 6.25 million reports. Against this background. fewer than 50 prosecutions and fewer than 10 convictions where the accused denied his guilt begins to look not quite so impressive. To quote Dr Mads Andenas, then Director of the Centre for European Law at King's College London, in a paper given at a conference on insider dealing held at the Institute of Advanced Legal Studies in February 1997:

> If you want to go to prison for insider dealing in the United Kingdom, it is possible. But you really had better confess.

There has been an increasing move, therefore, even among the former "criminal only approach" states, to introduce a civil and/or administrative regime. This, it is hoped, will achieve the results that the criminal justice system has not delivered. It has been said that, above all, the civil approach has one major advantage: greater ease of proof. In the criminal justice system, the various elements must be proven beyond reasonable doubt. Dr. Janet Dine has calculated that Part V of the Criminal Justice Act 1993 in the UK requires 54 different elements to be proven in order for a conviction to be secured. The following are just some of those that relate to a conviction for actual dealing:

- the defendant bought (or sold) securities;
- the defendant was in possession of the relevant information;
- the information related to the securities which the defendant bought/sold;
- the information was capable of affecting the price of those securities;
- the information had not been made public;

To the third, fourth and fifth of these must then, in each case, be added the further element that the defendant knew this: he knew that the information related to the securities, etc. Failure to prove just one element beyond reasonable doubt would mean the failure of the prosecution. It is perhaps not surprising that prosecutors were loath in such circumstances to risk the public resources involved in bringing a criminal case.

One approach taken, notably in the Netherlands, has been to remain with the criminal justice approach, but amend the law such that the offence is easier to prove.[2] There is a limit, however to the extent to which this can be done: if a conviction for

---

2 See pp. 71-72.

the offence can result in a person going to prison, in certain cases for several years,[3] it is only right that it be required that that conviction be on the basis of the strongest of proofs of guilt. If action was to be taken in cases where evidence could not be produced to this standard, other means needed to be found.

This means has been through the civil process. In the UK, a civil case, in contrast to the "beyond reasonable doubt test" of the criminal law, need only be proven on the balance of probabilities, i.e. 50.000001%.[4] The other Member States similarly impose less rigorous requirements. The consequences of a successful action will not involve a prison sentence, but they can include substantial fines. Thus, a way forward has been found whereby, although the defendant is dealt with perhaps less harshly than one would ideally like, he has not escaped scot free either. In view of this, and of the success of this approach not only within the EU but, perhaps with even greater publicity, in the United States, the UK and, more recently, Germany have now introduced wide-ranging civil measures to punish insider dealing, although other Member States still have yet to do so. As in the other "civil approach" Member States,[5] however, these new provisions are supplementary to the criminal justice regime: they do not replace it.

Although the measures are frequently referred to as civil, many of them are in fact more administrative in nature. For the most part, actions are brought not by alleged victims but by the financial services regulator. Indeed, it is very difficult to identify the victims of insider dealing (the offence of market manipulation, often grouped together with insider dealing, is of course a different matter).[6] Just as it is the regulator that brings the action, so the money that the defendant, following a successful case, is compelled to pay tends to be in the form of a penalty rather than damages. It is for this reason that this chapter has been entitled "Civil and Administrative Offences".

A final point that needs to be made before one examines each of the Member States in detail is that these civil/administrative measures are not always merely an alternative means of punishing the same offence. In some Member States, such as France or Ireland, the measures are very similar to their criminal counterparts and indeed an insider may find himself the subject of both a criminal prosecution and civil/administrative proceedings. Even there, however, there may be some differences. But in others, although there is some overlap, the criminal and civil

---

3 In the UK, insider dealing carries up to 7 years' imprisonment, in Ireland up to 10 years. For the full range of penalties in the various Member States, see the "Penalties" sections in Chapter 4.

4 That said, in the case of certain regulatory offences, a higher standard will be required: in general terms, the more serious the allegation, the higher the standard of proof. Even in the most serious cases, however, the standard will still fall well short of the criminal one of "beyond reasonable doubt".

5 With the partial exception of Germany and Spain.

6 For further discussion of the problems of identifying the victims, in the context of the UK's provisions for restitution orders in market abuse cases, see pp. 220-21.

offences are quite different; this is true of the UK's market abuse provisions and, far more strikingly, the Spanish legislation.

To date, as stated above, civil/administrative provisions have been introduced in seven Member States: France, Germany, Greece, Ireland, Italy (to a limited extent), Spain and the UK It is helpful, therefore, to examine each of these in turn.

France

The French administrative provisions are to be found in Regulation 90-08 of the COB, the Commission des Opérations de la Bourse (Stock Exchange Operations Commission). The Regulation's definition of inside information is the same as that in the criminal Article L465-1 of the Monetary and Financial Code; that of insiders is also similar, although it should be noted that the administrative definition also includes all persons holding privileged information as a result of the preparation or performance of a financial transaction.[7] More interesting is the way that the civil offence is phrased: persons holding privileged information are forbidden to exploit such information on the market, whether on their own behalf or that of another person. This reference to exploitation of the information is very similar to the terms "market abuse", used both in the new EU Directive 2003/6/EC and in the UK legislation, whose counterpart to insider dealing is "misuse of information". The French term, however, was introduced 10 years earlier.

Where offences are committed, the COB has the power to bring an action before the courts: Article 1 of the Regulation entitles it to appear on behalf of the State before any court or tribunal except a criminal court. (In criminal cases, the COB will pass its file to the public prosecutor.) It is, however, empowered simply to impose a sanction itself. A parallel may thus be drawn with the Financial Services Authority in the UK. Although civil or administrative sanctions cannot include a prison sentence, those who commit the offence of exploiting privileged information on the markets face identical fines to those provided for in the criminal legislation: up to €1,524,490[8] or 10 times the profit realised, whichever is the greater. In addition, where the offender is a shareholder, the COB may apply to the court for an order suspending voting rights. Finally, it may publish its decision. This power is invariably exercised and indeed the stigma resulting from the publication is seen as an additional penalty. A parallel may be drawn with the approach taken in the UK by the FSA and indeed the Investment Management Regulatory Organisation

---

7 Article 3.
8 Previously FF10 million. Following France's adoption of the euro, the approach regarding fines, and indeed all financial orders and awards by the courts, has generally been to retain the old amounts stated in French francs and then for the judges and lawyers to calculate the euro equivalent. The exception to this rule is where the order is made under provisions passed since the introduction of the euro, for example Article L465-1 of the Monetary and Financial Code, introduced partly on 15 November 2001, very shortly before the franc was replaced by the euro, and partly on 1 January 2002, the date of the euro's introduction.

(IMRO), one of the Self-Regulatory Organisations (SROs) that preceded it.[9] All these sanctions may be imposed on natural and legal persons alike.

Germany

The German civil provisions for insider dealing were only introduced with the amendment of the *Wertpapierhandelsgesetz* (Securities Trade Act) on 15 December 2004; prior to this, insider dealing was a solely criminal offence. Indeed, it is to be noted that actual dealing remains such.

Under the amended Act, however, unauthorised disclosure of inside information exposes the person responsible to regulatory liability.[10] The same applies to either encouraging a person to deal in insider securities or arranging for them to do so.[11] The provision is perhaps of particular importance in relation to secondary insiders, since they are only criminally liable if they actually deal. Primary insiders are, however, covered by both the criminal and the regulatory provisions.

In contrast to the other Member States that provide for civil liability for insider dealing offences, Germany neither provides for an unlimited fine, as in the UK, nor for a fine linked directly to the profits obtained, as in, for example, France or Greece. Rather, a maximum regulatory fine[12] of €200,000 is prescribed.[13] Because these provisions are so recent, however, it remains to be seen what the practice will be in terms of actual fines imposed.

Greece

The Greek legislation is almost a copy of the Directive and there is no difference whatsoever in terms of definition between the criminal and the civil/administrative provisions. The Epitropi Kefalaiagoras (Capital Markets Commission) does, however, have the power to impose administrative fines for insider dealing. These are between €29,347 and €2,934,702[14] or, if this is greater, up to five times the profits made by the insider. There have been very few cases to date, all of which have been dealt with by administrative fines rather than a criminal prosecution. These fines have, however, been substantial. In the first case brought by the Capital Markets Commission, *CMC v Trifon and others*, decided on 14 March 1997, the fines imposed ranged from Drs. 100 million to Drs. 600 million, the approximate equivalent of between €293,500 and €1.76 million. That said, the profits that the

---

9 All the SROs published notices of their decisions. IMRO, however, provided the best access to the public of their notices, although, like the other SROs, it never imposed a penalty for insider dealing.
10 Securities Trade Act, para. 39(2)3.
11 Securities Trade Act, para. 39(2)4.
12 *Geldbuße*, in contrast to the criminal *Geldstrafe*. The terms *Geldbuße* and *Bußgeld* appear, however, to be used interchangeably.
13 Securities Trade Act, para. 39(4).
14 Previously between Drs. 10 million and Drs. 1,000 million.

insiders had made between them through the transactions concerned amounted to over Drs. 8 billion.[15]

Ireland

Ireland, in section 109 of the Companies Act 1990, provides true civil liability for insider dealing. It adopts the same definition of the offence as the criminal provisions in section 108; indeed, it refers to them. However, in contrast to its counterparts in other Member States, the section does not provide for a regulator to take action; rather it gives a right of action to the victims. The definition of such a victim is simple: any party to the transaction who was not in possession of the inside information and who suffers loss as a result of any difference between the price he paid for the securities and the price for which they would have been likely to have been bought or sold if the information had been generally available. Where, therefore, an insider buys securities just before news is announced that increases their price, the insider will be liable to compensate his counterparty for the increase in the price that, on this basis, he should have paid in the first place. Similarly, where he dumps securities just before bad news relating to them is announced, he will be liable to refund his counterparty the difference between the inflated price for which he sold them and their actual worth following the news breaking.

The same liability is imposed on those who encourage another person to deal on the basis of inside information or who disclose such information without authorisation: any of the three criminal offences in section 108 will attract the civil liability in section 109.

This liability is explicitly stated to be without prejudice to any other liability that the insider may incur. The section uses the phrase "any other cause of action", which would imply a further civil liability. This may perhaps be for misrepresentation: it is not without reason that insider dealing and market manipulation are often viewed together. But it would seem clear that the civil liability also applies irrespective of any criminal liability. The Irish legal system is, like that of England and Wales,[16] a common-law system; indeed, Ireland inherited the system from its British former rulers. Under the English system, it is accepted as normal that a person who commits a criminal offence that causes loss or harm to another person is also liable to a separate civil action brought by the victim.[17] Similarly, it is becoming increasingly common for victims, where a prosecution either fails or is not brought in the first place, to make use of the lower standard of proof to bring a civil action. It would seem to follow that this approach could also be taken in Ireland.

---

15 Approximately €23.5 million.
16 Although the legal systems of England and Wales and of Northern Ireland are common-law, that of Scotland is not.
17 In contrast, in France, a civil-law jurisdiction, the judge in the criminal trial may directly award damages to the victim, who is separately represented throughout the proceedings.

An attractive feature of this provision is that it is uncontroversially fair. It has been a criticism of the civil sanctions of regulatory authorities that they allow those authorities to penalise a person even though their evidence against him is weak. This provision does not do that: the action is brought by the victim, not the regulator, and the aim is to compensate, not to punish. The role of the State as punisher remains firmly in the criminal sphere. A further advantage is that the loser is compensated fully. In certain jurisdictions,[18] the regulator imposes civil penalties (or alternatively brings an action) on behalf of a wide range of alleged victims; this can mean, however, that each individual victim receives only part, very possibly a small part, of their actual loss.

There are, however, also disadvantages. The principal one is, of course, that, since the action is brought by the victim rather than by the State on their behalf, redress is only open to those victims with the means to sue. Those who do not have such means, particularly where the alleged offender is not an individual but a substantial corporation, will remain uncompensated.

Also, however, the damages awarded will merely deprive the offender of his illicit profit. He is not actually any worse off. As such, the deterrence is minimal. If a person knows that, if he engages in insider dealing, the worst that can happen to him is that he will be forced to pay compensation such that the deal is on the same basis that it would have been if he had waited until after the relevant information became public, what reason does he have not to try it? There are, of course, the severe criminal penalties prescribed in section 108 of the Act: the prison sentence is the most severe of any Member State. But, as discussed above, the criminal provisions have the problem of the higher standard of proof, which all too often a prosecutor finds it impossible to meet. It could therefore be argued that a true deterrent would be an additional power for a regulator to bring civil proceedings. This could be on behalf of the victims but it could also be used as a means to penalise the offender where a criminal prosecution is viewed as impractical.

Italy

The Italian legislation does not prescribe civil or administrative sanctions for insider dealing as such. Even following the introduction of new legislation in 1998 and its amendment in 2002, the three substantive offences remain criminal offences and are dealt with accordingly. In contrast to the position in France, however, the offences – even though they lead to a criminal prosecution – are investigated by the CONSOB.[19] The CONSOB Resolution of 14 November 1991 hence prescribes heavy fines for the frustration of an investigation: refusal to co-operate with such an investigation or, in purported co-operation, providing false information to the CONSOB carries a fine of

---

18 For example, South Africa and, possibly, the UK: see pp. 220-21.

19 Commissione Nazionale per la Società e la Borsa (National Company and Stock Exchange Commission).

between €5,164.57 and €129,114.22.[20] In addition, public sanctions are imposed and the defendant will be required to pay the costs of the CONSOB action.

An exception to this approach concerns offences following board meetings. Article 2(3) of Law No. 157 of 17 May 1991 provided that, where a board meeting passes a resolution capable of affecting the price of securities, a controlling shareholder, director, liquidator, officer, supervisory board member or auditor of the company concerned who dealt in the relevant securities was liable to increased criminal penalties.[21] The CONSOB Resolution provides that where such persons refuse to co-operate with the CONSOB, they are not merely liable to an administrative fine but commit a separate criminal offence, carrying a prison sentence of up to 3 months. In one sense, this appears quite harsh. It should, however, be considered that in the UK, criminal penalties may be imposed on anyone, regardless of their position, who fails to co-operate with a Financial Services Authority investigation, particularly if they provide it with false or misleading information. Furthermore, the maximum prison sentence is 2 years.[22] There is evidence that this broader approach may now be taken in Italy as well. Law No. 157 has been replaced with new legislation, which, instead of singling out particular categories of insider, merely provides that where, *inter alia*, "the personal circumstances of the offender" mean that the normal criminal fine is inadequate, the fine may be trebled.[23] Since this may be seen as the successor to Article 2(3) of the old Law, it is possible that it may be used to impose criminal liability on anyone who fails to co-operate, certainly if they are in a senior position.

Spain

With the exception of the new market abuse provisions in the UK, the Spanish administrative provisions relating to insider dealing are arguably the most significant of those of any Member State. The Spanish criminal provisions for insider dealing

---

20 Previously between 10 million and 250 million lire. This Resolution was of course passed before the introduction of the euro on 1 January 2002, but even the most recent legislation, dated 11 April 2002, continues to cite levels of fines in Italian lire rather than euro.

21 See pp. 127-28.

22 General failure without reasonable excuse to provide information, either to the FSA itself or to an investigator appointed by it, may result in an action before the High Court (or, in Scotland, before the Court of Session) which in turn may lead to the person concerned being treated as though they were in contempt of court: s. 174, Financial Services and Markets Act 2000. Although such contempt is not technically a criminal offence, it nonetheless carries criminal penalties: up to 2 years' imprisonment and/or an unlimited fine. Actually providing false information to the FSA, or to its appointed investigator, is a criminal offence. In the context of an investigation, it carries up to 2 years' imprisonment and/or an unlimited fine (s. 177(4) of the Act); in a more general context, it carries an unlimited fine only (s. 398).

23 Article 180, Legislative Decree 58 of 24 February 1998, as amended by Legislative Decree 61 of 11 April 2002. For more details on this provision, see pp. 127-28.

are extremely restrictive, applying only to certain specified types of primary insider and, even then, only where a minimum profit has been made (or loss avoided).[24] In contrast, the administrative provisions of the *Ley del Mercado de Valores* (Securities Market Law) are extremely wide-ranging. Article 81.2 of the Law prohibits "any person who possesses inside information" from dealing on the basis of it. It does not matter whether the dealing is direct or indirect or on the insider's own account or that of a third party: it is forbidden. Nor does it matter how the insider came by the information: there is in this respect no distinction between primary and secondary insiders. The person who obtains inside information through his work, the friend he deliberately tips off, the taxi driver, the waitress or barman serving insiders who are careless with their talk: all are covered. The only test is: did the person, when he dealt in the securities in question, possess inside information relating to them?

Since the provisions apply to "any person", liability may accrue to natural and legal persons alike. Where, however, the offence is committed by a legal entity, Article 95 of the Law provides that, in certain cases, persons holding administrative or management responsibility in the corporation may be held liable instead of the legal entity itself. It should be noted that this applies to anyone exercising such a role: they need not necessarily be formal members or officers of the corporation. A comparison may be drawn with the position of shadow directors in the UK. More generally, liability may be imposed jointly and severally on the individuals and the legal entity concerned. As is seen below, however, where a legal entity is found to have committed an insider dealing offence, the fine can be extremely severe.

Just as any person in possession of inside information is prohibited from dealing on the basis of it, so anyone possessing such information (regardless of how they came by it) is prohibited from passing that information on to another person or from encouraging another person to deal on the basis of it.[25] As in all Member States, there is the necessary proviso that, to be prohibited, the disclosure must be unauthorised: Article 81.2 states that a person is prohibited from communicating inside information to a third party "unless in the normal course of his employment, profession or duties".

Thus far, the Spanish provisions are very similar to those of the Scandinavian Member States, particularly Denmark, albeit that these adopt an entirely criminal approach while, as has been seen, that of Spain is almost entirely civil. It is interesting, therefore, to compare the penalties. In Denmark, insider dealing offences can result in a prison sentence, but the maximum sentence is quite low: 18 months. Similarly, in Sweden and Finland, it is 2 years.[26] The fine, however, is unlimited. In Spain, any

---

24 See p. 75.

25 Since these two are separate offences both under the Directive and in the national legislation of all Member States, the distinction between them is discussed in Chapter 4.

26 In Sweden, this is for normal cases. For the full range of penalties under the Swedish legislation, see pp. 131-32. The low prison sentences, especially compared to those provided for in Member States such as Ireland or the UK, is in keeping with the comparatively lenient approach taken generally by the Scandinavian criminal justice systems.

of the three substantive insider dealing offences are classified in Article 99(o) of the Law as "very serious offences" against the market. As such, Article 102 prescribes a minimum fine of €30,050,61.[27] The maximum is not unlimited, as in Scandinavia (and indeed the UK), but, as in France and Greece, directly linked to the profits made: it is five times the profit. Where the offence is committed by a legal entity, however, the maximum fine is even higher: 5% of the corporation's capital or, where the corporation is part of a group, 5% of the capital of the entire group. In certain cases, these fines may be imposed personally on those who held management or administrative responsibilities in the corporation and who colluded in the offence.

This is not necessarily the end of the matter, however. Where the case is considered to justify it, the defendant may be suspended or even disqualified permanently from trading on the securities markets.[28] In addition, they may be disqualified for 5 years from holding the office of director. Depending on the circumstances of the case, this disqualification may either be total, like its counterpart in the UK under the Company Directors Disqualification Act 1986, or relate solely to the company concerned. It could be argued that a 5 year suspension is not that draconian a penalty. In the UK, disqualification may be for up to 15 years, while in Belgium, it may be permanent. Indeed, the Belgian provisions include a mandatory life disqualification from both holding the office of a director (of any company) and from continuing to practice in the financial sector.[29] It could, however, in response be argued that it is sufficient when seen in the context of the other sanctions that can be imposed. A company director who uses his company to commit insider dealing offences may, after all, face a fine that could easily bankrupt him; similarly, any insider dealer can be banned from the financial markets for life. Hence the suspension from acting as a company director may merely be a small added punishment, after which he can be allowed to return to earning a living in a sector that will be less likely to lend itself to similar offences in the future.

The above offences apply to any person. The Law contains an additional provision, however, which applies solely to primary insiders, in particular those who obtain inside information through their work. Article 81.1 provides that "any person who, by virtue of the exercise of his employment, profession, position or duties, possesses data or information relating to [securities] markets" is under a duty to safeguard it. This "safeguarding" responsibility is a general catch-all measure; the Law cites the following specific aspects of it:

- preventing inside information from being used in an unconscionable manner;
- taking such measures as are required to prevent or avoid such misuse;
- reporting any such misuse;

---

27 Previously Pts. 5 million.

28 A comparison may be drawn with the Financial Services Authority's powers to withdraw, either permanently or for a stated period, authorisation to engage in a regulated activity: see pp. 221-22.

29 Through the minimum prison sentence prescribed: see p. 124.

- taking action to put right any consequences brought about by the misuse.

This clearly does not preclude such a person from the proper disclosure of the information in the normal course of his work. Nor, it is explicitly stated, does it alter his duty to co-operate both with the courts and with administrative authorities as required under the law. But it does mean that he is responsible for the information with which he is entrusted – and which he entrusts to others. If a colleague to whom he has disclosed inside information abuses it, he cannot turn a blind eye. Indeed, he is responsible for his colleague's offence: the obligation to take action to put right the consequences make this clear. It would seem, therefore, that anyone handling inside information through their work is required to make a judgment call as to the use to which their colleagues or other professional contacts may put it, i.e. whether that use will remain within permitted bounds.

Of the other Member States, only France has a similar provision. The discussion of the rationale for such a provision, however, is much the same and the comments made in relation to the French provisions in Chapter 4[30] therefore apply equally to those of Spain. There is an important difference between the two, however, with regard to how they are penalised. Not only is the French provision a criminal one, carrying a potential sentence of imprisonment, the sentence prescribed is identical to that for actual dealing. It could be considered, therefore, that the French legislator has not seen any significant difference between a primary insider who allows another person to deal on the basis of the inside information and one who actively encourages him to do so. In contrast, the Spanish penalty for failing to safeguard inside information is lower than for actual dealing. Whereas actual dealing offences are classified as "very serious offences", failure to safeguard inside information is classified as merely a "serious infringement". It therefore carries a minimum fine of only €12,024.24[31]; the maximum is €30,050.61, which is the minimum fine for "very serious offences".

United Kingdom

For some considerable time, the UK was, like Germany, firmly in the category of Member States that dealt with insider dealing solely by means of the criminal justice system. Under the regime of the Financial Services Act 1986, the detailed regulation of the financial services industry fell, for the most part,[32] to the Self-Regulatory Organisations or SROs. Two of these, the Securities and Futures Authority (SFA) and the Investment Management Regulatory Organisation (IMRO), prohibited insider dealing in their Rules, but in practice, this was totally unenforced. When asked in

---

30   See pp. 138-39.
31   Previously Pts. 2 million.
32   A few institutions were regulated directly by the Securities and Investments Board (SIB), but these were very much the exception. Lawyers and accountants were regulated by their own professional bodies, designated Recognised Professional Bodies (RPBs).

1997 for their record of disciplining persons caught engaging in insider dealing, the SFA stated that this was a very serious offence against the market and they would therefore deal with it very severely. Their Board Notices, however, did not reveal a single case. IMRO were more candid: insider dealing was indeed prohibited in their rules, they said, but it was also a criminal offence and they therefore left enforcement up to the police. In any case, the remit of the SROs only extended to their own members; anyone else fell under the authority of the criminal law alone.

This changed at the turn of the Millennium: the Financial Services and Markets Act 2000 came into force on 1 December 2001.[33] Amid considerable publicity and discussion, Part VIII of FSMA, as the Act soon became known, introduced a new offence of "market abuse". Essentially, this consisted of two offences: insider dealing and market manipulation. Both of these had previously been criminal offences and they remained so: Part V of the Criminal Justice Act 1993 remained on the statute book, while the criminal offence of market manipulation was re-created in FSMA 2000.[34] In contrast, market abuse was an explicitly civil/administrative concept. To emphasise the distinction, new terms were devised for the offences that it covered: "misuse of information", "giving a false or misleading impression" (sometimes referred to as misleading statements and practices) and "distortion of the market". This book, however, is confined to insider dealing and hence misuse of information: market manipulation, although linked to insider dealing, is not only a separate offence but a separate subject for study in its own right. Although part of what follows applies equally to misleading statements and practices, it is on misuse of information that the comments will focus.

One basic point needs to be made at the outset. Unlike the Rules of the SROs, these provisions apply to everyone. The Financial Services Authority is not a club with jurisdiction only over its members, it is a statutory body with jurisdiction over the whole financial services sector. In the context of its task of reducing financial crime,[35] this extends to the entire public. Regardless of whether they have or have not received authorisation from the FSA to engage in a regulated activity, if a person – any person – commits an offence of market abuse, the FSA therefore has the power to deal with them.

So, to the definition of market abuse itself. This is set out in section 118(1) of the Act:

... behaviour (whether by one person alone or by two persons jointly or in

---

33 For the most part: certain provisions came into force earlier, although none relating to any form of abuse of the financial markets.

34 S.397.

35 FSMA 2000, ss. 2(2)(d), 6. As regards what is meant by "financial crime", s. 6(3)(b) explicitly states that it includes "misuse of information relating to a financial market".

concert),

(a) which occurs in relation to qualifying investments traded on a prescribed market ...

(b) which satisfies any one or more of the conditions set out in subsection (2); and

(c) which is likely to be regarded by a regular user of that market who is aware of the behaviour as a failure on the part of the person or persons concerned to observe the standard of behaviour reasonably expected of a person in his or their position in relation to the market.

Condition (a) is fairly uncontroversial, since "qualifying investments" cover all the types of security covered in insider dealing legislation elsewhere, including the Directive itself: shares, bonds, options, futures, future rate agreements (FRAs), etc. "Prescribed markets" similarly covers all the significant securities exchanges of the UK. What is potentially more controversial is the term "behaviour". At first glance, such a word does not appear to give cause for comment; subsection (10), however, defines it as covering both action and inaction. The significance of this is underlined in the policy on penalties set out in section 123 of the Act.[36]

Condition (c) is more complex. At first glance, it is a variant of the "reasonable man" test, but on closer analysis, it is not quite as simple as that. The "regular user" is just that: he is not merely a member of the public who invests from time to time, the oft-cited Aunt Agatha. Furthermore, he is not just a regular investor in general but a regular user of the particular market on which the (alleged) behaviour took place. It is recognised that behaviour can vary according to the market in question: what is appropriate on the metals futures market may not be so on the stock market. Not only must he deal regularly on that market, subsection (10) makes clear that he must deal regularly in the particular investments which the behaviour in question concerned. Thus, the judgment is that of someone who is well-used to dealing on that specific market and is therefore familiar with the kinds of behaviour that are and are not normal practice on it. Finally, unsurprisingly, subsection (10) also states that he must be reasonable.

Condition (b) refers to subsection (2), which in turn sets out the three types of market abuse, referred to by some commentators as the three limbs. As mentioned above, that which relates to insider dealing is termed "misuse of information". It is expressed in subsection 2(a) as follows:

the behaviour is based on information which is not generally available to those using the market but which, if available to a regular user of the market, would or would be

---

36 See pp. 215, 217-18.

likely to be regarded by him as relevant when deciding the terms on which transactions in investments of the kind in question should be effected.

There is considerable overlap between this and the definition of insider dealing set out in Part V of the Criminal Justice Act 1993. The behaviour must, however, be based on information "not generally available to those using the market", not simply "not publicly available". This may be splitting hairs: it is established that, if information is available through a system such as Bloomberg, it is publicly available for the purposes of the Act, even though most members of the public, including many who invest on a reasonably regular basis, never see or use such systems. More significant are the references to the information being "likely to be regarded by [the regular user of the market] as relevant" and to that relevance being "when deciding the terms on which transactions in investments .... should be effected". This is far wider than the test that the information must be capable of influencing the price. To a professional investor, as the "regular user" will, in practice, be, the price of an investment is but one of the terms on which the transaction will be effected. Others will include the number of securities to be purchased: certain information may not cause an investor to offer a substantially lower price, but it may give him cause for the extra caution that leads him to purchase a smaller quantity than he would otherwise have done. Similarly the time at which the transaction, and subsequent transactions linked to it, are to take place: this will be particularly important in relation to options, futures and FRAs.

The definition is supplemented by the Code of Market Conduct, which the FSA is required to issue under section 119 of the Act in order to provide guidance. This Code specifies kinds of behaviour which the FSA considers to constitute market abuse and also those which it does not. The latter is important: section 122 makes clear that if the Code states that a given type of behaviour does not amount to market abuse, that is definitive. No other test is then applied. In all other respects, the Code is simply to be relied on for general guidance. The sweeping effect of any safe harbours contained in the Code demonstrates graphically that those relying on it for guidance will not only be those judging a case in the future:[37] they will also include those who operate on the market and wish to establish whether a given form of conduct will be lawful or not.

The Code is not, however, set in stone: it is open to the FSA to amend or replace it as and when it sees fit. Should it do so, however, it is obliged to publish the new

---

37 That is, the FSA's Regulatory Decisions Committee or members of the Financial Services and Markets Tribunal. The Regulatory Decisions Committee (RDC) is a branch of the FSA, kept separate from the investigatory arm, which decides whether a penalty for market abuse should be imposed and, if so, what the amount should be. The Financial Services and Markets Tribunal is a tribunal to which appeals against any significant decision made by the FSA (not merely in relation to penalties) may be made as of right. It is set up under FSMA 2000 as part of the Courts Service, and hence the Department of Constitutional Affairs (previously the Lord Chancellor's Department) and is therefore totally independent of the FSA itself.

version. Furthermore, when assessing whether a given form of behaviour constituted market abuse, it will be the Code that was in force at the time of the behaviour in question that will be looked to for guidance.

Where the FSA considers that market abuse has taken place, it may impose one or more of a range of sanctions. That of imposing a financial penalty is the measure which has received the greatest publicity, but it has been rightly pointed out that this is but one of the sanctions available.[38] Since, however, it is this that has attracted most discussion, it is helpful to begin with the financial penalties.

Section 123 of FSMA 2000 states that if the FSA "is satisfied that a person is or has engaged in market abuse ... it may impose on him a penalty of such amount as it considers appropriate." Such a penalty may similarly be imposed on a person "who, by taking or refraining from taking any action has required or encouraged another person or persons to engage in behaviour" which, if that person had engaged in it himself, would have amounted to market abuse. This latter provision is sweeping: it is the closest that any UK provision relating to insider dealing (or similar conduct) comes to the French and Spanish obligation to safeguard inside information and prevent others from misusing it.

Essentially, therefore, the sanction for committing market abuse is a civil/regulatory fine. Indeed, in the earlier drafts of the Bill that ultimately became the Act, the term "civil fines" was used. It was felt, however, that the European Court of Human Rights, or even national courts,[39] might rule, on the basis of this, that, despite the explicit use of the word "civil", the measure was in fact criminal in nature.

A fine is, after all, an essentially criminal sanction: its purpose is to punish wrongdoing. Civil measures are designed to remedy a loss or harm suffered by someone and the damages awarded are, for the most part, calculated on the basis of the seriousness of the harm suffered, not the wickedness of the person or act that led to that harm. Even the higher sums awarded under the system of so-called "punitive" or "exemplary" damages are merely designed to prevent the defendant from making an overall profit from his wrong, not to punish him as such. In contrast, the fines/penalties imposed for market abuse are precisely designed to punish.

Nonetheless, non-criminal fines have been accepted and recognised in the UK for many years without attracting the attention of Strasbourg. The SROs, under the 1986 regime, regularly imposed fines on those who broke their rules and regulatory bodies, such as the General Council of the Bar and the Law Society, still do so, as do, albeit on a smaller scale, public libraries. All of these, however, have a common feature: their jurisdiction is limited to their members. The SROs were indeed regulators with considerable powers, but the persons and institutions they governed were members: they had joined the organisation and that organisation imposed sanctions, essentially,

---

[38] For example, in the introduction to ch. 13 of *Freshfields Bruckhaus Deringer on Financial Services: Investigations and Enforcement* (2001), Butterworths.

[39] Since October 2000, when the Human Rights Act 1998 came into force, the UK's national courts have had not only the power but the duty directly to enforce, as domestic law, the provisions of the European Convention on Human Rights.

as a club penalising breaches of its rules.[40] The same principle applies to the Law Society: all solicitors are members of it and hence it has the power to discipline them. Even their ultimate sanction, termination of authorisation, was (and still is in the case of professional bodies) technically merely expulsion from the club: it just so happened that membership was a requirement in order to exercise that particular profession/type of business.

In contrast, the FSA has the power, when dealing with cases of market abuse, to take action against any offender, regardless of who they are.[41] Unlike the rules of a club, which one makes a choice to accept when one becomes a member, no one has any choice whether or not they come under the market abuse provisions. Fines that may be imposed on any member of the general public are generally criminal.

It is perhaps noteworthy that Germany also has two specific terms for criminal and administrative fines:[42] *Geldstrafe* and *Geldbuße* respectively. One could take the view, however, that altering the terminology is mere window dressing and that a measure whose purpose is to punish and which is applicable to any member of society is by definition criminal in nature. Indeed, a number of speakers discussing these issues have warned that the adoption of the term "penalty" may not be sufficient to avoid the application of the European Convention on Human Rights and hence the Human Rights Act 1998. The issue is an important one for two reasons. Firstly, if the market abuse provisions are held to be criminal in nature, the criminal standard of proof will be demanded. This, of course, would defeat almost the entire object of the legislation! Worse, it could be argued that the "reasonable regular investor" test is too ill-defined to be an acceptable basis for criminal liability.

But secondly, crucially, if the market abuse sanctions are criminal in nature, this will severely restrict the FSA's investigative powers. As with the Department of Trade and Industry (DTI), the Serious Fraud Office and certain other organisations, the right to silence applicable in police interviews does not apply to FSA investigations. Failure to answer questions in a police interview may result in inferences being drawn by the prosecution and thereby the jury when the case comes to trial. Failure, without reasonable excuse, to answer the questions of the FSA, or those of an investigator appointed by it, is an offence in its own right and may result in up to 2 years' imprisonment or an unlimited fine, quite apart from any sanctions imposed for

---

40 Indeed, it was said in the financial services community that a direct consequence of this was that the SROs viewed with distinct disapproval any attempt to appeal against their sanctions: it was felt that persons and institutions were members of the club and should therefore accept the club's decisions.

41 This is separate from their extensive disciplinary powers and sanctions over those persons who are authorised to engage in a regulated activity. Those provisions are contained in the Rules and, to an extent, Guidance in the FSA's Handbook and, like the SRO Rules that went before them, do apply only to authorised persons.

42 Although Germany does not punish insider dealing itself with administrative fines, it does use them to deal with encouraging to deal and unauthorised disclosure, as well as to address minor offences such as failure to report promptly significant developments: see pp. 205 and 224-25.

the offence that was being investigated. When the DTI, which investigated insider dealing before the regime under FSMA 2000 was set up, used these powers to question those involved in the takeover of Distillers by Guinness in 1986 and then used the information they gave in the prosecution case against them, this was ruled illegal by the European Court of Human Rights.[43] The Court established that no one may be compelled to provide information that is then used in a criminal prosecution against them. The principle has not been applied to civil or administrative proceedings, but it may be seen that it will be if those proceedings are viewed as, in fact, criminal, whatever title happens to be given to them.

It is in fact clear that this was an important consideration when the legislation was being drafted. Although the market abuse provisions are explicitly not criminal in nature, the *Saunders* protection applies equally to them. Section 174(2) of FSMA 2000 states that where a statement is given under an order from either an FSA-appointed investigator[44] or the FSA itself, evidence relating to it may not be adduced by the prosecution or the FSA in either criminal proceedings or proceedings relating to a penalty for market abuse. Nor may any question be asked in relation to the statement. The only exceptions to this rule are where the defendant is being tried not for the offence originally investigated but for perjury or where he himself has already adduced evidence relating to the statement. Both of these are, however, standard exceptions under the general rules of criminal procedure; indeed, they are in keeping with the proviso that the use of the statement must comply with all rules concerning the admissibility of evidence in the circumstances in question.[45] The extension of the *Saunders* rule to market abuse proceedings, even though *Saunders* specifically related to criminal prosecutions, would seem to indicate a doubt even in the Government's mind as to whether such proceedings are in fact truly civil/administrative in nature.[46]

Where the FSA is satisfied that a person has engaged in market abuse, it may impose on him a financial penalty "of such amount as it sees fit". Although this appears fairly arbitrary, it is not, in fact. It was a criticism of the 1986 regime that the fines, and indeed other sanctions, imposed by the SROs were arbitrary: the "gentleman's club" mentality did not encourage scrutiny of the rationale of the type or level of sanction imposed. This is certainly borne out by the notices of the sanctions: even those issued by IMRO, the most informative of the SROs, did not explain clearly and explicitly the link between the circumstances of the case and the level of fine it imposed. FSMA 2000 sets out to ensure that this type of criticism cannot be levelled at the new system. In the Code of Market Conduct, referred to

---

43 *Saunders v United Kingdom* 23 EHRR 313, 17 December 1996.

44 This also applies to investigators appointed by the Secretary of State, who have precisely the same powers as those appointed by the FSA.

45 S.174(1).

46 The FSA may avoid this problem by choosing to conduct a non-compelled interview, i.e. one in which its powers to require answers to its questions are not invoked. In such interviews, the person questioned retains the right to silence and, therefore, any answers he does give are admissible as evidence against him in a criminal prosecution.

above, the FSA is also required to issue a statement of its policy as to the imposition of penalties, including the specific levels that will be imposed in different types of cases.[47] Three criteria are explicitly cited: the actual harm caused to the market by the behaviour in question, whether the behaviour was deliberate or reckless and finally, significantly, whether the person on whom the penalty is to be imposed is a legal entity or an individual. As with the Code, it is open to the FSA to amend or replace this policy, but, if it does, it must publish the new version.[48]

Section 123(2) states that the FSA must not impose a penalty on a person if it is satisfied either that he believed on reasonable grounds that his behaviour did not constitute market abuse or that he took all reasonable measures to avoid engaging in market abuse. It is a little strange that such a harbour is phrased in this way. It is to be noted that neither of these two criteria constitute an actual defence. In contrast to the position with types of behaviour approved by the Code, it is not stated that, in such cases, the person concerned is not to be regarded as having engaged in market abuse. Rather, it would appear, he has engaged in it. But nor is his state of mind mitigation in the true sense: it does not merely reduce the penalty that he would otherwise suffer, it removes the liability to a penalty completely. There are two major consequences. Firstly, it enables the FSA to deal with the offence in some other way (notably by a published statement), but secondly, it leaves the defendant vulnerable to the certain other measures that can be taken in cases of market abuse, notably disciplinary measures.[49]

Before looking at these, however, brief mention should be made of the interaction between these provisions and those of the criminal law. As seen above, there is considerable overlap between the market abuse offence of misuse of information and the criminal offence of insider dealing. Cases will therefore not infrequently arise which could be dealt with by either means. This is recognised in the Act, which, however, merely provides that the Treasury may issue guidance to the FSA as to how it should proceed in such cases. For some considerable time, this raised the question whether this meant that a suspected insider dealer would run the double risk of being both prosecuted and having imposed on him a penalty for market abuse. The fact that the FSA has the power to bring criminal prosecutions in cases of insider dealing[50] was one factor that led to this unease, although the example of other jurisdictions, both inside and outside the European Union, was another. In France, the defendants in the *Delalande/Synthélabo* case were the subject of both a criminal prosecution and civil proceedings brought by the COB. Similarly, a prosecutor in South Africa has stated, albeit informally and hence "off the record", that "in appropriate cases",

---

47 FSMA 2000, s.124.

48 The current policy is to be found in chapters ENF 14 and, to an extent, ENF 15 of the FSA Enforcement Manual.

49 See pp. 364–65.

50 FSMA 2000, s.402(1)(a). Note: this power applies in England and Wales and in Northern Ireland, but not in Scotland, where prosecutions must be brought by the Crown Office in the normal manner.

she would prosecute an insider dealer notwithstanding that he had already, in respect of the same offence, been fined civilly by the Financial Services Board.[51] The FSA addressed this concern by senior representatives stating on a number of occasions at conferences and other events at which the new measures were discussed that they would not in fact prosecute and bring proceedings for market abuse against the same offender in relation to the same offence. Nothing to this effect was, however, stated in writing and doubt therefore remained. The matter has, however, now been addressed in paragraph ENF 15.7.4 of the Enforcement Manual, part of the FSA's Regulatory Handbook. This states categorically that it is the FSA's policy not to impose a sanction for market abuse where a person is being prosecuted for an offence of market misconduct (such as insider dealing), or has been finally convicted or acquitted (following the exhaustion of any appeal processes) of such an offence, arising out of essentially the same allegations. Similarly, where a financial penalty for market abuse has been imposed on a person, it is the FSA's policy not to prosecute them on the basis of essentially the same allegations. That said, it is, as stated above, open to the FSA to change this policy at any time: it remains to be seen whether it will do so. The current version of the Handbook is dated January 2005.

The FSA has not, however, restricted itself in relation to other types of parallel proceedings. Although it is the most widely publicised, a financial penalty is not the only non-criminal weapon in the FSA's armoury. Two other measures, of considerable significance, are restitution orders and disciplinary measures. The latter, as under the 1986 regime, may only be brought against authorised persons, i.e. persons who have received a permission from the FSA to engage in a regulated activity (or firms from another EEA[52] Member State operating under a passport through the Investment Services Directive).[53] The former, however, like penalties for market abuse, may be imposed on any person, although their operation differs slightly in respect of authorised and non-authorised persons.

Where a person has engaged in market abuse (or, by either their action or inaction has encouraged another person to do so) and, as a result, either that person has made a profit or other persons have suffered some kind of loss or harm, the FSA may apply to the High Court[54] for a restitution order.[55] The Court then makes an award for such amount as it considers just, taking into account the profits made and/or loss or harm caused. As with financial penalties, such an order may not be made where the Court

---

51 In fact, however, insider dealing in South Africa is in practice very rarely dealt with by means of a criminal prosecution: the civil measures under the Insider Trading Act 1998 are considered far more effective. It should also be noted that in France, the *Delalande/Synthélabo* case was an exception: there, too, cases are generally dealt with by one means or the other, not both.

52 European Economic Area, i.e. the 27 EU Member States plus Iceland, Liechtenstein and Norway.

53 Council Directive 93/22/EEC.

54 In Scotland, the Court of Session.

55 FSMA 2000, s.383.

finds that the person either believed on reasonable grounds that their behaviour did not amount to market abuse or made a diligent effort to avoid engaging in it.

Although the amount awarded is payable to the FSA in the first instance, it may not keep the funds but must pay them out to such "qualifying persons" as the Court may direct. Section 383(10) of the Act defines who will constitute "qualifying persons". Where persons have suffered loss, the qualifying persons are those victims. This would seem to apply more, however, in cases of misleading or distorting the market than those of insider dealing: it remains controversial who, if anyone, is a victim of insider dealing.[56] It will therefore be the issue of distribution of profits that is more likely to be applicable. In such cases, the subsection states that the qualifying persons are those to whom the profits "are attributable".

The fact that removal of profits is described as "restitution" at all is striking: a senior officer of one City institution has commented that the provision is not restitution at all, but confiscation. Certainly, it bears strong similarities both to the civil recovery, and indeed criminal confiscation, provisions of the Proceeds of Crime Act 2002, although the proceeds of both of these are payable to the state (albeit a designated Fund). It is, however, perhaps even closer in nature to the system of civil fines that are imposed in South Africa under the Insider Trading Act 1998; these are similarly not retained by the Financial Services Board but distributed to the alleged victims.

But to whom are these profits attributable? The South African approach is to divide them between all persons who, within 3 days of the trade in question, traded in the relevant securities but in the opposite direction (i.e. bought when the insider sold or vice versa).[57] Given that FSMA 2000 specifically provides already for those who are held actually to have lost out, this would seem to be a not unreasonable model, although, given that the profits to be restored are not multiplied in the UK, each individual investor is unlikely to obtain much of a windfall!

Another approach might be to take the approach of a constructive trust, arguing that the insider held the information on trust. In the case of an employee, it would be on trust for the employer; in that of an agent or professional advisor (perhaps a lawyer), it would be on trust for the client. With an agent or contractor such as a lawyer, this would appear to be a simple application of the principle established in *Boardman v Phipps*[58] or *A-G for Hong Kong v Reid*.[59] Similarly, where the offender is a primary insider, it would seem uncontroversial. But with secondary insiders, it is less straightforward. Where a waitress deals on the basis of information overheard from her less than discreet clients, is it reasonable that the restaurant should benefit? (It is, after all, her employer and it was her job there that enabled her to make the

---

56 See Chapter 1.

57 A comparison may therefore be made with the Irish provisions, although, as noted above, in Ireland, it is not a state regulator but the individual investor who brings the proceedings.

58 [1966] 3 All ER 721.

59 [1994] 1 AC 324; [1994] 1 All ER 1.

profit.) Taking this principle even further could mean that, in theory at least, where the person overhearing the careless talk is the taxi driver, the profits are owed, again under a constructive trust, to the very persons whose carelessness led to the information being leaked! It is likely that in fact, in such circumstances, the Court would attribute the profits not to the individuals in the taxi but to their employer(s), but the point does show the limits of the doctrine.

In some cases, the source of the information will not be clear. With secondary insiders, the nature and timing of their dealing may raise a strong suspicion that they were privy to inside information, but where they came by it may be impossible to determine. It is one thing to penalise persons on less than overwhelming evidence – this is the very point of such measures – but the Court may be less than willing to attribute funds elsewhere on the same basis. Since the Act does not give guidance as to where profits are in fact attributable, it is possible that, in such cases, the Court could award the funds to the FSA as the representative of the market. But this is unlikely to be what Parliament intended. In any event, as with so much under FSMA 2000 and the new regime that it has introduced, it is likely that this issue will only be resolved once a number of cases have been brought and an authoritative ruling been made.

In the case of an authorised person, the FSA need not apply to the Court, but may make the order directly.[60] The same conditions apply, however, as with an order made by the Court.

Finally, there is the possibility of disciplinary action. This may only be taken in respect of an authorised person. It will, however, in some cases be the most draconian of the sanctions: not only may the FSA impose disciplinary fines (as opposed to financial penalties), it may also, under section 45(2) of the Act, vary or remove the person's permission to engage in a regulated activity. This may be done either in the interests of consumers or if one of the threshold conditions are not met. Most of the threshold conditions are not applicable to this book, but one, the requirement to be a fit and proper person, is of considerable importance. Schedule 6, paragraph 5 states that:

> The person concerned must satisfy the Authority that he is a fit and proper person having regard to all the circumstances including ...
>
> (c) the need to ensure that his affairs are conducted soundly and prudently.[61]

This condition is also applied, under paragraph 7, to EEA firms. The FSA states explicitly that, when deciding whether this condition is met, they will have regard to, inter alia, whether a firm "conducts, or will conduct, its business with integrity and in compliance with proper standards".[62] It is extremely unlikely that the FSA will be

---

60 S.384.

61 Incorporated also into the Threshold Conditions in the FSA Regulatory Handbook as COND 2.5.1.

62 COND 2.5.4(2).

of the opinion that this is true of a person who has engaged in market abuse. Since to engage in a regulated activity, which covers the entire financial services sector, without either permission, authorisation or an exemption (unlikely to apply here) is a criminal offence carrying up to 2 years' imprisonment,[63] it may be seen that this will involve the ending of a person's entire career.

Failure to Report Significant Developments

Article 7 of the Directive prescribes that, in addition to refraining from engaging in the substantive insider dealing offences, all undertakings whose securities are listed on a publicly-regulated market within the European Union have a duty to announce in a timely fashion any major development that is both price-sensitive and is not already publicly known.[64] The rationale for this is clear: once price-sensitive information has been published, insiders no longer have the opportunity to "steal a march" on the public and deal on the basis of the information under unfairly advantageous conditions.

In contrast to the dealing offences, all Member States have implemented this provision by means of regulatory, rather than criminal, measures. Two reasons may be identified. Firstly, it could be argued that this is an administrative measure and its breach is a negligent regulatory breach rather than a crime of deliberate wickedness. This does not entirely explain the approach, however. The UK imposes, in respect of a number of offences, criminal liability on those who are merely negligent: in the area of financial services, money laundering is an important example. France imposes criminal liability on certain types of primary insiders for failure to prevent others from using inside information illicitly. It is more likely that the rationale is based not so much on the state of mind of the offender as the degree of harm that the offence is likely to cause. Insider dealing causes a specific harm: a loss of general confidence in the market and a placing of investors who happen to be outside the privileged circle at a definite disadvantage. Provided that insider dealing is prohibited, it could be argued that the mere failure to disclose promptly significant developments affecting the undertaking concerned merely causes a slight impairment to the efficient running of the markets. Where the withholding of the information is not merely negligent but has a distinct purpose to deceive, this will constitute a range of separate offences ranging from fraudulent trading to market manipulation, which do carry severe criminal penalties.

But perhaps more significant is the second factor: the provision explicitly refers to undertakings, rather than to individuals. In the legal systems of a number of Member States, criminal liability may only be imposed on natural persons: corporate liability is reserved for the civil and regulatory arenas. Since, unlike the actual

---

63 FSMA 2000, s. 23(1).
64 For the definitions of "price-sensitive" and "publicly known", see Chapter 3.

dealing offences, this offence can only be committed by corporate entities,[65] it will follow that it will be dealt with in the way most commonly used for them.

Since it is a regulatory offence, failure to comply with the notification requirements generally carries an administrative fine.[66]

In Austria, section 82(6) of the *Börsegesetz* (Stock Exchange Law) requires issuers of securities listed on a stock exchange to inform both the public and the stock exchange of any circumstance capable of affecting, in either direction, the price of its securities. This notification must not only be timely; the section requires it to be immediate.

In Belgium, the Royal Decree of 18 September 1990 requires corporations to publish all facts and decisions of which they are aware and which could affect the price of their securities. There are, however, a number of exceptions to this rule. One which has been the subject of comment by practitioners is that rumours are not covered. This can be explained, however, by the rationale that it is only facts and decisions which are required to be published and that rumours are not facts.[67] On this analysis, rumours are therefore not in fact an exception to the rule. More important is the "holding exception": information held by a holding company on the companies in its group is viewed differently to normal types of information.[68] In addition, under the Decree, where a company's management is of the view that publication of the information would be harmful to the company's interests, it may apply to the Banking and Finance Commission for an exemption from the obligation to publish it. This seems at first to be a strange provision: there may be a range of circumstances in which publication of information would be highly detrimental to a company but this does not mean that it is not in the interests of the investing public or indeed of the public at large. The examples in the United States of Enron and WorldCom come to mind. The safeguard remains, however, the requirement that an exemption be sought from the Belgian regulator, the Banking and Finance Commission: the decision not to publish is not one which the company is permitted to make alone. The balance of the company's and the public interest and therefore the objective test as to whether the information should be published is thus weighed by the regulator. Although general publication of information is a regulatory requirement, it should be noted that failure to provide information to the Banking and Finance Commission when required, or indeed providing it with false

---

65 Although the term "undertaking" in European Community law covers any kind of business entity, including sole traders, the duty in practice is placed on corporate entities: sole traders are unlikely to issue securities which are traded on publicly regulated markets.

66 With certain exceptions: see below.

67 The requirement that inside information, in order to be covered by the Directive, and hence the implementing national legislation, be precise is discussed further in Chapter 3.

68 For a discussion of the "holding exception", a concept unique, among the Member States, to Belgium, see pp. 89-92.

or misleading information, is a criminal offence carrying between 1 and 12 months' imprisonment and also a fine of between €250 and €50,000.[69]

Denmark, in section 27(1) of the Securities Trade, etc, Consolidated Act,[70] requires that all issuers of securities publish information on "essential aspects concerning the company which may be assumed to be significant to the pricing of the securities". Publication must be immediate. Failure to publish as required may result in the withdrawal of authorisation to carry on business on the Danish securities markets.[71]

In Finland, Chapter 2, section 7 of the Securities Market Act requires all issuers of securities to inform promptly the regulator responsible for the trade in question of all their decisions. They must also report any other information relating either to the issuer itself or to its activities that is capable of having a material influence on the price of the security in question. As in Belgium, however, there is provision for an issuer to apply to the Financial Supervision for an exemption from this requirement where publication would either not be in the public interest or would be seriously detrimental to the issuer.[72] The exemption must, however, be sought as soon as the duty arises. Where no exemption is granted, it is then for the regulator in question, on receiving the information, to publish it "without undue delay".

Unusually among the Member States, France does not explicitly require the publication of price-sensitive information. Failure to publish such information in a timely manner is only an offence where it leads directly to an insider dealing offence. The situation can therefore be envisaged where a company officer does not disclose the price-sensitive information promptly, but rather deals on the basis of it; alternatively, where another person deals on the basis of it and it is alleged that the officer who should have made the disclosure has thus failed in his duty to prevent misuse of the information. In both of these scenarios, however, the officer who failed to make the announcement will be guilty of a substantive insider dealing offence. In not imposing a specific duty to publish price-sensitive information, it could be argued that France is in fact in breach of the Directive, although no action appears ever to have been taken.

The German provision is found in paragraph 15 of the Securities Trade Act. Every issuer of securities on a German exchange must publish any fact, not yet in the public domain, which becomes available to it in the course of its business and which, because of its relevance to the issuer's net worth or merely to the general course of its business, is capable of significantly influencing the price of its securities. It should be noted that it is not merely facts relating to the issuer directly which it must publish, but any fact of which it receives knowledge, provided that the fact meets the other criteria. In addition, where the security in question is a bond, facts must

---

69 Article 190, Law of 20 December 1995. Given the consequences of a prison sentence of 3 months or more in Belgium (see p. 124), even moderate cases will therefore result in the persons responsible being permanently disqualified from the financial sector.
70 Consolidated Act No. 168 of 14 March 2001.
71 Ss. 93(1), 92(1).
72 S. 11.

be published which are capable of influencing not just the price of that bond but the likelihood of the issuer being able to comply with its obligations under it. That said, the two issues are inextricably linked: should it be suspected that the issuer of a bond is unlikely to be able to meet its obligations, the bond will rapidly fall sharply in value, quite possibly becoming worthless. As an additional provision, before the fact is announced to the general public, it must be notified both to the Board of the organised market in question[73] and to BaFin.[74] The specific means of disclosure are important. Publication of the information in some other form before the announcement has been made in the required format is itself an offence, as is failure to notify the Board of the stock exchange or BaFin before making the general announcement.[75] Any of these offences is punishable with an administrative fine of up to €1 million.[76] It may be noted that this is five times as high as the maximum fine for secondary insiders who either disclose inside information or encourage or arrange the purchase or sale of insider securities.

As with much of the other anti-insider dealing legislation, the Greek implementation of Article 7 of the Directive is virtually identical to the text of the Article itself. It is, however, supplemented by Decision No. 86 of the Capital Markets Commission of 15 October 1996. This prescribed that failure to notify the Commission of the purchase of securities constituting more than 1.5% of the share capital of company listed on the Athens Stock Exchange is an offence carrying a fine of between €4,402.05 and €46,955.25.[77]

Although it gained independence from the UK in 1922, it was only in 1996 that Ireland set up its own stock exchange; up to then, Irish companies continued to be listed, and their securities traded, on the London Stock Exchange. Even after 1996, the Listing Rules of the London Stock Exchange continued in force in Ireland, although in the UK itself, the "Yellow Book" has since been replaced with new rules following the transfer of the UK Listing Authority to the Financial Services Authority in 2001. Paragraph 9.1 of the Yellow Book, as adopted by the Irish Stock Exchange, prescribes that issuers must notify the Company Announcements Office without delay of any major new developments in its sphere of activity, not in the

---

73 Not only does Germany, like several Member States, have a number of different exchanges trading different types of securities and commodities, it has a number of separate stock exchanges: several of the *Länder* have their own, although of course that in Frankfurt is by far the largest and most significant.

74 Federal Financial Services Supervision Authority.

75 Para. 39(2)5.(a), (b).

76 Para. 39(4), Securities Trade Act. In the previous version of the Act, i.e. that before the amendment of 15 December 2004, the different offences carried different levels of fine. Now, however, they all carry the same maximum fine, although, as this is the maximum, not mandatory, level, it may well be that a different level will still in practice be imposed for, say, publication of the information in the wrong format than for failing to publish it at all. Only after a number of actual cases will it be possible, however, to discern a policy for certain.

77 Previously Drs. 1.5 million and Drs. 16 million respectively.

public domain, which may, by virtue of their effects on the assets, liabilities, financial position or general activity of the issuer:

- lead to substantial movement in the price of its securities; or
- in the case of debt securities, either lead to substantial movement in their price of affect the ability of the issuer to honour its obligations.

Similarly, where the issuer's directors become aware that there is a substantial change in its financial position or in its operations and that this may lead to a significant movement in the price of the securities, they are to notify the Company Announcements Office of this without delay.[78] The same information is also to be notified to any other exchange on which the issuer's securities are listed. As with the rules of many securities exchanges, the sanction is the withdrawal from the exchange of the listing of the securities in question.

The Italian provisions are found in Article 66 of CONSOB Regulation 11971 of 14 May 1999.[79] This, by reference to Article 114.1 of the Consolidated Law on Financial Intermediation,[80] requires that issuers of financial instruments and their controlling managers inform the public, by means of a press release, of events occurring either in the issuers themselves or in their subsidiaries, which have not been made public but which, if they were, would be likely to have a significant effect on the price of the listed financial instruments. The press release is to be in a form that allows readers quickly and easily to assess not only the information but also the impact that the development is likely to have on the price of the issuer's securities. It must be made to the market management company, which in turn is immediately to make it available to the public, and also to two news agencies. Where the announcement is made during trading hours, there is an additional requirement that the press release be sent to both the CONSOB and to the market management company at least 15 minutes before it is issued.

The Luxembourg provisions, contained in Chapter 6, Article 9 of the Ministerial Regulation of 25 October 1996 on the approval of the Rules and Regulations of the Luxembourg Stock Exchange are as the Directive: they require issuers of units and securities to disclose any information that has not been made public but which is capable of influencing the price of their securities. They do not contain any specific variations in the way that the legislation of certain of the Member States considered above do.

In the Netherlands, section 46b of the Securities Trade Act, as amended, obliges both issuers of securities corporately and their managing and supervisory directors personally to notify the Securities Supervision Board of all information concerning

---

78 Paragraph 9.2.

79 As amended by CONSOB Resolutions 13605 of 5 June 2002 and 13616 of 12 June 2002.

80 Legislative Decree No. 58 of 24 February 1998, as amended by Legislative Decree No. 61 of 11 April 2002.

transactions in their securities. This is supplemented by the Listing Regulation of the Amsterdam Stock Exchange, which, like its counterparts in other Member States, requires issuers of securities to publish information that is as yet non-public but which may have a material influence on the price of their securities.

In Spain, similarly, issuers are required to publish non-public information capable of affecting the price of their securities. Unlike some Member States, however, there is detailed guidance as to what types of information need to be disclosed. In 1990, the Governing Body of the Madrid Stock Exchange in a Guidance Note listed the following as being subject to disclosure:

- nominal increases or decreases in the value of the security (whether or not these lead to an actual change in capital);
- mergers and acquisitions involving at least one listed company;
- take-over bids;
- acquisition or transfer of significant shareholdings or of shareholdings of credit institutions;
- any substantial change in the nature or class of listed securities;
- the calling of a General Shareholders' Meeting; and
- any litigation or other judicial proceedings, completed or ongoing, which may have a significant effect on the issuer's financial position.

This is now complied with by notifying the regulator, the National Securities Market Commission.[81] The Commission then passes the information on to the public by means of a daily bulletin. It should be noted that this duty applies whether the securities are listed or not. Where, however, they are listed, the issuer, as in certain other Member States, may apply to the Commission for the information not to be published on the grounds that this would damage their interests. Such an application must, however, be made immediately. Where, however, the securities are unlisted, the option of applying for non-publication is not provided.

As regards sanctions for non-compliance, in addition to an administrative fine, there is the possibility of suspension from trading on the securities markets.

In Sweden, the Rules of the Financial Inspection[82] impose a general requirement on issuers to report to the exchange or, where appropriate, other marketplace, any decision or other event that is capable of affecting the price of their securities. Where the issuer has subsidiaries, this applies to decisions or events affecting the securities price of any company in the group. The actual obligation is placed on the board members, Managing Director and Deputy Managing Director of either the subsidiary or the parent company as the case may be. As in some other Member States, an exemption may be granted by the exchange concerned should disclosure of the information be damaging to the company's interests.

---

81 Comisión Nacional del Mercado de Valores (CNMV). Article 82, Securities Market Law.

82 Ch. 2, paras. 15 and 21.

In the UK, the Listing Authority was transferred in 2001 from the London Stock Exchange to the Financial Services Authority. Although new listing rules have been produced administratively by the FSA, much of what was formerly contained in the Yellow Book is also found in Part VI of the Financial Services and Markets Act 2000. Section 80(1) of the Act imposes a general duty of disclosure in the listing particulars, notably:

> all information that investors and their professional advisors would reasonably require ... for the purpose of making an informed assessment of
>
> a) the assets and liabilities, financial position, profits and losses and prospects of the issuer of securities and
>
> b) the rights affecting the securities.

Section 81 then provides that where there is any significant change in the above information, or in the information required either under the listing rules or by the competent authority,[83] details must be submitted to the FSA and, if it approves them, then be published. The same applies regarding any significant new matter that arises which would otherwise have been required to be included in the listing particulars. "Significant" is defined as assisting investors and their advisors in forming the assessment described in section 80(1). It will be seen that this is far more wide-ranging than merely matters capable of affecting the price of the issuer's securities, although it will be seen that any such matters will come within the scope of what is required.

No specific penalties are prescribed for non-compliance with these requirements; section 100 of the Act merely states that, when deciding what penalties to impose, the FSA is to have regard to the expenses that it has incurred, or expects to incur, in fulfilling its duties as the listing authority.[84] Furthermore, any penalties recovered are to be used for the benefit of issuers of securities admitted to the official list.[85]

---

83 That is, the FSA: s. 72.
84 S. 100(1).
85 S. 100(2).

Chapter 8

Conclusion: A Model for Enforcement

As has been seen throughout this book, while considerable steps have been taken in recent months to combat both insider dealing and money laundering, these measures have drawbacks. In certain cases, they do not offer a full solution, while in others, they actually create further problems. It is recognised that any measure that effectively controls insider dealing or money laundering, or indeed any type of economic crime, will inevitably come at a cost, not only for law enforcement but for the financial services sector and their clients as well. What is less acceptable is that part of that cost should be unnecessary. In this final chapter, therefore, it is attempted to propose a model for controlling both insider dealing and money laundering in a way that will maximise effectiveness while removing unnecessary burdens on the legitimate players in the financial markets. Indeed, part of the removal of unnecessary burdens will be the incorporation of safeguards to protect the innocent and ensure compliance with the European Convention on Human Rights, to which all 27 Member States of the European Union are signatories.

That said, by no means all in the current system is wrong. Much that has been introduced is both effective and fair. In some cases, particular Member States have good provisions that are not found across the European Union but which other Member States would do well to emulate. It is therefore hoped that what will emerge will be a mixture of the best of the good and an amendment of the not so good.

It has also been seen that the problems of insider dealing and money laundering are closely linked, never more so than in the UK following the introduction of the Proceeds of Crime Act 2002. They do, however, retain different features (particularly in Spain, where the involvement of the criminal law in the fight against insider dealing is particularly small). It is therefore proposed, as in the rest of this book, to deal with them separately.

Insider Dealing

Definition of Offence

The arguments as to whether insider dealing should be prohibited are thankfully now largely consigned to history: there is a general consensus that it is wrong and therefore should not be permitted. There do remain some who claim that insider dealing is a victimless crime, but few, if any, continue to promote the argument of

Manne and others that it is positively beneficial. The question is, therefore: given that we agree that insider dealing is wrong and should be prohibited, how should we deal with it?

Firstly, the distinction between primary and secondary insiders should be abolished. In fact, some Member States do not in their legislation make such a distinction, but a number do, as does the Directive itself. This is unhelpful for a number of reasons. Firstly, it complicates the offence unnecessarily. In addition to the other elements that need to be proven, the prosecutor or regulator must show not only that the person was in possession of inside information relating to the securities in question but that they obtained it in a particular manner. If they fail to do this, it will mean that certain types of offence, notably the unauthorised disclosure of inside information, cannot be established. Even where the offence is that of actual dealing, prohibited in all Member States to primary and secondary insiders alike, the failure to prove that the defendant obtained the information through their employment, office or position can still have an impact. In Austria, for example, it will halve the maximum sentence that can be imposed, while in Spain, it will mean that only regulatory proceedings may be brought: a criminal prosecution will not be possible.

Secondly, few primary insiders deal themselves: they know that to do so invites detection and prosecution. Some have, whether through carelessness, stupidity or downright arrogance, but they are the minority. Even in the *Pechiney*[1] case in France, the act of the primary insiders (directors of the company concerned) was to instruct others to execute the actual transaction.[2] Drawing a distinction between the primary insider and their secondary insider accomplice therefore fails to recognise the reality of how insider dealing is, for the most part, committed.

Thirdly, to remove the distinction between a primary and secondary insider circumvents the discussion as to what is meant by obtaining inside information "in the course of their employment, profession or duties". Does it mean that the defendant's work must be such as will, because of its intrinsic nature, inevitably cause him to come into possession of inside information or will anyone who comes into possession of inside information through their work (for example, a cleaner, waitress or taxi driver) be covered?[3] If there is no distinction, it will not matter. The question will simply be: did the defendant possess relevant inside information?

Fourthly and finally, there is no real basis for arguing that a secondary insider or tippee is any less culpable than a primary insider. True, they do not abuse a position of trust in the same way that a primary insider does, but, as just seen, they often assist another to do so. Without the primary insider passing on the information,

---

1 Cour de Cassation, Criminal Division, 26 October 1995.
2 Furthermore, this case comes into the category of carelessness: the defendant failed to realise firstly that a call from a public telephone could be monitored and secondly that, even if that call was the only act that took place on French territory, an offence under the French insider dealing legislation would be committed.
3 For a detailed examination of this issue, see Chapter 2.

the secondary insider could not have dealt; equally however, but for the secondary insider's undertaking the actual transaction, the dealing could not have taken place without being very swiftly detected.

A far simpler approach is that taken in, for example, Denmark and the Spanish civil measures: a person who is in possession of inside information is prohibited from dealing in the securities to which it relates, encouraging another person to do so or disclosing that information to any third party other than in the legitimate and authorised course of their employment or profession.

The question of the defendant's state of knowledge must of course be examined: was he aware that the information that came into his possession was inside information? All Member States require actual knowledge to be proven, at least in their criminal provisions. This does make the offence extremely difficult to prove in all but a few cases. True, where a professional is careless enough (or perhaps stupid enough!) to deal themselves in securities in relation to which they demonstrably had inside information, they can easily be brought to book. But few do this: most arrange for others to deal on their behalf. Strict liability, however, goes too far the other way. It is therefore suggested that the appropriate *mens rea* should be suspicion, possibly supplemented with "or had reasonable grounds to suspect". The market abuse provisions in the UK under the Financial Services and Markets Act 2000 come close to this, but place the burden of proof on the defendant: a person will not be held to have in engaged in market abuse if they show that they believed, on reasonable grounds, that what they did did not amount to market abuse. This makes the task of bringing a case considerably easier for the prosecutor/regulator. It is well recognised that suspicion is almost as difficult to prove as knowledge: how can a court or regulator accurately see into a person's mind? Reasonable grounds for suspicion, however, is an objective test and hence one easier to meet.

Criminal or Civil Enforcement?

Having defined the offence, the question then arises whether it should be dealt with by means of criminal or civil/administrative measures? In general, the approach of the UK and certain other Member States, such as France, is a good one. As has been seen, the criminal provisions are inadequate on their own and there is much to be said for the arguments of Professor Rider and others that the criminal law will always be ill-suited to deal with insider dealing. But it is right, as Rider himself has acknowledged in a number of conference presentations, to keep the criminal sanctions as an option. It is submitted that the Spanish approach goes too far. Very probably, the criminal provisions will over time rarely be used (as indeed they are in practice rarely used at present). But the fact that they can be used, that those who engage in insider dealing know that there is a risk of being prosecuted, does provide a deterrent that mere civil sanctions do not.

There are two reasons for this. Firstly, there is the threat of imprisonment. It is true that the over-use of open prisons for financial criminals softens this: the confinement of Saunders and his colleagues in Ford open prison caused particular public outcry and it is similarly arguable that the system in Sweden that allows many prisoners to go home for the weekend does much to reduce the pain of going to jail. But nonetheless, the threat of imprisonment is, for many persons, a deterrent in a way that a fine would not be. This is perhaps particularly true of economic criminals, who are, for the most part, middle-class professionals from law-abiding backgrounds. Certain types of offences are often committed by persons who have seen family members and friends also prosecuted for similar offences and hence may regard imprisonment as simply one of life's risks. This is, however, rarely true of economic criminals. For them, the threat of imprisonment is a decided deterrent.

The second reason is that a criminal conviction carries a stigma that a regulatory ruling or even a civil judgment does not. Whether a person does or does not have a criminal record is commonly used to judge their character. As a barrister, I am required as a rule of professional conduct to inform both the Bar Council and my Inn of Court if I am convicted of a criminal offence. I am not obliged to inform them if I am fined by the Financial Services Authority.[4] The common term "convicted criminal" implies that, once a person has been convicted of an offence, he remains a criminal all his life, irrespective of whether or not he re-offends. Immigration services and prospective employers take a far closer interest in whether a person has any criminal convictions than if they have suffered regulatory or disciplinary sanctions[5] – the list goes on. The effect of this stigma, and the threat of it, is therefore considerable.

Even where it is decided that a given offence will be dealt with through civil, rather than criminal, means, the fact that the behaviour in question constitutes a criminal offence tends to increase the seriousness with which it is viewed; conversely, the fact that it only carries regulatory or civil liability tends to reduce it. In the few cases where this is not the case, where the public strongly disapprove of a given type of behaviour but it is dealt with relatively leniently (in their eyes), this leads to public unease: in the UK, one is well accustomed to public complaints at apparently short prison sentences,[6] community service orders and the like.

Before moving on to the civil approach and the issues that arise in connection with it, a few remarks should be made on the approach taken in relation to the prison sentences. In some Member States, the maximum sentences for insider dealing are quite severe, for example 7 years in the UK and 10 years in Ireland. This would seem

---

    4   They may well find out by other means and, if they do, take action, but it is still viewed less seriously.

    5   Employers within the financial services sector will also be interested in regulatory sanctions, since it will have a bearing on a person's authorisation to engage in financial services business. Outside that sector, however, it is commonplace for a job application form to enquire about criminal convictions, but rare indeed for it to mention regulatory offences.

    6   For example, the sentence of 18 months passed on Jonathan Aitken in June 1999 for perjury, a sentence which the trial judge, incidentally, said was relatively severe in view of Aitken's involvement of his daughter Victoria. It is arguable that the outcry that followed this sentence was one reason for the rather more severe sentence, of 4 years, passed on Lord Archer for a similar offence just over 2 years later.

reasonable, although to date, neither jurisdiction has actually imposed sentences approaching these. In others, however, they are far lower: 2 years in Austria for primary insiders (only 12 months for secondary insiders), and 12 months for all insiders in Belgium.[7] Although it is true that prison sentences generally are shorter in some Member States than in others,[8] it does potentially raise the suspicion that, in at least some Member States providing for short prison sentences for insider dealing, the offence is perhaps not viewed as seriously, by the legislators at any rate. Also necessary to take into consideration is the fact that a number of Member States have a system of almost automatic remission, provided that the prisoner behaves relatively well. In both Germany and the UK, a prisoner is generally released after serving two-thirds of his sentence,[9] a marked contrast to the US approach of requiring prisoners to serve 85% or even longer. In order to reflect the seriousness of insider dealing, it is therefore suggested that the maximum sentence for insider dealing, across the European Union, should be at least 5 years.[10] This should apply to both primary and secondary insiders: as seen above, it is submitted that the distinction between primary and secondary insiders be abolished.

Although it is therefore important to retain the threat of a criminal prosecution, the civil approach is an important supplement to it. It is recognised that it is extremely difficult to prove all the elements of insider dealing beyond reasonable doubt (although as the figures show, it can occasionally be done). Yet there are decided reservations on human rights grounds to accepting a lower standard of proof for an offence for which the suspect can be sent to prison. The trend, seen now in several of the Member States and which will increase further with the implementation of the Market Abuse Directive, to adopt civil offences of insider dealing is therefore to be welcomed.

Having established that it is appropriate to have in place both criminal and civil measures in this area, the question then arises as to how a given defendant should be dealt with. In France, as in South Africa, the law allows a "both and" approach: pursuing a defendant through one part of the justice system is not a bar to pursuing him, in respect of the same offence, through the other. In contrast, in the UK, at least at present, the Financial Services Authority is compelled to choose one path

---

7   For details of the sentences available in the various Member States, see Chapter 4.

8   The UK is famous for imprisoning a higher percentage of its population even than Luxembourg.

9   In the UK, this applies where the sentence is of 4 years or more and parole may be granted even before the two-thirds mark is reached. Where the sentence is less than 4 years, the release is after one-half of the sentence has been served.

10 This would also achieve a lesser disparity between penalties in different Member States, something explicitly called for in para. 39 of the Preamble to the Market Abuse Directive. Although this paragraph, like the Directive as a whole, specifically refers to administrative measures and sanctions, it is submitted that the principle could also usefully be applied to the criminal sphere.

or the other.[11] The "both and" approach has serious problems of double jeopardy. Although it is well established in some jurisdictions that a person can be prosecuted, sued and, in some cases, disciplined in relation to the same offence,[12] these three measures are designed to do different things: criminal penalties punish on behalf of the state, i.e. society in general, civil penalties recompense a victim's loss and generally have nothing whatsoever to do with punishment,[13] while disciplinary measures punish on behalf of a specific group of which the offender is a member, not society as a whole. In contrast, administrative sanctions have much the same purpose as criminal penalties, to punish on behalf of society: although the means are different, the purpose is the same.

This is underlined by the practice followed in those jurisdictions that do follow the "both and" option. In France, although in the case of *Delalande/Synthélabo*, the defendant was both pursued administratively and subsequently prosecuted, this has proved the exception, not the rule. Furthermore, in that case, although the criminal trial resulted in a conviction, no sentence was passed other than an order to pay costs: the administrative fine of FF 10 million already imposed was judged adequate. Similarly in South Africa, although prosecutors have informally stated that they would be quite prepared to prosecute an insider dealer who had already been fined by the Financial Services Board, this has to date never actually happened.

An "either or" approach is therefore more appropriate. It should, however, be stated with greater certainty than in the current UK provisions. Since the ruling out of parallel proceedings is only found in the FSA Enforcement Manual, it can easily be changed. In the model proposed here, it would be established in the legislation itself. Guidance could be drawn from the confiscation/civil recovery approach under the Proceeds of Crime Act 2002, under which the civil recovery procedure may only be effected if there is no realistic prospect of a criminal conviction. For the present purposes, cases of misuse of information, i.e. market abuse, that fall outside the criminal definition of insider dealing would obviously satisfy this.[14] Alternatively,

---

11 Although the Financial Services and Markets Act 2000 does not preclude a "both and" approach, para. 15.7.4 of the Financial Services Authority's Enforcement Manual states that it is the FSA's policy not to both prosecute and impose a penalty for market abuse in respect of the same allegations.

12 In France, it is much rarer for a criminal defendant also to be sued by his victim, since French criminal courts are permitted to award civil damages that are far more extensive than the English compensation orders. For this reason, the victim (unlike in England and Wales) will regularly have separate legal representation at the criminal trial.

13 This is particularly true in England and Wales, where the courts generally award "punitive" or "exemplary" damages only to prevent the defendant making a net profit, for example a newspaper publishing a defamatory article. The approach in the United States contrasts with this: courts in a far wider range of cases will, when assessing damages, consider a defendant's culpability.

14 Since, in such cases, no criminal offence will have been committed, civil recovery under the Proceeds of Crime Act 2002 will not be possible since, as with confiscation under the Act, the property in question must derive from a criminal offence: s.241.

a provision could simply state, "A person shall not be prosecuted for an offence under Part ... of this Act where proceedings for misuse of information have been brought against that person arising from the same allegations. No proceedings shall be brought against a person for misuse of information where that person has been prosecuted for an offence under Part ... of this Act in respect of the same allegations."

Civil/Administrative Sanctions

As at present, civil/administrative proceedings should result in a financial penalty. The issues under the European Convention on Human Rights that arise from the use of the term "fine" in such cases are recognised and the term "financial penalty" should therefore remain. In Germany, the problem is avoided by the use of two words for "fine", one criminal, one administrative: where the languages of other Member States have similarly distinct terms, they should be used.

Restitution orders should not, however, be available. Such orders are entirely right and proper in cases where there are identifiable victims, for example in cases of market manipulation. This will include "negative insider dealing", i.e. publishing lies, then trading on the benefit. They are not, however, appropriate for insider dealing itself, which is in any case treated as a separate offence. As discussed in Chapter 1, while insider dealing is clearly wrong, those who claim it has no clear victims have a point. The market does indeed lose, but not in identifiable financial terms. The Irish and indeed South African approach that the "losers" are all those who dealt in the securities in question, but in the opposite direction, over the relevant period is unsatisfactory. Misuse of information should therefore be a separate category of market abuse with restitution orders excluded.

Insider dealers should, however, be forced to disgorge their profits. In criminal cases, this is simple: an increasing number of Member States have provision to confiscate profits as an ancillary measure to a criminal sentence. In civil cases, there are a number of possible ways of achieving this other than the current UK system of restitution orders. One is to provide for a direct link, explicitly stated in the legislation, between the profits obtained and the financial penalty imposed. It should not be a vague principle as in "the Authority shall take into account"; rather, as is already the case in France, Greece and Spain, the maximum penalty should be quoted as a specific multiple of the profits made. The South African model, providing for an exact correlation, is perhaps too rigid: there should be room for discretion to reflect the particular circumstances of the case. Furthermore, the funds from the penalties should go to the state in some form, not the market players.

Another solution is simple confiscation, either criminal or civil, in addition to the fine or other sanction. In the UK at present, this is provided: civil recovery will allow confiscation of profits even without a criminal conviction. The problem with this, however, is that there must be evidence that the assets do derive from criminal conduct: even the term "unlawful conduct" in Part 5 of the Proceeds of Crime Act 2002, dealing with civil recovery, is defined in terms of a criminal offence rather than having the usual civil meaning. Although a specific criminal offence need not be proven, it remains the case that civil recovery, as it currently stands, will not be available where the conduct is identifiable and does not constitute a criminal offence, as in some cases of misuse of information. For such a system to work in relation to insider dealing, therefore, it would need to be available in relation to the proceeds not only of a criminal offence, as at present, but of any act that is prohibited under the criminal, civil or administrative law.

A third option would be a civil action brought by the regulator on behalf of the market, the system used in the United States. This certainly works well; indeed, the United States is probably more successful at bringing insider dealers to book than any other jurisdiction. It does, however, have the conceptual problem that if insider dealing is conceived to be a tort, in respect of which an action can be brought, then under the principles certainly of English law, some loss or damage must not only be shown but quantified.[15] As seen, it is very difficult to determine what, in financial terms, such a loss is. Some have assessed it as the difference between the price at which the other, innocent, investors dealt and that at which they would have dealt had they, too, been party to the inside information: Ireland currently takes this approach. Certainly they would have got a better deal had the information already been published. But is it true to say that their loss is attributable to the insiders? Had every insider complied with the prohibition and refrained from dealing until the information was published, would those outside the circle not still have dealt? If their transactions were executed without any influence from the insiders' activities, those activities are not the cause of their loss. This being the case, to bring an action on their behalf would seem ill-conceived. Furthermore, if the real objective is to deprive the insider dealers of their profits, rather than to compensate the other investors, the damages obtained should go to the state, not to anyone else.

This being the case, providing for the maximum fine to be a multiple of the profits obtained (or loss avoided) would seem to be the preferable option. As to what that multiple should be, this is more difficult, since it will need to achieve two objectives in one: to extract the insiders' profits and also to punish them. One could argue that those in particular positions of trust (directors, professional advisors, etc.) should be dealt with more harshly than certain other insiders (such as junior employees) and hence a high multiple, such as ten, is appropriate. On the other hand, such senior figures are likely to have dealt on a larger scale and hence five or even three times will still amount to a heavy fine. Although there is something to be said for having a multiple of ten, given that, as a maximum fine, it will only be imposed in the worst cases, it is also arguable that the maximum fine should not be so high that it will only exceptionally be imposed, hence five might be appropriate. A possible model might therefore be taken from the Spanish and Swedish concept of "serious" and "very serious" offences: in most cases, the multiple could be five, but in aggravated

---

15 English civil procedure allows for punitive damages rather more restrictively than that in the United States.

cases, notably where the defendant was in a position of particular trust, it could rise to ten.

Money Laundering

In many ways, the UK's Proceeds of Crime Act 2002, discussed in detail in Chapter 5,[16] is a good workable model for anti-money-laundering legislation. Few, if any, pieces of legislation are, however, perfect and there are a number of issues that still need to be addressed.

Terrorism and Other Crimes

As already noted, while the laundering of drug trafficking offences and other types of crime are brought together under the Act, "terrorist money laundering", i.e. the handling, etc. of property linked to terrorism, remains outside its scope, dealt with separately under the Terrorism Act 2000 (as amended by the Anti-Terrorism, Crime and Security Act 2001). The argument for having separate offences of money laundering and terrorist money laundering, owing to the different natures of the two, has been discussed.[17] But it does create problems.

The approach is certainly useful to deal with actual money launderers, who can be shown to have known precisely what they were doing. It is no problem to charge them under the appropriate law: the Proceeds of Crime Act 2002 or the Terrorism Act 2000. With financial intermediaries, however, it is more problematic. Again, where they know precisely what they are doing, the matter is simple: in such cases, they will be launderers in the same category as their clients. The problem comes with the large majority of defendants, who merely suspect. With them, the problem of the dichotomy of two separate pieces of legislation remains. It was previously seen under the dichotomy, which existed before the coming into force of the Proceeds of Crime Act 2002, between drugs and so-called "all crimes" laundering. There may be evidence that the financial intermediary suspected that there was something wrong with either his client or the transactions that he was asked to execute, but how is the prosecutor to prove the nature of his suspicion? Did he suspect that the funds were linked to terrorism or to some other form of crime?

One may consider the following scenario. A financial intermediary regularly executes transactions between his client's account and that of a company in Pakistan and it is hard to see that these transactions have a clear commercial purpose. Certainly, there is evidence that the intermediary was suspicious. But did he suspect that these monies were funding Islamic terrorism or that they were simply linked to trafficking in heroin and cannabis? It will be a crucial issue: on this will depend what charge is to be brought. When interviewed, he denies being suspicious of anything (as he is likely to do). If he is charged with terrorist money laundering

---

16 See pp. 157-73.
17 See pp. 173-75.

under the Terrorism Act 2000, his counsel may well argue that there is no clear evidence that he suspected that the funds were linked to terrorism; for all we know, he may have suspected that his client was a drug trafficker. But if he is charged under the Proceeds of Crime Act 2002, the court will be told that, for all we know, he may have suspected that they were linked to terrorism. In this particular case, evidence may be given by an officer of the Serious Organised Crime Agency, or possibly Special Branch, to the effect that drug trafficking in the Golden Crescent is controlled by Al-Qaeda and, therefore, if the intermediary suspected that the funds were linked to drug trafficking, this amounted to a suspicion that they were linked to terrorism. Hence a charge under the Terrorism Act 2000 may be proven in any event. But the defence counsel will say that there is no evidence that the intermediary knew that: he is a banker, not an intelligence officer. Nor will placing alternative counts on the indictment avail: in order to convict of either of them, the jury will need to be satisfied of their choice beyond reasonable doubt.

Until early 2003, this difficulty frequently confronted prosecutors forced to choose between the Drug Trafficking Act 1994 and the Criminal Justice Act 1988: did the banker suspect his client of, for example, trafficking in drugs or human beings? That dilemma disappeared with the creation of an all-encompassing series of offences in the Proceeds of Crime Act 2002 and it is submitted that the same could be done with relation to terrorist money laundering. It is proposed, therefore, that a single offence be introduced of receiving, etc, property "where the person knows or suspects it to be criminal property or terrorist property". This would, at a stroke, remove the requirement for the prosecution to prove whether the intermediary suspected that the assets were linked to terrorism or to another form of crime. Provided that it could at least be shown that he suspected that they were linked to one or the other, he would be convicted.

Very little else would need to be amended to fit in with this. "Criminal property" and "terrorist property" have already been clearly defined, hence the use of these terms would suffice.[18] Further, the laundering offences under the Proceeds of Crime and Terrorism Acts carry the same maximum sentence, hence there would be no sentencing complications for the legislator. There could admittedly be for the judge, who might wish to sentence a person who had been assisting terrorists rather more harshly than one who had been laundering the property of an "ordinary decent criminal".[19] But Parliament, in providing for identical sentences, would not appear to have necessarily concurred. Violent gang crime that has a close connection to drug trafficking but none at all to any political or ideological organisation may be seen as an equal threat in the UK, as in much of Europe, to that of terrorism. In

---

18 Save for the amendment to the definition of "criminal property" suggested on other grounds below.

19 This term was first used in the 1970s by law enforcement officers in Northern Ireland in order to distinguish between the paramilitaries and those who had nothing to do with them but engaged in traditional forms of criminality, such as tax evasion, car theft and the like, merely to line their own pockets.

any case, a policy could still be maintained that, where a prosecutor was able to present evidence that the intermediary suspected the property to be of one type or the other, he should do so for the assistance of the court. The combined offence would, however, mean that there would not be a risk of a complete acquittal (or even inability to bring the case in the first place) where this could not be done.

Further justification for this combined approach may be found in the 2005 Directive. Article 1(1) provides simply that "Member States shall ensure that money laundering and terrorist financing are prohibited." It was not felt necessary to have two provisions, one prohibiting money laundering and the other prohibiting terrorist financing: they are dealt with, jointly, in not just a single Article but a single sentence. There are separate provisions relating to the respective definitions of money laundering and terrorist financing,[20] just as there will need to be in national legislation, because of the difference in their nature. The actual prohibition, however, is combined.

Similarly, the provision could be retained that, where the defendant is an authorised financial intermediary, actual suspicion need not be proven provided that it can be shown that he had reasonable grounds to suspect. Indeed, the combined offence would make this easier: there will be many circumstances where a financial intermediary will have reasonable grounds to suspect that something is amiss, but not necessarily what that something is.

Definition of "Criminal Property"

The Criminal Justice Act 1988 referred to property derived either from an indictable offence[21] or from an act committed outside the United Kingdom which, had it been committed in the UK, would have constituted an indictable offence. The Proceeds of Crime Act 2002 continues this, but adds, as predicate crimes, not only drug trafficking offences but also summary offences. It also refers to acts which constitute a criminal offence in any part of the United Kingdom. Given that summary offences are now included, this produces an unfortunate result: the proceeds of what is a quite legitimate act in one jurisdiction of the UK but which is prohibited in another will, at least technically, become criminal property. An example concerns the sale of alcohol. In Scotland, pubs are generally permitted to stay open until around midnight and there are proposals to extend these hours even further. In England and Wales, however, "closing time" is generally 11.00 pm; even the recent liberalisation of this merely give greater discretion to local authorities. This will mean that if a Glasgow pub sells alcohol after 11.00 pm, as it is perfectly permitted to do, the proceeds will be property derived from an act which is an criminal offence in certain parts of the UK, i.e. those parts of England and Wales where licensing hours are not extended. As such, it will be criminal property. Not only will it be criminal property "south of

---

20 Articles 1(2) – 1(3) and Article 1(4) respectively.
21 Except drug trafficking offences, which were dealt with separately under the Drug Trafficking Act 1994.

the border", it will even be criminal property in Scotland if the person handling the money is aware, as many Scots are, of the stricter English licensing laws.

One is assured that prosecutors are all too few in number and overloaded as it is and hence will in practice not expend time and resources bringing money laundering charges in such a case. Further, a jury would in such circumstances be very likely simply to refuse to convict. This may indeed be so, but it does not alter the fact that the provision is ill-conceived. At the very least, the Act should require, for property to constitute criminal property, that the act from which it is derived be a criminal offence in the part of the United Kingdom in which it is received. Preferable would be a provision to the effect that criminal property must be derived from an act which is a criminal offence throughout the UK.

As the European Union becomes an ever more closely-knit entity, there may well be an argument for a similar provision in relation to other EU Member States. In Spain, insider dealing is only a criminal offence in very limited circumstances. The definition under the UK's Criminal Justice Act 1993, however, as in other Member States, is far less restricted. Should a person in Spain therefore engage in insider dealing and make a profit of €150,000, he will have committed an act that constitutes not just an offence in the UK but quite a serious one. Yet in Spain, where the act was committed, it is only an administrative offence.[22] Hence, should the profits be paid into his account in Madrid, no offence will be committed. But should they then be transferred to an account in London, the bank will be guilty of money laundering unless it can show that it had no reason to suspect that anything was amiss.

Some might argue that this is fair enough: the fact that the Spanish take a relaxed view of insider dealing and its proceeds does not mean that the British need to. When the Criminal Justice Act 1993, which inserted the money laundering provisions into the Criminal Justice Act 1988, was drafted, Parliament very deliberately covered funds derived from acts that it was not prepared to tolerate even though other jurisdictions might: the example generally cited was overseas corruption.[23] The other jurisdictions contemplated very possibly did not include EU Member States, but there are a number of examples: not only insider dealing in Spain, but prostitution (and indeed selling cannabis) in the Netherlands, publishing pornography in Denmark, Germany and Belgium, etc. If the UK disapproves of such activities, it is perhaps not unreasonable that it should seek to hinder the money flows from them.

But such an approach hardly assists continued European integration. It is one thing for one Member State to prohibit acts which others are prepared to tolerate: specific provision is made under European law for such laws to protect public health, morals and even public policy. Indeed, there are parallels in multi-jurisdictional

---

22 Since the profits are well below the €450,760 threshold: see p. 115.

23 It was perhaps ironic that, between the coming into force of the Criminal Justice Act 1993 and that of the Anti-Terrorism, Crime and Security Act 2001, a London banker who knowingly invested bribes received by, for example, a government minister in the Republic of Congo was liable to up to 14 years' imprisonment while, as a matter of English law, his colleague who paid that bribe in order to secure a contract committed no offence!

states, never mind regional entities such as the European Union. In the United States, gambling is permitted in the state of Nevada but illegal in Minnesota,[24] while China's "one country, two systems" approach is well known. It does, however, go a step further to impose criminal liability on a person in one Member State who receives the proceeds of an act which takes place in another Member State and is quite legal there.

Part of the problem is that the Directive does not provide a definite list of predicate offences: it merely states that "all serious crimes" should be covered, leaving it very much up to Member States to decide what a serious crime is. The revised form of the Forty Recommendations of the Financial Action Task Force go further, providing that predicate offences should include all offences which carry a maximum sentence of at least 1 year's imprisonment and the 2005 Directive mirrors this.[25] Since, however, sentencing policy varies widely between the Member States, this is of only limited help when seeking to establish an EU-wide policy. The minimum list that the Directive does give is certainly a starting point, although it is submitted that it should be expanded: for a start, all fraud should be covered, not merely that perpetrated against the EU budget.[26] But any list of specific offences will be unacceptable not only to the UK but also to France, where predicate crimes are defined as any *crime* or *délit*, essentially the same definition as the old UK "indictable offences". A wide definition will, however, not appeal to Luxembourg, which prefers the specific list approach. The solution would therefore appear to be a two-tier approach. In the first instance, Member States would be free to determine their own list, although the FATF principle of including any offence which may attract at least 1 year's imprisonment in the state in question would seem to be a sound one.[27] But this would then be subject to a rule that, where the act from which the property is derived (a) took place in another EU Member State and (b) did not constitute a criminal offence there, the property shall not be deemed to be criminal property. This need not be so controversial: a parallel may be drawn with the approach taken by the French Penal Code to offences committed abroad. Where a French national commits an act which constitutes a *crime*, the most serious category of criminal offence, they are guilty of it under French law just as though they had committed the act on French territory. Where, however, the act merely constitutes a *délit*, they will only be guilty if it is also a criminal offence in the jurisdiction where it was committed.[28] The same

---

24 Even within states, there are differences: in the State of Utah, for example, beer may be sold in Salt Lake City but not in Washington County.

25 Or a minimum sentence of 6 months: Article 3(5)(f). The Preamble to the 2005 Directive makes clear that a key aim in introducing a new Directive was that EU standards should match those of the FATF: para. 5.

26 This restriction remains in the 2005 Directive: Article 3(5)(d).

27 In any case, no Member State would wish to find itself non-compliant with the FATF Recommendations!

28 Article 113-6. As an exception to this rule, all *délits* punishable with imprisonment are covered where the victim is a French national: Article 113-7.

approach could be taken across the Union in relation to predicate offences for money laundering.

It should be stressed that, in order to protect the public health, morals, policy, etc, of the various Member States, this principle would only apply to money laundering offences. Where, for example, a person purchased pornographic material that is legal in Denmark but prohibited in the UK, they would commit a criminal offence if they imported it into the UK or obtained it in the UK, directly or indirectly, from the importer. But the offence would be one of evading the prohibition on the importation of (or possessing) obscene material, not of handling criminal property.

Protection of Brokers, etc, under Insider Dealing Laws

The issue relating to brokers and other intermediaries who possess inside information in relation to given securities and who are then instructed to purchase those securities is delicate, but would seem to be satisfactory. In cases where the client is not himself in possession of inside information (or at least the broker has no reason to suspect that he is), the broker need fear nothing. He is not guilty of insider dealing, by reason of the exception provided for such cases; nor is he guilty of receiving criminal property, since he has no reasonable grounds to suspect his client of being guilty of any offence. Where, however, he does so suspect, he will not be able to execute the transaction as, if he does, he will be guilty, when he buys the securities, of receiving criminal property. This is arguably as it should be: the whole point of the new provisions is to prevent persons, particularly financial services professionals, from assisting in the commission of a criminal offence. The fact that the broker in such a case will now be guilty of money laundering, rather than merely aiding and abetting insider dealing, as under the previous regime, and that he will therefore face a potential prison sentence of exactly double, may seem harsh, but it is quite clearly what was intended.

Application of Precautionary Measures

The requirement that all professionals within the financial sector, i.e. banks, investment firms, lawyers, accountants and the like, obtain particulars of identity when commencing a business relationship is sound. Similarly, little criticism can be made regarding the requirement for additional identification to be made when a transaction is to be executed which has a value of €15,000 or more. It does mean that a certain amount of unnecessary paperwork will need to be undertaken: when a customer, for example, purchases or sells real property[29] or even a moderate business enterprise pays its suppliers. But the benefits of monitoring reasonably large transactions probably outweigh such inconvenience.

---

29 Certainly in the UK, it is difficult to imagine any house, or even flat, with a value of less than £10,300, the approximate equivalent of €15,000.

What gives greater cause for concern is the much more limited application to dealers in high value goods, such as jewellers. It is of course accepted that many jewellers sell items with a range of values and hence that certain of the transactions which they process involve amounts far smaller than is the case within the financial sector. Clearly, little will be achieved by requiring formal identification to be recorded every time a customer buys a £50 chain. But it is nonsense that a customer who purchases a €20,000 piece of jewellery in cash will need to present formal identification but one who makes a similar purchase with a credit card (which may not necessarily be issued by a bank in a "safe" jurisdiction) will not. Further, there are arguably reasonable grounds for suspicion when anyone makes a purchase of even €5,000 in cash, yet, given the terms of the Directive, a jeweller would be on fairly safe ground if they claimed that the mere fact that it was in cash and for such an amount did not arouse their suspicions. It is therefore suggested that, as with financial institutions, dealers in high value goods should be required to obtain and record identification in relation to all purchases or sales with a value of €15,000 or more, regardless of how payment is made.

Where transactions are in cash, it is suggested that the threshold for requiring identification should be far lower than €15,000. The threshold of €2,000, as now required of casinos,[30] might be appropriate: at most €5,000 would be. This should apply not simply to dealers in high value goods but to all institutions covered by the Directive, including bureaux de change. The latter, of course, have a particularly high volume of customers undertaking one-off transactions. Until relatively recently, it was a routine requirement throughout most of Europe to present a passport when exchanging any amount of currency, however small; it would not seem unreasonable to restore this requirement for cash transactions above €2,000.

It should be stressed that it is not being suggested that cash transactions of these amounts should be prohibited. It is recognised that certain sectors, such as the second-hand car trade, frequently deal in cash even where payments of several thousand euro are involved. It is also recognised that, as more people from more countries travel internationally, there will be bona fide travellers to EU Member States who, because credit cards, electronic bank transfers, etc, are rare in their home jurisdiction,[31] are accustomed to conducting all their business in cash and carry appropriately large sums. For global commerce to be maintained, they must continue to be permitted to do so. When they do, however, it is not unreasonable to ask them to present suitable forms of identification. A comparison could be made with the currency import/export legislation of the United States and France. In the United States, under the Bank Secrecy Act, imports or exports of currency with a value of more than $10,000 must be reported to the Financial Crimes Enforcement Network (FinCEN), a division of the US Treasury. Similarly, under the French Customs

---

30 Article 10(1). This is an increase on the previous threshold of €1,000, provided for in the 2001 Directive.

31 China is a notable example, but far from the only one.

Code,[32] imports or exports of cash exceeding €7,600 must be declared to Customs. Provided that such a report/declaration is made, however, the actual import/export of the currency is totally permitted.[33] The same approach could be taken with large cash transactions.

It is therefore suggested that all cash transactions above a €2,000 threshold incur an identification requirement; indeed, this would arguably be appropriate not merely for the business sectors covered by the Directive but for all businesses.[34] It is recognised, however, that a number of cash transactions are carried out by established customers, particularly at financial institutions, in respect of whom identification will already have been obtained. This will, for example, be the case with shops and restaurants who bank much of their takings, and similarly pay their staff, in cash. In such cases, the existing threshold of €15,000 would be appropriate. The exemption could easily be drafted: it would merely state that, where the institution or business has an ongoing business relationship with the customer, and evidence of his identity has therefore already been obtained and recorded, further identification shall only be required when transactions, whether in cash or otherwise, are carried out to a value of €15,000 or more.

Casinos are ideal smurfing centres and a threshold value, which will trigger customer identification requirements, is pointless, regardless of the level at which the threshold is set.[35] It is accepted that casinos do monitor their customers, for security reasons, through close circuit TV cameras and also that regular customers, who join the casino as members, will be caught by the requirement to obtain identification when commencing a business relationship. This will, however, not completely solve the basic problem: it is still too easy for a person to slip through the net. It is therefore suggested that it should be not simply an option but a requirement that all customers should be identified on entering the casino. This is already the case in the UK, and indeed in Malta, one of the new Member States that acceded to the EU in May 2004; it is suggested that it be a requirement across the Union.

Current Trends

The above is the ideal: it may be useful, however, to consider what developments there are likely to be in the near to medium future.

---

32 *Code des Douanes.*
33 Save where the money is known or suspected to be linked to a criminal offence.
34 Save for casinos: see below.
35 They have also been recognised for some time as presenting significant opportunities for money laundering. See, for example, Leong, A.V.M. (2003-04) "Macau Casinos and Organised Crime" 7 *Journal of Money Laundering Control* 298.

Civil Enforcement of Insider Dealing Legislation

It has been noted that there has been a historical divide between the Member States in relation to the punishment of insider dealing: some have taken a purely criminal approach, while others have supplemented this with civil/administrative measures. Spain chose to take an almost exclusively civil approach, but at the time was exceptional in doing so.

There are already signs, however, of a change of emphasis. Although the Insider Dealing Directive continues to have a major influence on the control of the offence across Europe, the impact of the Market Abuse Directive, which has now replaced it, is likely to increase. This in turn will lead to greater use of civil/administrative provisions, such have already been seen in Germany and the UK. Indeed, it will mean that they will need to be introduced in those Member States that currently take a solely criminal approach to insider dealing, such as the Scandinavian states or Portugal.[36]

The question for the future, however, is: will the new civil/administrative provisions merely supplement the existing criminal measures or will they actually replace them, at least in part? The new legislation in the UK, which came into force in December 2001 and that in Germany, introduced 3 years later, would seem to provide two possible models. As discussed above, there is much to be said for maintaining criminal sanctions in parallel with the civil/administrative approach: these achieve certain things which administrative fines do not. Further, the experience of the UK and, even more, France demonstrates that the two systems can work quite well in parallel. Even the United States, often cited as the leading example of controlling insider dealing through civil measures, has not seen fit to abandon the criminal measures altogether: prosecutions continue in appropriate cases. Also in favour of the continuation of criminal sanctions is the fact that the majority of the Member States, although not required to do so, have provided for them in their legislation, even where they introduced civil sanctions as well.

The new German approach should not, however, be dismissed as an aberration. Germany is, after the UK, the leading financial centre of Europe. The continued interest of the Deutsche Börse in purchasing the London Stock Exchange only serves to underline this. A change of approach in Germany is therefore likely to have a considerably wider impact than one in Spain. Secondly, it is noticeable that, where jurisdictions provide for a "twin track" approach to insider dealing, it is in practice the civil measures that are used. The United States and France are important exceptions, but they are exceptions. In Greece, heavy administrative fines have been imposed, but there have been no criminal prosecutions. The Insider Dealing Directorate of

---

36 Art. 14 of the Market Abuse Directive requires administrative sanctions, in addition to any others that may be imposed, for insider dealing. It is implied that the grounds are that administrative proceedings are faster and therefore more efficient than a criminal prosecution: para. 38 to the Preamble. See Rider, B.A.K., Alexander, S.K. and Linklater, L. (2002) *Market Abuse and Insider Dealing*, Butterworths, p. 74.

the South African Financial Services Board similarly reports considerable success in civil actions against insider dealers while, again, very few criminal prosecutions have to date been brought. These are perhaps relatively minor financial centres in global terms, but the same pattern may be observed in the UK: since the introduction of the market abuse provisions in December 2001, there have been a number of successful civil actions brought by the Financial Services Authority, but no criminal prosecutions. One may suspect that the FSA's initial non-response to the question of whether both criminal and civil proceedings would be brought in respect of the same offence was not, as some feared at the time, because it wished to keep its options open, but rather because it felt it was of limited relevance. It did not matter whether parallel proceedings would technically be available because the plan in practice was to concentrate on civil enforcement.

It is true that Germany has not abolished criminal enforcement completely. Those who actually deal face prosecution and a prison sentence, as may a primary insider who commits any of the insider dealing offences. Germany does, however, illustrate a trend. It was open to the legislator to follow the approach of certain other Member States and impose the same sanctions, criminal or civil, on any person who commits any of the offences. It chose not to do so. Rather, it reserved criminal sanctions for the most serious cases, while creating the option to bring civil proceedings in all but the most egregious. Although the new legislation has been in force for only a few months and it is therefore too soon for cases under the new regime to be reported, it is likely that the approach in Germany will in practice now mirror Spain, setting a strong example to the rest of Europe.

In contrast, however, it is likely that, in the UK, the restitution order in cases of misuse of information[37] will rarely if ever be used, since it is difficult to see what purpose it may serve. It cannot be defended as a means of depriving the insider dealer of the profits of his offences in the way that civil recovery is, since, unlike sums taken through civil recovery, the proceeds are specifically not to be given either to the Treasury or to any regulator, but to some third party. It will generally be very difficult to justify why a given third party has been chosen as the beneficiary, something that could all too easily form the subject of a judicial review application.

In any case, it is arguable that the financial penalties imposed for market abuse are the true counterparts to civil recovery: they can be set at a level to deprive the offender of the proceeds of the abuse and, at the same time, the monies paid are retained by the Financial Services Authority as part of its funding. They have the added advantage that they do not require a court action: even where the offender is not an authorised person, they are imposed by the FSA directly.[38] Given this, it is likely that restitution orders will in practice be reserved for cases of misleading

---

37 In contrast to misleading practices, which can give rise to clearly identifiable, individual victims.

38 The case may be appealed to the Financial Services and Markets Tribunal, but, at "first instance", it is the FSA itself that decides what penalty to impose.

Customer Identification

The means by which an institution identifies its customers needs to be addressed. Most Member States[39] have a national identity card, which must be carried by all persons at all times as a legal requirement. For some time, it seemed increasingly likely that the UK would follow suit: one of the first announcements made by Charles Clarke, on becoming Home Secretary in December 2004, was that he would continue David Blunkett's plans to introduce it. The debate centred primarily on whether, in the long term, the card would become compulsory or remain purely voluntary. Although the prevention of money laundering has not, to date, been among the grounds given for its introduction, it is of relevance. If a national identity card is introduced with features including, as proposed, the holder's fingerprint and iris scan, it will soon be regarded as the standard "satisfactory evidence of the customer's identity". It would seem difficult to argue that a card with such features is not "reasonably capable of establishing that the applicant for business is the person he claims to be". The range of alternative identity documents currently accepted would therefore be likely to diminish and, even if holding the card were not actually a legal requirement, it would become difficult to operate without one.

Particularly if the card proved successful in assisting financial institutions to identify their customers both more simply and more effectively, pressure for the Republic of Ireland, as the one remaining Member State without such as card, also to adopt this measure would then inevitably grow, if only through action at EU level.

In practice, however, the identity card debate quietened during early 2005, due possibly to the Government's wish not to add to the list of controversial measures in the run-up to the general election.[40] The proposals returned following the election, although dispute as to the actual cost of the card, combined with doubts as to whether it would be effective in achieving its stated aims, namely of preventing terrorism and organised crime, have also come to the fore. Opposition to the card by both the Conservative and Liberal Democrat Parties remains and it is therefore uncertain what precise future the plans will have.

Meanwhile, particularly for non-nationals, or possibly non-residents,[41] the passport will continue to be the form of identification required. There is therefore a risk that the difficulty of bank staff discerning a valid from a forged passport from,

---

39 All except the Republic of Ireland and the UK.

40 It was reported that the Bill introducing identity cards has been among a number of measures sacrificed in preparation for the election: *Guardian*, 16 March 2005.

41 Certain Member States, such as Germany and Belgium, issue identity cards to all legal residents, whether they are citizens or not. (Clearly, a separate class of card is issued to non-citizens.) It is now planned that the UK will follow this approach, although whether other Member States will do so is less certain.

say, Kazakhstan, Uruguay or even Ghana will remain. As the general standard of identification expected rises, it is therefore possible that there will be pressure on institutions to move from one copy of the "passport handbook" in the legal department at headquarters to several copies, distributed among the branches and made easily available to all staff dealing directly with clients.[42] This pressure may be applied directly by the Financial Services Authority; even if it is not, however, it is likely that, should an institution be found to have accepted a false passport, the explanation that the relevant staff at the branch had no means of verifying it is unlikely to impress.

For an institution with a large network of branches[43] to supply every branch with a copy of the handbook may, however, prove impractical and expensive. The trend, already noticeable, for foreign nationals only to be dealt with by certain branches is likely to intensify, with perhaps only one branch per large town or city dealing with such clients and none at all in the smaller centres. This will inevitably lead to added inconvenience for non-residents seeking to conduct financial business.[44]

Financial Cost of Compliance

The issue of the costs of regulation needs attention. The cost of compliance with the anti-money-laundering regime, even before the added burden of the Proceeds of Crime Act 2002, was calculated at around £650 million per year, but this is only part of the overall compliance costs. To the larger institutions, this is simply an inconvenience, albeit not one they gladly endure. For the smaller firms, however, now making up 97% of all firms regulated by the Financial Services Authority,[45] it potentially makes it difficult for them to remain in the industry. In January 2005, therefore, the FSA announced in its Business Plan that it would undertake a study of the costs of compliance with the requirements of the Financial Services and Markets Act 2000. Particular attention was to be given to smaller firms, as well as wholesale firms operating in internationally competitive markets. Quite what was meant by the latter was, however, unclear: it could be argued that most, if not all, markets are

---

42 The "passport handbook" is in fact a manual rather than handbook. It contains facsimiles, produced with the assistance of the various Embassies, of genuine passports from every jurisdiction as an aid to financial institutions, especially banks, to recognise fakes. In practice, however, institutions tend to save money by purchasing only one copy, which is then kept in the library of the legal department at their headquarters, rather than being readily available to the staff in the network of branches, who are arguably more likely to need to use it on a day to day basis.

43 For example, the "High Street" banks.

44 This trend has already started. It is increasingly difficult for, for example, overseas students to obtain bank accounts or even travel insurance; the Money Laundering Regulations are frequently pointed to by institutions to explain their change of policy.

45 FSA Press Notice FSA/PN/027/2005, 3 March 2005. Smaller firms were explicitly stated to be "central to the FSA's priorities" for 2005-06 in the FSA Press Notice FSA/PN/009/2005.

now internationally competitive. It did indicate, however, that the FSA is starting to take on board the very real concerns of many in the industry that the cost to them of compliance is simply too high. The fact that the study was to be conducted in conjunction with the Financial Services Practitioner Panel, a body independent of the FSA, showed that the industry was genuinely represented. The announcement in May 2005 that the firm of Deloitte was to undertake some of the research for the study underlines this. A criticism that one could make, however, is that reference was only made to the FSMA 2000 regime, no mention being made of the costs of compliance with the Proceeds of Crime Act 2002, the Money Laundering Regulations 2003 and, of increasing importance now, the Terrorism Act 2000. It may, however, be that the study will ultimately deal with these issues, although there is been little sign of this from the FSA to date.

In any event, it does suggest that the regulatory culture is changing. Formerly, the attitude was perceived to be, "Being in the financial services industry is a privilege which carries responsibilities: if you want the privilege, you should be pleased to accept the costs." It could be argued that the change from firms receiving "authorisation" under the Financial Services Act 1986 regime to their being granted "permission" under the current system supports this. The new study suggests, however, that the FSA is more accepting of the view that the financial services sector is an industry, a highly important part of the British economy, and, as such, it should be supported and assisted, not overburdened.

The balance is never an easy one. It will be recalled that one of the objections raised in Europe for many years against the outlawing of paying bribes to foreign public officials was that not only were such "commissions" necessary if one was going to do business in certain jurisdictions but important business would simply be lost to firms from states which took a more liberal approach.[46] If one accepts, as it is suggested that most would, that the four regulatory objectives of market confidence, public awareness, protection of consumers and reduction of financial crime are desirable, it must be recognised that these will come at a cost to the financial sector. In the area of fighting organised and economic crime, in particular, the industry does have a part to play. The question, however, is how great that cost and that part should fairly be.

Enforcement Process

Even more significant, arguably, is the FSA's announcement of a review of its enforcement process, announced on 2 February 2005.[47] The review will be wide ranging, covering in particular:

---

46 Conversely, it could be argued that one of the reasons that the United States pressed so hard for other jurisdictions to adopt legislation in line with its own Foreign Corrupt Practices Act was to cease US firms losing out, because of the Act, to foreign competition.
47 FSA Press Release, "FSA announces scope of enforcement processes review", 2 February 2005, FSA/PN/014/2005.

- the processes followed by supervisors, enforcement staff and decision-makers when considering possible breaches of statutory or regulatory requirements, and the nature and extent of the communications and interactions between them;
- the role and involvement of senior FSA management throughout these processes;
- options for making regulatory decisions based on a fair procedure by persons separate from the investigators; and
- the accountability of decision makers to the FSA Board.[48]

The FSA openly state that this review will incorporate "the lessons learned" from the comments made by the Financial Services and Markets Tribunal in the Legal and General case. This case involved mis-selling of pensions rather than any of the offences considered in this study, but the Tribunal's findings do raise issues of general application. In particular, they focus on how the FSA makes out its case. The FSA had found defects in the Legal and General procedures and stated that these defects had led to the selling of pensions to persons for whom they were not suitable. The Tribunal agreed. It found, however, that there were only eight cases in which pensions had been mis-sold rather than 60 as alleged by the FSA. The FSA had extrapolated the extra cases on the basis of "common sense", not actual evidence: it had concluded that the defects it discovered (and which the Tribunal confirmed) must have led to rather more occasions of mis-selling than those it actually proved. An analogy could perhaps be drawn with the assumptions made under the Proceeds of Crime Act 2002 in relation to persons enjoying a "criminal lifestyle"; the difference, however, is that those assumptions are explicitly endorsed by legislation, while the FSA's very similar logic was not. The Tribunal held that the fine should have been based on the number of cases for which there was actual evidence, not the number the FSA had calculated. As such, the £1.1 million imposed was too high. The situation was exacerbated by the fact that the sample of customers the FSA reviewed was unduly low in the first place: general conclusions could therefore not reasonably be drawn from it.

The Future

The review of procedures announced, however, goes rather further: in essence, all significant aspects of FSA investigations and enforcement will be considered. The views of institutions, and indeed consumers, are being invited: further guidance for their comments was issued on 15 March 2005. In the meantime, however, certain tentative remarks/predictions may be made.

Certain aspects of the way in which the FSA was set up, and the procedures within which it was to operate, were a response to the perceived unfairness of the

---

48 FSA Statement, "Enforcement process review", 23 February 2005, www.fsa.gov.uk.

SRO system that preceded it. The result may have been an improvement in some ways, but the industry is still not entirely satisfied. Whereas the complaint against the SROs' disciplinary system was that they operated like clubs and therefore expected those against whom they acted to take their medicine without argument, that against the FSA is that, to quote one leading City compliance officer, "it thinks it's a police force." Not only a police force, it might be added, but one with the power, following arrest, to issue proceedings and even pass sentence.

Already the "sentencing" arm of the FSA, the Regulatory Decisions Committee, is organisationally separate from the investigators: although the men and women who go through the firm's files and question its staff then form a view whether or not there has been a breach of the rules (or indeed legislation), they do not make a formal finding as to guilt, let alone determine the penalty. The suspicion remains, however, that the members of the Committee, which does have this function, could be unduly influenced by the views of the investigators, who are, after all, their colleagues. In 1998, the Court of Appeal ruled that Lord Goddard, Lord Chief Justice, was wrong to state that evidence given by a police officer was by definition to be given credibility.[49] It may be that a similar issue will now arise in relation to the Financial Services Authority.

In reviewing the nature and extent of communication between the FSA supervisors, enforcement staff and decision makers (i.e. those who make a formal finding), procedures could be implemented to ensure a greater degree of independence. The question will remain, however, of state of mind. Can any disciplinary committee or tribunal be truly independent when those putting "the prosecution case" are members of the same organisation? A comparison could perhaps be made to military courts-martial: a study of the percentage of convictions and acquittals before these could perhaps be informative to the present discussion,[50] as could the number of court-martial convictions subsequently overturned by the Court of Appeal.[51] Within the private sector, it is difficult to see how the problem can be surmounted: it is inevitable that those presenting allegations to a disciplinary hearing within a firm, for example, will be colleagues of those deciding on them. The situation with a regulator, however, is, it is submitted, different. It may be that the Regulatory Decisions Committee may need to be separated from the FSA and made a separate tribunal. The FSA would then present its case to this tribunal in the way that the COB, for example, presents cases to courts in France.

This is particularly important in relation to the offences raised in this book. All but a few of them are capable of being prosecuted – indeed, by the FSA – as criminal

---

49 *R v Bentley* [1998] *The Times*, July 31. Bentley had in fact been executed, following his conviction, some decades earlier; the case had been brought, however, by his sister in order to clear his name.

50 Although the defence counsel at a court-martial is sometimes a civilian barrister, both the prosecutor and the judges are invariably military officers.

51 An appeal from a conviction before a court-martial lies not to another military tribunal, but, as with the civilian Crown Court, to the Court of Appeal.

offences. The fact that the FSA may choose instead to bring regulatory proceedings[52] does not detract from the seriousness of the charges. If it is accepted that an offence that could send a person to prison merits a tribunal that is institutionally separate from the investigators, it is suggested that the same is true of an offence that can drive a person out of his industry. Within a firm, a decision to fire an individual may make it very difficult for him to obtain another job within the same sector, but he does not commit a criminal offence if he succeeds. With a regulatory decision, the stakes are higher. As the whole area of the FSA's disciplinary procedures comes under review, it may be that an independent tribunal will be called for at "first instance" as well as at appellate level.

As the UK remains the leading financial centre of the European Union, it may well be that the outcome of the review may have an effect on the way financial services offences are dealt with in other Member States. Equally, the experience of other Member States may assist in establishing a way forward for the FSA's disciplinary system. In France, as in many civil law jurisdictions, the prosecutor is a judicial office: reference is made to "the magistrates of the bench and the magistrates of the prosecutor's office".[53] Although, however, the judge and the prosecutor are colleagues, this does not lead to allegations of undue influence. Indeed, the French *juge d'instruction* (investigating magistrate) is often far more robust in dismissing a weak prosecution case at an early stage than an English magistrate.[54]

The area of human rights is likely to remain a major area of concern and development. It would be surprising if the increased attention given to the Human Rights Act 1998 as a result of terrorist cases does not spread to the area of financial crime. Again, there may well be influence in this area from other Member States, particularly some of those which acceded since 2004. These may prove wary of any provisions that erode the protection of human rights, due to their recent experience of abuses. Estonia, Latvia, Lithuania and Slovenia, in particular, only emerged as independent democratic states in 1991, a full two years after the revolutions elsewhere in Central and Eastern Europe. The new Member States may be expected to have an important influence on the shaping of future legislation at EU level. The influence of the new democracies can only grow further with the accession of Romania and Bulgaria.[55] The trend for over 10 years now has been that national legislation to

---

52 As, for example, in the Northern Bank case in August 2003.

53 *Magistrats du siège et magistrats du parquet.* In civil law jurisdictions, the judiciary is entirely separate from the legal profession: from law school onwards, the training and career path are different for the two, to the extent that a person who later wishes to change from one to the other needs to undertake substantial re-training.

54 It is a criticism often made of lay justices in England and Wales that, particularly if the alleged offence is serious, they are reluctant to take the responsibility of dismissing the case, preferring to leave this to the Crown Court. In contrast, the high conviction rate (over 90%) in France has been explained, at least in part, by the fact that cases likely to result in acquittal are not permitted to reach the trial stage in the first place.

55 It may be that the accession of Turkey, which continues to have a rather more authoritarian law enforcement culture, will move the debate the other way. Turkey's

combat financial crime, not least insider dealing and money laundering, is led by European initiatives. It is not inconceivable, therefore, that some of the objections raised in this book may be addressed by trends from the east.

To conclude, the efforts to control both insider dealing and money laundering across the European Union may be described as "a work in progress". Much has been achieved and is of considerable value. Significant parts, however, still need to be changed if they are to be, at the same time, just and effective. The move towards civil, rather than criminal, enforcement of insider dealing is already observable and is likely to become the favoured approach in the future, although amendments to the current structure would be desirable. In the area of money laundering, also, there are a number of measures which, it is submitted, need further improvement. It may be that, in time, entities such as the European Union and the Financial Action Task Force will not be as swift to adopt each other's measures without due consideration of the drawbacks, but this particular lesson would not appear to have been learned yet.

Meanwhile, the area of regulatory enforcement is coming under consideration. A reprimand from the Financial Services and Markets Tribunal in the UK has led the Financial Services Authority to institute a review of its procedures at a time when the area of human rights is having increasing influence. The outcome may have an effect across the European Union, which itself will continue to expand.

All of this will take time. Much of the legislation, at both EU and national level, is new and it has yet to be seen how it will work in practice. There is likely to be room for further study and comment for some considerable time to come.

---

accession remains, however, uncertain and, even if it does accede, it will be one voice among 28, possibly more. A group of ten could still be persuasive.

Bibliography

Alexander, R.C.H. (2004) "The 2003 Money Laundering Regulations" 8 *Journal of Money Laundering Control* 75.
Archbold: Criminal Pleading, Evidence and Practice (2005).
Ashe, T.M. and Counsell, L. (1993) *Insider Trading*, 2nd Edition, Tolley Publishing Company Ltd.
Attorney-General's Committee, Report of the on Securities Legislation in Ontario ("Kimber Report") (1966).
BBC News, "Howard unveils Tory asylum plans", 24 January 2005.
Bell, R.E. (2000-01) "An Evolving Series of Proceeds of Crime Models" 8 *Journal of Financial Crime* 21.
Bell, R.E. (2002-03) "The Prosecution of Lawyers for Money Laundering Offences" 6 *Journal of Money Laundering Control* 17.
Bell, R.E. (2003-04) "The Seizure, Detention and Forfeiture of Cash in the UK" 11 *Journal of Financial Crime* 134.
Blair, W. (ed.) (2002) *Banking and Financial Services Legislation*, 3rd Edition, Butterworths.
Brindle, M. (2001-02) "The Liabilities of Financial Intermediaries and Their Advisors for Handling the Proceeds of Crime" 9 *Journal of Financial Crime* 227.
Burchell, J.M. and Milton, J. (1997) *Principles of Criminal Law*, 2nd Edition, Kenwyn: Juta.
Clerk, J.F. (2000) *Clerk & Lindsell on Torts*, 18th Edition, Sweet & Maxwell.
Davidson, N.R.W. (2004-05) "Third Party Liability: The Risk of Being Sued by Those Damaged by Regulatory or Enforcement Action" 12 *Journal of Financial Crime* 209.
Davies, P.L. (ed.) (2003) *Gower and Davies: The Principles of Modern Company Law*, 7th Edition, Sweet & Maxwell.
Dersowitz, R.S. (2002) *Federal Bodysnatchers and the New Guinea Virus: Tales of Parasites, People and Politics*, W.W. Norton & Co.
Duderstadt, I. (1996-97) "Implementation of the Insider Dealing Directive in the United Kingdom and Germany" 4 *Journal of Financial Crime* 105.
Ellinger, E.P., Lomnicka, E. and Hooley, R.J.A. (2002) *Ellinger's Modern Banking Law*, 3rd Edition, Oxford University Press.
Farrar, J.F., Furey, N., Hannigan, B. and Wylie, P. (1998) *Farrar's Company Law*, 4th Edition, Butterworths.
Financial Action Task Force (2001) Report 2000-2001.
Financial Action Task Force (2001) "Review to Identify Non-Cooperative Countries or Territories: Increasing the Worldwide Effectiveness of Anti- Money Laundering

Measures", June 2001.
Financial Action Task Force (2003) "Review to Identify Non-Cooperative Countries or Territories: Increasing the Worldwide Effectiveness of Anti- Money Laundering Measures", June 2003.
Financial Services Authority (2005) "FSA announces scope of enforcement processes review", Press Release, 2 February 2005.
Financial Services Authority (2005) "Enforcement process review", Statement, 23 February 2005.
Financial Services Authority (2005) "FSA begins cost of regulation study", Press Notice, 3 March 2005.
Fishman, J. (1993) "A comparison of enforcement of securities law violations in the UK and US" 14 Co. Law 163.
Forman, C. (1989) "Insider Trading, Illegal in US, is Customary in Europe", *Asian Wall Street Journal*, 9 February 1989.
Freshfields Bruckhaus Deringer on Financial Services: Investigations and Enforcement (2001) Butterworths.
Gilligan, G.P. (1999) *Regulating the Financial Services Sector*, Kluwer Law International.
Givel, M.S. and Glantz, S.A. (2002)"Political Reform and Tobacco Control Policy Making in Mississippi From 1990 to 2001", Center for Tobacco Research and Education, University of California, San Francisco, Paper MS2002.
Goode, R. (2004) *Commercial Law*, 3rd Edition, Penguin.
Graham, T., Bell, R.E. and Elliott, N. (2003) *Money Laundering*, Butterworths.
Grant, M. and Talbot, L. (1999-00) "Chinese Walls" 7 *Journal of Financial Crime* 336.
Gregory, S. (2003) *Forget You Had A Daughter: Doing Time in the Bangkok Hilton*, Vision Paperbacks.
Gully-Hart, P. (2004-05) "The Risk of Being Sued by Those Damaged by Regulatory or Enforcement Action: Over-regulation of Financial Services?" 12 *Journal of Financial Crime* 246.
Hayton, D.J. (2003) *Underhill and Hayton: Law of Trusts and Trustees*, 16th Edition, Butterworths.
Herzel, L. and Harris, D. (1989) "Do we need insider trading laws?" [1989] Co. Law 34.
Hinterseer, K. (2002) *Criminal Finance: the Political Economy of Money Laundering in a Comparative Legal Context*, Kluwer Law International.
Jefferson, M. (1995-96) "Corporate Criminal Responsibility – Ascription of Criminal Liability to Companies" 3 *Journal of Financial Crime* 275.
Jerez, O. (2002) *Le Blanchiment de l'Argent*, Revue Banque.
Johnstone, P. and Haines, J.D. (1998-99) "Future Trends in Financial Crime" 6 *Journal of Financial Crime* 269.
Johnstone, P. and Haines, J.D. (2001-02) "Human Rights and the Restructuring of Financial Services Regulation in the UK" 9 *Journal of Financial Crime* 179.
Kennedy, A. (2004-05) "Justifying the Civil Recovery of Criminal Proceeds" 12

Journal of Financial Crime 8.
Lastra, R.M. (1996) *Central Banking and Banking Regulation*, London School of Economics and Political Science.
Law Society of England and Wales, *Guide to Professional Conduct*.
Leong, A.V.M. (2003-4) "Macau Casinos and Organised Crime" 7 *Journal of Money Laundering Control* 298.
Levitt, A. (1998) "A Question of Integrity: Promoting Investor Confidence by Fighting Insider Trading", SEC Conference, 27 February.
Lorie, J.H. and Niederhoffer, V. (1968) "Predictive and Statistical Properties of Insider Trading" 11 *Journal of Law and Economics* 35.
Loss, L. (1970) "The Fiduciary Concept as Applied to Trading by Corporate Insiders in the United States" 33 *Modern Law Review* 34.
Maitland-Hudson, A. (1991) *France: Practical Commercial Law*, Longman.
Manne, H.G. (1966) "In Defence of Insider Trading" 44 *Harvard Business Review*, No. 6, 113.
Manne, H.G. (1966) *Insider Trading and the Stock Market*, Collier-Macmillan.
McLean, L. (1998) *The Guv'nor*, Blake Publishing Ltd.
Morton, J. (2003) *Gangland: The Lawyers*, Virgin Books.
Newman, J.C. (1994) *French Tax and Business Law Guide*, CCH Editions.
O'Neill, S. and Lister, D (2005) "MI5 Given Task of Boosting Intelligence on Money Making", *Times*, 25 February 2005.
Peacock, D. (1996-97) "France: Insider Trading: The Court of Cassation's Judgment on What Qualifies as Privileged Information" 4 *Journal of Financial Crime* 85.
Performance and Innovation Unit (PIU) Cabinet Office (2000) *Recovering the Proceeds of Crime*.
Pfeil, Ursula C. (1996) "Finanzplatz Deutschland: Germany Enacts Insider Trading Legislation" 11 *Am. U.J. International Law and Policy*, 137.
Png, C.-A. (2000-01) "Financial Services Regulation and Liability of Corporations" 8 *Journal of Financial Crime* 47.
Preston, E. (2002-03) "The USA PATRIOT Act: New Adventures in American Extraterritoriality" 10 *Journal of Financial Crime* 104.
Quinn, S.E. (1993) *Criminal Law in Ireland*, 2nd Edition, Irish Law Publishing.
Rakoff, J.S. and Eaton, J.C. (1995-96) "How Effective is US Enforcement in Deterring Insider Trading?" 3 *Journal of Financial Crime* 283.
Rider, B.A.K (1995-96) "Civilising the Law – The Use of Civil and Administrative Proceedings to Enforce Financial Services Law" 3 *Journal of Financial Crime* 11.
Rider, B.A.K. (2000) "The Control of Insider Dealing – Smoke and Mirrors!" 19. *Dickinson Journal of International Law* 1.
Rider, B.A.K. (1978) "The Fiduciary and the Frying Pan" 42 *The Conveyancer* 114.
Rider, B.A.K. (1999-2000) "The Price of Probity" 7 *Journal of Financial Crime* 105.
Rider, B.A.K., Abrams, C. and Ashe, T.M. (1997) *Financial Services Regulation*,

CCH Editions.

Rider, B.A.K., Alexander, S.K. and Linklater, L. (2002) *Market Abuse and Insider Dealing*, Butterworths.

Rider, B.A.K. and Alexander, R.C.H. (1998) "The Regulation of Financial Markets With Particular Reference to Market Abuse", Report of Criminal Law Session of Fifteenth World Congress on Comparative Law.

Rider, B.A.K. and Ashe, T.M. (ed.) (1995) *The Fiduciary, the Insider and the Conflict*, Brehon Sweet & Maxwell.

Rider, B.A.K. and Ashe, T.M. (ed.) (1995) *Money Laundering Control*, Round Hall Sweet & Maxwell.

Rider, B.A.K. and Ffrench, H.L. (1979) *The Regulation of Insider Trading*, Macmillan.

Robbins, S.G. (1966) *The Securities Markets: Operations and Issues*, Collier-Macmillan.

Rutledge, G.P. and Haines, J.D. (2001) *Electronic Markets*, Butterworths Compliance Series.

Schumpeter, J.A. (1942) *Capitalism, Socialism and Democracy*, Taylor Francis Lit., reprinted Routledge (1994).

Sealy, L.S. (2001) *Cases and Materials in Company Law*, LexisNexis UK.

Small, R.G. (2001) *Path dependence and the law: A law and economics analysis of the development of the insider trading laws of the United States, United Kingdom and Japan*, PhD thesis, University of London.

Turkson, E. (1997-98) "South Africa: Money Laundering" 5 *Journal of Financial Crime* 393.

US Senate Select Committee on Securities and Exchange, Report (1974).

Van Duyne, P.C. (2003) "Organizing cigarette smuggling and policy making, ending up in smoke" 39 *Crime, Law and Social Change* 285–317.

Vogel, S.K. (1996) *Freer Markets, More Rules: Regulatory Reform in Advanced Industrial Countries*.

Wright, R. (1999-2000) "Banking on Secrets – The price we all pay for secrecy and confidentiality in the face of international organised and economic crime" 7 *Journal of Financial Crime* 304.

Wu, H.K. (1968) "An Economist Looks at Section 16 of the Securities Exchange Act of 1934" 68 *Columbia Law Review* 260.

Zekos, G. I. *Insider Dealing / Trading – An Economic Overview of an Established Offence*. Published on Internet at http://members.fortunecity.com/gzekos/insider.htm.

Index

A-G for Hong Kong v Reid 16, 162
absolute privilege 198
allowing to deal 138–9, 210–11
Amalgamated Metal Trading Ltd. v City of London Police Financial Investigation Unit and others 195–6
Austria
    dealing
        exemptions 117–18
        penalties 123
    inside information 85–7
    insiders 47–51
    legal entities 48–9
    price-sensitive information, reporting 223
    primary insiders 47–8, 85–6
    secondary insiders 47, 48
    securities 86–7

Bank of Scotland v A 195
Belgium
    dealing
        exemptions 117
        penalties 124
    financial instruments 87–8
    holding companies 91
    holding exception 89–92
    inside information 87–92
    insiders 51–4
    legal entities 53–4
    money laundering, imprisonment 148
    price-sensitive information, reporting 223–4
    primary insiders 51, 52
    secondary insiders 51–2
    securities 87–8
Boardman v Phipps 16–18, 161
Bray v Ford 14–15
breach of trust 18
brokers *see* financial services
bubbles in security prices 9
bureaux de change 151–2, 153–6, 243

C v S 193
capital flight 22–3
casinos 153–4, 244
Cayman Islands 34
China, financial crimes 149
Chinese walls 14, 185
City Press affair 42
civil fines 215, 220
civil recovery 235–7
Code of Market Conduct (Financial Services Authority) 79–80, 120
companies *see* legal entities
Compliance Officers, money laundering 188
confiscation 235–6
Cook v Deeks 16
corporations, criminal liability 49–50
corruption 146–7, 249
    proceeds of 23
Council of Europe 32
crime
    disruption of 26
    proceeds of 23–5
criminal liability, legal entities 47
criminal offences, economic motivation 23–4
criminal property 157–8, 160–63, 189–90, 239–42
customer identification 150–51, 153–5, 243–4, 247–8

dealing 114–16
    exemptions 116–21
    federated states 116
    fines 122–3
    inside information 118–19
    local authorities 117–18
    penalties 121–3
        Austria 123
        Belgium 124
        Denmark 124–5
        Finland 125
        France 125–6

Germany 126
Greece 126
Ireland 127
Italy 127–9
Luxembourg 129
Netherlands 129–30
Portugal 130
South Africa 124
Spain 131
Sweden 131–2
United Kingdom 132–5
public debt management 116–18
United Kingdom, specialist defences 119–21
defamation 197–8
Denmark
dealing, penalties 124–5
inside information 66, 92–4
insiders 54–5
legal entities 55
market information 92–3
price-sensitive information, reporting 224
price sensitivity 93
publication of information 92
securities 93–4
unlisted securities 94
directors, disqualification 210
disruption of crime 26
drug trafficking 146, 165
economic motivation 23–4

EEA (European Economic Area), money laundering 164
employee rewards 3–6
encouraging to deal 135–7
penalties 137–8
England and Wales see also United Kingdom
legal entities 50
ethical investment 42
EU see European Union (EU)
European Economic Area (EEA), money laundering 164
European Union (EU)
budget fraud 146–7
compliance with legislation 32
corruption 146–7
financial regulation 31–2

fraud 146–7
insider dealing 31
money laundering 145–56
bureaux de change 153–6
casinos 153–4
customer identification 150–51, 153–5
financial institutions 151–2
high value dealers 152–3
imprisonment 148
preventative measures 150–51
reporting suspicious transactions 151
staff training 151
threshold 152, 155
organised crime 146–7
prospective members 32
ex parte James 15

facilitator liability 27–8, 166
FATF see Financial Action Task Force (FATF)
fiduciary duty 14–19
Financial Action Task Force (FATF) 32–5
Hong Kong 33
money laundering, predicate offences 241–2
Non-Compliant Countries and Territories (NCCT) 33–5
regional groupings 33
financial confidentiality 22
financial crimes 26
financial embargoes 23
financial institutions see financial services
financial instruments see securities
financial intermediaries see financial services
financial regulation
European Union (EU) 31–2
France 183
Spain 183
United States 28–31
financial services
absolute privilege 198
advice to clients 186
Chinese walls 185
conflicts of interest 185
constructive trustee liability 192–7
defamation 197–8

disclosure 193–4
insider dealing 181–8, 242
  for clients 184–5
  by employees 183–4
money laundering 188–99
  civil litigation 191–7
  cost of compliance 191, 248–9
  professional confidentiality 192
  qualified privilege 197–8
  regulators 183
  reputational risk 198–9
  tipping off 193
Financial Services and Markets Act 2000 13, 77–80, 186–7, 212–22
  authorised persons 219
  disciplinary system 221–2, 251–2
  misuse of information 213–14
  prescribed markets 213
  price-sensitive information, reporting 228
  qualifying investments 213
  regular users of markets 213
  restitution orders 219–21
Financial Services and Markets Tribunal 214
Financial Services Authority (FSA) 171
  advice to clients 186
  Code of Market Conduct 79–80, 120, 187
    market abuse 214–15
    penalties policy 217–18
  disciplinary action 221–2
  enforcement process 250
  investigations 208
    right to silence 216–17
  jurisdiction 212
  Legal and General case 250
  money laundering 156
  parallel proceedings 219–22
  penalties 217–18
  public statements 187
  Regulatory Decisions Committee (RDC) 214
  restitution orders 219–21
  sanctions 215–16, 217–18
Finland
  dealing, penalties 125
  inside information 94–5
  insiders 55–6

legal entities, criminal liability 55–6
price-sensitive information, reporting 224
secondary insiders 55
securities 95
unlisted securities 95
France
  allowing to deal 138–9, 211
  currency import/export 243–4
  dealing
    exemptions 117
    penalties 125–6
  financial instruments 97–8
  financial regulation 183
  inside information 53, 95–8
    incidental acquisition 59–60
    price sensitivity 96–7
  insider dealing
    administrative provisions 60–61, 204–5
    civil provisions 60–61
    criminal provisions 56–60
    parallel proceedings 218–19, 234
    penalties 57–8, 61
  insiders 56–61
  judiciary 252
  legal entities, criminal liability 56–7
  misappropriation of privileged information 20–21
  money laundering 146
  offences committed abroad 241
  Pechiney case 98, 125
  price-sensitive information, reporting 224
  primary insiders 61
  privileged information 20–21, 95–8
  professions 56, 60, 73
  recel 58–60, 116, 126
  secondary insiders 58–9, 61
  securities 97–8
  shareholders 58, 60
fraud 146–7
  insider dealing as 116
FSA *see* Financial Services Authority

gambling 11 *see also* casinos
Germany
  administrative fines 216
  advisory bodies 64

dealing
  exemptions 118
  penalties 126
derivatives 99
enterprises connected with issuers 63
financial analyses 99–100
forecasts 99–100
inside information 62, 98–101
insider dealing
  civil provisions 205, 245–6
  criminal provisions 245–6
insider facts 61, 83
insiders 61–6
  threefold test 64–5
journalists 65
legal entities, criminal liability 66
market manipulation 99–100
money laundering 146
  identification of customers 150–51
penalties 66
price-sensitive information 100–101
  reporting 224–5
primary insiders 61–2, 65
professions 63–4
publication of information 101
secondary insiders 61–2, 65–6
securities 99
shareholders 63
Weru case 126
Gibraltar 34
government officials as insiders 41
Greece
  dealing, penalties 126
  inside information 102
  insider dealing
    administrative provisions 205–6
    employees of financial institutions 184
  insiders 66
  price-sensitive information, reporting 225
  securities 102
Guernsey 34

H. M. Customs & Excise, money laundering 156
Hong Kong, Financial Action Task Force (FATF) 33
Human Rights Act 1988

financial crime 252–3
market abuse 216

identity cards 247
industrial espionage 27
information as property 160–61
inside information
  Austria 85–7
  Belgium 87–92
  definition 83
  Denmark 54, 66, 92–4
  Finland 55, 94–5
  France 53, 95–8
  Germany 62, 98–101
  Greece 102
  holding companies 89–92
  incidental acquisition 42–6
    France 59–60
  Insider Dealing Directive (89/592/EEC) 83–5
  Ireland 102–3
  Italy 103–4
  knowledge of confidentiality 37–8, 231
  Luxembourg 104–6
  Netherlands 106–7
  Portugal 107
  price sensitivity 93, 96–7, 100–101, 108, 109–10, 110–11
  as property 160–61
  securities 85
  significant effect 84
  Spain 53, 66, 108
  strict liability 37–8
  Sweden 108–10
  unauthorised disclosure 139–42
  United Kingdom 110–11
insider dealing *see also* allowing to deal; dealing; encouraging to deal; inside information; insiders; *and by names of countries*
  administrative offences 201–4, 233–5
    parallel proceedings 218–22
  administrative sanctions 235–7
  civil enforcement 245–7
  civil offences 201–4, 233–5
    parallel proceedings 218–22
  civil sanctions 235–7
  clients of financial institutions 184–5
  compliance 181–8

Index

confiscation 235–6
convictions 78, 122, 201
criminal offences 113–14, 231–3
   parallel proceedings 218–22
defences 189–90
definition 184, 229–31
economic arguments for permitting 3–10
employees of financial institutions 183–4
enforcement 231–5
   civil 245–7
financial services 181–8, 242
as fraud 116
grounds for prohibition 10–21
holding companies 91
imprisonment 231–3
international pressure for control 28–35
legal entities 47
Money Laundering Directives 148–9
offences 163–4
parallel proceedings 218–22
partnerships 182–3
profits, disgorgement 235–7
reasonable grounds for suspicion 231
regulation 201, 207
repeated 26–7
restitution orders 219–21, 235
thresholds 149
victims of 2
Insider Dealing Directive (89/592/EEC)
   compliance 181–8
   English translations *ix*
   inside information 83–5
   insiders 38–46
   professions 43–4
   shareholders 38–40
   significant developments 222
insider facts 61, 83–4 *see also* inside information
insiders 37
   Belgium 51–4
   Denmark 54–5
   Finland 55–6
   France 56–61
   Germany 61–6
   government officials 41
   Greece 66
   Insider Dealing Directive (89/592/EEC) 38–46

Ireland 67–9
Italy 69–71
journalists 41
Luxembourg 71
Netherlands 71–2
Portugal 72–5
primary *see* primary insiders
secondary *see* secondary insiders
shareholders 58, 60, 63, 75, 81
Spain 75–6
Sweden 76–7
United Kingdom 77–80
United Kingdom government 41
Investment Services Directive (93/22/EEC) 31–2
investor confidence 11–12
Ireland
   dealing, penalties 127
   government officials 68
   inside information 102–3
   insider dealing, civil liability 206–7
   insiders 67–9
   journalists 68
   legal entities, criminal liability 69
   money laundering, imprisonment 148
   price-sensitive information, reporting 225–6
   secondary insiders 68
   securities 102–3
Isle of Man 34
Italy
   CONSOB (National Company and Stock Exchange Commission) investigations 207–8
   dealing
      exemptions 117
      penalties 127–9
   financial instruments 104
   inside information 103–4
   insiders 69–71
   price-sensitive information, reporting 226
   professions 70
   public officials 70
   securities 104
   unlisted securities 104

ex parte James 15
Jersey 34

jewellers 152–3, 243–4
journalists
   Germany 65
   insiders 41–2
   Ireland 68
   Sweden 109

Keech v Sandford 14

Law Society 10–11
Legal and General case 250
legal entities 48–9
   criminal liability 47, 48–50
      Austria 48
      Belgium 53–4
      Denmark 55
      England and Wales 50
      Finland 55–6
      France 56–7
      Germany 66
      insider dealing 47
      Ireland 69
      Portugal 75
      South Africa 57
      Spain 76
      Sweden 76–7
      United Kingdom 78
   criminal sanctions 50–51
looting, proceeds of 23
Luxembourg
   dealing, penalties 129
   inside information 104–6
   insiders 71
   money laundering 146
   price-sensitive information, reporting 226
   securities 106
   unlisted securities 106

Mahon and another v Rahn and others (No. 2) 198
Manne, Henry 3–7
market abuse 78–9, 120, 132, 186–7, 212–22
   administrative sanctions 245
   as criminal offence 216–17
   disciplinary action 221–2
   parallel proceedings 218–22
   restitution orders 219–21

Market Abuse Directive *ix*, 245
market information 9–10, 92–3
   defence 119–21
market liquidity 12
market makers 119
market manipulation 42, 99–100
market volatility 6–7, 9
Marshall Islands 34
misappropriation of privileged information 19–21
misleading behaviour 42
misuse of information 79, 213–14, 235, 246–7 *see also* market abuse
MLROs (Money Laundering Reporting Officers) 167–8, 188–9
Monaco 34
money laundering *x*, 143–5
   absolute privilege 198
   bureaux de change 153–6, 243
   cash transactions 243–4
   casinos 153–4, 244
   civil litigation 191–7
   compliance 188–99
      cost of 191, 248–9
   Compliance Officers 188
   constructive trustee liability 192–7
   criminal property 239–42
      receipt of 189–90
   customer identification 150–51, 153–5, 243–4, 247–8
   defamation 197–8
   definition 22, 143, 145
   disclosure 193–4
   European Economic Area (EEA) 164
   European Union (EU) 31, 145–56
   financial institutions 151–2
   Financial Services Authority (FSA) 156
   France 146
   Germany 146
   H. M. Customs & Excise 156
   high value dealers 152–3, 243–4
   imprisonment 148
   international pressure for control 28–35
   jewellers 152–3, 243–4
   Luxembourg 146
   minors 154
   offences 146–7
   passports 155–6, 247–8
   precious metal dealers 165

predicate offences 241–2
preventative measures 150–51
Proceeds of Crime Act 2002 (UK) 143, 157–73
professional confidentiality 192
qualified privilege 197–8
reasonable grounds for suspicion 165–6
reasons for prohibition 24–8
reporting 151, 165–9
    cost of 191
reputational risk 198–9
terrorism 173–9, 237–9
Terrorism Act 2000 (UK) 178–9
theories of legitimisation 21–4
threshold 152, 155
tipping off 193
training 151, 189
United Kingdom 156–79
USA PATRIOT Act 2001 30
young adults 154
Money Laundering Directives 143, 145–56, 239
    compliance 188–99
    insider dealing 148–9
Money Laundering Reporting Officers (MLROs) 167–8, 188–9
money transmission services 151–2

National Criminal Intelligence Service (NCIS) 168–9, 193–4
Nauru 34
NCCT (Non-Compliant Countries and Territories, Financial Action Task Force) 33–5
Netherlands
    confiscation 130
    dealing, penalties 129–30
    inside information 106–7
    insiders 71–2
    price-sensitive information, reporting 226–7
    securities 106–7

OECD *see* Organisation for Economic Co-operation and Development
Office of Public Prosecutor of Ghent v Bekaert and Storme 52

Organisation for Economic Co-operation and Development (OECD), Financial Action Task Force (FATF) 32–5
organised crime 146–7
Oxford v Moss 20, 161–2

parallel proceedings 218–22, 233–5
partnerships, insider dealing 182–3
passports 155–6, 247–8
Pechiney case 98, 125, 230
Portugal
    dealing, penalties 130
    inside information 107
    insiders 72–5
    legal entities, criminal liability 75
    primary insiders 72–3
    professions 73–4
    public officials 74
    secondary insiders 74–5
    securities 107
price-sensitive information, reporting 222–8
primary insiders 81, 158, 230–31 *see also* insiders; secondary insiders
    Austria 47–8, 85–6
    Belgium 51, 52
    France 61
    Germany 61–2, 65
    Portugal 72–3
    Spain 75, 210–11
    Sweden 76–7
    United Kingdom 77–8
privileged information, misappropriation 19–21
proceeds of crime 23–5
    public opinion 27
Proceeds of Crime Act 2002 (UK) 143, 157–73
    adequate consideration 173
    civil recovery 235–6
    criminal conduct 157, 159
    criminal property 157–8, 160–63, 239–40
        receipt of 189–90
    defences 158, 167, 171–3, 189–90
    information 160–61
    jurisdiction 158
    mixed property 158
    Money Laundering Reporting Officers (MLROs) 167–8

moratorium on transactions 170
nominated officers 167–8
offences 158–63
police 172
precious metal dealers 165
receivers 172
reporting 165–9
   civil liability 170–71
   tipping off 169–70
professional confidentiality 192
professions 43–4, 56, 60, 63–4, 70, 73–4
public confidence in securities markets 12–13
public opinion on proceeds of crime 27
publication of information 92, 101, 109

qualified privilege 197–8

RDC (Regulatory Decisions Committee) 214
receivers 172
recel 58–60, 116, 126
Regal (Hastings) Ltd. v Gulliver 15–16
regulators for financial services 183
Regulatory Decisions Committee (RDC) 214
restitution orders 219–21, 235, 246–7
role models 27–8

Saunders v United Kingdom 217
SEC v Texas Gulf Sulfur Co. 10
secondary insiders 44–6, 81, 230–31 *see also* insiders; primary insiders
   Austria 47, 48
   Belgium 51–2
   fiduciary duty 19
   Finland 55
   France 58–9, 61
   Germany 61–2, 65–6
   Ireland 68
   Italy 71
   Portugal 74–5
   Spain 75
   Sweden 77
   United Kingdom 78
secret trusts 22
securities
   Austria 86–7
   Belgium 87–8

   Denmark 93–4
   Finland 95
   France 97–8
   Germany 99
   Greece 102
   inside information 85
   Ireland 102–3
   Italy 104
   Luxembourg 106
   Netherlands 106–7
   Portugal 107
   price bubbles 9
   Spain 108
   Sweden 110
   United Kingdom 111
   unlisted 85, 94, 95, 104, 106
securities markets, public confidence 12–13
securities regulation 13–14
securities trading 3–5
Self-Regulatory Organisations (SROs) 215–16
serious fraud 147
Seychelles 21, 35
share-tipping 41–2
shareholders 81
   France 58, 60
   Germany 63
   Insider Dealing Directive (89/592/EEC) 38–40
   Spain 75
significant developments, reporting 222–8
SOCA (Serious Organised Crime Agency): 144, 151, 167, 168-9, 171, 172, 189, 193, 238
solicitors 10–11
South Africa
   civil fines 220
   dealing, penalties 124
   Insider Trading Act 1998 40
   legal entities, criminal liability 57
   parallel proceedings 218–19
Spain
   allowing to deal 210–11
   dealing
      exemptions 117
      penalties 131
   financial regulation 183
   inside information 53, 66, 108
      price sensitivity 108

insider dealing
  administrative provisions 75–6, 208–11
  as criminal offence 98, 115
  criminal provisions 75
  legal entities 209, 210
  unauthorised disclosure 209
 insiders 75–6
 legal entities, criminal liability 76
 price-sensitive information, reporting 227
 primary insiders 75, 210–11
 secondary insiders 75
 securities 108
 shareholders 75
speculators 7–9
SROs (Self-Regulatory Organisations) 215–16
strict liability 37–8
Sweden
 dealing, penalties 131–2
 financial instruments 110
 inside information 108–10
  price sensitivity 109–10
 insiders 76–7
 journalists 109
 legal entities, criminal liability, 76–77
 price-sensitive information, reporting 227
 primary insiders 76–7
 publication of information 109
 secondary insiders 77
 securities 110

takeovers 121
Taylor v Serious Fraud Office 198
terrorism
 money laundering 173–9, 237–9
 proceeds of crime 175
Terrorism Act 2000 (UK) 173, 175–9
 defences 178, 179
 fund raising 175
 funding arrangements 176
 juries 177
 money laundering 178–9
 reasonable cause for suspicion 176–7
 terrorist property 178–9
The Regulation of Insider Trading (Rider and Ffrench) *viii*

tippees 44, 45, 46, 48, 59 *see also* secondary insiders
tipping off 169–70, 193
Turkey 253

Ukraine 34
unauthorised disclosure 139–42
United Kingdom
 alcohol licensing laws 51, 239–40
 civil recovery 235–6
 Code of Market Conduct (Financial Services Authority) 79–80
 confiscation 124, 133–5
 criminal property 157–8, 160–63, 189–90, 239–40
 dealing
  penalties 132–5
  specialist defences 119–21
 demutualisation 108
 fraud, serious 147
 identity cards 247
 inside information 110–11
 insider dealing
  civil provisions 211–22
  convictions 78, 201
  criminal provisions 77
  parallel proceedings 219–22
 insiders 77–80
  government officials 41
 legal entities 50
  criminal liability 78
 market abuse 78–9, 120, 132, 212–22
  as criminal offence 216–17
 market information defence 119–21
 market makers 119
 misuse of information 79, 246–7
 money laundering 156–79
 price-sensitive information 110–11
  reporting 228
 price stabilisation rules 121
 primary insiders 77–8
 restitution orders 124, 246–7
 secondary insiders 78
 securities 111
 serious fraud 147
 takeovers 121
United States
 civil recovery 235–7
 currency import/export 243

financial regulation 28–31
insider dealing 181–2
money laundering 30
unlisted securities 85, 94, 95, 104, 106
U.S. v Newman 19–20, 26–7
U.S. v O'Hagan 20

U.S. v Vincent F. Chiarella 19
USA PATRIOT Act 2001 30

Weru case 126
Wu, Hsiu-kwang 7–9